Planning the American Indian Reservation

Planning the American Indian Reservation

From Theory to Empowerment

Nicholas Christos Zaferatos

Foreword by
Brian Cladoosby

Syracuse University Press

First Edition 2015
15 16 17 18 19 20   6 5 4 3 2 1

Figures, photographs, and tables are provided by Nicholas C. Zaferatos unless otherwise noted. Portions of this book were derived from the author's previously published articles in "Tribal Nations, Local Governments, and Regional Pluralism in Washington State: The Swinomish Approach in the Skagit Valley," 2004, *Journal of the American Planning Association,* (Winter) 70 (1): 81–96; "Planning the Native American Tribal Community: Understanding the Basis of Power Controlling the Reservation Territory," 1998, *Journal of the American Planning Association,* 64 (4): 395–410; "Developing an Effective Approach to Strategic Planning for Native American Indian Reservations," 2004, *Space and Polity,* (Winter) 8 (1), by permission of the publisher © 2012 Taylor & Francis Ltd, http://www.tandf.co.uk /journals; "Appropriate Technologies in the Traditional Native American Smokehouse: Public Health Considerations in Tribal Community Development," Nicholas C. Zaferatos and Mary Ellen Flanagan, 2001, *American Indian Culture and Research Journal,* 12 (3): 69–93, by permission of the American Indian Studies Center, UCLA © 1996 Regents of the University of California; and "Environmental Justice in Indian Country: Dumpsite Remediation on the Swinomish Indian Reservation," 2006, *Environmental Management,* 38 (6): 896–909, by permission of the publisher, Springer Science+Business Media.

∞ The paper used in this publication meets the minimum requirements of the American National Standard for Information Sciences—Permanence of Paper for Printed Library Materials, ANSI Z39.48-1992.

For a listing of books published and distributed by Syracuse University Press, visit www.SyracuseUniversityPress.syr.edu.

ISBN: 978-0-8156-3393-8 (cloth)   978-0-8156-5318-9 (e-book)

Library of Congress Cataloging-in-Publication Data
Zaferatos, Nicholas C. (Nicholas Christos)
    Planning the American Indian reservation : from theory to empowerment / Nicholas Christos Zaferatos ; foreword by Brian Cladoosby. — First edition.
        pages cm
    Includes bibliographical references and index.
    ISBN 978-0-8156-3393-8 (cloth : alk. paper) — ISBN 978-0-8156-5318-9 (e-book)
1. Indian reservations—United States.   2. Indians of North America—Government relations—1934–   3. Indians of North America—Politics and government.   4. Tribal government—United States.   I. Title.
E93.Z34 2015
323.1197—dc23   2014047740

Manufactured in the United States of America

Nicholas Christos Zaferatos, PhD, AICP, is a professor of urban planning and sustainable development at Huxley College of the Environment, Western Washington University. His teaching emphasis in urban planning, sustainable development, Native American planning, and environmental policy complements his regional and international teaching and research interests. Since 2005, Dr. Zaferatos has directed several Mediterranean teaching and research programs in sustainable development. He directed the Kefalonia Program in Sustainable Community Development (Greece) and currently serves as director for the Sustainable Ithaca Program (Greece). Professor Zaferatos also serves as the president and CEO of A World Institute for a Sustainable Humanity—Hellas, a not-for-profit organization promoting sustainable community development in the Mediterranean region. His professional practice in urban planning spans over thirty-five years and includes planning and executive positions and civic appointments on planning boards and commissions with local, regional, and Native American governments.

Contents

List of Illustrations   *ix*

List of Tables   *xi*

Foreword, BRIAN CLADOOSBY   *xiii*

Preface   *xvii*

1. Introduction and Overview: *The Work of Tribal Planning*   *1*

Part One. *The Setting for Native American Reservation Planning*

2. An Overview of Federal Indian Policy and the Evolution of the Tribal Political Community   *13*

3. The Context of Tribal Sovereignty   *35*

4. The Tribal Cultural Community   *72*

Part Two. *Theories and Models Empowering Tribal Planning*

5. The Tribal Political Economy and Its Underdevelopment   *95*

6. Identifying Oppositional Forces in Tribal Planning   *123*

Part Three. *The Dimensions of Tribal Planning*

7. An Adaptive and Contingent Model of Tribal Planning   *145*

Part Four. *Case Studies in Mediating Tribal Planning Relationships*

8. Mediating Tribal-State Conflicts
   Experiences from Washington State   *165*

9. Regional Pluralism: *The Skagit Valley Experience*   *209*

10. Appropriate Technologies and the Native American Smokehouse   *237*

11. Environmental Justice on the Swinomish
Indian Reservation   *262*

12. Conclusion   *287*

Acknowledgments   *295*

APPENDIX 1: Federal Court Decisions   *297*

APPENDIX 2: Federal Statutes   *301*

References   *309*

Index   *329*

Illustrations

1. Alienation of the tribal political community   *109*
2. Modified Indian alienation model   *110*
3. Pre-alienation model   *111*
4. Post-alienation model   *111*
5. Model of tribal political action   *149*
6. The dimensions of tribal planning   *153*
7. Tribal community development planning framework   *159*
8. Ceded territories of western Washington State   *169*
9. Tribal planning model depicting the negotiative approach   *208*
10. Swinomish Indian Reservation and surrounding region   *211*
11. Aerial view, Swinomish Indian Reservation   *216*
12. Tribal planning model illustrating the Swinomish tribe's strategic approach   *235*
13. Exterior view, Swinomish Indian smokehouse   *238*
14. Ceremonial room interior and upper bleacher seating area   *241*
15. Main ceremonial room air quality test sampling locations   *245*
16. Interior roof in ceremonial room showing smoke hole   *246*
17. Smoke dispersion from a cooler fire mixed with ambient room air   *252*
18. Installation of air inflow pipe and fire pit vault   *254*
19. Ceremonial room showing test fire   *258*
20. Relating the smokehouse experience to the tribal planning model   *260*
21. Superfund excavation of PM Northwest site in progress   *283*
22. Correlating environmental justice to the tribal planning model   *285*

Tables

1. Effects of Federal Indian Policy   17
2. A Comparison of Values, Attitudes, and Behavioral Attributes   82
3. Responses to Indian Incorporation   118
4. Matrix of Oppositional Forces in Indian
   Community Development   124
5. Forms of Non-Indian Opposition to Tribal Governance   129
6. Principles and Imperatives of Tribal Self-Determination   156
7. Puget Sound Area Indian Reservation Characteristics   170
8. Summary of State-Tribal Conflicts   177
9. Tribal-Local Government Cooperation since 1980   206
10. Swinomish Intergovernmental Cooperative Agreements   220
11. Respirable Particulate Concentration, September 1997
    Concept Tests   251
12. Respirable Particulate Concentration   256
13. Swinomish Environmental Management Agreements   271
14. Integrated Site Assessment Findings   278

Foreword

THE SWINOMISH TRIBE will be forever grateful to "Nick en um," our tribe's playful reference to Nick Zaferatos, our first professional land use planner, and the team of professionals he helped recruit. Together, they provided invaluable advice and guidance to the tribal council at a time when our tribe was still trying to recover from the era of assimilation and termination and develop a long-term strategy to regain control of our land, our lives, and our culture. Nick was a careful listener, learned about our ways, learned about our culture, and adapted the tools of planning to help guide us through a process that let us define our community vision and strategically plan for the next seven generations.

When Nick arrived, we were still hunkered down on the Swinomish Reservation trying to avoid the melting pot of mainstream America, and most of all, the local governments that surrounded us, and we were dealing with ongoing bigotry toward our children in public schools, gunfire from non-Indian fishermen upset with the 1979 Supreme Court decision upholding the *Boldt Fishing Case*, and nearby towns passing resolutions asking Congress to abrogate Indian treaty rights. But this was not our heritage and not our way. Coast Salish Tribes had always traveled and traded up and down Puget Sound, along the Strait of Juan de Fuca, down the Pacific Coast to Oregon, and across the Cascade Mountains to eastern Washington. We had well-defined relationships with our tribal neighbors and trading partners who recognized our home territory, honored our usual and accustomed fishing areas, and facilitated our seasonal travel to distant places. Still, those boundaries and relationships shifted over time—even before European contact—in a dynamic political and cultural equilibrium that tribal nation-states have always operated within.

What Nick brought to Swinomish in 1980 was a new way of thinking "Swinomish" that recognized the changing fabric of our region, the different competing forces, and new obstacles to tribal governance. In post-assimilation-and-termination America, Nick offered us a process to articulate our dream for the tribal community, chart out a pathway to lead us there, and, along the way, overcome the historical status quo that had been slowly shifting away from us for 150 years.

As we shifted our sights outward beyond the Reservation, we found both hostility toward us and a willingness to work with us as regional partners in a world of increasingly complex regional issues—population growth, water shortage, crime, education, and health. The hostility was born from a sense of historical entitlement to the encroachment on Indian lands and resources that non-tribal communities benefited from and the resistance to any change that required effort or expense. The willingness to work together came from the immediacy of pressing regional issues that required our neighbors to forget—or put aside—the "turf issues" of jurisdiction and government control and focus instead on the collective resources that could be used to combat the common threats to our respective communities. Cooperation on law enforcement was an early victory where county and municipal police agencies saw the benefit of working with tribal law enforcement to combat crime—particularly drug crime—and of supporting the return of criminal jurisdiction, which had been taken over by the state during the termination era, back to federal and tribal governments through federal retrocession. The Swinomish Police Department today is one of only a handful of tribal police departments nationally that has been certified as meeting the standards set by their state association of sheriffs and police chiefs.

What we saw when we looked out from the Reservation was a world of "stakeholders." Initially angered by the refusal of our jurisdictional neighbors to meet with us "government-to-government," we eventually came to realize that many of the political leaders of these communities saw their role as overseeing a diverse group of stakeholders—private and sometimes non-profit public interests—rather than working with other governments to define and protect a common "public interest." On the

Reservation, that's all tribal leaders thought about: what's best for the community as a whole, how to provide a safety net of social services for those who could not afford them, how to protect Mother Nature, and how to live in balance with all that the Creator had provided. We found that this approach conflicted in many ways with the stakeholder process that operated off Reservation—there were no simple "split-the-difference" solutions for us when it came to salmon or other natural resources that had minimum survival needs and could not be sustained on an arbitrary half of whatever was at stake. In the stakeholder process, we sometimes appeared unreasonable, wanting too much and unable to "get along," but we stayed engaged and did the best we could to bridge this political and cultural divide.

Over the years, our comprehensive planning strategy has been grounded upon educating our political counterparts, negotiating in a world of stakeholders, being generous in spirit while maintaining a clear focus on the long-term goals and needs of our tribal community, and litigating tribal issues only as a last resort. Because of the continual loss of tribal rights in the past, litigation has occasionally been necessary to change the historical status quo and shift the momentum back in a direction that will restore—rather than continue to diminish—tribal communities, their cultures, and the natural resources that sustain them. Selective and often successful litigation has had the added benefit of enhancing our role as a "stakeholder" and our ability to work with our neighbors, reach appropriate accommodations, and advance our tribe's wellbeing in a way that also benefits the region and the collective public interest. Our challenge is to use this newfound strength to work with regional governments and stay out of court as much as we can.

Nick's book on tribal planning provides an invaluable handbook and reference for tribal governments and other planners and policy makers that interact with tribes. It describes the complex conditions that face tribal nations today and includes methods and approaches to tribal planning that can be used to promote long-term sustainable development in a variety of tribal settings. His insights about the practice of tribal planning present a new way of thinking about—and effectively overcoming—the many challenges that we tribal nations will inevitably continue to face in our pursuit of economic independence and self-determination.

Brian Cladoosby
Chairman, Swinomish Indian Tribal Community
President, National Congress of American Indians

Preface

IN THE LATE WINTER OF 1980, having recently completed a graduate degree in planning, several limited term planning experiences with local governments and a small consulting firm, I came across a job announcement by the Swinomish Indian Tribal Community in Washington State for a "planner." For many years, I had been interested in Native American issues, especially and after having worked as a consultant on a few projects with Washington tribes. Therefore, I decided to submit my application and see where this might lead.

Shortly thereafter, I was invited to the Swinomish Indian Reservation for an interview. I had several other job interviews with local and state agencies during that same period, but I was not sure whether I was really interested in working with those agencies. There was a special quality that I experienced during the Swinomish interview that was absent during my other interviews. I felt immediately comfortable in the presence of the interview committee, which was comprised of members of the Swinomish tribe's governing council as well as several tribal elders. Their handshake was soft and sincere. Genuine kindheartedness emanated from them as they introduced themselves and spoke about the conditions facing their reservation community. The interview, itself, primarily consisted of a conversation about the people of Swinomish, their history, their enduring hardships, and their aspirations. They talked about what they thought they needed from a planner, considering that planning was still relatively new to Swinomish. They had previously received a federal grant that funded a planner to work, for the most part, on economic development projects. Subsequently, a second grant paid for a consultant to write a draft comprehensive land use plan and a zoning

ordinance. Despite these opportunities, the tribe's experience with planning their reservation was still in its infancy stage. The tribe had not yet
begun to think about how to govern its reservation in a comprehensive
manner, because until that time, reservation governance had largely been
a matter of state or county regulation with virtually no tribal involvement. The tribe, like all Native American Nations, had just emerged
from a two-decade period during which the federal policy of termination
largely decimated tribal political authority. The interview committee
spoke about the environmental problems on the reservation that needed
to be addressed. They voiced concern about how the reservation's non-
Indian resident population had grown rapidly over the years and had
eclipsed the Indian population by a four-to-one margin, due to Skagit
County's zoning policies, which favored suburban development along
the reservation's scenic marine shoreline. They stressed the importance
of fishing and the need to expand the tribe's fishing economy, particularly in light of the *Boldt Fishing Case*, a federal court ruling—subsequently upheld by the Supreme Court—that affirmed the tribal treaty
fishing right. They spoke of their aspirations to build boat docks, finance
a tribal fishing fleet, and reopen a defunct fish processing plant. They
stressed the importance of resuming the construction of a commercial
building that would be used as a tribal restaurant and beginning work
on a planned industrial park, two federally funded projects intended to
expand the employment base on the reservation. They talked about their
housing needs and the priority to plan for more tribal housing within the
ancestral village. They spoke of their dream to construct a *smokehouse*,
the Swinomish peoples' traditional house of worship. They also asked if
I knew much about planning in Indian country, to which I answered, "I
have had a few limited experiences and I am very motivated." We spoke
for several hours and I left feeling very good about the interview and
especially about the people I met. I couldn't help but wonder what my life
would be like if I was offered, and accepted, the job.

It was on a Thursday afternoon, a few days after the interview, that
the phone rang and I was offered the job of tribal planning director. I
accepted the job offer with elation and gratitude and agreed to begin work
on the following Monday morning. I mentioned to my wife, Cynthia,

that I sensed that this was going to be a very special and life-changing experience, despite the fact that I really had very little to base my expectations on.

On Monday morning, I arrived at the tribal administration building to meet with the former general manager. He welcomed me to the job and provided a bit of an orientation, mentioning Public Law 280, the Indian Reorganization Act (IRA), and a few other federal statutes that I was hardly familiar with. He wanted me to understand that Swinomish was an "IRA-280" tribe. Then he explained that the tribe had just recently dismissed nine of its former core staff, including their former planner. There had been a political scandal of sorts and the tribal council, the Swinomish Indian Senate, decided to release the staff that consisted largely of non-Indian professionals.

After about one half hour, the former general manager showed me to my office and my orientation was concluded. There I was, sitting in one of the eight offices that enclosed a large open space that was filled with desks and filing cabinets, occupied by the tribal accounting department. My new office contained a federal-surplus metal desk, a phone, three chairs, a bookcase, and a large black and white aerial photograph of the reservation which was leaning up against the wall. There was no computer, only an IBM Selectric typewriter. The almost empty bookcase held several grant files and a stack of copies of the Swinomish Comprehensive Plan, which had been prepared by a consulting firm and paid for as part of a Housing and Urban Development (HUD) section 501 planning grant. The plan had been adopted by the Swinomish Indian Senate just one year earlier. HUD's section 501 program authorized tribal governments to be eligible to apply for these grants, thereby constituting the first instance of federal support for reservation comprehensive planning.

As I contemplated my new surroundings, I realized that there was no other planning staff. It was just me. I was the planning department of the Swinomish Indian Tribal Community.

I quickly learned about the IRA, Public Law 280, as well as many other federal acts of Indian assimilation and termination and began to understand the enormity of the role those laws played in shaping Indian societies and tribal governance. I was beginning to understand not only how the function of tribal planning could be used to bring about the protection and development of the tribal homeland for the benefit of Swinomish Indians, but, also, how to cultivate social and political justice in light of a history of political violence. Until this time, my perspective had been limited to what I had learned in my planning classes and by my experiences in municipal and county planning agencies. Several questions percolated through my mind. Are tribes to replicate what local governments do, or is there more to this work? Where do tribes stand in terms of having the authority to plan? What is their ability to enforce laws enacted under their own tribal constitutions, especially with regard to non-Indians and non-Indian owned reservation lands? What points of tension would likely arise if tribes sought to disrupt the balance of state and county power operating on reservations? How do I learn what I need to learn to be an effective planner in Indian country?

Again, the year was 1980 and, frankly, the American planning profession hadn't, to this point, shown much concern for planning in Indian country. There was little, if anything, available in the planning literature to guide our work. As I met planning colleagues from other tribes, I soon realized that tribal planners were mainly involved with writing grants for housing, economic development, and infrastructure projects. Most of the work in tribal planning, in the late 1970s and early 1980s, was driven by federal funding incentives from the Department of Commerce's Economic Development Administration (EDA), HUD, the Indian Health Service, and the Bureau of Indian Affairs. EDA funded my position, as well as many other tribal planning positions in the nation, in an effort to help tribes develop an economy to alleviate chronic unemployment. Their key strategy at the time was to establish industrial parks and tourism projects on Indian reservations as a way to infuse private capital into reservation economies. This objective was supposed to solve the persistent problem of reservation poverty. A study funded by the Ford Foundation later evaluated the EDA strategy. Entitled "The Gift That Hurt," it chronicled the overwhelming disaster of a strategy that resulted in financial losses on many reservations. Despite HUD's brief period of funding reservation planning and EDA's often misguided support of Indian economic development, there was a virtual absence of comprehensive planning in Indian country in the decade that followed the enactment of the federal Indian self-determination policies of the early 1970s.

It wasn't immediately obvious then, but we, as Indian Country planners, were about to embark on one of the most ambitious journeys in American planning history—at Swinomish and on most other tribal reservations throughout the nation. Tribal planning, I began to realize, was about to experience an awakening. In the absence of a comprehensive federal approach to help tribes begin the activity of reservation planning, it was evident that the search for a tribal planning methodology would have to emerge through on-the-ground, experiential practice.

Within my first year, I participated in recruiting key tribal staff, including an in-house attorney, an assistant planner, a social services director, a housing director, and a financial comptroller, as well as a few other key administrative positions. By the time I left Swinomish, after twenty years in my dual role as planning director and general manager, the tribal administration had grown to number several hundred, and became one of the largest employers in Skagit County. Many of my original cohort of professional colleagues are still employed by the tribe, with several approaching thirty-five years of gratifying and effective service to the community. In 1999, when I assumed a university appointment as a professor of urban planning, the tribe's planning department had expanded to more than a dozen planners plus a portfolio of consultants. Our law department had five in-house attorneys who managed several litigation projects. Our public works department was operating reservation-wide public works, including utility services to most of the non-Indian residential community. We became engaged in all matters of reservation planning: long range, strategic, regulatory, intergovernmental coordination, economic development and gaming, cultural resources protection, habitat restoration, water and air quality management, hazardous waste cleanup, housing development, urban design, community development, shorelines management, public works, and the co-management of off-reservation natural resources. For a relatively small reservation community, planning had evolved into a very complex system.

When I first began working for Swinomish, my chairman was Robert "WaWalton" Joe Sr., with whom I worked very closely for nearly two decades. He provided visionary direction and bestowed his wisdom with great humility. We became brothers. Our council consisted of dedicated leaders whom I greatly respected. Of the hundreds of council votes that I witnessed, including decisions on many contentious issues, I cannot recall a single vote that was not unanimous. That is the Swinomish way. And that is no doubt the reason why so much was accomplished during a relatively short period. My relationship with the council was always one based on trust and honesty. When I hired Brian Cladoosby, one of the council members, to work as my assistant general manager, I explained to him that his job assignment would be straightforward: "learn everything about your tribe as quickly as possible so that you can assume the role of general manager." Brian later responded that he didn't want my job. Rather, he aspired to one day become the chairman of his tribe. He did that, and so much more. In 2013, Chairman Brian Cladoosby was elected by the national tribal leadership to the presidency of the National Congress of American Indians.

This book is about lessons learned regarding tribal planning, in an effort to make the work of tribal planning more comprehensible. The first section of the book attempts to explain the essential context under which tribal planning occurs. The second section examines political theories that I believe are crucial for discerning the conditions that thwart the ability of tribes to manage their reservation homelands. A strategic planning model based on anticipatory and contingent approaches to planning, as a way to deal with the persistent conditions of conflict and uncertainty that surround tribal planning, is presented in the third section. The book concludes with several case studies from my own experiences at Swinomish and with tribes throughout Washington State. In each case study, I draw parallels to the planning model and to the strategies that were used to overcome resistance to the tribe's management of its reservation affairs. What I have learned about tribal planning is a composite of my experiences at Swinomish, my work with other tribal planners and leaders, and my doctorate studies at the University of Washington. My dissertation focused on the evaluation of planning approaches for overcoming conflicts that tribal nations face. Much of what I learned came not so much from the contemporary planning literature, which had published little in the field of tribal planning, but rather, from other social sciences fields. The works of political social theorists and philosophers, Michel Foucault, Jurgen Habermas, Leonie Sandercock, Manuel Castells, Constantinos Doxiades, and even Hippodamus of Melitus, have influenced my thinking far more than the conventional planning literature has.

In addition to being versed in the methods and processes of planning, the work of tribal planning is also fundamentally about being devoted. By being devoted, I refer not only to the advocacy that is necessarily inherent in our work throughout Indian country, but also to the importance of being personally impassioned about the work. Those who are honored with the responsibility of working on behalf of tribal interests recognize how exceptionally resilient these tribal societies are. How can we be anything other than humbled by the charge we are entrusted with: to help protect irreplaceable tribal homelands that were repeatedly diminished over the ages through unjust public policy actions; to work toward the reservations' continuous sustainability for the seven generations to come; to face and overcome the historic bigotry and political violence that Indian people have been and, sadly, are still subjected to; to confront the unrelenting resistance to a tribe's right to govern its people and its territories without further infringement; to help a people that have been so neglected by mainstream society, and by our own American planning profession, so that they may one day realize a blessed community created by their own hand and through their own vision.

There is a Greek word, *philotimo*, that, for me, describes what working for Indian people is all about. Though it is widely considered to be untranslatable, the literal translation of philotimo means "friend of honor." Perhaps it is difficult to accurately translate because it represents the highest of all Greek virtues. Its meaning implies a standard of living for each individual of a community that is based on the deepest-felt sense of gratitude. Philotimo means never doing enough for your community and always placing the interests of the community before the self. It is expressed through continuous acts of sacrifice, generosity, and respect. This explains why it is so rare to encounter the conditions of homelessness in Indian country that have become so prevalent in other American communities. This is not because Indians don't know poverty. It is that their generosity and their deep sense of responsibility to their families and to their community means that no one is left to suffer alone. It is the tradition of the Indian potlatch. It is the embodiment of deeply honoring all the people of the community, as well as the natural world that sustains the community. Working in Indian country means to work within a society that has the deepest sense of philotimo.

I dedicate this book to my Swinomish mentors and friends, the late Chairman Robert "WaWalton" Joe, Sr., the Swinomish people, and to my Swinomish staff colleagues who worked tirelessly and who provided such wise advice as, together, we formulated the strategies that helped the tribe overcome many difficult problems. Each of these individuals helped teach me what the work of tribal planning is about. This book is dedicated, as well, to the planners working in the service of Native nations and indigenous peoples throughout the country and the world. Your work is of the utmost importance.

Planning the American Indian Reservation

1

Introduction and Overview

The Work of Tribal Planning

THIS BOOK is about planning in Native American Indian reservations. It is written from a perspective of tribal empowerment. As tribal planners, the approaches that we use in our service to tribal communities must be grounded and well informed by the particular planning situation found in each individual reservation, a situation that has largely been shaped by a methodical policy history that simultaneously eroded tribal political authority and fragmented many of the reservation homelands that were originally reserved for exclusive tribal use. As planners, we are challenged to continuously identify the problems and constraints that our constituent communities face; the obstacles that stand in the way of advancing a community's goals. However, we must also be vigilant not to accept the erosive policies of the past as static, discovering, instead, how to use the tools of planning to bring change to the planning situation itself in order to enable the attainment of a tribe's goals. We begin to understand the true power of planning when it is applied as an instrument of change that empowers communities. Effective tribal planning can alter the nature of the political landscape and help to rebalance the uneven relationships that have been formed between tribal governments and their non-tribal political counterparts. Tribal planning's overarching objective is to assist tribes as they transition from passive objects of historical circumstances into principal actors in shaping their future reservation communities. Tribal planning is primarily concerned with making plans and charting a course for the future. However, as it undertakes plan making, it must simultaneously reconcile the disruptive histories that have impeded its progress. It is the

1

attribute of reform that largely defines the process of tribal planning in its quest for social and economic equity, political justice, and cultural survival. This book seeks to make evident the work of tribal planning.

Introduction

In simple terms, planning is concerned with both imagining a desired future and selecting the best means to attain that future. Planning seeks to improve the social, economic, and ecological conditions of a community. The task remains, at best, a difficult undertaking, as American society's inherent plurality and the differentiation of community needs have led planners to focus increasingly on the specific needs of distinct social groups, particularly groups that have previously been underrepresented in American planning practice. This book aims to promote planning's effectiveness in improving the conditions of one of the most underrepresented segments of the American community, the Native American Indian reservation community. Native American Indian reservation planning is one of the most challenging and poorly understood specializations within the American planning profession. In fact, and as a result of the assertion of tribal interests in the mainstream political landscape challenging the balance of state power relations, the profession of planning has generally failed, until quite recently, to pay sufficient attention to the needs of tribal communities. In some instances, it has even inadvertently impeded the progress of planning in those communities, planning that tribes sorely need to improve the conditions of their reservation communities, which continue to rank among the most disadvantaged in American society.

Despite federal efforts during the past century that simultaneously sought to assimilate and then to terminate tribal societies and their reservation homelands, tribal communities, miraculously, continue to exist, and, in an increasing number of cases, to prosper. American Indian tribes always have possessed sovereign powers of self-government over their internal affairs and over their lands—sovereign powers that support their continued existence. Over time, however, other governments (including federal, state, and local governments) have encroached on tribal self-governing powers. Today, tribes' specific authority over reservation lands and resources are often unclear. Contemporary development of Native American communities continues to be adversely affected by a long-standing history of past federal Indian policy, jurisdictional conflicts in state-tribal relations, and the incorporation processes of the US political economy.

As a starting point for supporting the work of planning in Native American Indian reservations, this book attempts to unveil the complex context of tribal planning as a step toward informing its practice. The externally induced, and often turbulent circumstances that tribes face in their pursuit of improved reservation conditions, include seemingly insurmountable obstacles that continue to frustrate tribal governments as they plan their communities' futures. As professionals, we need to do far better in developing a more insightful understanding about the conditions facing tribal planning in order to help reconcile the barriers that prevent tribes from attaining their long sought-after futures. In the following chapters, I examine the context under which tribal planning occurs, introducing new approaches that are informed, in part, by planning's own theoretical traditions, in order to make the conditions that impede tribal development more decipherable. This book examines these problems by emphasizing a greater understanding of the historical oppositional forces that have been imposed upon tribal nations and their territories—forces that continue to obstruct tribal communities. In order to further a tribe's self-determination, planning should be grounded in a tribe's own historical experience from which effective planning strategies can be formulated. This book approaches tribal planning as a fundamental exercise in political sovereignty development.

The Particular Case of Tribal Planning

Native American Indian tribes have been subjected to various states of crisis since their earliest contact with Western civilization. Historically, treaty-making separated Indian people by removing Native communities to isolated reservation territories, thereby allowing the progressive development of their ceded lands. For more than one and a half centuries, tribes have coped with a shifting federal Indian policy that has resulted in a diminishing of their ability to exercise self-governance over their societies and over their self-reserved territories. The tribal pursuit of self-determination became increasingly complicated by a long series of impediments that emerged throughout the tribes' historic contact with American society. These impediments also contributed to a reservation condition characterized as politically and economically *underdeveloped*. An understanding of the nature of these circumstances helps to inform planning's ability to devise strategies to effectively advance tribal objectives. Since 1970, the implementation of the federal self-determination policy pledged federal commitment to the strengthening of tribal self-governance and the lessening of federal management of tribal affairs, which, previously, had stifled tribal control over Indian resources and promoted dependency rather than self-sufficiency. United States self-determination policy was first articulated in 1970 by President Richard Nixon and subsequently enacted as the Indian Self-Determination and Education Assistance Act of 1975 (Pub. L. No. 93-638), which fundamentally reaffirmed tribal rights and authority. The national policy promotes Indian self-governance by affirming the right of tribes to decide their collective future. The dependent-sovereign polity of tribes is a fundamental quality that distinguishes tribes from all other American communities.

This book examines the evolving context of tribal sovereignty by exploring the historical events that created a complex reservation situation that both diminished tribal self-governance and allowed for the encroachment by non-tribal interests into tribal affairs. The effects of these historic processes are manifested through the concept of *incorporation*. The US political economy's incorporation of tribal territory has been primarily exercised through resistance to and denial of tribal authority. In many cases tribal reservation jurisdiction has been supplanted by state and local jurisdiction, resulting in ongoing conflict and complex litigation. The chapters in this book explore the conditions that thwart the advancement of tribal development and suggest approaches for making tribal planning more effective. For tribes to overcome the forces that obstruct their own development, interventions that emanate from a tribe's own political authority is first required. This presumes, of course, that tribes possess sufficient powers of self-government.

Overview of the Chapters

Part 1 describes the setting for Native American reservation planning in a series of chapters that establishes the context for tribal planning. The persistence of political interventions that confront tribal authority are viewed in terms of a dialectical relationship between tribal interests and the competing interests of federal, state, and local governments, as well as of private interests. The nature of this political conflict is explored through an historic analysis in chapter 2, "An Overview of Federal Indian Public Policy and the Evolution of the Tribal Political Community." Federal Indian policy and federal case law decisions describe the causal events that have shaped the tribal setting.

"The Context of Tribal Sovereignty," chapter 3, expands an understanding of the nature of tribal political authority. Throughout this book, I argue that the ability of a tribe to plan and exercise control over its territory is a fundamental and necessary attribute of self-government. This chapter helps to clarify the status of tribal sovereignty based upon the extent of regulatory powers that tribes are believed to possess. Of primary concern in tribal planning is the ability of a tribe to govern reservation land use, manage the reservation environment, develop its reservation economy, and preserve its cultural integrity.

In chapter 4, "The Tribal Cultural Community," I consider, in a generalized manner, the nature and qualities of tribal culture and their importance as central attributes in tribal planning. Differing philosophical ideologies that are prevalent in mainstream American and tribal societies are examined in order to illustrate that differences do exist and that those differences influence how a tribe may prioritize its community goals. Cultural differences can also contribute to dissonance with non-Indian societies that can, in turn, contribute to conflict. In undertaking the examination of tribal cultural values, I am cautious to point out that broad differences may exist among tribes, and among different cultural groups within individual tribes. The discussion details the fundamental belief systems that have been distinctly associated with many modern Indian societies, and that have, at times, been in conflict with the norms of non-Indian society.

In part 2, theoretical models are explored in order to understand the particular conditions that are found in tribal planning situations. In chapter 5, "The Tribal Political Economy and Its Underdevelopment," the US political economy's overarching presence in tribal affairs is viewed as a pervasive obstacle confronting tribal development. A community's ability to manage its resources is essential if it is to overcome poverty and ensure its future prosperity. This chapter examines several theories of community development that help to explain the causes that contribute to the persistent conditions of underdevelopment in tribal communities. The discussion examines the processes that led to the alienation and underdevelopment of reservation economies and equates the alienation process to historic events that were imposed upon tribes by external political and economic interests. As a prerequisite to furthering reservation development and tribal self-determination, successful tribal planning must have the capacity to identify and overcome the interferences that occur in tribal affairs.

Within the practice of tribal planning, obstacles are inevitably encountered that must be addressed through a cogent planning strategy. Obstacles that are present in the tribal planning situation are complex and often difficult to ascertain. The types of obstacles that operate within the tribal territory are described in chapter 6, "Identifying Oppositional Forces in Tribal Planning," as largely exogenous, emanating from forces that are external to the tribe. To illustrate their effects upon the tribal political community, and to make them more transparent, these obstacles are identified in a general framework.

In part 3, chapter 7, "An Adaptive and Contingent Model of Tribal Planning," a framework for Native American Indian reservation planning is proposed that aligns a tribe's community development objectives with its historic experiences and its political capacity. The approach emphasizes the consideration of external forces that interfere with a tribe's affairs, thereby producing both a dynamic and conflictive planning environment. Adaptive and contingent planning approaches are particularly useful in evaluating such dynamic planning environments. These approaches provide a systematic process for assessing political conflicts that affect a reservation community before tribal strategies are selected and implemented to overcome conflicts and attain desired outcomes. Criteria are first presented to describe the salient components of tribal self-determination. A planning model is then presented to portray the forms of obstacles that may be encountered in tribal planning. The model provides a logical framework for evaluating alternative planning approaches in order to anticipate and resolve, or avoid, conflict. The model is not intended as a blueprint for tribal planning, but, instead, as a general procedure for guiding a tribe's plan development process. It provides for the systematic assessment of a tribe's capacity to formulate and implement planning strategies, to assess and modify those strategies based on the anticipation of conflict, and to evaluate outcomes.

In part 4, four case studies are presented illustrating tribal experiences in resolving conflicts in tribal planning and in improving relationships between tribes and surrounding political communities. The cases address tribal relations with federal, state, and local governments, as well as internal conflicts within a tribe's own competing policies. Particular attention is focused on the strategies used to bring about innovations in public policy that resulted in strengthening tribal interests and promoting more equitable relations with non-tribal governments. In each of these case studies, I use a phenomenological approach, which simultaneously combines the perspectives of observer and participant in the evaluation of each planning experience, based on my prior involvement as the planning director and general manager of the Swinomish tribe. The case studies are used to reflect the application of the general planning model presented in chapter 7. The case study experiences are not intended as a demonstration of universal applicability, but, rather, to reflect the particular circumstances and outcomes of the affected tribal communities and their non-tribal political counterparts.

In chapter 8, "Mediating Tribal-State Conflicts: Experiences from Washington State," the shift in public policy from adversity to cooperation is reviewed through several examples that illustrate the development of new forms of state-tribal relations. The chapter highlights dispute resolution experiences affecting land, natural resources management, and public services that led to meaningful and improved intergovernmental relations with tribes. A typology of state-tribal conflicts reflecting the state's general interests in tribal affairs is also presented. The chapter explores the circumstances that encouraged the emerging preference in Washington State to mediate conflicts through cooperative approaches as an alternative to litigation and highlights several statewide planning experiences that successfully resolved conflicts through agreements. Although a variety of dispute resolution methods have been successfully employed in tribal/non-tribal relationship building, this chapter emphasizes the particular mediation approach that emerged in Washington State in the years following the federal district court's ruling in *United States v. State of Washington* that affirmed tribal treaty fishing rights and mandated the state to meaningfully involve tribes in the management of natural resources.

Chapter 9, "Regional Pluralism: The Skagit Valley Experience," demonstrates how effective tribal planning can resolve an array of reservation regulatory and development problems. The chapter reviews the events that led to improved regional cooperation in land use planning and in the administration of public services in the Skagit Valley region of Washington State. When the Swinomish Indian Tribe realized that it could not successfully achieve its reservation development goals in isolation from the surrounding region, its strategic approach was to bridge relations with surrounding communities by entering into formal agreements. The result was to pave the way for a new form of political pluralism in the region that would advance tribal interests while simultaneously helping to achieve Washington State's growth management goal for consistency in regional planning. The chapter concludes with lessons that can be applied to other regions that face similar opposing interests in the development of coordinated land use policy.

Overcoming the long suppression of traditional Indian spiritual practice is an important objective in tribal community development. However, these practices can be frustrated when conventional building and public health and safety standards are applied that do not take into account the particular aspects of Indian culture. In chapter 10, "Appropriate Technologies and the Native American Smokehouse," the Swinomish Indian Tribe's attempt to reconcile its own building code compliance as it commenced the construction and operation of a long-anticipated traditional ceremonial smokehouse is presented. The celebrated resumption of smokehouse activities, however, presented new environmental health risks that were not adequately anticipated and that required remediation. In a previously published article co-authored with Mary Ellen Flanagan (Zaferatos and Flanagan 2001), I examined how the tribe was able to overcome building and public health code conflicts that prohibited structures with open fires through the tribe's own ability to modify those standards and how the associated health risks posed by open fire burning can be mitigated with the assistance of technical assistance partnerships. The case study illustrates how appropriate technologies can be applied in tribal community development in a manner that respects cultural values and ceremonial practices. Moreover, the experience demonstrates how tribes can reconcile their internal conflicts with respect to the attainment of both cultural preservation goals and conventional public safety requirements.

During the past two decades, considerable national attention has focused on the environmental pollution inequity that persists among the nation's poorest communities. Despite these efforts, the struggle to attain environmental justice among tribal nations is more than a matter of equitably enforcing national laws. It is also a matter of honoring the promise that Native American homelands would forever be sustainable through the federal trust duty of protecting Indian lands and natural resources. Of equal importance is the federal promise to assist tribes in managing their reservation environments under their own reserved powers of self-government. Chapter 11, "Environmental Justice on the Swinomish Indian Reservation," traces the tribe's two-decade struggle in pursuit of reservation environmental justice. The PM Northwest Inc. (PMNW) dumpsite is located within the boundaries of the Swinomish Indian Reservation in Washington State. Between 1958 and 1970, PMNW contracted with local oil refineries to dispose of their hazardous wastes in the reservation dumpsite. Almost twenty years would pass before the tribe was able to persuade the US Environmental Protection Agency (EPA) that it had a fiduciary responsibility and that a cleanup action under the Comprehensive Environmental Response, Compensation, and Liability Act (CERCLA) was warranted. The chapter reviews the enduring struggle to achieve Indian environmental justice in the Swinomish homeland, a process that was dependent upon the concurrent development of the tribe's own political and environmental management capacity, as well as EPA's acknowledgment that Indian environmental justice is integrally linked to its federal trust responsibility.

Part ONE

The Setting for Native American Reservation Planning

2

An Overview of Federal Indian Policy and the Evolution of the Tribal Political Community

A BASIC PREMISE of federal Indian law is the right of Indian self government based on the principle that a tribe's political authority is inherent and has never been extinguished.

The term "Indian tribe" has several meanings. Ethnologists define a tribe as a group of Indians[1] sharing a common heritage and a distinct language. At the most basic level, a tribe is considered "a group of Indians that is recognized as constituting a distinct and historically continuous political entity for some governmental purpose" (Canby 2009). Recognition depends on the purpose for which the status of Indian tribe is asserted. A tribe is normally recognized to exist by the federal government if Congress or the President "has historically created a reservation for the tribe and the U.S. has had some continuing political relationship with the tribe" (Newton 2012). The Department of the Interior requires federal recognition as a prerequisite for a tribe's entitlement to federal Indian services.

---

1. The term "Indian" can be defined in both an ethnological (racial) or a legal sense. Ethnologists classify a person as being Indian, i.e., as belonging to a distinct race of people, only when that person has greater than one-half Indian blood quantum. Federal laws define an Indian as anyone of Indian descent and may specify a minimum blood quantum to be considered as an Indian for purposes of those laws. Still other federal laws define an Indian as anyone who has been accepted as a member of a "federally recognized" Indian tribe, pursuant to the tribe's eligibility requirements for enrollment.

Federal recognition may be derived from a treaty, statute, or executive or administrative order based on a previous relationship with the tribe as a distinct political entity. These events constitute the existence of a special relationship between the federal government and the tribe. To qualify for federal recognition, a tribe must satisfy five requirements as established by the Department of the Interior:[2]

1. The group can be identified by historical evidence, either written or oral;

2. Its members are descendants of an Indian tribe that inhabited a specific area and who continue to inhabit a specific area in a community viewed as American Indian and distinct from other populations in that area;

3. The Indian group has maintained governmental authority over its membership and has been an autonomous entity throughout history, including the present;

4. The group membership is composed principally of persons who are not members of any other tribe; and

5. The tribe has not been the subject of congressional legislation expressly terminating its relationship with the federal government.

Denial of federal recognition does not alone disqualify Indian people from participating in federal Indian programs. Indian persons can enforce a treaty that their ancestors entered into with the United States even though the federal government refuses to recognize the existence of that tribe.[3] Tribes have often been defined by their political identity. For example, when several ethnological tribes were placed within the same reservation, they often assumed a single political identity. Single ethnological tribes that were dispersed to different reservations often acquired

---

2. In 1978, the Department of the Interior published criteria for the acknowledgment of the existence of tribes not previously recognized. See 25 C.F.R. § 83 (1994).

3. The Ninth Circuit Court of Appeals found "the failure of the federal government to recognize a particular group of Indians as a tribe cannot deprive that group of vested treaty rights. The group must have maintained itself as a distinct community identifiable to the group named in the treaty" (*United States v. State of Washington*, 641 F.2d. 1368 (9th Cir. 1981)).

separate political identities. Although the terms *nation, tribes,* and *band* have been used interchangeably in treaties and statutes, a treaty tribe may no longer possess its original form of self-governing authority if its governmental structure has been altered under Congress's plenary powers.

Indian tribes derive their governmental powers for determining their collective welfare from three basic sources: treaty rights, federally conveyed rights, and retained inherent sovereignty. Prior to the treaties, as sovereign political entities, the tribes exercised absolute autonomy of choice in decision-making. The treaties served both to limit sovereignty and to affirm rights and powers. The federal history of post-treaty relations, however, has been inconsistent regarding the treatment of tribes as legitimate governments, as evidenced during the 1950s to 1960s termination era. Since 1970, the adoption of federal self-determination policy and enactment of subsequent legislation has once again reaffirmed tribal rights and authority. Self-determination policy promotes Indian self-governance by affirming and supporting the right of tribes to decide their collective future. The dependent-sovereign political nature of tribes is a fundamental quality that, among other characteristics, distinguishes tribes from other American cultural communities.

It is estimated that prior to the arrival of Europeans, more than 400 independent tribal communities existed. By 1900, the combination of war and disease reduced a population of more than one million Indians to less than 300,000. Since 1900, the Indian population has increased to 2.9 million.[4] Currently, 566 Indian tribes are federally recognized, including more than 200 village groups in Alaska.[5] The number of Indian reservations (including federal and state recognized reservations, pueblos, rancheros, and communities) total 334. While American Indian reservations[6]

4. U.S. Census. 2010. "Selected Population Characteristics for American Indian and Alaska Native Areas. Summary Population and Housing Characteristics." U.S. Bureau of the Census: Washington, D.C.

5. Federal Register, Volume 77, Number 155, dated August 10, 2012 (77 Fed. Reg. 47868).

6. "Indian Reservation" defines the area of land set aside by the federal government for the use, possession, and benefit of an Indian tribe or group of Indians. Most

cover approximately fifty-six million acres, with reservations varying in size from the fifteen million acre Navajo Indian reservation to the one acre Golden Hill Indian reservation in Connecticut, many reservations contain a high percentage of land that is owned and occupied by non-Indians. Only 140 of the 334 reservations have an entirely tribally owned land base.

Indian persons have the lowest life expectancy of any group in the United States. American Indian life expectancy is only two-thirds that of the non-Indian population. Indians also suffer from a high rate of unemployment and fall below the national average of income, quality of housing, and education. Indians continue to be the most impoverished and economically deprived segment of our population. The major social and economic problems facing Indian people today are a result of the complex pattern of laws, particularly federal laws, that have dominated Indian life (Pevar 2012). Paradoxically, while federal laws are intended to benefit the welfare of Indians, they have caused both political and economic dependencies as the economic survival and social welfare of Indians continue to depend upon federal assistance. The conditions of tribal communities today are inextricably linked to 200 years of federal Indian policy and regulation.

To understand the present situation that tribal communities face, an understanding of the historical events that have led to their current political status is essential. Past federal Indian policy inconsistencies have shifted dramatically between two prevailing and opposing public policy positions. One prevailing position regarded tribal communities as enduring political entities with a protected territory, while the other sought the decline or elimination of tribes, the removal of their territories from trust protection, and the assimilation of their members into mainstream society. These two contradictory positions regarding Indian affairs have continually shaped legislation, court decisions, and the federal administration

---

reservations were created through congressional acts, a federal treaty, presidential order, or other act of Congress. All land areas contained within the exterior boundaries of an Indian reservation are also referred to as "Indian country."

of Indian affairs. These policy shifts have occurred abruptly over time, resulting in a disruption of the social and political cohesiveness of tribes. Table 1 summarizes the effects of the major federal Indian policy periods on the tribal political community.

TABLE 1 Effects of Federal Indian Policy

US Policy Event	Period	Effect of Policy on Indian Territory
Independence Period	1492–1787	Isolationism; recognition of tribal self-governance and autonomy
Early Period Agreements	1787–1828	Introduction of trade relations
Relocation Period	1828–1887	Treaty-making; reservation of tribal lands as exclusive Indian territories
Allotment and Assimilation Era	1887–1934	Introduction of private land ownership; subdivision of communally held lands; procedure for trust to fee conversion of Indian lands; immigration of non-Indians to Indian reservations
Indian Reorganization Period	1934–1953	Reconstitution of Indian territory and tribal self-governance
Termination Era	1953–1967	Disbanding political authority of certain tribes; foreclosure of tribal territories and full assimilation into US political economy
Self-Determination Era	1968–	Reconstitution of tribal territory; affirmation of tribal sovereignty and self-governance
Self-Governance Period	1990–	Further promotion of tribal self-governance through "treatment as a state" delegation for federal program responsibility

Source: Nicholas C. Zaferatos.

Overview of Federal Indian Policy Periods

The Tribal Independence Period: 1492–1787

Prior to, and immediately following contact with non-Indian society, each tribe exerted autonomy over its own territory and conducted its affairs subject to its own form of government, cultural values, and language. Treaties and agreements were made between the early settlers and neighboring tribes, and goods were exchanged for non-Indians to acquire title to Indian lands, as well as to foster friendship. However, as these early settlements grew, conflicts began to emerge over the control of land.

Early Agreements with Tribal Sovereigns: 1787–1828

During the seventeenth century, both British and Spanish colonies began negotiating treaties with Indian tribes, thereby granting tribes a sovereign status similar to their relations with the colonial governments (American Indian Lawyer Training Program 1988). Britain and its colonies entered into treaties with a number of tribes. The British Crown's relationship with Indian tribes constituted a formalized relationship that regarded the tribes as foreign states. As the colonists encroached upon Indian territories, an imminent threat of conflict emerged as the Crown assumed the role of protector of the tribes from the colonialist encroachment. As a result, during the colonial revolution against Britain, many tribes aligned themselves with the Crown (Pevar 2012). To avoid potential Indian conflict, feared to be disruptive to colonial settlement after Independence, the US Constitution clarified the federal government's role with respect to its future relationship with the tribes. Congress was granted constitutional powers to regulate commerce with the tribes, and the president was authorized to enter into treaties with the consent of the Senate.[7] The US government regarded Indian tribes as having a status similar to that of a foreign nation, and efforts were made to solidify their political allegiance. The Northwest Ordinance of 1787,[8] ratified by Congress in 1789, declared

---

7. U.S. Const. art. I, § 8, cl. 3; art. II, § 2, cl. 2.
8. Act of August 7, 1789, 1 Stat. 50.

"the utmost good faith shall always be observed towards Indians; their land and property shall never be taken from them without their consent."

The First Congress established the basis of Indian policy with the passage of the Trade and Intercourse Acts between 1790 and 1834.[9] The purpose of these acts was to physically separate Indians from non-Indians and to subject the interaction of these groups to federal control. The acts established the first boundaries of Indian country[10] and served to protect Indian interests in a number of ways: non-Indians were prohibited from acquiring Indian lands or from settling or entering upon those lands for purposes of hunting or grazing; trading with Indians was controlled through federal licensing and regulation; and crimes and takings by non-Indians against Indians were prohibited under federal laws that provided for federal compensation to injured Indians. The Trade and Intercourse Acts did not interfere with the commerce among Indians, which was deferred to the tribes. These protections, however, were often ignored as the federal government overlooked the forcible, illegal taking of title to Indian lands by non-Indians that continued throughout this period.

The Relocation Period: 1828–1887

Federal Indian policy shifted in 1828 when Andrew Jackson announced the federal goal of the removal of eastern Indian tribes to the west. This relocation or "removal" policy became the "dominant federal Indian policy of the 19th century" (Deloria 1985). In 1830, Congress passed the Indian Removal Act that authorized the president to negotiate with eastern tribes for their relocation to areas west of the Mississippi River. Many tribes that were previously granted permanent reservations in Arkansas, Kansas, Iowa, Illinois, Missouri, and Wisconsin were forced to move to the Oklahoma Indian Territory. The federal intention of reservation

9. 1 Stat. 137, 1790; and 4 Stat. 729, 1834.

10. "Indian country" refers to all lands under the supervision of the US government that have been set aside for the use and benefit by Indians. Indian country incorporates Indian reservation lands as well as other lands existing outside Indian reservations under federal jurisdiction which are dedicated for Indian use. Congress first used the term in 1790 (18 U.S.C. § 1151) to describe the territory controlled by Indians.

relocation was to remove Indians from the settlement territories and force them to cede most of their previously occupied lands in exchange for a reservation of smaller territories. Concurrently, following the discovery of gold in California in 1848 and increased non-Indian settlement, western tribes were similarly subjected to removal policies.

One century after Congress passed the Northwest Ordinance of 1787 that acknowledged the sovereign integrity of Indian tribes, Congress sought to diminish the status of tribal sovereignty. In 1871, Congress ended the practice of treaty-making with tribes[11] and abandoned its treatment of tribes as independent nations. Thereafter, federal dealings with tribes occurred through the passage of statutes that, unlike treaties, did not require tribal consent. Existing treaties, however, would continue to remain intact. Reservations created after 1871 were established through statute or by executive order, the intent of which was to separate Indians and non-Indians. Congress enacted a number of laws during the mid-nineteenth century that sought to increase federal control over Indians and to promote their assimilation into non-Indian society. The emphasis of these laws and subsequent programs was directed toward educating and "civilizing" Indian youth. By 1887, more than 200 Indian schools were established by the federal government that prohibited Indian youth from speaking their Native languages and from practicing their social and religious traditions.

Parallel to the emerging policy of Indian removal, the Supreme Court was formulating its own Indian legal doctrines that would have a long term influence on Indian law. The shaping of both federal Indian law and policy was largely influenced by three Supreme Court opinions written by Chief Justice John Marshall. Collectively referred to as the *Marshall Trilogy*, the decisions included *Johnson v. McIntosh*,[12] *Cherokee Nation v. Georgia*,[13] and *Worcester v. Georgia*.[14] In the first of these major decisions

11. 16 Stat. 544, 566, codified as 25 U.S.C. § 71.
12. 21 U.S. (8 Wheat.) 543 (1823).
13. 30 U.S. 1 (1831).
14. 31 U.S. (6 Pet.) 515 (1832).

relating to a tribe's legal and historic relationship to the land, the court recognized the right of Indians to their land. However, this right was viewed as an occupancy right as opposed to an ownership right, with the title to the land held in trust by the United States. The doctrine of "Indian title" became one of the most controversial doctrines in Indian law.

In *Johnson v. McIntosh*, the court considered whether a non-Indian who had purchased land from an Indian tribe had indeed obtained valid title, as the purchaser could only acquire that interest which the tribe itself could legally sell. The Supreme Court held that the purchaser did not acquire valid title since the tribe no longer owned the land. The court ruled that by virtue of Europe's discovery and conquest of the North American continent, the US government had become the owner of all the land within the United States. The court went on to rule that Indians retained a "right of occupancy" of their ancestral homelands, a right that was superior to all claims other than those of the federal government. The federal government could extinguish this *Indian title*,[15] but, until it did so, Indians had the right to remain on their original homelands (Pevar 2012). The Court thereby established four principles of Indian title":[16]

1. The federal government acquired ownership of all land within the United States by discovery and conquest;

2. Indians retain a perpetual right to live on their ancestral homelands until Congress decides to take this land for other purposes;

3. Indian title is a possessory interest, and Indians have a right to possess the ancestral homelands, but not to own them unless Congress grants the Indians title; and

4. Indian title cannot be sold by Indians without authorization from the federal government.

Between 1828 and 1830 the state of Georgia enacted a series of laws that divided the Cherokee tribal territory among several counties, extended

---

15. "Indian title" is also referred to as "aboriginal title" or "Indian right of occupancy."

16. The doctrine of Indian title continues to serve as an important tribal protection. Federal courts have recognized that tribes can eject persons, including state and local officials, from lands claimed under Indian title.

state law into the Cherokee territory, invalidated Cherokee law, and made it a criminal offense for the Cherokees to act in a governmental capacity. The Cherokees brought suit[17] in the Supreme Court in *Cherokee Nation v. Georgia*. Chief Marshall determined that the tribe had demonstrated that it was a "state" and "a distinct political society separate from others, capable of managing its own affairs, and governing itself," as the treaties between the tribe and the US government had recognized. However, Marshall determined that the tribe could not constitute a "foreign" state:

> Though the Indians are acknowledged to have an unquestionable, and, heretofore unquestioned, right to the lands they occupy, until that right shall be extinguished by a voluntary cession to our government; yet it may well be doubted whether those tribes which reside within the acknowledged boundaries of the United States can, with strict accuracy, be denominated foreign nations. They may, more correctly, perhaps, be denominated domestic dependent nations. They occupy a territory to which we assert a title independent of their will, which must take effect in point of possession, when their right of possession ceases. Meanwhile, they are in a state of pupilage; their relation to the United States resembles that of a ward to his guardian.[18]

Marshall had established the judicial basis for supporting the future protection of tribal sovereignty by recognizing the status of tribes as *domestic dependent nations*. This characterization of tribes as *wards* of the federal government provided a basis for the protection of tribes by the federal government and reaffirmed the tribal right to self-government. In *Worcester v. Georgia*,[19] the Court found that the treaties, along with the Trade and Intercourse Acts, "manifestly consider the several Indian nations as distinct political communities, having territorial boundaries, within which their authority is exclusive . . . , in which the laws of Georgia

17. The ability of the Cherokee tribe to bring suit was based on its "foreign state" status within the meaning of article III, section 2, of the US Constitution defining judicial power.

18. 30 U.S. (5 Pet.) at 17.

19. 31 U.S. (6 Pet.) 515, 557 (1832).

can have no force." Marshall's ruling in *Worcester* established the foundations of jurisdictional law that excluded a state's power over Indian affairs. The ruling, however, did not alter the administration's policies of removal, as virtually all of the tribes located east of the Mississippi River were relocated to the west.

The Allotment and Assimilation Period: 1887–1934

During the 1870s, two contrary public opinions emerged with respect to the conditions of Indians and their reservations. Sympathetic views toward Indians raised moral concern about the impoverished conditions most Indians faced on reservations. Adversarial views objected to large reservation territories that prohibited non-Indian settlement. The two disparate viewpoints resulted in the General Allotment Act of 1887,[20] also known as the Dawes Act. Both legal historians and the tribes consider this to be one of the most disastrous periods of Indian legislation in US history. Initial support for passage of the act reflected growing public sentiment toward improving Indian conditions and assumed that, if Indians were given the opportunity to cultivate privately owned land, they would assimilate into American society as productive farmers. Tribal governments were viewed as obstacles to individual Indians being able to assimilate and, hence, succeed within American society.

The effects of the act, however, were to diminish the role of tribal governments, to abolish Indian reservations, and to force Indians to adopt the agrarian and private property values integral to non-Indian society. Congress divided communally held tribal lands into separate "trust allotments,"[21] transferring to each eligible tribal member a trust title right to an individual parcel, and providing for the disposition of surplus parcels to non-Indians. Generally, allotments of 160 acres were made available to each family head and eighty acres distributed to other individuals.

20. 24 Stat. 388, as amended, 25 U.S.C. § 332–58.

21. "Trust allotments" refers to federal land that has been set aside for the exclusive use by an Indian, who is called the "allottee." A restricted allotment consists of land requiring federal approval before it can be sold, leased, mortgaged, or encumbered.

Title to the allotted land was to be held in trust by the United States for a period of twenty-five years, after which time the land was to be conveyed to the Indian allottee in fee simple title, free of encumbrances. It was the congressional intent that Indians be protected from state taxation during this transitional period to Indian private ownership. The act also conveyed US citizenship to Indians upon receiving allotments and subjected Indians to state criminal and civil law.[22] Furthermore, the secretary of the interior was authorized to negotiate with tribes for the disposition of any excess lands that remained after allotments, providing for non-Indian purchase of, and settlement on, those surplus lands.

The act was imposed upon the tribes without the consent of either the tribes or the affected individual Indians. The immediate effect of the act was a rapid decline in the amount of Indian held land, from 138 million acres in 1887 to forty-eight million acres in 1934 (Pevar 2012). A large percentage of the original land base was sold to non-Indians as tribal surplus. The balance was subsequently sold by allottees when, after the twenty-five-year trust period expired, their lands became subject to state taxation and intestacy laws that created a highly fractionated ownership pattern that made the use and management of the land difficult. With the transfer of ownership from Indian trust to fee allotments, many reservations became checkerboard configurations of Indian and non-Indian ownership.

While the objective of separating Indians from their lands was largely successful, the effect of the policy of Indian assimilation was later viewed as disastrous, as a majority of Indians did not wish to abandon their communal societies and adopt Western values. Since most of the reservation land base was unsuitable for small scale agriculture—a form of economic production that was alien to them—many impoverished Indians either voluntarily sold their land parcels to white settlers or, unable to pay state-imposed real estate taxes, lost their land in foreclosure. Tribal governments

---

22. In 1924, Congress passed a statute conferring citizenship to most Indians born within the United States (8 U.S.C. § 1401 (b)), completing the process of granting citizenship to Indians, and the additional complicating effect of subjugating Indians as citizens of the states where they resided.

and their isolated communities became disrupted by the sudden presence of increasing non-Indian populations within the reservations and by the significant shrinkage of the tribal community's territorial homeland. The legacy of the General Allotment Act has contributed greatly to the destruction of Indian culture and persists as an ongoing obstacle as tribes work to strengthen self-government, maintain social cohesiveness, and achieve economic improvement.

The Indian Reorganization Period: 1934–1953

A major reversal of federal Indian policy was introduced in the early 1930s due, in part, to the diminished demand by non-Indians for Indian lands and resources during the Great Depression. Public opinion at the time favored a radical new policy. The Meriam Report of 1928[23] documented the failures of federal Indian policy during the Allotment Period and promoted a new direction that supported a reversal of federal policy. In 1934, John Collier,[24] commissioner of Indian affairs and a firm supporter of Indian reform, declared a new federal position toward tribes: "No interference with Indian religious life or expression will hereafter be tolerated. The cultural history of Indians is in all respects to be considered equal to that of any non-Indian group."

In June 1934, Congress passed the Indian Reorganization Act[25] (IRA), also known as the Wheeler-Howard Act. The express purpose of the IRA was to "rehabilitate the Indian's economic life and to give him a chance to develop the initiative destroyed by a century of oppression and paternalism."[26] The IRA was founded on the principle that the indefinite existence of tribes was both likely and morally just. The act sought to protect the remaining tribal territories and to assist in establishing a more effective governing structure to promote their self-governance.

23. Institute for Government Research (IGR). 1928. *The Problem of Indian Administration*. Washington, DC: IGR.

24. Commissioner of Indian Affairs. 1934. *Annual Report*, p. 90. Washington DC: Office of the Commissioner of Indian Affairs.

25. 25 U.S.C. §§ 461 et seq.

26. H.R. Rep. no. 1804, 73d Cong. 2d sess., p. 6 (1934).

The IRA formally ended the practice of allotment of tribal lands to individual Indians and authorized the secretary of the interior to add additional lands to existing reservations, to create new reservations for landless tribes, and to restore tribal ownership to any land that had been removed as surplus under the General Allotment Act and not sold to non-Indians. The act also extended the trust period for allotments that still remained in trust. To strengthen self-governance, the act authorized tribes to organize and adopt constitutions and bylaws subject to the ratification by the tribal membership and the subsequent approval by the secretary. The IRA established a $10 million revolving credit fund to incorporated tribes and required the secretary of the interior to provide Indian hiring preference within the Bureau of Indian Affairs in order that Indians may influence the formulation and administration of federal Indian policy.

Passage of the IRA resulted in an increase of Indian landholdings between 1935 and 1953 of more than 2 million acres, as well as the accompaniment of reservation improvements in health facilities, irrigation works, housing, schools, and roads. While the act was effective in reversing the further erosion of tribal territories, provisions for encouraging tribal adoption of governing structures were less successful. The constitutional model of government encouraged by the act was based on the US constitutional model, a model regarded as unsuitable by many tribes. Hence, approximately one half of the tribes rejected reorganization under the act and chose instead to retain their inherent form of self-government.[27] Tribes that incorporated under the Indian Reorganization Act adopted standardized charters that allowed the tribes to engage in economic activities within a corporate framework.[28] The significance of the act is highlighted by its support of tribal self-governance.

27. The IRA provided that tribes could vote not to be governed by its provisions and many tribes rejected the application of the act. These tribes retained their aboriginal form of self-government, and their governing actions are generally not subject to secretarial approvals. While some non-IRA tribes operate similarly to IRA governments, others continue to operate under unwritten customary laws.

28. Corporate powers were conferred to the chartered tribal corporations. However, many powers, including the pledging of tribal assets, remained subject to secretarial

The Termination Period: 1953–1967

During this period, Congress abruptly abandoned its policy of supporting tribal self-governance and also ended its commitment to improving the Indian economic condition. A new policy direction emerged that focused on the collapse of cohesive tribal unity. Congress sought to terminate the federal trust relationship and all associated benefits and services provided to Indian tribes and to force the dissolution of their reservations. In 1953, Congress adopted House Resolution 108, which established the policy of termination, seeking to make "Indians subject to the same laws and entitled to the same privileges and responsibilities as other citizens of the United States, and to end their status as wards of the United States."[29] Under the policy, several tribes were terminated by statute, thus ending their special relationship with the federal government and fully subjecting them to state laws. Further, their lands were converted to private ownership and often sold to non-Indians. Despite Congress's expressed purpose of "freeing" the Indians from burdensome federal control, the results were generally tragic. Concurrent with Congress's goal of termination, the Bureau of Indian Affairs encouraged Indians to relocate from the reservation, with incentives provided under the Interior Department's Indian relocation programs. These programs offered funding assistance to Indians seeking employment in urban areas. However, unemployed reservation Indians who relocated to target cities often became part of the urban poor and suffered the additional social trauma associated with cultural dislocation.

Congress furthered the termination policy in 1953 with the enactment of Public Law 280.[30] The statute extended state civil jurisdiction[31]

---

approval. The corporate power subjecting the entity to lawsuits continues to concern many tribes that are reluctant to waive their sovereign immunity.

29. H. Cong. Res. 108, 83rd Cong., 1st Session. 67 Stat. B132 (1953).

30. Pub. L. 280, 67 Stat. 588 (1953), codified as amended in 18 U.S.C. §§ 1161–62, 25 U.S.C. §§ 1321–22, and 28 U.S.C. § 1360.

31. Federal courts later defined "civil jurisdiction" to mean only *adjudicatory jurisdiction* (civil causes of action and state laws that govern how a court makes decisions) and not *regulatory jurisdiction*.

to Indian country in five states, and conferred full criminal and partial civil jurisdiction over Indian reservations.[32] The law also consented to the assumption of jurisdiction by any other state that agreed to assume such jurisdiction by either statute or by a state constitutional amendment. Consent of the concerned tribes was not required. Public Law 280 altered the division of jurisdiction among the federal government, the states, and the tribes in those states where it applied and severely diminished tribal authority.

State governments, which historically resisted tribal sovereignty within their territorial limits, had long sought to gain control over Indian resources and Indian people (Champagne and Goldberg 2012; Cline 2013). Since Public Law 280 transferred powers and responsibilities from the federal government to the respective states, an anomaly was created in which tribal governance oversight was granted to the historic adversary of tribal interests. However, assumption of Public Law 280 jurisdiction by the states did not entirely extinguish the federal trust relationship. The act disclaimed any grant to the states over the powers to tax Indian properties held in federal trust or the assumption of treaty rights held in hunting or fishing. A later court decision in *Bryan v. Itasca County*[33] held that the law had not conveyed to the states general regulatory power in Indian country. Public Law 280 represented only a partial step toward termination by eroding certain immunity from state powers previously enjoyed by the tribes. The state obligation under Public Law 280 was eventually ignored by the states because the delegation of authority required substantial enforcement responsibilities without the ability to generate a compensating tax revenue. The tribes viewed Public Law 280 unfavorably and objected to any reversion of federal powers to the states, absent their expressed consent (Goldberg 2009, 2010).

---

32. The law transferred state jurisdiction to all Indian country within the five states of Nebraska, Wisconsin, California, Oregon, except the Warm Springs Reservation, and Minnesota, except the Red Lake Reservation.

33. *Bryan v. Itasca County*, 426 U.S. 376 (1976).

Tribal Self-Determination Period: 1968 to Present

In 1958, the Senate Committee on Interior and Insular Affairs, in an attempt to reverse the loss of Indian lands to non-Indian ownership, persuaded the secretary of the interior to declare a moratorium on the further sale of Indian land, pending an evaluation of the extent of Indian land losses. The study found that the loss of approximately 2.6 million acres of Indian land occurred between 1948 and 1950, and an additional 1.8 million acres had been transferred to non-Indian ownership between 1953 and 1957. The results of the evaluation recognized the "potentially disastrous" effects of termination and hastened Congress's disillusionment with termination policies.[34] One of the earliest formal repudiations of termination occurred on September 18, 1958, when, in a radio address, Interior Secretary Seaton called for the end of "coercive termination." Seaton[35] advocated against the further termination of Indian tribes unless

> [s]uch tribe or group has clearly demonstrated first, that it understands the path under which such a program would go forward, and second, that the tribe or group affected concurs in and supports the plan proposed. . . . To me it would be incredible, even criminal, to send an Indian tribe out in the streets of American life until and unless the educational level of that tribe was one which was equal to the responsibilities which it was shouldering.

In the 1960s presidential election campaign, John F. Kennedy stated that, if elected:[36]

> There would be no change in treaty or contractual relationships without tribal consent and there would be protection of the Indian land base, credit assistance, and encouragement of tribal planning for economic development.

34. Chairman of the Senate Committee on Interior and Insular Affairs, 85th Cong., 20 Sess., Memorandum: Indian Land Transactions XVII.

35. From Seaton's broadcast address, KCLS radio, Flagstaff, Ariz., and transcribed in 105 Cong. Rec. 3103 (1959).

36. S. Rep. no. 994, 87th Cong., 1st Sess., part I, at 801 (1961).

President Kennedy's later appointment of Stewart Udall as secretary of the interior led to the creation of a special Interior Department task force to address Indian affairs. The task force recommended a shift in policy from termination of the federal trust relationship to the development of human and natural resources on Indian reservations. Kennedy also sought to include Indians within his "new frontier" social and economic programs that led to expanded BIA services in education, vocational training, housing, and community development. The idea of self-determination gained further support during President Johnson's administration by including Indians within the "Great Society" legislation.[37] In 1966, President Johnson appointed the first Native American to the post of commissioner of Indian affairs. Under Robert Bennett's leadership, tribes were encouraged to contract with the BIA to administer on-reservation federal Indian programs.[38]

In 1968, in an effort to repudiate the policy of assimilation, Congress passed the Indian Civil Rights Act.[39] The act imposed upon the tribes the requirements of the Bill of Rights and constitutional restraints in their governmental actions, as similarly imposed upon the states by the Fourteenth Amendment. Through statute, the Indian Civil Rights Act imposed

---

37. In President Johnson's 1968 Indian policy speech entitled "Special Message to the Congress on the Problems of the American Indian: the Forgotten American" (1968, Pub. Papers, Part I, at 335), he proposed "a new goal for our Indian programs: A goal that ends the old debate about 'termination' of Indian programs and stressed self-determination; a goal that erases old attitudes of paternalism and promotes partnership and self help. An opportunity to remain in their homelands, if they choose, without surrendering their dignity; an opportunity to move to towns and cities of America, if they choose, equipped with the skills to live in equality and dignity."

38. Tribes were included in many legislative programs under the "War on Poverty" years in the 1960s. In 1961, the Department of Housing and Urban Development (HUD) extended eligibility for public housing assistance to Indian reservations. HUD established tribal housing authorities to operate low rental and mutual help housing projects. In addition to the BIA and Indian Health Services, the Office of Economic Opportunity provided broad services to Indians and reservations in the 1960s.

39. 82 Stat. 77, 25 U.S.C. §§ 1301 et seq.

the requirements for the protection of free speech, free exercise of religion, and due process and equal protection under the law. The act's passage presumed the continued existence of tribal governments in contrast to the preceding policy of termination. The act amended Public Law 280 to prohibit any further state assumption of civil and criminal jurisdiction in Indian country without the express approval of the tribes[40] and provided for state retrocession from such jurisdiction.

In the same year, President Nixon commissioned a report on the state of Indian Affairs. The "Josephy Report" contained recommendations based on the "Indians' own expressed desires and proposals for solutions to their needs" and encouraged a policy of Indian self-determination (Josephy 1971). The newly accepted goals of Indian control over both planning and administration of Indian programs represented the cornerstone of Nixon's "Special Message to Congress" of July 8, 1970,[41] wherein he formally pronounced the new federal Indian policy. Nixon criticized past policies toward Indians and praised the "Indian's history of creativity and survival despite overwhelming obstacles."[42] He called for the rejection of termination and paternalism policies, because they ignored the moral and legal obligations inherent in the special relationship between tribes and the federal government and resulted in the erosion of Indian initiative and morale. Urging Congress to pass a resolution that expressly repudiated the termination policy in House Concurrent Resolution 108, he simultaneously advocated new legislation that would empower Indian communities to assume control of their programs and their political affairs. The new self-determination Indian policy statement reinstated the trust relationship between the federal government and the tribes and

40. 25 U.S.C. §§ 1321–22, 1326.

41. See Richard M. Nixon, 1970, "Special Message on Indian Affairs," July 8, in *Public Papers of the Presidents of the United States, 1970*. 564–67 and 576.

42. Ibid. President Nixon expressly denounced the termination policy in 1970 and stated: "This, then, must be the goal of any new national policy towards Indian People: to strengthen the Indian sense of autonomy without threatening his sense of community."

encouraged further congressional legislation to provide for greater tribal self government.[43]

The Indian Self-Determination and Education Assistance Act of 1975,[44] recognized as the pivotal centerpiece legislation supporting Indian self-government since the IRA, provided the instrument that allowed tribes to directly administer the federal government's Indian programs within their reservations. The Self-Determination Act reflected a fundamental philosophical change concerning the administration of Indian affairs: that tribal programs should be funded by the federal government, but the programs should be planned and administered by the tribes themselves.

In 1983, President Reagan reaffirmed the federal government's policy of promoting tribal self-determination and echoed President Nixon's reversal of the termination policy:[45]

This administration intends to restore tribal governments to their rightful place among the governments of this nation and to enable tribal governments, along with state and local governments, to resume control over their own affairs.

The self-determination policy is premised on the ideal that tribes constitute legitimate basic governmental units and seeks to strengthen tribal self-governance. The self-determination policy has been reaffirmed by executive orders under presidents George Bush,[46] William Clinton,[47]

43. See 116 Cong. Rec. 23258.

44. Pub. L. No. 93-638, codified at 25 U.S.C. §§ 450f et seq., and in sections of chapters 5, 25, 42, and 50 U.S.C.

45. Ronald Reagan. 1983. "Presidential Statement on Indian Policy," January 24. *Weekly Compilation of Presidential Documents* 98.

46. George Bush. "Statement by the President of June 14, 1991 Reaffirming the Government to Government Relationship between the Federal Government and Tribal Governments." Los Angeles: Office of the Press Secretary.

47. See William J. Clinton, 1994, "The President Memorandum of April 29, 1994," 59 Fed. Reg. 22951, May 4; Executive Order No. 13084, Fed. Reg. 63:96; Presidential Documents, 27655–57, May 19, 1998.

George W. Bush,[48] and Barack Obama,[49] promoting the government-to-government relationship between the federal government and tribal governments and the exercise of inherent sovereign powers of tribes.

Reconstituting the Tribal Territory

The self-determination era brought about critical reforms in an attempt to help correct some of the most harmful effects that resulted from assimilation and termination policies. One of the important reforms witnessed during this period was the reconciliation of the long-standing tribal claims to aboriginal land titles. Beginning in the late 1970s, Congress authorized the first of a series of land claim settlements by enacting the Rhode Island Indian Claims Settlement Act. The act made approximately 900 acres of state and private land available to a state-chartered, Indian-controlled corporation that was authorized to manage the settlement lands, and appropriated $3.5 million to purchase the private portions of the settlement lands. In return, the tribe consented to extinguish its land claims within Rhode Island and all potential damages based on those claims. Similarly, the Alaska Native Claims Settlement Act (ANCSA), enacted by Congress in 1991, represented a major settlement by Alaska Natives seeking to resolve their aboriginal land claims. The act extinguished all claims based on aboriginal right, title, use, or occupancy of land or water areas in Alaska in return for the transfer of $462,500,000 of general treasury funds into a separate Alaska Native Fund.[50] Alaska was divided into twelve geographic regions, each containing a regional corporation, and village corporations were established for eligible Native groups. The regional corporation supervised the distribution of funds

---

48. See George W. Bush, Executive Order 13175 of November 6, 2000; Fed. Reg. 65:218 Presidential Documents, Nov. 9, 2000; Executive Order 13336 of September 23, 2004; Fed. Reg. 69:87, May 5, 2004.

49. See Barack Obama, 2009, "Memorandum for the Heads of Executive Departments and Agencies," 74 Fed. Reg. 57881 (Nov. 5, 2009).

50. An additional fund of up to $500,000,000 was to be deposited into the fund from mineral royalties.

to village corporations and to individual member stockholders. The act also distributed more than 40,000,000 acres of land to the corporations. Between 1978 and 2006, more than sixteen settlement acts of Congress were authorized, with many claims, as of yet, still unresolved. As with the Alaska Native Claims Settlement Act, Congress tends to prefer restructuring tribal governmental status with a tribal corporate structure, often with the condition that state jurisdiction becomes applicable. While the settlement of land claims is a positive step toward righting past wrongs toward Native peoples, the further diminishment of the inherent sovereignty of those affected tribes,[51] as a condition of the settlement agreements, remains troublesome to many tribes.

Conclusion and Implications for Planning

This chapter introduced the idea of tribal sovereignty as an evolving political conception that has been continually shaped and reshaped by federal policies and legal doctrine. The effects of these inconsistent federal policies and legal decisions have often been contrary to the current policy of Indian self-determination and have resulted in diminishing the tribal land base and weakening tribal powers of self-governance. In combination, these events have created a tumultuous planning environment characterized by jurisdictional uncertainty. The confusing jurisdictional ground upon which tribes conduct their community development planning continues to be contested whenever a tribe's control over its lands and resources is challenged. In subsequent chapters, the implications of conducting tribal planning under the conditions of jurisdictional uncertainty are more fully addressed, as are suggested pathways that tribes can pursue to increase their political authority and to establish greater clarity in order to enable tribal planning to become more effective.

---

51. In 1998, the Supreme Court held in *Alaska v. Native Village of Venetie Tribal Government* (118 S.Ct. 948, 140 L.Ed.2d 30. 1998) that the Neets'aii Gwich'in Indians land was no longer "Indian Country" as the Alaska Native Claims Settlement Act revoked the Venetie Reservation status.

3

The Context of Tribal Sovereignty

In 1832 Chief Justice Marshall declared that "Indian Tribes were distinct political communities having territorial boundaries, within which their authority is
exclusive, and having a right to all the lands within those boundaries, which is
not only acknowledged, but guaranteed by the United States."

THE ABILITY OF A TRIBE to exercise control over its territory is arguably
the most fundamental precondition necessary for effective tribal planning.
This chapter clarifies the status of tribal sovereignty and the civil regulatory authority that tribes are understood to possess over their territorial
resources. Of particular concern to tribal planning are the limitations
placed on a tribe's ability to regulate land use and economic activities,
manage environmental quality, and restrict the conduct of private activities of Indians and non-Indians within the boundaries of a reservation.

The Status of Tribal Sovereignty

The unique relationship between the United States and Indian tribes has
shaped the evolution of Indian law and the development of the doctrine of
tribal sovereignty. While the relationship may have first been introduced
as a means with which to control tribes, their lands, and their natural
resources through subjugation, it is now held that the Indian federal trust
relationship is the basis for the federal protection of Indian resources as
well as for the continuation of federal aid for the management of those

Epigraph from *Worcester v. Georgia*. 31 U.S. (6 Pet.) 515, 557 (1832).

resources. Congress established its special authority over Indian affairs under the Indian Commerce Clause of the Constitution,[1] which empowers Congress to "regulate commerce with foreign nations, and among the several states, and with the Indian Tribes." Together with the power to enter into treaties, this Constitutional clause forms the basis for broad federal power, which the Supreme Court has interpreted as *plenary*, or having full authority over tribes. The concept of a special plenary federal power over Indian affairs has long been established as a cornerstone of Indian law and federal Indian policy. The extent of those plenary powers, however, is limited by the application of the trust doctrine.

Congress's extensive power over the tribes includes the ability to terminate tribes, although compensation must be paid for lands that belonged to a terminated tribe. Though Congress may unilaterally abrogate treaties, the courts have required that Congress express itself clearly before abrogation can be upheld. Further, Congress may revoke regulatory jurisdiction from the tribes and place such power with federal, or under special circumstances, state governments. The dominance of Congress in establishing policies over tribes is underscored by the fact that the Supreme Court has never set aside any act of Congress as being beyond the scope of Congress's power over Indian affairs.[2]

Doctrine of the Federal Trust Responsibility

The Supreme Court in *United States v. Mitchell*[3] reaffirmed the principle of an "undisputed existence of a general trust relationship between the U.S. and the Indian people." The Supreme Court first recognized the existence of a trust relationship in its earliest decisions that interpreted Indian treaties.[4] In almost all of the treaties entered into between 1787 and 1871, Indians ceded their land territories in exchange for promises, including

1. U.S. Const. art. I, § 8, cl. 18.
2. Western Governors' Association (WGA). 1989. *Staff Report on State-Tribal Cooperation.* Denver, CO: WGA.
3. 463 U.S. 206, 225 (1983).
4. See *Cherokee Nation v. Georgia*, 30 U.S. 1 (1831); *Worcester v. Georgia*, 31 U.S. 515 (1882).

the guarantee of a permanent reservation for the tribes and the federal protection of their safety and well-being. The Supreme Court has held that such promises establish a special trust relationship, characterized as that of *ward* and *guardian* and implying the continued promise to create "a duty of protection" toward Indians.[5]

Subsequent Supreme Court decisions reaffirmed the status of tribes as self-governing entities. These precedent-setting decisions interpreted the treaties as well as other federal Acts as protecting the status of tribes as distinct political communities possessing self-governing authority within their respective territorial boundaries. The Trade and Intercourse Acts (Prucha 1970) prohibited the sale of Indian land without federal consent, thereby establishing tribal territorial rights as trust beneficiaries of the United States. This doctrine of trust over Indian resources extended federal protection of Indian landownership from intrusion by state control and subsequent non-Indian settlement. The trust relationship also created a federal responsibility for the maintenance of Indian lands and natural resources. The administration of the trust responsibility has currently been extended beyond the Department of the Interior and the Department of Justice to include the entire federal administration due to the proliferation of federal programs that affect Indians and Indian tribes.[6] Since the 1970s, each of these federal agencies has been directed to establish its Indian policy with respect to the federal trust relationship and based on a government-to-government relationship.

The basis of this special relationship implies that Indians would trust that the US government would fulfill the promises it made in exchange for Indian secession of lands. The federal government's obligations to honor this trust relationship and to fulfill its treaty commitments are hence

5. In *U.S. v. Kagama*, 118 U.S. 375, 384 (1886).

6. See Barack Obama, "Memorandum for the Heads of Executive Departments and Agencies, Presidential Order of November 5, 2009," published at 74 Fed. Reg. 57879 (November 9, 2009); and William J. Clinton, "Government-to-Government Relations with Native American Tribal Governments. The President Memorandum of April 29, 1994," published at 59 Fed. Reg. 22951 (May 4, 1994).

referred to as the *trust relationship* (Pevar 2012).[7] In 1977, the American Indian Policy Review Commission (1976, 130) expressed the nature of the trust obligation as follows:

> The purpose behind the Trust Doctrine is and always has been to ensure the survival and welfare of Indian tribes and people. This includes an obligation to provide those services required to protect and enhance Indian lands, resources, and self government, and also includes those economic and social programs which are necessary to raise the standard of living and social well being of the Indian people to a level comparable to the non-Indian society.

However, the history of federal Indian policy demonstrates the US government's continuous failure to faithfully observe its trust commitments to tribes. In spite of the fact that Congress has a responsibility to fulfill this nation's treaty commitments, it has broken nearly all of its Indian treaties. Furthermore, during the 1950s termination era, Congress abolished more than 100 tribal governments.

Origins of Tribal Sovereignty

Tribal sovereignty generally refers to the inherent right to self-govern, which has never been relinquished. In Chief Justice Marshall's opinion for the majority in *Johnson v. McIntosh*,[8] the Supreme Court held that tribes had no power to grant lands to anyone other than the federal government. By establishing limitations on tribal sovereignty, the Court later emphasized the affirmative governmental power of tribes. In *Cherokee*

---

7. Pevar (2012, 27) observes that "the courts have extended the trust responsibility in three respects: First, federal statutes, agreements and executive orders, can create trust obligations as the treaties also can. Second, the trust obligation may include implied, not just express, commitments. For example, when a treaty promises a tribe it can use its reservation for 'Indian purposes,' this obligates the government to protect the Indian's right to hunt and fish on that land. Finally, the trust responsibility imposes an independent obligation upon the federal government to remain loyal to the Indians and to advance their interests, including their interests in self-government."

8. 21 U.S. (8 Wheat.) 543 (1823).

Nation v. Georgia,[9] the Court held that tribes qualified as separate *states* and further characterized the tribes as *domestic dependent nations.* For 150 years following the Cherokee cases, no additional limitations on tribal sovereignty were found to further restrict the domestic dependency status of the tribes. However, in *Oliphant*,[10] the Supreme Court raised the issue of the Suquamish Indian Tribe's power to exercise criminal jurisdiction over non-Indians on its reservation. The tribe, which relied on its inherent sovereignty, argued that no treaty or act of Congress extinguished its criminal-law authority over non-Indians. But the Supreme Court held that the exercise of criminal jurisdiction over non-Indians was "inconsistent with the domestic status of the tribes" (Pevar 2012). By creating the possibility of further judicial limitations on tribal sovereignty, the *Oliphant* decision posed a threat to tribal autonomy. Where it cannot be shown that a tribal interest is affected, the court in *Montana*[11] held that a tribe lacked inherent powers to regulate hunting and fishing by non-Indians on non-Indian owned land within a reservation.

Due to their status as domestic dependent nations, tribes have also lost their inherent power to regulate liquor sales on reservations.[12] In contrast, the Court in *United States v. Wheeler*[13] found that tribes retain the power to prosecute their own members and that the taxation of non-Indian activities on the reservation was also consistent with a tribe's domestic dependent status.[14] The general attributes constituting tribal sovereignty (Canby 2009) can be summarized as follows:

1. Indian tribes possess inherent governmental powers over all internal affairs;

2. The states are precluded from interfering with the tribal exercise of self government; and

9. 30 U.S. (5 Pet.) 1 (1831).

10. *Oliphant v. Suquamish Indian Tribes*, 435 U.S. 191 (1978).

11. *Montana v. United States*, 450 U.S. 544, 564–65 (1981).

12. See *Rice v. Rehner*, 463 U.S. 713, 726 (1983).

13. *U.S. v. Wheeler*, 435 U.S. 313, 327 (1978).

14. In *Washington v. Confederated Tribes of the Colville Indian Reservation*, 447 U.S. 134, 152–54 (1980).

3. Congress has plenary power to limit tribal sovereignty.

Tribal governments are not comparable to local governments, which derive their authority directly from states. In order for a municipality to enact regulations, it must be shown that the state has conferred such power to that municipality, as the state is the sovereign body that possesses those powers. A tribe, conversely, retains its own sources of governing powers. For example, a tribe's power to levy a tax is not subject to challenge, on the grounds that Congress has not conveyed such powers to the tribe. The tribe, as a sovereign polity, generally needs no authorization from the federal government to exercise its powers.[15] However, the exercise of tribal sovereign power has been challenged, and in some cases, limited, prompting continuous clarification by the courts.

An important distinction to consider in understanding tribal authority is whether a limitation exists that would prevent a tribe from acting or whether any authority exists that would permit a tribe to act. The courts have generally found that "as a sovereign, it is free to act unless some federal intrusion has affirmatively modified that sovereignty."[16] Tribal sovereignty has also been used to prevent the intrusion of state jurisdiction within Indian country. Two consequences result from tribal powers being inherent rather than conferred by the federal government. The provision of the Bill of Rights that restricts the federal government neither applies to the tribes, nor does it violate the Fifth Amendment provision against double jeopardy for the tribe and the federal government to prosecute a defendant for the same offense. As independent sovereigns, the courts have affirmed that tribes are able to defend their public policies.[17]

Tribal sovereignty has also operated by deterring state intrusion into Indian country with certain restrictions. The Supreme Court has consistently prohibited state law from applying to Indians in Indian country. In

---

15. This is the general rule, notwithstanding provisions of the Indian Reorganization Act of 1934 requiring certain tribes to obtain secretarial approval to exercise certain governmental actions.

16. *National Farmers Union Ins. Co. v. Crow Tribe*, 471 U.S. 845, 852–53 (1985).

17. See *U.S. v. Wheeler*, 435 U.S. 313 (1978).

Williams v. Lee,[18] a unanimous court ruled that state courts have no jurisdiction over a civil claim by a non-Indian against an Indian for a transaction arising on the Navajo reservation (Pevar 2012). The court held that state law had application only where "essential tribal relations" were not involved and that absent governing acts of Congress, the question has always been whether the state action infringes on the "right of reservation Indians to make their own laws and be governed by themselves."[19] State interference would undermine the tribal court authority over reservation affairs and thereby infringe on the right of Indians to govern themselves. The Supreme Court in *McClanahan*[20] held that state law would only be permitted into Indian country if two conditions were met: the intrusion would not interfere with tribal self-government and non-Indians were involved. The court also found that the State of New Mexico[21] could not tax the income of an Indian that was earned on the reservation:

> State jurisdiction is preempted by the operation of federal law if it interferes with or is incompatible with federal and tribal interests reflected in federal law, unless the state interests at stake are sufficient to justify the assertion of state authority.

The ruling in *William v. Lee* that state law may not interfere with tribal self-government continues to remain in effect today as an independent test to be applied along with preemption analysis.[22] However, tribal self-government no longer appears to be defined to include anything that affects Indian interests (Canby 2009). As a result, most cases involving the application of state law in Indian country are decided on preemptive grounds.[23]

---

18. 358 U.S. 217 (1959).

19. In *Williams v. Lee*, 358 U.S. 220, 223.

20. *McClanahan v. Arizona State Tax Commission*, 441 U.S. 164 (1973).

21. *New Mexico v. Mescalero Apache Tribe*, 462 U.S. 324, 224 (1983).

22. Established in *New Mexico v. Mescalero Apache*.

23. In *Strate v. A-1 Contractors*, 520 U.S. 438 (1997) the Court held that when a traffic accident occurs on a public highway located within a reservation and maintained by the state, civil action against negligent non-tribal members falls within state or federal

The power of the federal executive branch is limited, as well, by the trust relationship, where the courts have held executive officials to strict fiduciary standards in their management of Indian trust resources.[24] The courts have also mandated that absent congressional authorization, federal agencies cannot subordinate the interests of Indians to other public purposes.[25] The legal representation of Indian interests represents another important aspect of the federal trust responsibility, where the United States attorney is held responsible for representing Indians and tribes in all suits "at law and in equity."[26]

In the early 1900s, the trust relationship was viewed as a form of transitional protection during a period that emphasized the assimilation of Indians into mainstream society. In recent years, however, the trust relationship has become redefined as a doctrine that supports progressive federal legislation enacted for the benefit of Indians and tribes, and constitutes the basis for the current federal Indian policy of self-determination. It is widely viewed that the trust relationship has developed into a permanent doctrine of federal Indian policy that serves to guide the future development of both Indian policy and Indian law.

Tribal Political Authority

Tribal governmental powers are generally understood to be inherent powers of a limited sovereignty that have never been extinguished by the tribes. In *United States v. Wheeler*,[27] the Supreme Court found that tribal governments, because they possess attributes of sovereignty over their

---

regulatory and adjudicatory governance and tribal courts may not exercise jurisdiction in such cases.

24. The Supreme Court decisions in *Seminole Nation v. United States*, 316 U.S. 286, 296–97 (1942) and *United States v. Payne*, 264 U.S. 446, 448 (1924) have required officials of the United States to maintain "obligations of the highest responsibility and trust" and "the most exacting fiduciary standards" in carrying out their trust responsibility to Indians.

25. *United States v. Winnebago Tribe*, 542 F.2d 1002 (8th Cir. 1976).

26. 25 U.S.C. § 175.

27. *U.S. v. Wheeler*, 435 U.S. 313 (1978).

members and their territory, are unique. Powers not limited by federal statue, by treaty, or by restraints implicit in the federal trust relationship remain with tribal governments.[28] Inherent tribal powers of self-government enable tribes to fully exercise most forms of civil jurisdiction over Indians and non-Indians alike (Rosen 2007; Wilkinson 2005).[29] The following summarizes the range of tribal powers, recognized under federal law, that constitute tribes as fully autonomous political communities:

1. *Power to Establish a Form of Government.* Federal law provides Indian tribes the authority to adopt any form of government appropriate to their practical, cultural, or religious needs. Tribes are not required to adopt forms of government modeled after the US government since the tribes are not limited by the US Constitution and are therefore not subject to such principles as the separation of powers or the religious establishment clause (AILTP 1988, 36). The most widely accepted form of tribal governmental structure was adopted under the Indian Reorganization Act (IRA), and those tribes exercising self-governance under IRA constitutions are founded, not on the delegation of congressional powers, but, rather, on their inherent powers of sovereignty. The courts have also consistently upheld non-IRA forms of tribal governmental structure as valid.

2. *Power to Determine Membership.* A fundamental power of tribal government is the right to determine its membership, which confers the rights to vote in tribal elections, to hold office, and to receive proprietary

---

28. Limits to tribal sovereignty have been established to include the power to self-alienate tribal lands or the power to make treaties with foreign nations (American Indian Lawyer Training Program [AILTP] 1988, 35).

29. Notwithstanding situations where a tribe's reservation becomes reduced or excluded from "reservation status," resulting in the further diminishment to a tribe's power of self-government. The United States Supreme Court in *Hagen v. Utah*, 510 U.S. 399 (1994), ruled that portions of the Uintah and Ouray Reservation had been diminished when the reservation was open to non-Indian settlement, and that such lands were no longer located within the reservation. The court ruled that tribal jurisdiction within the exterior boundaries of said reservation applies only to tribal members and tribal or trust lands. In *South Dakota v. Yankton Sioux Tribe*, 522 U.S. 329 (1998), the Supreme Court decided that much of the tribe's reservation status ended during the 1890s when the tribe sold portions of the reservation land to the government.

interests in tribally held resources. Under the Civil Rights Act of 1968, tribes are also not required to comply with the concept of equal protection and due process in determining membership.

3. Police Power. The exercise of tribal authority to legislate and enforce civil and criminal laws over their territories represents a fundamental power of tribes' status as autonomous political communities. Tribal political authority encompasses the power to regulate the conduct of individuals within a tribe's jurisdiction, to determine domestic rights and relations, to dispose of non-trust property and establish rules of inheritance, to regulate commercial and business relations, to generate tax revenues for the operation of essential governmental services, and to administer justice though law enforcement and tribal court systems. Tribal authority to regulate land use through zoning has also been upheld as an important component of territorial control.[30]

4. Power to Administer Law and Order. Although tribes have the authority to administer civil and criminal justice in Indian country, criminal jurisdiction has been limited by the Indian Civil Rights Act and denied in certain applications over non-Indians under the *Oliphant v. Suquamish Indian Tribe* decision.[31] The power of tribes to exclude persons from within their territory is an inherent right of sovereignty. The exclusionary power is viewed as a means of protecting tribal communities against undesirable persons who may threaten their well-being. The power to exclude, however, has been limited to rights retained by non-members, including the right to access and occupy lands on the reservation owned in fee patent.[32]

30. *Knight v. Shoshone and Arapahoe Indian Tribes*, 670 F.2d 900 (10th Cir. 1982); *Santa Rosa Band v. Kings County*, 532 F.2d 655 (9th Cir. 1975); *Snohomish County v. Seattle Disposal Co.*, 70 Wash. 2d 668, 425 P.2d 22 (Wash. 1967), *cert. denied*, 389 U.S. 1016 (1967).

31. 435 U.S. 191 (1978).

32. The Supreme Court held in *Nevada v. Hicks* (533 U.S. 353. 2001) that tribal authority to regulate state officers in executing process related to the off-reservation violation of state laws is not essential to tribal self-government. It also ruled that Congress has not limited the states' inherent jurisdiction on reservations regarding off-reservation violations of state law.

5. *Sovereign Immunity.* Tribes possess the power to establish governmental and business organizations for the purpose of managing tribal resources and assets. Tribally chartered businesses retain exemptions from federal income taxation and immunity from suit unless such immunities are expressly waived. Indian tribes cannot be sued without their waiver of sovereign immunity, and the courts have generally upheld that business contracts with tribes alone are insufficient to waive sovereign immunity from suit without prior congressional approval.[33] The principle that tribal governments and their agencies possess sovereign immunity from suit has been established in a number of court rulings.[34] However, tribes are not deemed to be immune from suits by the federal government.[35] Certain tribes have formed tribal corporations pursuant to chapter 17 of the Indian Reorganization Act of 1934, which authorizes the secretary of interior to issue corporate charters to tribes, which confer specific powers in order to conduct corporate business. Many of those charters include the power to "sue and be sued." Several courts[36] have interpreted this provision to constitute an authorized waiver of tribal immunity, while other courts[37] have held that the clause in the corporate charter does not waive the tribe's general immunity.

6. *Tribal Civil Jurisdiction over Non-Indians.* Tribal authority to regulate non-Indians on non-Indian reservation lands has resulted in a contentious situation for tribes in their ability to manage the reservation environment. An important precedent was established in 1981 by the Supreme Court in *Montana v. United States,* where the Court defined a standard test to evaluate an action that threatens or has some direct effect

33. In a related matter, the Court in *Match-E-Be-Nash-She-Wish Band of Pottawatomi Indians v. Patchak,* Nos. 11-246 and 11-247, 132 S. Ct. 2199, 183 L. Ed. 2d 211 (U.S., 2011 Term, decided June 18, 2012), ruled that the United States had waived its sovereign immunity to permit actions against the United States for taking land into trust for Indian tribes.

34. See *Santa Clara Pueblo v. Martinez,* 436 U.S. 49, 58 (1978).

35. *U.S. v. Yakima Tribal Court,* 806 F.2d 853, 861 (9th Cir. 1986), *cert. denied,* 107 S. Ct. 2461 (1987).

36. *Frontenelle v. Omaha tribe,* 430 F.2d 143 (8th Cir. 1970).

37. *Atkinson v. Haldane,* 569 P.2d 151 (Alaska 1977).

on the political integrity, the economic security, or the health or welfare of a tribe. Generally, wherever an action threatens a tribal interest, the courts have affirmed a tribe's authority. In a subsequent 1982 decision[38] the court further upheld a broad view of tribal civil authority over non-Indians on non-Indian land under the *Montana* "tribal interest" test, which involved a zoning dispute. Historically, the courts have upheld the principle that state law does not apply to Indian affairs in Indian country without express congressional consent. Congress's broad powers under the Indian Commerce Clause have been regarded by the courts as the constitutional authority that preempts the state's exercise of governmental authority in favor of tribal self-government. Unless Congress expresses a clear intent to permit the application of state regulation over a particular Indian activity, state regulation is presumed preempted.[39] In *Washington v. Confederated Tribes of the Colville Indian Reservation*,[40] the Supreme Court provides guidance as to when tribal powers apply to non-Indians by recognizing that tribal authority is divested only when its exercise is inconsistent with overriding federal interests: "tribal sovereignty is dependent on, and subordinate to, only the federal government, not to the states."

7. *Taxation and Regulation in Indian Country.* The federal taxing power applies in Indian country with respect to both Indians and non-Indians. There are certain types of income earned by Indians that Congress has elected not to tax, including income from allotted trust land and income derived from treaty guaranteed fishing resources. It has long been

38. *Knight v. Shoshone and Arapahoe Indian Tribes*, 670 F.2d 900 (10th Cir. 1982).

39. Public Law 280, enacted by Congress in 1953, exemplifies such an express delegation by transferring the jurisdictional authority over most crimes and certain civil matters to six states. Public Law 280 was amended in 1968 to require tribal consent to further state jurisdiction in all future cases. However, no tribes have since consented. The amendment also permitted states to retrocede criminal or civil jurisdiction acquired under Public Law 280. Public Law 280 specifically excluded the regulation and taxation of trust land and exempted the hunting and fishing rights of Indians. In *Santa Rosa Band v. Kings County*, the court confirmed that Public Law 280 did not transfer regulatory powers over Indian reservations to the states.

40. 447 U.S. 134 (1980).

held that states do not have the power to exercise taxation of Indian trust lands. This exclusion, mandated by Congress, was included in certain western state constitutions as a condition for admission into the Union. The primary limitation is that a state may not tax when the subject matter is preempted by federal law. The exercise of a tribal taxing authority does not necessarily invalidate a state tax, regardless of whether it results as a double tax burden that disadvantages those who deal with tribes. The authority of a state to regulate within Indian country is similar to a state's taxing powers, and the preemption test established in *New Mexico v. Mescalero Apache Tribe*[41] is often relied upon by the courts, which established that state jurisdiction is preempted by federal law if it interferes with federal and tribal interests, except in cases where the state interests are sufficiently at stake to justify its authority.

Until recently, it was assumed that the states possessed little regulatory powers within Indian country. When on-reservation conduct exclusively involving Indians is at issue, state law is generally not applicable, since the state's regulatory interests are likely to be minor and "the federal interest in encouraging tribal self-government is at its strongest."[42] The Supreme Court held in *Bryan v. Itasca Country*[43] that the destruction of tribal governments will likely result "if tribal governments and reservation Indians were subordinated to the full panoply of civil regulatory powers, including taxation, of state and local governments."

8. *Intergovernmental Relations between Tribes and States.* Agreements between tribes and states provide an effective avenue for addressing the conflicts that arise from the complexities inherent in past federal policy and laws. Initially, Congress authorized intergovernmental agreements in the Indian Child Welfare Act of 1978, which provided for cross-deputization by commissioning officers of the other jurisdiction to act as agents under their authority. In the event a tribe lacks criminal jurisdiction over non-Indians, such an agreement provides a tribal police officer

41. *New Mexico v. Mescalero Apache Tribe*, 462 U.S. 324, 334 (1983).
42. *White Mountain Apache Tribe v. Braker*, 448 U.S. 136, 144 (1980).
43. 426 U.S. 373 (1976).

who is cross-deputized under state and federal law, with the authority to both arrest a non-Indian who commits a crime within the reservation and to deliver the arrested person to state or federal officials. Civil regulatory agreements have also been executed in a number of areas to promote greater cooperation among state, local, and tribal governments in the areas of child welfare protection, co-regulation of gaming activities, the provision of utilities, and land use regulation and enforcement. Tribes have attained clear judicial and legislative recognition of their governing authority to support a broad spectrum of powers that are linked to their inherent sovereignty.

Regulating the Reservation Territory

As a consequence of the inconsistencies in federal Indian policies that created a complex composition of land ownership conditions on many reservations, tribal efforts to operate reservation planning programs continue to be both challenged and resisted. Further complicating reservation governance has been the growing opposition to tribal jurisdiction by non-Indian landowners who demand state or local government intervention to shield them from tribal jurisdiction.

Historic events that originated with the General Allotment Act of 1887 established two irreversible conditions that have complicated reservation property interests. First, the act introduced individual Indian ownership to the once communally owned reservations. Second, it authorized the transfer of federal trust parcels to non-Indian fee ownership. The act encouraged settlement onto reservations by non-Indians, constituting a property rights situation that was no longer limited to tribal interests alone. As many reservations today exhibit some degree of land ownership fractionalization, a plurality of property rights interests have emerged to create divisive obstacles to a tribe's exclusive territorial control. While it has long been recognized that the tribes retain inherent rights to regulate their territories, the allotment and subsequent occupancy of reservation lands by non-Indians pose new challenges to the exclusive jurisdiction of tribes over their reservations (Johnson 1988). Questions also arise regarding the applicability of state and local zoning laws over reservation lands that are owned and occupied by non-Indians.

As part of the policy's scheme to incorporate Indians and their resources into the assimilated US political economy, the Allotment Act first introduced Indians to the Anglo concept of private land ownership. The act established a system of land allocation that further removed portions of the reservation lands as *surplus*. These surplus lands, available for non-Indian ownership and occupancy, facilitated the process of incorporating reservation resources into the political economy.[44] The resultant Indian reservation resembled a patchwork of land ownership, comprised of trust lands held by the federal government for the tribes, allotted lands held in trust for individual tribal members, fee land held by non-Indians, federal public lands, and state and county lands.

Recent Supreme Court rulings have further limited a tribe's authority to exercise civil jurisdiction over non-Indians. A 2012 court of appeals decision in *Evans v. Shoshone-Bannock Land Use Policy Commission*[45] overturned an earlier district court decision to dismiss an injunction filed against the Shoshone-Bannock Land Use Policy Commission and the Fort Hall Business Council for attempting to enforce tribal building permit requirements on a non-tribal resident. The Ninth Circuit Court

---

44. Several court rulings clarified the limits of tribal authority over lands that were removed from trust ownership or were thereafter considered to be non-reservation or non-"Indian Country" lands. The courts in *South Dakota v. Bourland*, 508 U.S. 679 (1993) and *Hagen v. Utah*, 510 U.S. 399 (1994) ruled that when reservation surplus lands are restored to the public domain, reservation status is thereby terminated. *Bourland* held that any treaty rights of the Cheyenne River Sioux Tribe to regulate non-Indian hunting and fishing were abrogated when treaty lands were taken to create a reservoir under the Flood Control Act. The opinion reflects the presumption that the loss of tribal title divests a tribe of its regulatory power. *Solem v. Bartlett*, 465 U.S. 463 (1984) is considered the Supreme Court's leading ruling regarding reservation disestablishment, reflecting congressional or executive actions that divested lands of their trust or restricted status where tribes may therefore lack jurisdiction over non-Indian activities within their reservation boundaries. These cases imply that tribes may lack power over non-Indian activities on reservation fee lands unless they can demonstrate their interests under *Montana* and *Brendale* rules.

45. *Evans v. Shoshone-Bannock Land Use Policy Commission*, No. 13-35003 D.C. No. 4:12-CV-00417-BLW (9th Cir. Dec. 5, 2013).

of Appeals reversed the decision of the district court by finding the tribe lacked the power, under the particular circumstances of the case, to regulate the land use of the non-Indian plaintiff. In *Bugenig*[46] the courts also ruled against a tribe's jurisdiction over a reservation non-member when it found its exercise of power was beyond what is necessary to protect tribal self-government or inconsistent with the dependent status of the tribes. The court found that Congress can make express delegations of power to Indian tribes to regulate the actions of non-tribal members, but because of the general presumption against tribal jurisdiction over non-members, such delegation must be "express."

In *Montana v. United States*,[47] the court ruled that the Crow Tribe did not have the authority to regulate hunting or fishing by non-Indians on non-Indian fee lands within the reservation. A general principle was established in *Montana* that, absent congressional delegation, Indian authority did not extend "beyond what is necessary to protect tribal self-government or to control internal relations" (Goeppele 1990). The courts decided in *Montana* that tribes have been divested of their sovereignty to regulate relations between Indians and non-Indians by virtue of their dependent status and that the exercise of tribal authority beyond what is necessary to defend tribal self-government is inconsistent with the dependent status of tribes. However, *Montana* provides two important and broad exceptions, or tests, to its ruling, whereby a tribe's authority may apply to non-Indians:

• A tribe retains its authority to regulate the activities of non-members who have entered into consensual relations with the tribe or its members through commercial dealings, contracts, leases, or other arrangements;

• A tribe retains its regulatory authority over the conduct of non-Indians on fee lands when that conduct threatens or has some direct effect on the political integrity, the economic security, or the health or welfare of the tribe.

46. *Bugenig v. Hoopa Valley Tribe*, 266 F.3d 1201 (9th Cir. 2001).
47. 450 U.S. 544 (1981).

The scope of the second exception is comparable to the traditional scope of authority of the police powers.[48] After *Montana*, subsequent lower court decisions granted tribes authority over non-Indians under the second *Montana* exception where the non-Indian activity was found to threaten the integrity of the tribe and its resources. The Tenth Circuit Court in *Knight v. Shoshone and Arapahoe Tribes*[49] also upheld tribal zoning authority over non-Indian fee lands, as it found that no competing county zoning ordinances existed to restrict land use on non-Indian fee lands on the reservation.

The *Brendale* Decision

The Yakima Tribe brought suit in federal court to prohibit the application of county zoning laws regarding two areas of the reservation designated by the tribe as "closed" and "open" to development. In its adopted zoning ordinances of 1970 and 1972, the tribe established five categories of land use districts: agriculture, residential, commercial, industrial, and restricted. The closed areas were restricted to the harvesting of wild crops, grazing, hunting and fishing, and camping due to their important religious and spiritual significance to the tribe. Construction in this area was limited to the tribe and the Bureau of Indian Affairs (BIA) in association with natural resource management activities. Yakima County had regulated land use since 1946 and had only applied its zoning to fee lands on the reservation. The county zoning designation for the closed areas was "forested watershed," which permitted a range of uses including residential development, campgrounds, lodging, restaurants, and general stores.

Brendale[50] is comprised of two distinct cases. In the first case, Philip Brendale, a non-member Indian, sought to subdivide his 160-acre fee

---

48. The authority of police powers is defined as that which "enables the people to prohibit all things inimical to comfort, safety, health, and the welfare of society" (*Drysdale v. Prudden*, 195 N.C. 722, 143 S.E. 530, 536 (1928)).

49. 670 F.2d 900 (10th Cir. 1982).

50. *Brendale v. Confederated Tribes and Bands of Yakima Indian Nation*, 492 U.S. 408 (1988).

simple landholding into two parcels to be used for trailer sites and recreational cabins. This land was located within a portion of the Yakima Indian Reservation's "closed area," which contained approximately 3 percent in fee lands and where access by the general public had been restricted since 1972. Brendale's proposed subdivision conformed with Yakima County zoning, but conflicted with the tribe's "closed area" zoning designation.

The second case involved Stanley Wilkinson, a non-Indian fee land-owner, who proposed subdividing a thirty-two acre parcel into twenty parcels in the area designated by the tribe as "open." Approximately one half of the "open" area was held in fee ownership with prevailing uses consisting of rangeland, agriculture, residential, and commercial uses. Unlike the closed area, non-members were not restricted from this area where the county or local municipalities provided urban services. Most of the fee land lay within the three state-incorporated towns of Toppenish, Wapato, and Harrah, where neither the tribe nor the county regulate land use. The remainder of fee land was largely scattered among the trust lands. Eighty percent of the population within the open area was non-Indian. Tribal zoning of the Wilkinson parcel was agriculture, allowing a minimum lot size of five acres. County zoning designated the parcel for "general rural" use, allowing a minimum lot size of one acre. Similar to Brendale's petition, the proposed subdivision conformed with county regulation but conflicted with tribal zoning codes.

The federal district court held that the tribe had authority to zone non-member fee lands in the closed area, but not in the open area. On appeal, the Ninth Circuit Court held that land use authority over both the open and closed areas fell within the second *Montana* exception.[51] The court implicitly equated the existence of inherent tribal sovereignty with the limits of police power.[52] The Ninth Circuit ruling further found that tribal authority to zone the property would advance the goal of "systematic and

51. *Confederated Tribes and Bands of the Yakima Indian Nation v. Whiteside*, 828 F.2d 529 (9th Cir. 1987).

52. Brendale and the county argued that Public Law 280, as implemented in Washington State by Wash. Rev. Code 37.12.010, divested the tribe of authority to regulate non-Indians on fee land on the reservation. The Ninth Circuit rejected this view, noting that

coordinated planning" and, in considering both county and tribal interests, found that the "strength of tribal interests over the closed area justi-
fied exclusive tribal zoning of Brendale's property." The court remanded
the case involving Wilkinson's property to the district court to balance
tribal and county interests in zoning non-member fee lands located in
the open area. The Ninth Circuit Court held that the tribe's governmental
authority is derived implicitly from its status as a dependent sovereign and
explicitly from its treaty and ruled (at paragraph 28):

> Yakima Nation has exclusive authority to zone tribal trust land, which
> constitutes nearly all of the closed area and over half of the open area.
> Although the fee land owned by non-Indians is clustered primarily in
> one part of the reservation, the reservation still exhibits essentially a
> checkerboard pattern. If we were to deny the Yakima Nation the right to
> regulate fee land owned by non-Indians, we would destroy their capac-
> ity to engage in comprehensive planning so fundamental to a zoning
> scheme. This we are unwilling to do.

The United States Supreme Court agreed to hear the case on appeal
and narrowly held that the tribe lacked authority to regulate the non-Indian
owned lands in the "open area." The Court ruled that the tribe retained
authority to zone non-member lands in the closed area of the reservation,
but had lost the authority to control such lands in the open area.[53] The
Court also reaffirmed the tribe's authority to retain exclusive power to regulate Indian trust lands on the grounds that state authority to regulate such
lands had been "preempted by extensive federal policy and legislation."[54]

Public Law 280 grants state courts jurisdiction over civil litigation but does not change
tribal regulatory authority (Johnson 1988, 167).

53. Basing his dissenting opinion on a broader interpretation of *Montana*'s second
exception, Justice Blackmun supported the tribe's right to zone all reservation fee lands,
as the loss of the long-term benefits of comprehensive land management would represent
a significant impact on tribal interests. He further rejected the notion of concurrent tribal
and county zoning jurisdiction of non-member lands as being unworkable.

54. See also *Santa Rosa Band of Indians v. Kings County*, 532 F. 2d. 655, 658 (9th Cir.
1975) Cert. Denied, 429 U.S. 1038 (1978).

The Court construed *Montana*'s second exception narrowly and concluded that the tribe's authority did not extend over all activities listed within the exception, but was instead dependent upon specific circumstances. It further ruled that a tribe has authority over a proposed land use on non-Indian land only insofar as it threatens a tribe. With the absence of such threat, the land use control would revert to the non-Indian local government. Rather than support tribal authority, the ruling allowed the tribe the right to sue based on a "demonstrably serious impact" to their political integrity, economic security, or their health and welfare.[55] In considering the authority of the tribe to zone non-member lands, Justice Stevens found that their power had systematically diminished due to specific acts of Congress, such as the Allotment Act, and the absence of tribal regulation of non-member lands. Justice Stevens concluded that the tribe had authority to zone Brendale's property in the closed area due to the circumstance that non-members owned very little land in the closed area. Further, by restricting access to the closed area, the tribe was able to exercise its basic power to exclude, thereby preserving the power to define the essential character of that area. Justice Stevens concluded that the tribe lacked the power to zone non-member land in the open area since nearly 50 percent of the open area contained non-member fee lands and because the tribe had not established "the essential character" of the land by restricting access to it.[56]

The *Brendale* opinion challenged basic principles of land use planning by allowing for an uncoordinated land use management system within the reservation. A fundamental principle of land use planning is that it retains comprehensiveness and prospectiveness. Under Justice White's approach, the county had jurisdiction over predominately non-member fee land reservation areas while the tribe retained authority over predominately tribal lands. Justice White prescribed a means for resolving differences between

55. *Brendale*, 109 S.Ct. at 3008.

56. The court further raised an important concern regarding non-member representation in tribal government by acknowledging that the non-member population constituted 80 percent of the open area population, of which the majority population could not vote in tribal elections.

conflicting land use policies of the two governments by only allowing for a tribe-initiated federal nuisance-type lawsuit to prevent a proposed development. This approach to conflict resolution is inconsistent with comprehensive, prospective planning. "Essentially, this sets land use planning on reservations back to the pre-*Euclid* era,[57] when nuisance actions for overtly harmful uses were the primary means of controlling the use of private property" (Goeppele 1990, 425).

The Court's support of tribal zoning over fee lands in the closed area was based on the "pristine" environment that the tribe maintained in that area. This would suggest that tribes might be subjected to losing their ability to meaningfully "define the essential character" of their reservation when any land use changes from a pristine character. If development within pristine areas of a reservation equates to a loss of tribal authority over that area, a paradox is presented in the legal argument by linking the advancement of tribal economies through reservation development to the inadvertent diminishment of inherent tribal authority. The Supreme Court's complex decision was summarized by Weaver (1990) as follows:

JURISDICTION IN THE "OPEN AREA":

• The tribe does not have authority to zone fee land within the open area.

• The General Allotment Act diminished the treaty reserved power to exclude non-Indians from fee lands on the reservation and the exclusion power no longer serves as a basis for tribal power to zone fee lands in the open area.

• Absent of express congressional delegation, tribal sovereignty beyond that which is necessary to protect tribal self-government or to control internal relations is inconsistent with the tribe's dependent status.

• Under *Montana*, the tribe has a protected property interest in land use activities on the reservation, but the county's zoning impact must be "demonstrably serious" and must "imperil the tribal integrity, economic security, or health and welfare" before the tribe may seek protection in federal court.

---

57. *Euclid v. Ambler Realty Co.*, 272 U.S. 365 (1926).

• Exercise of Yakima County zoning over non-Indian fee land in the open area does not alone imperil the tribe's interests.

JURISDICTION IN THE "CLOSED AREAS":

• The tribe may zone fee land in the closed area.

• This authority is based on the tribe's maintenance of the "essential character" of the area through the exclusion power. The power to zone is incidental to its power to continue to preserve that character.

• The power to exclude derives from express treaty provisions and its inherent sovereignty.

Hence, *Brendale* establishes a test for determining the effect of tribal regulatory control versus county powers. Under the ruling, tribal regulation of non-members' use of fee land on a reservation is dependent upon the following conditions:

• Whether the activity occurs within a reservation area in which the tribe can demonstrate that it has maintained the "essential character" of the reservation;

• Whether the activity to be regulated on fee land "imperils the political integrity, the economic security, or the health or welfare" of the tribe;

• The manner by which the particular fee land passed out of trust;

• Whether the particular non-Indian has entered into a contractual or consensual relationship with the tribe or its members.

An underlying principle of zoning is that, while the value of private property may be affected by certain imposed use restrictions, private landowners receive a reciprocal benefit by being assured of predictable and compatible adjoining land uses. When two governments pursue independent and checkerboard zoning schemes, individual landowners may lose the protection of reciprocal benefits as a consequence of the restrictions placed on their property. *Brendale* creates further legal uncertainty as it fails to provide a clear test for determining the extent to which fee lands on the reservation would remain subject to tribal authority. Rather than referring to a clear standard, courts applying Justice Stevens's approach rely only on a list of factors to determine when tribes retain authority over non-member lands on the reservation. As the courts continue the process of dividing reservations into dual jurisdictional areas, the concept of reservation cohesiveness is at risk and the search for a unitary doctrine supporting a consistent tribal regulatory authority over the tribal territory becomes more difficult.

The uncertainty created by *Brendale* is also at odds with the fundamental principles of land use planning and growth management that promote jurisdictional coordination in regional land use planning. *Brendale* promotes an opposing precedent by fragmenting the reservations into zoning checkerboards without offering solutions or clear guidance as to how tribes and local governments might cooperate in order to achieve a long-term vision for consistency in regional planning. This situation becomes further complicated in states with growth management laws that often direct governments to cooperate with regards to land use planning, yet fail to specifically acknowledge tribes as legitimate participants in regional planning.

Controlling the Reservation Environment

In contrast to matters concerning land use jurisdiction, where the federal government does not assert an explicit interest or standard for land use planning, the enactment of comprehensive federal environmental legislation that began in the 1960s represents the assertion of a national interest over state interests in order to ensure that all areas of the nation are uniformly protected from air, water, hazardous waste, and solid waste pollution. For purposes of administration, Congress instructed the United States Environmental Protection Agency (EPA) to delegate its authority to carry out federal environmental policies to qualifying states. In the absence of state regulatory jurisdiction in Indian country, however, Congress retained its federal responsibility for the protection of the reservation environment, thus creating a multiple-jurisdiction system for the administration of the nation's environmental laws. Given that environmental problems are rarely contained within political boundaries, conflicts may arise when multiple jurisdictions simultaneously administer environmental protection programs within a common region. Industrial and other developments on lands adjacent to a reservation that are managed by a state program may pose a potential risk of degradation to reservation environmental quality. Timber practices on upstream riparian lands, for example, may threaten tribal fisheries. Since both tribal and state governments share a common concern for compliance with federal environmental standards, the protection of the environmental quality of reservations poses a coordination challenge among the fiduciary responsibilities of the federal government, the states, and the tribes. Each may be engaged in administering environmental protection programs in overlapping regions, sometimes applying discrepant standards.

In 1984, the EPA sought to clarify the role of tribes in the administration of federal environmental policies when it adopted an Indian policy establishing a tribe's authority to conduct reservation-wide environmental programs similar to those delegated to the states. Congress later amended most federal environmental statutes to provide a mechanism for the EPA to fund tribes, as it had previously funded states, to enable them to develop programs to protect their territories. However, the authority granting a delegation of program responsibility to the tribes occurred one and a half decades after the initial enactment of the legislation. As a result of the exclusion of tribes in the early period of environmental program development, tribal lands were often ignored, the tribal role in implementing federal programs was not well defined, and the tribal capacity to operate such programs was largely undeveloped.

The EPA Indian policy statement provided the necessary guidance for the administration of environmental programs on Indian lands, under the terms of the agency's directives:

• The EPA will work with tribes on a government-to-government basis;

• The EPA will recognize tribal governments as the primary authority for implementing federal environmental programs on tribal lands;

• The EPA will take affirmative steps to assist the tribes in assuming regulatory responsibility for reservation lands; and

• The EPA will encourage cooperation between the tribes and the state and local governments in the implementation of federal environmental programs.

In November 1985, the EPA adopted its "interim strategy" for the implementation of the EPA Indian policy. The strategy recognized that forcing tribal governments to act through state governments that cannot exercise jurisdiction over Indian tribes was an ineffective way to implement national environmental programs and conflicted with the federal trust responsibility. To exercise the trust duty, the secretary of the Department of the Interior had been designated as the federal trustee for Indian tribal resources.[58] The United States Supreme Court has since upheld the federal trust obligation for the protection of Indian resources as a fiduciary duty to Indian tribes,[59] while Congress has affirmed the treatment of tribes as states for the purposes of implementing environmental programs[60] under a variety of environmental statutes.

Sources of Tribal Environmental Authority

Tribes derive their power to regulate activities that threaten to degrade tribal lands, waters, and resources from three principal sources. The first of these sources is their proprietary rights. The courts have affirmed common law tribal proprietary, aboriginal, and reserved water rights[61] and held that the creation of Indian reservations necessarily included the implied reservation of a proprietary water right.[62] Without such a reserved water right, the reservation would be of no value. A corollary to the reserved water right is the right to water of undiminished quality. This right of quality protection is derived from the "equitable apportionment doctrine" that imposes a duty on sister states to protect water quality and prevent the diminishment of quality enjoyed by neighboring states.

The second source is the inherent sovereignty that tribes possess to protect their lands. Inherent tribal sovereignty provides for the exercise

58. Exec. Order No. 12580, § 5(d), 52 Fed. Reg. 2923, 2926, (January 29, 1987).

59. See *United States v. Mitchell* (*"Mitchell II"*), 463 U.S. 206, 224; *Blue Legs v. BIA*, 867 F.2d 1094 (8th Cir. 1989).

60. The federal courts, in *Arizona Public Service Co. v. EPA*, 211 F.3d 1280, 1300 (D.C. Cir. 2000), were called upon to determine whether a provision of the Clean Air Act delegates to Indian tribes the authority to enforce the Clean Air Act on non-member fee-owned land within a reservation. The court of appeals upheld the provision as a delegation based on its review of specific language in the statute that it found to establish an express delegation.

61. See *County of Oneida v. Oneida Indian Nation*, 470 U.S. 226 (1985).

62. In *United States v. Winters*, 207 U.S. 563 (1908).

of police powers and civil regulatory controls to protect the health, safety, and welfare of the reservation population from threats imposed by environmental pollution. The exercise of the tribe's civil regulatory authority is derived from its own constitution, and extends to both its members and to its territory.

In addition to their proprietary rights and inherent sovereignty over their lands, tribes may request delegated authority under federal environmental laws. Congress reaffirmed the EPA's policy of working on a government-to-government basis with tribes when it amended the provisions of the Safe Drinking Water Act in 1986; the Comprehensive Environmental Response, Compensation, and Liability Act in 1986; and the Clean Water Act in 1987.[63] The amendments recognized the EPA's obligation to treat tribes as states and provided for the delegation of responsibility for implementing environmental programs and regulating the reservation environment to tribes.

EPA's interim final rules, released in 1988 and 1989, established the criteria for tribes to qualify for "treatment as a state" under the Clean Water Act, the Public Water System (PWS) program, and the Underground Injection Control (UIC) program under the Safe Drinking Water Act. Once a tribe qualifies, they are eligible to receive funding to develop reservation-wide environmental protection programs.

Cooperative Mechanisms in Environmental Protection

Agreements between tribes and state governments to cooperate in the administration of environmental programs have begun to emerge in a

---

63. Under section 518, the 1987 amendments to the Clean Water Act directed the EPA to promulgate regulations that treated tribes as states for implementing a variety of Clean Water Act programs. Programs included in section 518 are Title II (construction grants), section 104 (research, investigations, and training), section 106 (grants for pollution control), section 303 (water quality inventory), section 308 (inspections, monitoring and entry), section 309 (federal enforcement), section 314 (clean lakes), section 402 (National Pollution Discharge Elimination System), and section 404 (dredge and fill material). Section 518 further directs the Environmental Protection Agency to establish a mechanism to resolve conflicts resulting from differences between state and tribal water quality standards.

number of states, among the most ambitious efforts are those occurring in Washington State. The Washington Timber, Fish and Wildlife Agreement represented one such agreement that involved the participation of the tribes, state agencies, the private timber industry, and the environmental community. Addressing the regulation of timber practices on private and state lands to protect tribal and non-tribal fisheries interests and wildlife habitat concerns, the agreement served as the foundation for the promulgation of regulations by state agencies. Washington State has also entered into an agreement with the Puyallup Tribe regarding the implementation of the federal Resource Conservation and Recovery Act on trust and non-trust lands within the reservation. The Colville Tribe entered into an agreement with the state regarding a procedure by which water pollution would be cooperatively regulated within the reservation boundaries. In another example of environmental program cooperation, the Swinomish Indian Tribal Community entered into a tri-lateral agreement with Washington's Department of Ecology and the EPA to cooperatively administer permit activities under the National Pollution Discharge Elimination System, forming a partnership that relies upon the technical assistance provided by the state to support tribal recommendations to the EPA on reservation pollution discharge permits. Under the agreement, the EPA would retain permit issuance responsibility until such time that the tribe enacts its water quality standards and applies to EPA for program delegation.

As tribes assume greater responsibilities under federal environmental programs, the need to develop technical capabilities also increases. States, having received program development funding assistance from the EPA for several decades, can assist tribes by fulfilling technical capacity gaps to supplement the development of tribal programs. In return, the states would benefit by helping to develop tribal environmental programs that foster consistency in environmental standards, thus overcoming problems associated with trans-boundary issues. The protection of the environmental quality of reservations is fundamental to the continued survival of tribal communities and the maintenance of a healthy reservation community. Inter-jurisdictional cooperation, promoted under the EPA Indian policy, provides opportunities to strengthen tribal governance over Indian territory while simultaneously fostering regional cooperation and policy consistency among tribal, state, and local governments.

Economic Development and Taxation

Economic development is a primary means for alleviating the chronically depressed economic conditions that persist on most Indian reservations, where more than 39 percent of reservation Indians live below the federal poverty line—four times that of the national average (Harvard Project on American Indian Economic Development 2008). Emerging tribal development models emphasize the importance of generating reservation economies while concurrently developing the tribal social community in order to reverse the pervasive conditions of reservation underdevelopment and lessen dependency on external assistance (Anderson and Parker 2008). The development of a self-sustaining tribal economy requires access to affordable private capital,[64] a skilled labor force, competent management, and access to markets. The encouragement of private investment is also an important component in the development of Indian reservations (Cornell 1987, vi). Relying on tribal inherent governing powers and proprietary reservation resources, reservation conditions can be improved through the dual process of expanding the reservation economy and establishing a stable reservation tax base. The attributes of tribal sovereignty provide the necessary legal foundation with which to support the development of reservation economies.

The two governmental principles of taxation power and tax immunity combine to provide powerful tools for structuring a revenue system to support reservation economic development. In addition to a tribe's inherent authority to tax and regulate economic activities, tribes also possess significant tax immunities as a result of their sovereignty. Tribally owned reservation businesses are exempt from federal income tax, and state tax laws generally do not apply to tribal businesses or to trust properties. The

---

64. In 1997, the First Nations Development Institute (FNDI) estimated the annual financing needs in Indian country between $17 and $56 billion for basic infrastructure, facilities, housing, and enterprise development.

development of the reservation economy is greatly advantaged through the application of these governmental exemptions (Endreson 1991; Harvard Project on American Indian Economic Development 2008). In 1982, the Supreme Court in *Merrion v. Jicarilla Apache Tribe*[65] upheld a tribe's power to levy a tax as a fundamental exercise of its tribal sovereignty:

> The power to tax is an essential attribute of Indian sovereignty because it is a necessary instrument of self-government and territorial management. This power enables a tribal government to raise revenues for its essential services. The power does not derive solely from the Indian tribe's power to exclude non-Indians from tribal lands. Instead, it derives from the tribe's general authority, as sovereign, to control economic activity within its jurisdiction, and to defray the cost of providing governmental services by requiring contributions from persons or enterprises engaged in economic activity within that jurisdiction.

The authority to apply tribal taxation ensures that economic activity occurring within the reservation will result in measurable benefit to the reservation community while also providing the taxed entity the reciprocal protection necessary to sustain the activity. Tribes, like other forms of government, rely on their ability to raise revenues in order to operate essential governmental services. These services include tribal courts and agencies to enforce tribal laws, the delivery of services to reservation residents and businesses through the provision of fire, police protection, and social services, and the development of a reservation infrastructure necessary to support the growth of the reservation economy. These efforts, however, are often frustrated by the intervention of state taxation powers. Tax conflicts occur when a state attempts to collect taxes either from non-Indian businesses operating on the reservation or from transactions between tribal or Indian businesses and non-Indians. Tax conflicts can impact reservation economic activity in several ways, depending on the nature of the activity being taxed, the rate of the taxes imposed, and the

---

65. *Merrion v. Jicarilla Apache Tribe*, 455 U.S. 130 (1982); see also *New Mexico v. Mescalero Apache Tribe*, 462 U.S. 324, 332 (1983).

competitiveness of the market in which the taxable activity competes (Endreson 1991, 3). To advance their economic development objectives, it is necessary that tribal governments resolve state taxation conflicts in order to attract capital financing and investment and to ensure a stable reservation business environment. The resolution of tribal-state conflicts has come about through litigation as well as through cooperation.

When such conflicts are litigated, a balancing test is often applied by the courts to determine whether states can tax or regulate non-Indians who engage in commerce with Indians. The legal test[66] balances federal and tribal interests against those of the state and considers the degree to which each government regulates and provides services to the activity that is taxed. The risks associated with litigation include double taxation, an outcome where both a state and a tribal tax may be applied simultaneously, resulting in reservation businesses becoming less competitive and discouraging further private investment. Litigation can also increase tensions between states and tribes that could adversely affect other efforts in tribal-state cooperative endeavors. The limitations, costs, and risks associated with litigation have led many tribes to explore other options for resolving tax conflicts, including cooperative agreements.

The process frequently used to initiate cooperative agreements begins with government-to-government talks that enable tribal and state leaders to directly discuss their respective needs for revenue generation, their economic development objectives, and the practical, political, and economic concerns that arise from tax conflicts. Cooperative solutions may prove more favorable than adversarial approaches, as the need for tax revenues is common to all governments. Negotiations involving tax agreements have focused on three issues that arise when a tribe and a state seek to tax and regulate the same activity. The first issue concerns the economic impacts associated with double taxation when both governments impose a similar tax on the same activity. The second issue concerns the regulatory confusion and inefficiencies that result when different governments tax

---

66. See *White Mountain Apache Tribe v. Bracker*, 448 U.S. 136 (1980); *Washington v. Confederated Tribes of the Colville Reservation*, 447 U.S. 134 (1980).

and regulate the same activity without regard to the other. The third issue concerns each governments' interest to ensure a reasonable competitive balance between its own business entities and those of the other government. Virtually every state that coexists with an Indian tribe has entered into some form of taxation arrangement with tribes. Examples include agreements for sharing tax revenues from cigarette and tobacco products, motor vehicle fuel sales, and revenue sharing from sales, business, and income taxes (Harvard Project on American Indian Economic Development 2008, 73).

The use of tax incentives can help overcome obstacles to attracting capital to the reservation economy. Tax incentives for Indian reservations include incentives that encourage employment and business development on reservations and incentives that target passive investment capital. Incentives attracting passive investments are provided through the issuance of tax-exempt bonds, under the Indian Finance Act of 1974, for the provision of essential governmental services, such as reservation infrastructure. The federal 1987 Omnibus Reconciliation Act, however, has limited tax incentives intended to attract passive capital investment for reservation economic development. The act requires the use of private activity bonds under restrictive terms, often limiting their general utility.[67] Even with expanded permitted uses, questions regarding the efficacy of these bonds to attract passive capital have been raised because the cost of such bonds continues to be determined by capital markets that are subject to market influences and investor perception of risk, which tends to be relatively high for reservation investments (Harvard Project on American Indian Economic Development 2008).

To overcome the obstacles in attracting financial capital to the reservations, several tribes have established Native American community development financial institutions (CDFIs) formed either under a tribe's governmental authority or as nonprofit organizations. Their primary

---

67. For example, the act required that 95 percent of the net proceeds of the sale of such bonds must be used for an on-reservation manufacturing business, which is both owned and operated by the tribe.

activities are to finance small businesses and to provide technical assistance for business startups. These entities have also begun to provide financing for other forms of reservation development, including housing development and land acquisition. In addition, tribes and Indian individuals now control several banks and credit unions. In 2001, a consortium of twenty-one tribes and Alaska Native corporations created the Native American Bank, a nationally chartered bank, to provide lending to tribes for economic and community development (Harvard Project on American Indian Economic Development 2008, 131).

The Case of Indian Gaming Enterprises

Federal gaming legislation illustrates an example of congressional infringement upon a tribe's ability to establish gaming enterprises under its inherent governmental authority. The intervention by Congress over a tribe's right to expand its economy through gaming is due, in part, to the interests expressed by the states that impose regulatory restrictions on gaming operations in their states and by the private gaming industry that has generally perceived Indian gaming as a competitive threat to their industry. Federal gaming legislation serves to restrict the types and scope of gaming enterprises conducted by the tribes in what has become, in recent decades, the fastest growing component of tribal economic development.

The emphasis on gaming development by tribes is attributed to a number of factors. First, gaming enterprises tend to be labor intensive, with many of the required skills acquired through relatively short-term tribal training programs. Second, profit levels from gaming operations tend to significantly exceed profit levels from other types of economic activities and are therefore viewed to be more effective in meeting the chronic revenue needs of tribes. As a tribally owned enterprise with restricted market competition, tribal investment in gaming generally does not face the higher risks associated with the startup of other businesses, and market competition tends to occur on a regional, rather than a local scale (Cookson 2010). This allows tribes to establish a definitive market share relatively free from market competition, with the exception of other tribal gaming enterprises. Such limited private competition enables tribal enterprises to maximize their return on investment, produce net profits to support tribal services, and generate greater social benefits such as increased tribal employment.

The economic and fiscal impacts of gaming on Indian reservations occur on a number of levels. A survey of eighty-one Indian gaming enterprises in 1993 estimated total gross annual wagering revenues for class II and class III gaming exceeding $7.5 billion. By 2007, Indian gaming revenues increased to more than $26 billion (National Indian Gaming Commission 2010; Center for Applied Research 1993). Indian gaming also contributed to the growing reservation-state economy as a substantial portion of new personal Indian income, whether earned from gaming or from other tribal enterprises, ultimately enters the state economy through tribal household expenditures. Consumer spending by tribal members and tribal governments acts as a direct stimulus for job and income growth in non-Indian communities. The National Indian Policy Center (1993, 15) estimated that in 1990, Indians contributed more than $21 million in state sales tax revenues nationwide.

In 1988, Congress passed the Indian Gaming Regulatory Act (IGRA),[68] which established the statutory basis for the operation, regulation, and protection of Indian gaming. The act establishes three distinct classes of gaming. Class III gaming is defined in section 2703 (8) of the act to include casino-type games, electronic games, and other forms of gaming that are not classified as class I or class II. IGRA allows class III gaming on Indian lands subject to conformance to a tribal ordinance and further requires that the activities be conducted under the terms of a tribal-state compact. Tribes wishing to engage in class III gaming must initiate a request with the state to commence compact negotiations subject to review and approval by the secretary of the interior. IGRA requires that states negotiate "in good faith" with the initiating tribe. If the state does not respond in good faith to the tribal request for compact negotiation, the tribe may commence action against the state in federal district court.[69]

---

68. 25 U.S.C. sec. 2703.

69. If the district court finds that the state has failed to negotiate in good faith, the court may order the state and the tribe to conclude a compact within sixty days. If an

By 2006, of the approximately 367 Indian gaming enterprises operating nationally, the majority were operating under the provisions of tribal-state compacts, representing 224 tribes in 28 states (Harvard Project on American Indian Economic Development 2008).

Litigation related to the act has occurred in more than twenty states, as well as in the District of Columbia. Eleven states have either raised state sovereign immunity defenses under the Eleventh Amendment of the US Constitution or under the defense of reserved powers granted to states under the Tenth Amendment. Most of these cases were filed by tribes following the refusal of states to enter into negotiations under the good faith negotiation provision of the act. Certain cases involved the forms of class III games sought by the tribes and the wagering limitations sought by the state on the tribal gaming activity.[70]

Conclusion and Implications for Planning

The management of the reservation territory is of paramount importance to the sustainability of tribal communities. The historic diminishment of a tribe's governing authority, however, creates a tribal planning situation that is embroiled in questions regarding the ability of a tribe to control its future development. This chapter demonstrates that the tribes clearly possess the power to regulate Indians in Indian country and, under certain circumstances, may regulate its members outside the reservation when important tribal interests are at stake, such as treaty fishing by its members. In addition, tribes also possess substantial powers to regulate non-Indian activities in Indian country that have a demonstrable effect on Indian interests. Since the 1970s, the implementation of the Indian self-determination policy throughout the federal system has resulted in

---

agreement is not concluded during this period, each party is required to submit its last best offer to a court appointed mediator who may select either the state or the tribal compact version. If the state does not consent to the compact chosen by the mediator, the matter becomes referred to the secretary of the interior who prescribes procedures consistent with the selected compact, the district court findings, the IGRA provisions, and relevant provisions of state law.

70. See Endreson (1993).

the restoration of many powers that had previously either been removed or were dormant. The development of a tribe's political capacity for self-governance continues to be influenced by both federal Indian policy as well as court decisions that delineate the balance of competing interests that operate within the tribal planning situation.

The lessons learned in the *Montana* and *Brendale* decisions provide guidance with respect to the extent of tribal regulatory authority over the activities of non-Indians. In *Montana*, tribal sovereignty is framed as a power that had been narrowed by virtue of a tribe's dependent status and that, without express congressional delegation, the exercise of tribal authority over the activities of non-Indians beyond what is necessary to defend tribal self-government may be found to be inconsistent with their dependent status. However, two important exceptions in the *Montana* ruling establish the circumstances where tribal authority may be found to be valid. These exemptions are important considerations in forming effective tribal planning strategies, particularly when non-Indian property interests are present:

• A tribe can regulate the activities of non-Indians who have entered into consensual relations with the tribe or its members through commercial dealings, contracts, leases, or other arrangements;

• A tribe also retains its inherent regulatory authority to regulate the conduct of non-Indians on fee lands when that conduct threatens or has some direct effect on the political integrity, the economic security, or the health or welfare of the tribe.

The second test serves as a central guiding principle in tribal planning. The extent to which a tribe defines its essential character, political integrity, economic security, and health and welfare, in consideration of all reservation interests, may well be the deciding point for defending a tribe's jurisdictional primacy, given that many reservations now contain a plurality of property rights interests. Justice Blackmun, in his dissenting opinion in *Brendale*, recognized the importance of the tribe's right to zone all reservation lands, including fee lands, as he found that the loss of the long-term benefits of comprehensive land management would represent a significant impact on tribal interests. However, *Brendale*'s defining test for determining the tribe's authority over certain fee lands was weighed against the tribe's inconsistency in providing equal services and protection to both the "open" and "closed" areas of the reservation, resulting in a decision that ultimately supported the county's authority.

The *Brendale* decision was based on a narrow set of factual and unique circumstances that may not necessarily represent the conditions found in other reservations. This raises several questions regarding the consequences of the decision as well as the important role that comprehensive reservation planning plays in strengthening tribal governance. For example, would the Supreme Court have affirmed tribal regulatory primacy had the tribe demonstrated a history of providing services and proactive planning that benefited the entire reservation community, rather than only that portion comprised mostly of tribal interests? Would the outcome have been different had the tribe established a reservation policy that defined the essential character of the reservation in terms of a plurality of interests? And, in response to the increase in non-Indian occupancy on many reservations, does the consideration of those non-Indian interests now constitute a prerequisite in tribal planning before a tribe can preempt the imposition of a county's jurisdiction? Lessons learned from the aforementioned cases represent a starting point for assessing how future courts might rule in balancing competing county and tribal jurisdictional interests. The successful reconciliation of the plurality of competing interests that occur in the reservation planning situation is the principal challenge to tribal planning.

In our effort to formulate more effective tribal planning strategies that empower tribal communities, the lessons learned from these rulings should be firmly incorporated as central considerations in tribal planning. Under the rulings, the key question regarding a tribe's ability to regulate reservation fee lands is dependent upon whether the activity affects the "essential character" of the reservation or imperils the political integrity, the economic security, or the health or welfare of the tribe. Based on these and other landmark rulings,[71] and combined with the tribal delegation of

---

71. See also *Cardin v. DeLaCruz*, 671 F.2d 363 (9th Cir. 1982), *cert. denied*, 459 U.S. 967 (1982); *Confederated Tribes and Bands of Yakima Indian Nation v. Whiteside*, 828 F.2d 529 (9th Cir. 1987).

authority under the federal environmental statutes, tribes retain a clear ability to apply their building, health and safety, environmental protection, and zoning regulations in a consistent manner throughout their reservations, provided they meet these legal standards. A reservation plan that inclusively addresses the broader needs of the reservation community may provide the strongest argument for the defense of tribal authority, and would be consistent with planning's overarching principle for the planning of diverse and inclusive communities. Approaches in pluralistic planning may best serve to resolve the dilemmas that challenge a tribe's ultimate ability to control the future development of its tribal community.

4

The Tribal Cultural Community

THIS CHAPTER examines the general social characteristics and cultural value systems that are reflected in Indian societies. It is important to be aware that differences exist between historic and contemporary Indian cultural value systems, as well as variances among different cultural groups and within individual tribal groups. The generalizations described reflect observations from previous anthropological work conducted primarily in the Coast Salish region of the northwestern United States. This discussion aims to highlight how the underlying belief systems that are common to modern Indian societies are distinct from, and sometimes in conflict with, the norms and social values found in non-Indian society.

The expression of a community's development goals is based upon the consensual belief systems that reflect the collective views of a community. Those views may pose a dialectic tension in relations between tribal communities and mainstream US society. Many of these tensions are manifested in cultural goal conflicts, especially as they relate to the use of land and natural resources (LeVine and Campbell 1972). For example, in order to safeguard fisheries habitats, Northwest tribes that possess treaty fishing rights have repeatedly emphasized the importance of preserving adequate in-stream flows to support fisheries in water resource allocation policy. This priority, however, has conflicted with the state's consideration of other non-tribal priorities regarding the allocation of water among competing user groups. According to the tribal view, past water allocation policies that have favored other competing uses have led to diminished fisheries resources. Recent tribal interventions involving litigation[1] against the State of Washington represent attempts by the tribes to protect their proprietary treaty rights by demanding a greater consideration for the protection of fisheries resources. Such interventions signify both the tribes' economic interests as well as their cultural preference for sustaining a fishery resource that has, in addition to its commodity value, a sustenance and spiritual value that is an essential part of its cultural belief system.

Ethnic Groups

An important distinction between cultures and ethnic groups was described by Barth (1969), who recognized that, while ethnic groups are the bearers of cultures, they are not limited to cultural groups. Ethnic groups are created when groups of people of common origin and background ascribe a common identity to themselves. Members of these groups define their social boundaries by adhering to specific cultural traditions. Anthropologists have historically focused attention on the differences between cultures, their historic boundaries, and their connections, but have not, until more recently, investigated the constitution of ethnic groups and the nature of the boundaries between them (Roberts 1975). Viewing Indian communities in terms of their ethnic development provides a more complete understanding of their ability to survive and adapt to new social circumstances, rather than merely describe their loss of aboriginal culture. In order to understand contemporary tribal community development, it is helpful to possess an historic understanding of their adaptation through their ethnic organization and their responses both to initial contact and to continued interaction with non-Indian influences. The distinction between understanding tribal communities as ethnic communities in contrast to cultural communities is further advanced by the processes of cultural disintegration, or the loss of aboriginal cultures, creative acculturation,[2] and bi-culturation (Swinomish 1991; Collins 1974; Amoss 1972).

1. See *Swinomish Indian Tribal Community v. Department of Ecology*, No. 87672-0 (Wash. Sup. Ct. October 3, 2013).
2. Roberts' analysis of ethnic evolution relies on a number of anthropological approaches, including the "ethnic stratification" and the "long term transformations" of

Roberts (1975, 8) describes an ethnic group as "the largest operating socio-political unit in an area that is recognized by the people themselves as something they belong to by virtue of where they live and what their origin is" and depicts the ethnic community as containing twelve central characteristics:

1. It is an "operating socio-political unit" containing a membership and a system of polity. This is distinguished from an ethno-linguistic category, which may not function as a community except with respect to sharing a language and other cultural features. The organization itself defines the function of its members and their engagement in a common activity.

2. It is a "coordinate unit" recognized by its members and given a name or a label. This distinguishes it from a culture or society. The boundary of an ethnic group is not always distinguished by a territorial borderline, but by the distinction made by the membership regarding the group's composition.

3. Members of an ethnic group distinguish themselves from other groups by their active participation in group activities or by a number of diacritica that help reinforce a sense of group identity. The diacritica may be cultural features, places of residence, and possession of cultural objects or specialized knowledge.

4. An ethnic group is an "original group," whose members share a common geographic or spiritual "home" as well as a common genealogical origin.

5. The size of ethnic units may vary, ranging from an extended family to an entire village.

6. Ethnic groups may experience frequent mobility among their membership and some may even be exogamous. Their boundaries are usually maintained, despite the flow of individuals across them. It has been argued that change of ethnic identity may require an individual to undergo a

---

systems of ethnic stratifications (Barth 1969), and the process of fusion, or the merging of ethnic groups (Paden 1970). Approaches by LeVine and Campbell (1972) on ethnocentricism further contribute to an explanation of how ethnicity and group boundaries have undergone evolution over time.

process of incorporation that may require generations of effort to change cultural values (Roberts 1975; Paden 1970).

7. Ethnic groups may be fragile and subject to recurrent dissolution and reconstitution of new group members, with small groups being the most unstable.

8. The more mobile their elements, the less ethnic groups develop profound cultural differences from one another.

9. Over a period of time, ethnic units may undergo transformations by taking in new members or redefining their boundaries. This may be accomplished through the process of cultural fusion, where two or more groups join to share a common identity, or through the process of cultural fission, the splitting apart of a single group.

10. Ethnic units may be found in sets of increasing inclusiveness, especially when fusion of several small coordinate units is occurring.

11. Ethnic units usually interact with each other.

12. Relationships between ethnic groups take many different forms.

Values Differences

In spite of the process of acculturation and the acceptance of many non-Indian values, important value differences prevail that contribute to the maintenance of an Indian ethnic identity. Northwest coastal tribal communities, like other Indian communities, continue to place a high value on family and community life (State of Washington 1971). Tending toward lifetime residency within their reservations, members of tribal reservation communities are generally characterized as less likely to relocate from their reservation communities than members of non-Indian communities. Tribal community members also tend to avoid isolation in urban areas, preferring to retain close associations with their well-developed familial community. Service to the community continues to be a common value emphasized by the community members; similarly, non-Indian values of individual achievement for material and financial gains are often replaced by cooperation. Roberts (1975, 338) observes that in many Coast Salish Indian communities "generosity brings more esteem than display of items of personal wealth, especially generosity in giving food and meals to large groups. Face to face contacts are highly valued over impersonal communication in writing." Northwest coastal tribes also show a greater reverence for spiritual knowledge gained through transcendental experiences than do non-Indians (Collins 1974). Even those members who may no longer participate in traditional religious activities, but instead, practice Western forms of religion, continue to acknowledge a strong personal association with traditional religion.

Indian people have objected to the assumption that the loss of Native cultures is either inevitable or desirable. Many view acculturation[3] as something undesirable and equate the acculturation process to "de-culturation," or the loss of a culture. Acculturation, which was thought to contribute to the long-standing ideal of the American cultural "melting pot," has recently been replaced by the preferential notion of a pluralistic American society, a notion that retains strong associations with cultural diversification. Bi-culturation, as an emerging concept, promotes the diversity in a society's culture by providing a positive model for cultural identity and a process for achieving dual cultural competence. A bi-cultural community actively seeks to retain its original cultural traditions, identity, beliefs, and set of values while learning to constructively cope within a mainstream society.

Indian views toward their land and natural resources distinctly differ from predominant non-Indian views. Indians tend to view their land holdings, whether held in individual trust allotments or as community owned trust lands, as a collective, rather than a private, financial asset (Ackerman 1981). This personal view is considered holistic as it integrates a religious value that regards the land as sacred. Land holdings are rarely sold for financial gain. Instead, many tribal communities emphasize the reacquisition of reservation lands that had previously been sold out of trust ownership. In addition, the land is perceived to be a permanent territorial homeland integrating the cultural continuity of the community with

3. The anthropological meaning of the term "acculturation" originally referred to the process of interaction between members of two different cultures, resulting in increasing familiarity and exposure to the foreign culture, the exchange of ideas, goods and technology, and consequent change in each culture. In the acculturation process, one culture usually dominates the other culture.

its polity. Fundamentally, the Indian land base is viewed as a social and political ecosystem that connects the community to its historical roots.

The Suppression of Indian Religion and Traditions

Early Anglo contact with Indian communities often resulted in misunderstanding about Indian traditions and evoked ethnocentric assumptions about the superiority of non-Indian culture. A presumption of cultural dominance over Indian values eventually led to the persecution of Indian religious practices. Early settlers rarely sought to understand Indian religion (LeVine and Campbell 1972; Collins 1974), and instead projected their own fears by misinterpreting Native practices as forms of devil worship, ignorance, or black magic. This lack of understanding of Indian religious traditions resulted in a similar rejection of tribal cultures in general:

> Most non-Indian cultures have little appreciation for the multiplicity and subtle complexity of Indian spiritual systems. Indian spirituality pervades many aspects of Indian culture. For thousands of years it has provided Indian people with a deeply spiritual outlook on life. These spiritual practices embody a deep contemplation of nature and the meaning of life and death and provide a set of socially constructive values by which Indian people traditionally conduct their lives (Swinomish 1991, 30).

The earliest settlers in the Northwest viewed Indian people as primitive and ignorant and regarded their values and religious beliefs as heathen. They relied upon their own technological superiority and ethnocentricism to persuade Indian people that "God was on their side." While many Indians publicly converted to Western religions, most continued to participate in traditional religious practice. Non-Indian society eventually used institutional mechanisms, including the passage of laws that prohibited Indian religious practices, to disrupt tribal cultural cohesion. Cultural continuity was further compromised by forcibly removing Indian children from their families and sending them to government operated boarding schools or by placing them in non-Indian foster and adoptive homes. During the late 1800s, it was declared illegal for Indians to practice any aspect of traditional religion, spiritual dances, or healing practices. Courts of "Indian Offenses" were established to punish those who persisted in practicing traditional beliefs. Indians were fined and imprisoned for possessing traditional spiritual regalia or for participating in traditional dances. The institutional mechanisms employed by the federal government were intended to humiliate Indian people and encourage them to reject their traditional ways as being primitive and evil.

As a result of persecution, Indians were forced to practice traditional Indian spiritualism in secrecy (Roberts 1975). The suppression of Indian religion eventually led to the diminishing of invaluable Indian knowledge and traditions. Indians who preserved spiritual knowledge became extremely reluctant to reveal what they knew and would often deny any association with that knowledge as a form of self, and community, preservation. Another significant effect of religious persecution was the loss of traditional medical and healing knowledge. Indian cultures have historically regarded their spiritual well-being as an inseparable part of their physical, emotional, and social well-being and have often relied on traditional spiritual healing practices to treat both physical and spiritual illnesses. The denial of traditional Indian religion was directly responsible for the disruption of Indian healing systems.

In the Northwest, the persecution of traditional Indian religious practices led to the formation of the Indian Shaker Church, which combined Christian beliefs with traditional Indian beliefs, including the retention of Indian healing traditions. The Shaker Church offered Indians a way of adapting to the prevailing Christian beliefs while preserving a strong sense of Indian identity and cultural independence. Similar forms of "Indian Christianity" also developed in other regions of the United States. While the legal practice of persecution of traditional religion was abated, following passage of the Indian Reorganization Act of 1934, prohibition of the practice was not formally repudiated until passage of the Indian Freedom of Religion Act of 1978.[4] However, by the mid-1900s, pervasive disruption of Indian cultures had already occurred. Many Indians had become ashamed of their Indian ways or had lost confidence in their traditions.

---

4. Indian Freedom of Religion Act, 92 Stat. 469 (1978) (codified at 42 U.S.C. § 1996).

Others had learned to cope with persecution, either by denying their association with traditions or by retaining their experiences by practicing in private, away from contact with non-Indians.[5]

Ethnic Fusion

The process of assimilating the cultural values and behaviors of various ethnic groups is depicted as a process of ethnic fusion and may include four distinct processes that affect the territorial boundaries of the ethnic group: boundary maintenance, fission, fusion, and intrusion.[6] Throughout the Northwest tribal region, Roberts (1975, 16) observed ethnic fusion as a prominent process affecting the identity of ethnic tribal groups. Fusion by semi-autonomous ethnic groups occurred both prior to and during the treaty-making period, which grouped bands of tribes together under different treaties and reserved common territories for their relocation. Seven distinct ethnic groups from the Skagit River region entered into the Treaty of Point Elliott as signators.[7] Article I of the treaty provided for the ceding of the Indian land territories, comprising an area that generally extends from the City of Tacoma to the Canadian border. Article II reserved four tracts of land as exclusive Indian territory, following US Senate ratification of the treaty, and the Indians consented to relocate to these reservations within a one-year period. The process of ethnic fusion initiated by the treaties resulted in the modern formation of the Northwest tribal communities

5. In 1987, the Church Council of Greater Seattle wrote a formal letter of apology to all Indian people, admitting the past insensitivity of Christian churches and pledging future support for and defense of Indian religious freedom (Seattle Archdiocese, Letter to Northwest Tribes 1987).

6. Boundary maintenance refers to the definition of ethnic identity unique from other groups. Fission refers to the splitting of a single ethnic unit into several parts with each subsequent part assuming a new ethnic identity. Fusion represents the merging of a group of ethnic units to form a new ethnic identity. Intrusion represents the migration of a new group into an ethnic community and fundamentally changing the identity of the original group.

7. These groups were the Skagit, Kikialus, Sah-ku-meh-hu, Me-sek-wi-guilse, Noo-qua-cha-mish, Swinamish, and Noo-wha-ah. Four other bands were indirectly represented or were protesting non-signators: Co-ba-ah-bish, Samish, Sba-le-och, and Mis-skai-whwa.

upon designated reservation territories. Eight specific ramifications resulting from the process of fusion are described by Roberts (1975, 398):

1. The individual members of the ethnic group established a collective
identity.

2. The frequency of their collective interaction resulted in increased
ethnic cohesiveness over time.

3. Members of different ethnic groups established functional economic and political links with neighboring groups and established common genealogical histories.

4. Value congruence strengthened as a reaction to the introduction of
threatening values represented by non-Indian settlers in the Northwest.

5. Members of the newly expanded ethnic group identified a shared
ethnic status and worked to improve the common control over their
shared assets and their ranking in relation to other ethnic groups.

6. Ethnic fusion was facilitated when commonly recognized leaders
emphasized their ethnic identity, service to the community, and the adoption of future-oriented goals toward group achievement.

7. The formation of a common reservation homeland territory bolstered the early identity for the fused ethnic group.

8. The subsequent reorganization of their government further fostered
cohesiveness of the ethnic group as a political community.

Community Values and Values Dissonance

The term "culture" refers to the underlying belief systems of a society
as reflected in its general lifestyles and as supported by a collective set
of social norms and ideals. Many contemporary Indian lifestyles can be
characterized as having a strong sense of family orientation, common
exchange and reciprocity among tribal members, and a shared collective experience, including being victimized by historic social prejudice.
Tribal societies continue to emphasize large community gatherings and
shared meals that foster cultural cohesion. These customs often extend to
other Indian societies by means of frequent travel within cultural circuits
(Amoss 1972; Collins 1974). The persistent presence of alcohol abuse and
the tragic effects of deaths and losses continue to bind the community,
which primarily relies on healing processes from within the community.

Many Indians continue to maintain separate social and economic lifestyles, often avoiding all forms of exchange with non-Indian society. Historic non-Indian prejudice has contributed to widespread distrust by Indians toward non-Indian society. The history of persecution, prejudice, loss of language, and other aspects of Indian culture has greatly influenced both the lives and viewpoints of tribal people. In spite of these historic influences, Indian communities have managed to retain their cultures through their resilient responses to loss and misfortune (Swinomish Tribal Mental Health Project 1991, 167).

Though having adapted to non-Indian work standards, many Indian people continue to prefer a lifestyle that is based on seasonal work patterns. In Coast Salish cultures, the winter season continues to emphasize commitments to spiritual values and family relations while the summer season is devoted primarily to the work of commercial fishing. "While a receptive or even fatalistic life view may be intrinsic to some Indian cultures, poverty, alcoholism, and social alienation are not. While many Indian people face severe economic and social conditions, these conditions must not be confused with Indian culture" (Collins 1974, 168). It has been widely recognized by Indian communities that the path toward a more secure identity and improvement of their collective well-being is integrally linked to the maintenance of their Indian culture. Thus, tribal members have increasingly relied upon the tribal governance structure to provide necessary protection from continued external disruptions to the community's social cohesiveness.

Ten behavioral characteristics that illustrate many of the fundamental differences in tribal community values and attitudes serve as a framework to depict the variances in cultural patterns between dominant European-American viewpoints and those of Native Americans. Since social values and attitudes provide the foundation for the articulation of a community's development goals, a comparison of the contrasting social characteristics that may contribute to the values dissonance between the Indian and non-Indian community is presented in table 2. Although each viewpoint can be construed as an overgeneralization, the comparison, nonetheless, is useful for contrasting social preferences that have been observed in each respective group.

TABLE 2 A Comparison of Values, Attitudes, and Behavioral Attributes

Values	American Indian Viewpoint	European-American Viewpoint
Cooperation	Historically regarded as necessary for community survival, cooperation is highly valued by the tribal community. Because of strong solidarity, competition within the group is rare. Cooperation is so significant that democracy is often practiced through participatory consensus rather than by majority rule.	Competition is highly valued. Competing with one's peers to prove oneself better is generally reinforced. Competitive achievement is often viewed as necessary for personal advancement and success.
Importance of Group Cohesiveness	Most Indians are not driven by ego and tend to strive for anonymity. They stress the importance of personal orientation in the group. The needs of the group are considered over those of the individual.	The concept of individualism is encouraged. The needs of the individual are often considered over those of the group.
Patience	Having patience to wait quietly is considered a virtuous quality. Evidence of this value is reflected in Indian works of art, such as beadwork, quilt work, or sand painting.	One is taught to not allow "grass to grow under one's feet." It is considered important to act quickly and with haste.
Modesty	The value of modesty is emphasized. Boasting and loud behavior that attract attention are discouraged.	It is an acceptable practice to draw attention to one's accomplishments.
Individual Autonomy	Respect for an individual's dignity and autonomy are greatly valued. Indian people avoid controlling the behavior of others and they are taught not to interfere in the affairs of others. Indian parents generally practice non-interference regarding their child's vocation.	It is acceptable to aggressively involve oneself in the affairs of others. Advice is freely given. Most non-Indian parents become involved in and influence their child's choice of careers.
Placidity	Placidity, the ability to remain quiet and still is highly regarded, as is the state of silence. Most Indians display	Action is valued over inaction. The person who gets thing done rapidly and moves on to

Values	American Indian Viewpoint	European-American Viewpoint
	few nervous mannerisms. When ill at ease, Indians observe in silence, while inwardly determining what is expected of them. Indians are slow to demonstrate anger or other strong emotions.	the next task is admired. Silence causes discomfort. When ill at ease, verbal activity increases as do bodily movements. Emotional reactions are almost immediately visible.
Savings	Indians traditionally haven't seen the value in amassing large quantities of goods, such as savings accounts or life insurance policies. This attitude reflects a past in which nature's bounty provided for one's needs.	Saving is a means of achieving increased status. One is taught to forgo present use of time and money for the anticipated satisfaction to be enjoyed at a later date. One is encouraged to invest in property and savings. The quality of "thrift" is admired and emulated.
Sharing	Generosity and sharing are greatly valued. Most Indians freely exchange property and food. The respected person is not one with large savings, but rather one who gives generously.	The value of sharing is recognized, but not strongly promoted. While the concept of sharing is advanced, it may conflict with the value of individual ownership.
Materialism	Acquiring material goods for status is not as important as being respected in the community. A "give-away" of blankets and money to honor others is a common occurrence. Upward social mobility within the non-Indian society is not actively sought.	Generally, success is measured by the amount of accumulated material goods. Acquiring material goods for the sake of ownership and status is encouraged.
Work Ethic	The Puritan work ethic is foreign to many Indians. A rigid work schedule was traditionally not part of the Indian system.	The Puritan work ethic, extolling the value of work for work's sake, is admired and encouraged.

Source: Nicholas C. Zaferatos.

A distinctive set of observed cultural values that reflect many Coast Salish tribal communities as well as other Indian communities throughout the nation is summarized below. These values reflect many of the important social attributes found among Indian peoples in tribal community settings (Amoss 1972; Collins 1974; State of Washington 1971; Swinomish 1991, 170):

Respectfulness. Respect toward others is of paramount importance in tribal life. Norms for social politeness and respect may be represented in subtle and complex ways that are often difficult for non-Indians to understand. Coast Salish people understand respect in terms of "knowing one's proper place in the social structure and that of other persons" (Roberts 1975, 170), with elders being especially recognized within the community. Respect is also shown through recognition of individual differences and the importance placed on individual experiences. Judgment of others is replaced with tolerance for individual differences and it is considered disrespectful to interfere with others' behavior and preferences.

Informality and Social Involvement. An important social value shared by many Indian communities is the informal nature of social interactions that serves to remove social status differences. Indian people may perceive formality, rigid time schedules, professional jargon, and Western fashion as a means of establishing a separate social status at the expense of others. Casual clothing is the preferred form of dress within reservation communities. Informality serves to convey a concept of respect and social equality.

Social Status. The social status of the Indian family, especially through ancestral lineages, contributes to the individual's social position within the community, and the behavior of an individual is viewed as a reflection of the entire family. In determining social status, acts of generosity and traditional knowledge of the community and its member families are held in high regard. As community historians, tribal elders are revered in their role as keepers of tribal history. Conversely, the social status of an individual that is based upon the notion of popularity is frowned upon and may result in the person being publicly shamed.

Inter-Family Relations. Many tribal communities include several family groups that retain prestigious social and political influence within the community. An individual member's political and social ambitions may be influenced by family loyalties, obligations, and conflicts. The tribal extended family tends to form a social nucleus whereby relations with other families tend to be cautious so as not to be offensive. Disrespect between families is discouraged so that inter-family rivalries, that may extend for generations and become disruptive to the cohesiveness of the entire community, are avoided.

Community Cohesiveness. Community gatherings of member families continue to constitute an important tradition among Indian tribes. The values placed on community sharing solidify the cultural sense of the entire community. Hospitality is highly valued and is typically extended by an entire community when hosting other communities. Opening one's home and giving gifts to guests is regarded as culturally important. Indian people often refer to this form of personal sharing as "Indian insurance." Reciprocal exchange and community support guarantee that families will not be abandoned when dealing with their own misfortunes. Acts of generosity are an ongoing integral component of community cohesiveness.

Community Decision-Making. Indian decision-making styles differ from non-Indian styles in a number of distinct ways. Indian people generally avoid exercising control over other individuals, tending to become more tolerant of differences rather than trying to change the opinions of others. Many Indian cultures place a greater value on social cooperation than on individual decision-making in order to ensure collective community cohesion. Decisions are typically made not by individual voting, but by consensus, only after family members have come to a mutual agreement.

Non-Self-Assertion and Noninterference. Indian people value group cohesiveness over individual achievement and teach their children not to compete against others or to stand out among their peer group. Adults may avoid excelling over others for fear of appearing superior, and they rarely assert themselves or their opinions over others. In traditional Indian societies an emphasis is placed on the avoidance of interfering in the affairs of other families, as the community reveres each family's right of self-determination. Social norms are informally reinforced within the Indian community through the use of shaming, withdrawal of approval, humor, and teasing, which affect the social rank of the individuals and their families.

Attitudes Regarding Time. The reference to Indian as people operating on "Indian Time" reflects an important cultural difference between most Indian and non-Indian people in their attitudes about punctuality. Creating schedules and making precise appointments are perceived to be foreign concepts that can interfere with forming meaningful relationships. Indian time refers to the priority of activities being adjusted to fit the time availability of its members rather than to a prearranged timetable. Indian people tend to exhibit great patience and faith that problems will be resolved on their own accord. In dealings with non-Indians, such attitudes may result in delays and may even lead to conflict, as the importance of punctuality is often replaced with the importance of participation. Shared social responsibility, particularly in times of social crisis, prevails over other matters.

Communications Patterns

Many Indian communities retain patterns of communication that are distinct from non-Indian forms. The languages spoken, use of intonations, subtle differences in meanings, physical gestures, facial expressions, use of humor, and the use of silence each represent a major component of speech that together form a community's system of communication. Where some Native languages have been partially or entirely lost, others have been revived and continue to be spoken, especially among tribal elders. For those communities that have lost their languages, a deep sense of loss, sadness, and shame may be experienced. The consequences of cultural deprivation, which began with the historic prohibition of the use of Native languages, have had devastating effects on many Indian people. Because Native languages are also perceived to be an important link to spiritual connectiveness, the loss of language may represent a severance to one's spiritual foundation (Roberts 1975). Many tribes have stressed the importance of Indian youth learning their Native language in order to more fully achieve a sense of community identity, which may not be adequately conveyed through the use of the English language.

While most Indian people have become fluent in the English language, verbal communication barriers continue to exist in dialogue between Indian and non-Indian communities. Indian forms of English speech often differ from the form spoken by the non-Indian community. According to Roberts (1975), one reason explaining the differences in Indian English is that the language was either learned as a second language or learned from grandparents whose primary language was Native. Such differences in accent and rhythm can persist over several generations.

Many Indian groups use terms and phrases that are often misconstrued by non-Indians, especially expressions that refer to their cultural traditions and are completely foreign to non-Indian society. For instance, Indian people may refer to home as "a place where they stay," connoting, in part, a different set of values toward the concept of home occupancy than that more commonly understood by the non-Indian community. The notion of "staying" at a home suggests a non-possessive concept that reflects a traditional value of sharing shelter with an extended family. Home ownership, in terms of Western concepts of equity accumulation, appreciation, and privacy, continues to remain a foreign concept to many individuals.[8] Understanding the culturally based meaning of such expressions is critical for bridging an understanding between Indian and non-Indian communities.

Indian people often express their cultural meanings by incorporating nonverbal communication as an integral part of their speech patterns. In certain situations, Indian people may tend to maintain long periods of sustained silence that may cause non-Indians to feel uncomfortable. These silent durations often reflect deep thought about what has been said or exhibit respect for the speaker. A common misconception of Indian people by non-Indians is that their silence indicates withdrawal or unfriendliness

---

8. In another example, following the death of a family member, an Indian person may express the need to "have some work done on the house," referring to the spiritual practice of removing any lingering spirits or danger from the house (Swinomish Tribal Mental Health Project 1991, 187).

when, in fact, the intention may be a display of acceptance and respect prior to responding. Listening carefully and paying close attention when someone is speaking continue to be important values encouraged by Indian society.

As a sign of respect, Indian speech emphasizes the virtue of patience. Dialogue tends to occur by taking turns rather than by interruptive conversation, a pattern that tends to be typical in non-Indian dialogue. It is considered impolite to interrupt a speaker, especially elders of the community. Often, long periods of dialogue may take place before more focused discussions regarding specific matters are attempted. Many Indian people accept the fact that sufficient time will be devoted to establishing a broad understanding of both the subject matter and the individual before any decision is made.

Misunderstandings may also occur in communications between Indian and non-Indian people when either the language or the silence is misinterpreted. Further, Indians may mistake the meaning of certain body language and physical gestures of non-Indians. Nonverbal communication may reflect significant cultural differences between Indian and non-Indian participants where neither may even be cognizant of the intent of the other, as the following forms of nonverbal communication illustrate (Swinomish Tribal Mental Health Project 1991, 189–93):

Eye Contact. In many Indian cultures, direct eye contact tends to be avoided because it is considered to be disrespectful, intrusive, or intimidating. This may be a result of the traditional large communal family living arrangements, where averting one's eyes helps protect the privacy of others. Some Indian people feel uncomfortable with non-Indians who look directly into their eyes while talking and may look down or look away from the speaker. This often represents a manner of respect and attentiveness rather than a sign of unfriendliness.

Handshakes. Traditional Indian hand shaking tends to be much gentler than the more assertive non-Indian handshakes, which often are intended to convey self-assurance and trust. In contrast, many Indians tend toward a gentle touching of hands with the purpose of receiving impressions about the other person's spirit and personality and allowing expression of themselves. It is not intended as an expression of dominance, self-confidence, or necessarily a wish for friendship. Misunderstanding and negative impressions may result from the different purposes and styles of such hand greetings, and may be damaging to any future relationship. The handshake can also play an important role in revealing the degree of knowledge and exposure a person has to the other culture. When a non-Indian shakes hands in a non-Indian manner, the Indian person may assume the non-Indian is likely to be unfamiliar with Indian culture. Alternatively, given an Indian form of hand grasp may indicate the non-Indian has some familiarity with and demonstrates a sincere effort to learn about and adapt to Indian ways. Likewise, while many Indian people adapt their handshake style to match non-Indian expectations, it does not necessarily mean that the Indian person is "acculturated," but rather, that he understands what is expected in the non-Indian context and chooses to adjust.

Social Exchange. Culturally significant social exchanges are manifested through both verbal and nonverbal communications. While many non-Indian gestures serve to reflect approval, agreement, recognition, and gratitude, no specific American gesture demonstrates the important Indian value of demonstrating thanks and giving honor, which continues to be prevalent in the Indian culture. Coast Salish people convey honor, recognition, and thanks by extending both arms forward with palms open facing upward, hands held in a natural and receptive position, and both arms moving up and down several times in a graceful gesture.

Expression of Emotion. A common stereotype of Indian people as being stoic and unresponsive is largely due to a misunderstanding about the ways in which Indian people express their feelings as well as a historic Indian mistrust of non-Indians. Some Indian cultures express feelings in more subtle ways than non-Indians do, with circumspect and self-containment, and strong outward expressions of feeling are viewed as self-indulgent, a sign of both weakness and self-centeredness. Negative feelings, in particular, may be expressed in a more subdued manner by Indian people. This may be because of social norms, which discourage confrontation, as well as the experience of a long history of accumulated

losses and grief. People who have suffered a great deal of trauma or deprivation may be less likely to demonstrate grief at a new loss than those who
have rarely faced a severe crisis.[9]

Conclusion and Implications for Planning

A community's values shape its vision for a desired future; its policies
direct resources toward the attainment of that future vision. Similarly,
tribes define their policies to reflect their community's values and vision.
It should be expected that the visions and policies of Indian and non-
Indian communities will differ, as they reflect different community needs,
priorities, and circumstances.

The previous chapter was concerned about questions regarding the
authority of tribal and non-tribal jurisdictions to simultaneously plan and
manage the reservation environment. This chapter concerns the content
of policies that are imposed in reservation communities and the relationship of those policies to the underlying differences that are rooted in contrary community visions. In planning Native American communities, a
cultural values dissonance occurs when discrepant policies are concurrently encountered, as demonstrated in the case of *Brendale*.

While most tribal-non-tribal land use policy conflicts focus primarily
on matters of jurisdiction, few efforts have been undertaken to understand
and reconcile the content of normative-based conflicts (Gardner 1980).
A communicative discourse that seeks to bridge Indian and non-Indian
future visions must deliberately attempt to avoid errors in communication.[10] Once it becomes understood that a values dissonance is likely to
occur within an inter-community dialogue, efforts can focus on avoiding

---

9. The Swinomish Mental Health Project (1991, 192) observed that "people who
grew up in families which were dysfunctional due to alcoholism or violence may have
learned to protect themselves by shutting down their feelings. Those not familiar with
Indian people may mistake courage, acceptance, or numbness stemming from emotional
overload for insensitivity or lack of caring."

10. Habermas (1979, 29) expresses the idea of communicative competence as the
ability to mutually understand others so that the parties engaged in dialogue can be in
accord with each other in a shared value orientation.

false conjectures about the other community. The ability to foster effective dialogue that communicates the cultural meaning of a community's policies may lead to new opportunities for developing improved relationships between tribal and non-tribal communities. Efforts that lead to a greater understanding about the needs of other communities help to promote mutual understanding, appreciation, and, eventually, the acceptance of a plurality of community visions (Bond 2011). The reconciliation of public policy differences is an important step toward developing consistency in regional policy and, ultimately, an acceptance of regional cultural diversity (Ashley and Hubbard 2004; Brand and Gaffikin 2007).

While conflicts inevitably result whenever inconsistent policies are concurrently applied to the same geographic region, the mere application of dual governmental policies, however, does not alone create conflict if the content of those policies are in agreement. When policies are consistent, they represent a condition of *jurisdictional concurrency*, as separate governments simultaneously apply different, but compatible, policies through their separate, and presumably valid, authority. The conditions of concurrent land use planning is more fully explored in chapter 9 as an alternative method to resolving situations where multiple jurisdictions operate within Indian reservations. More pertinent to this chapter is the correlation between a community's policy formulation and its social values and the importance of understanding, and appreciating, how normative differences in community visions may underlie opposing policies.

Part TWO

Theories and Models
Empowering Tribal Planning

5

The Tribal Political Economy
and Its Underdevelopment

THIS CHAPTER explores social and development theories from the field of political economy to explain the causes that generally contribute to the persistent conditions of underdevelopment in both nations and in communities. The analysis is extended to the particular conditions of underdevelopment that are found in tribal communities and equates the processes of Indian *alienation* and *incorporation* to a series of historic events that were imposed upon tribes, their lands, and their resources.

Beginning in the eighteenth century, much of the earliest work in the study of political economy focused on the role of the economy in shaping society.[1] Political economy theory has been closely associated with Marx's early work on class relationships and the role of capitalism in creating imbalanced societies (Marx and Engels 1978; Meszaros 1970). In the twentieth century, political economy theorists branched out beyond a strict orthodox view of economic theory to incorporate new concerns that extended to the social impacts associated with economic systems. These theorists, referred to as *post-structuralists*, pursued analysis of a community's development process that emphasized the relationship between economic and political systems and their direct impact on a society's social

1. Francois Quesnay founded the physiocratic school in the mid-1750s, introducing the first scientific approach to the study of political economy. Physiocracy economic theory viewed the wealth of nations as being derived from the value of land development. It immediately preceded the first school of classical economics that began with the publication of Adam Smith's *The Wealth of Nations* in 1776.

well-being. Such theories viewed the study of cultural development as no less significant than economic development. Veblen's (1919) work in the early 1900s focused attention on the behavioral effects of "greed and conspicuous consumption" in economic systems on the growing inequities in societies. Inspired by Marxian theory, the writers of the French school of political economy sought to identify the relationships between systems of accumulation and systems of social and political regulation (Boyer 1987, 1994). Later works by "world systems" and "autonomist" theorists called for a further shift in the study of political economy to a focus on the global conditions of social injustice (Wallerstein 1991). These various research approaches examined the network of connections that produce local and global conflicts, approaches that emphasized the human struggles of society rather than merely on mechanisms of economies (Hardt 2000).

Beginning in the 1960s, the influences of political economy discourse in planning occurred during the American planning profession's period of social reawakening with a proliferation of contributions by such notable planning theorists as Davidoff (1965), Dyckman (1983), Forester (1980), Friedmann (1987), Castells (1983), and later Boyer (1994), Sandercock (1998, 2003), and others. Since the 1990s, the focus of planning has shifted beyond these earlier theoretical works concerned with the causal relationships between planning, prevailing economic systems, and social equity systems to theories and principles of social capital development, environmental justice, and sustainable development. The political economy and development theories that seemingly reached their pinnacle during the 1980s are, nevertheless, just as relevant today in assessing the unremitting conditions of injustice that continue to persist in Native American communities.

An important characteristic in political economy theory is the concept of "praxis," an idea whose roots in the history of philosophy has influenced Marxian theory,[2] the Frankfurt school of critical thought,

---

2. Marx was concerned with praxis in his earliest work, a doctoral dissertation on Greek philosophy, which insisted that philosophy be made practical. His principal interest was to create an alternative to alienated labor. In Marx's view, capitalism freed

and other action-oriented research traditions. Praxis refers to the activity of individuals as the primary instrument for producing change in society. Where theory seeks truth, the goal of praxis is to achieve action. As the focus of planning progressed from physical form (city beautiful), regulation (city functional), and management (city efficient) in the late nineteenth and early twentieth centuries, to a concern for social planning and an emphasis in community participation and citizen action, praxis became an integral part of American planning.

In general, these development theories are chiefly concerned with how desirable change in society can best be achieved and draw from a variety of social science disciplines and approaches. The post-development theory school of thought emerged in the 1990s in reaction to prevailing neoliberal economic theories.[3] Its primary focus was to question the purported goals of mainstream economic theory as arbitrary, if not impossible, to achieve. According to post-development theorists, neoliberal theories have resulted in creating inequitable hierarchies of developed and underdeveloped nations, with the goal of underdeveloped nations presumed to be the achievement of full development status. Western lifestyle, viewed by post-development theorists, is seen to be neither a realistic nor a necessarily desirable goal for the world's underdeveloped population, especially when development is equated to the loss of a society's culture (Sachs et al. 2007). Post-development theory views Western notions regarding the conditions of poverty or "backwardness" as being culturally ethnocentric and Western-oriented and calls, instead, for a broader involvement by underdeveloped societies in determining their own appropriate standards of development. Post-development theorists propose a vision of society that is de-linked from world-controlled capital systems that dominate those

---

labor from the alienation of necessity only to replace it with a new form of alienation that included the reduction of labor power to a marketable commodity. His goal was to transform alienated labor into praxis, or free, universal, self-activity.

3. Neoliberalism is a political philosophy supporting free trade, competitive markets, government deregulation, and privatization to emphasize the role of the private sector in society's development.

societies and, instead, advocate structural changes among undeveloped nations that emphasize solidarity, reciprocity, and the maintenance of traditional culture and knowledge.

Human development theory, a branch of post-development theory, has more recently emerged to combine ideas of the post-development theorists with concerns for environmental justice, sustainable development, social equity, and welfare economics that maximize the value of human capital in an economy. Sen's (1999) work emphasizes the importance of human capital as a measurement of national achievement, in which human capital, rather than income, is the determinant of a society's well-being. This core idea also underlies the construction of the Human Development Index, a human-focused measure of development pioneered by the United Nations Development Program. Human development theory can be categorized as a form of social welfare economics, where the success of economic policies is based on the well-being of peoples.

These various theories of development are examined more closely in the following discussion in an attempt to discern the causes that are responsible for creating the imbalanced conditions of underdevelopment that are common in many reservation communities. As a prerequisite to advancing reservation development and tribal self-determination, tribal planning must successfully account for the causes that contribute to reservation underdevelopment in order to overcome their detrimental effects (Cornell 2007).

The Political Economy of Development and Underdevelopment

"Underdevelopment" refers to the disadvantaged economic conditions of a community caused by external causes rather than by its own pattern of development (Frank 1988). The arrival of dominant market economies to previously isolated or independent economies created an economic and social disruption that altered the historic coherence of societies that had once been self-contained. A new market relationship emerged to displace the self-sufficient economies in order to emphasize the production of marketable commodities. A community's economic future became increasingly dependent upon outside economic markets, particularly as external price movements increasingly determined the value of its products. Linkages to larger external markets encouraged the export of raw materials from undeveloped economies, resulting in a further dependence upon external markets. Economic assistance, in the form of loans and grants, often followed, promoting increased economic productivity in those secondary economies. However, as the dependency on external funding increased, these capital intensive productivity measures have often proved to be unsuccessful in returning economic benefits to the local community and have tended, instead, to contribute to social and economic tensions in those underdeveloped economies. Further, external financial assistance frequently required that certain conditions imposed on the recipient community be fulfilled. The technical assistance that commonly accompanied financing encouraged the adoption of policies attractive to the foreign economy, but not necessarily conducive to, or ideologically compatible with, the development of the local communities (Baran 1988). In order for underdeveloped communities to reduce their dependency on external economies and stimulate their economic and social progress, the nature of their relationship to external economic forces must be modified accordingly.[4]

Dependency, Social Movements, and Critical Theory

Several theories of underdevelopment provide a framework for understanding the historic separation and imbalances in the relations between tribal communities and the broader US political economy. These theories include: dependency, unequal exchange, urban marginality, and critical theory.

Dependency theory[5] characterizes the nature of relations between developed and underdeveloped economies in terms of a dependency of

4. Wilber (1988, 110) describes developed countries as "economies which were never under-developed, in that their growth was largely self-generated." Underdeveloped countries, in contrast, are characterized by their economic dependency that is linked to their relations with developed countries.

5. As developed by Frank (1988, 130), dependency theory was formulated as a reaction to the neoclassical economic view of development in which the condition of underdevelopment is viewed in terms of an economy comprised of two distinct sectors: a traditional, self-sufficient sector, and a modern, developing sector whose economies

capitalist relations. An integral component of capitalist relations involve conditions of unequal exchange in which the developed economy, referred to as the *core* economy, and the underdeveloped economy, or the *periphery*, is depicted as complementary opposites in their economic relationship. Dependency theory posits that, during the era of European capitalist expansion, most world economies became incorporated within the network of capitalist relations that has penetrated even the most isolated sectors of the underdeveloped world. The theory holds that to a large degree the present condition of underdeveloped nations is a product of the historical development of capitalism on a world scale. The key concept in the dependency model is the nature of the relationship of two trading economies, with one playing a dominant and subjugating role and the other a dependency role. This relationship has historically been manifested by colonies and the imperial powers that not only conquered them but also derived material benefit from their resources. In a modern sense, a similar relationship can be seen between an underdeveloped country that has formed a dependency through trade relations and a dominant trading market. The dependency invariably implies a relation of unequal power and control. Such a situation results in both a loss of sovereignty by the underdeveloped nation regarding its ability to control its own development and a diminished material benefit caused by the dependency. Thus, in dependency theory, capitalism is regarded as a system where power is primarily exerted over an underdeveloped trading partner through market exchange. Dependency theory[6] examines core-periphery structures as

---

operate independent of the other. While the modern sector is intertwined with the world capitalist market, capitalist market relations do not directly affect the traditional sector.

6. Closely related to dependency theory, the "metropolis-satellite" and "world-systems" theories of underdevelopment rely on Frank's (1969, 21–94) "development of underdevelopment" thesis to explain the root causes that contribute to the uneven development of lesser economies. Metropolis-satellite theory portrays economies in terms of rural poverty. World system theory maintains that the growth process of global capitalism divides the world's economies into three components: a core, a periphery, and a semi-periphery. Both theories contend that uneven development is the result of modern nation-states expanding internationally or regionally into undeveloped areas. As modern

the primary instrument for extracting economic surplus from its periphery and channeling this surplus to the world economy, thereby perpetuating underdeveloped conditions in the periphery.

Ideas pertaining to dependency and underdevelopment are further explored in the post-dependency model of "unequal exchange" (Amin 1976). The relationship between the core and the periphery promotes development in the core while, concurrently, blocking the progress of development within the periphery. As in dependency theory, unequal exchange theory is based on the presumption of a global capitalist system that contains the two divisions of a core and periphery, whose economies are viewed to be dynamically related. The theory stresses the importance of understanding the internal structure of the periphery countries in order to uncover the conditions that foster the continuation of these relationships. The central thesis of Amin's model is that a core and periphery dualism exists at each of three stages of capitalist development: mercantilist, pre-monopoly-competitive, and monopoly-imperialist. The complementary opposite relationship becomes prominent in the third stage when the periphery economy is no longer capable of altering its relationship to the core or to the conditions of its underdevelopment.

Similar to how imbalanced global relations are addressed in dependency theory, the theory of urban marginality (Castells 1983, 179) helps to explain the imbalanced domestic relations that occur within a single national economy. The theory attempts to explain conditions of poverty in terms of "urban margins," which result, in part, from social causes and political apathy. Urban marginality theory focuses on the phenomenon of urban poverty by examining the inability of both the market economy and public policy intervention to provide adequate access to the distribution of a community's economic benefits so that conditions of urban poverty can

---

nation-states expand, they rely upon resources extracted from undeveloped regions to fuel their continued development. This process results in an interruption to the natural course and timing of the development of these regions. Underdevelopment is the result of a lack of development in the peripheral economy and the imbalance of exchange that perpetuates underdevelopment.

be alleviated. In response to the discrepancy that exists among economic classes, social movements have emerged to react to the economic imbalances that contribute to poverty. By acting primarily within the realm of public policy, the goal of these social movements has been to build stronger economic and social communities. In addition to addressing economic justice, social movements have also reacted to institutions that deny poor communities access to opportunity.[7] Social movements do not pursue a change to political institutions, but, rather, seek to work within the existing status quo of political systems as agents of social reform. These movements attempt to overcome identified problems through a process of transforming structural hindrances that result in social problems rather than through the creation of a new normative vision of society.

The application of critical theory, as developed by Habermas (1979), helps to inform an understanding of the nature of conflicts that are encountered in Indian community development. Critical theory approaches are useful for identifying the complex nature of competing non-tribal interests that interfere in Indian affairs. They also provide a framework for understanding how institutionalized power structures have historically diminished tribal autonomy. The sources of these controlling influences, as in the core-periphery model, are external to the tribes and primarily act as extractive mechanisms to derive economic benefit from tribal territories.

Critical theory is fundamentally concerned with determining whose interests are being served by an action. Habermas argues that "[t]echnocracy hides the latent contradictions and conflicts of the capitalist state. Technical decisions are made, but the general public is unaware of their political content and of the political forces at work behind the scene" (quoted in Benveniste 1989, 75). For Habermas, a general crisis of legitimization occurs when a political system no longer delivers its promises of material sufficiency, social equity, or democratic rights. The approach's

---

7. Four principal processes that promote social change are change within an existing institutional power, change through revolutionary actions, change through social movements, and change through social mobilization and expanded community consciousness. Urban social movements employ each of these processes except actions that involve revolutionary tactics (Castells 1983, 322).

ultimate objective is a historically oriented analysis of contemporary society with the practical aim of critically examining the imbalances that are produced in the capitalist society (Habermas 1979, xiii).[8] Critical theory provides an approach for analyzing how power is produced through public policy and suggests that planning, as an instrument of public policy, can become more effectively used to overcome the imbalances associated with institutional mechanisms of power (Forester 1980, 275).

Understanding Indian Dependency

Dependency and critical theories provide approaches for examining the endemic impoverished conditions that persist in Indian communities so that the nature of Indian and non-Indian relations and their impact upon the conditions of reservation economies can be better understood.[9] Historically, federal Indian policy has been based on the acculturation approach to Indian ethnicity and poverty, which posits that before white contact, American Indians were backward and undeveloped and that the Indian condition would only improve through a process of full integration into the social and economic mainstream of US society. Acculturation theory is derived from modernization or *melting pot* theory, which argues that nation-building requires a process of integrating formerly diverse social groups into one political economic entity in order to produce a new shared sense of identity. Both acculturation and modernization theories, as applied to Indians through a series of major federal policy actions, have failed to successfully integrate those societies into the mainstream due to three main factors: the diverse ethnicity of Indian communities, the persistence of tribal sovereignty, and the underdeveloped conditions that Indians continue to face (Page 1985).

8. Critical theory is based upon a three-tiered research program comprised of a theory of communication, a theory of socialization, and a theory of social evolution. A principal assumption of critical theory is that social evolution is conceived as a learning process that is based on the presupposition that communication must be "comprehensible, truthful, and right." The search for consensual understanding is derived through general agreement by all participants regarding what constitutes "right."

9. See Page (1985), Rostow (1960), and Portes (1976).

The history of exploitation of Indian territories by the US political economy has resulted in the political oppression of Indians, a condition that can be perceived as a form of neo-colonial subjugation. The imbalanced influence over tribal resources is attributed to public policy and administrative institutions that have historically exercised control over access to Indian resources, most of which are held in trust ownership by the federal government. The history of federal-Indian relations has unilaterally been applied under the guise of "civilizing" reservation Indians for the purpose of facilitating the private economy's access to Indian resources. The most pervasive public policy actions included the General Allotment Act, which not only divided the Indian territory, but also provided a mechanism for the removal and sale of land to non-Indians, and the termination policies of the 1950s that hastened the erosion of Indian political control over the reservation territories.

As forms of internal colonies, Indian reservations are economically and politically dependent upon the federal government and the broader economy for goods and services. The political economy is comprised of a complex mix of economic interests, each of which has a particular interest in the development of the Indian territory and thus in maintaining an ongoing relationship with the Indian community. Those vested interests include the federal government, which serves as trustee and manager of the resource base; state and local governments, which directly benefit from the taxation of businesses; private industry that extracts reservation resources; and individuals who own private property on reservation lands. The private economy includes the institutional investment and banking sector, as well as individuals who view reservation development as a stimulus for their own economic interests. The pervasive role of the US political economy in reservation development is evidenced by the presence of reservation-based industries that are neither owned nor controlled by Indians. The extraction of raw materials and agricultural products by these industries are intended for productive use outside the reservations.[10]

---

10. Notably absent in the timber rich Indian territories of the Northwest are reservation timber manufacturing industries that continue to be located outside the Indian

Indian economic failure can, in large part, be attributed to the Bureau of Indian Affairs' historic encouragement of tribal dependency upon the political economy to develop Indian resources. The application of the dependency model of underdevelopment equates the lack of development, and hence the slow "acculturation" of Indians, to exploitation by the surrounding economy which appropriates Indian resources for its own development. In portraying the relationship between the reservation economy and the private economy as a "host-parasite" relationship, Wallerstein (1979, 1992) argues that opportunities for a tribal-controlled reservation development model grow increasingly unlikely unless such changes occur with the cooperation of the regional economies.[11]

The relationship between a tribal community and the external political economy is observed as conflictive, as the tribal community is often required to modify its own development policies in order to adjust to the impending demands posed by external economic forces. The economic conditions experienced by many tribal communities conform to a dualistic model comprised of an internal and socially cohesive community and an external economy that interfaces with the dominant political economy. The strong socially cohesive nature of tribes largely reflects the philosophical doctrine of collectivism. In contrast, the external political economy reflects the fundamentally incongruous ideological doctrine of individualism. Such an alien component contributes to a dualistic paradigm that invariably creates tension. The tribal collectivist philosophy,

---

economy. Extractive timber activities provide limited economic benefits to reservations as value added benefits are usually not present on the reservations.

11. Owens (1978, 62) warned that if reservation control of development is not attained "energy development will prove the latest and most devastating fiasco of federal Indian policy" and suggests the following prescriptive actions: (1) tribes must regulate business activities that take place on reservations; (2) tribes must establish access to financial benefits derived from resource utilization through taxation, production sharing, services contracts and hiring clauses; (3) tribes must develop capabilities to gain managerial control over those resource based enterprises; and (4) tribes must build a reservation commercial infrastructure within a more diversified and self-sufficient reservation economy.

as symbolized by the "potlatch," views resources as a community-owned asset. As such, the development of those resources is dependent upon consensual agreement regarding the changes that would be acceptable to the collective reservation community, as well as an expectation of equitable distribution of benefits to the entire community.[12] By retaining both proprietary rights to their territories and their inherent sovereignty, tribal communities are in a strong position to reestablish a productive and self-fulfilling economic structure that would enable them to discontinue their dependency and to instead fulfill many of their needs in accordance with their traditional community values. The creation and operation of new tribal corporations and enterprises exemplify recent practices in tribal community development based on these socializing principles of collectivism.

Alienation and the Incorporation of the Indian Political Community

A corollary to the view of underdevelopment is the concept of alienation, which implies a state of separateness that is experienced in different contexts, ranging from an individual's self-alienation from a community to institutional alienation, whereby entire social groups become alienated from larger societies. The term can also be applied to Indian territories that have been removed from federal trust ownership and transferred to fee simple title or removed from reservation status, hence, being alienated from federal trust protection and from tribal control. The processes that cause the separation of a tribe from its sovereignty and its territory constitute the most pervasive form of alienation. The concept of alienation emerges from a long history of literary works in treatises on law, economy, and philosophy that reflect the development of Western philosophy,

---

12. As an example, the Northwest treaty tribes fishing rights are held as a collective proprietary right. The distribution of the resource (harvest privileges to its members) is balanced with conservation requirements, reflecting the simultaneous goals of resource sustainability and individual and community equity. The annual "first harvest" is often dedicated to the tribal elders, a tradition observed for thousands of years.

from slavery to the transition to capitalism and socialism (Meszaros 1970, 27).[13] Marx's concept of alienation focuses on the individual's primary value as laborer. The key elements in Marx's theory of alienation are individuals, their labor, and capital, which, together, represent productive activity. Marx depicts the relationship between the individual, labor, and capital as a continuous interaction between each constituent part. The practice of separating individuals, their autonomous self, and their labor value is associated with early slavery periods as well as other forms of subjugated labor. This process reflects a tendency in early European traditions to exploit human resources by separating the individual from their free will.

The alienation model is applied to the Indian context by replacing the components of individual, labor, and capital in the Marxian "dialectic" relationship, in which the collective tribal community substitutes for the individual, and the assets of reservation resources substitute for labor. Since Indian labor historically had not been valued as a significant resource to the US political economy,[14] the natural resources contained within the Indian territory, instead, became the primary object of subjugation. The interests of the political economy, therefore, have been focused

13. Modern theories of alienation have been shaped by European philosophy, especially through the contributions of Feuerback, Hegel, and Marx, as well as by English political economy theory. Adam Smith expressed the concept of alienation in relation to the private ownership of property and forwarded the ideal that "everyone should be able to give and to alienate that which belonged to him" (Smith 1776, 342). Hobbes's (1651) contribution to English political economy literature through his notion of "universal saleability" was based on the premise that an individual had to first be converted into a commodity, and thereafter, as property for the duration of a contract term. This social order, as conceived by Hobbes, implied the supremacy of the master who possessed the power to sell, or alienate, his servant. The principal function of Hobbes's social contract was the introduction of a new form of feudal relations that established the right of certain individuals to control other persons.

14. Notwithstanding the inclusion of Native Americans in the early history of the US slave trade, generally occurring between the late fifteenth century and the early sixteenth century. See Gallay (2002).

on controlling Indian natural resources. The means for accomplishing such objectives are associated with the historical development of Indian federal policies, which enabled the political economy's access to, and control over, Indian territory.[15] The tribal political community, which possesses political sovereignty and property rights, however, stands between the political economy's free access to Indian territory. Figure 1 illustrates the operation of the US political economy as it alienates tribes from their control over reservation resources.

The US political economy's view of reservation natural resources as an alienable and salable commodity contrasts with the traditional Indian view of the reservation as an inalienable and collective homeland, which is inseparable from tribal cultural identity. Tribal communities that have been subjected to the intervening forces of the political economy are depicted as alienated by means of their diminished political sovereignty over their territories. For tribal communities to recover their self-determination, the forces that alienated tribes from their former autonomous states must be identified and considered within a framework of historic circumstances and events. The two principal factors that cause Indian alienation are forces that diminish tribal sovereignty and forces that reduce the federal trust obligation to protect a tribe's political authority and its trust resources. When unabated, these forces continue to impede the development of tribal self-governance. The removal of intervening forces through assertive tribal action is, therefore, a necessary precondition for reversing Indian alienation and advancing tribal community development. The characteristics of the forces that are imposed upon a tribe's sovereignty and its territory can be expressed as follows:

• *External*: forces that intervene and are exerted from beyond the control of a tribe;

• *Historic*: forces representing the aggregate of actions that have taken place over an extended period of time;

---

15. As a trustee, the federal government maintains a fiduciary role and ultimate control over Indian trust resources.

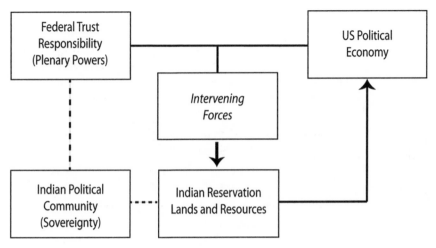

1. Alienation of the tribal political community.

- *Economic*: forces reflecting economic interests that operate within the Indian territory for the purpose of extracting Indian resources for the benefit of non-Indian interests, largely represented by the private economy;
- *Political*: forces manifested through political means, including executive acts and laws enacted through the plenary powers of Congress, leasing rights granted by federal trust agencies, and the intervening powers of state and local governments.

Over time, and to varying degrees, these intervening forces have contributed to the alienation of Indian territories. The creation of state political enclaves within a reservation represents a form of state usurpation of tribal authority,[16] an authority antithetical to the original purposes of reservation creation. The intrusion of state jurisdiction onto the reservations, often facilitated by acts of Congress, continues to threaten a tribe's political integrity and its social and economic cohesion. Consequently, tribal

16. As an example, the establishment of a state municipality or a county water or sewer district whose boundaries lie within a reservation boundaries creates, in effect, an enclave of state jurisdiction embedded within the tribal political territory.

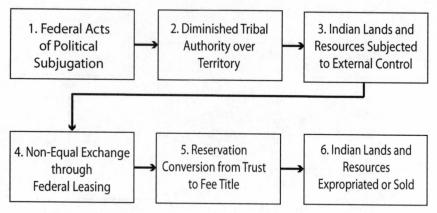

2. Modified Indian alienation model.

territorial resources are the principal assets that have become alienated from tribal control. A conception of Indian alienation is further illustrated in figure 2.

The objectification of Indian resources[17] as a commodity for expropriation is a function of the degree of authority exercised by a tribe in relation to other forces that are simultaneously exerted over those resources. Figure 3 illustrates a simplified pre-alienation representation of the relationship between a tribe and its territorial resources.

Figure 4 depicts a post-alienation representation of competing tribal and non-tribal interests over the utilization of reservation lands and resources. The model delineates the effects of intervening forces, represented by the political economy, and facilitated by past federal policies that weakened tribal sovereignty, as well as state political intervention that challenge a tribe's authority to the control its reservation resources. The federal trust responsibility is depicted as passive when it fails in its duty to protect Indian resources from external interferences. The outcome is a

17. Indian resources include reservation lands and natural resources, as well as off-reservation treaty property resources, which in some cases involve tribal hunting, fishing, cultural, and shellfish harvest rights, which are generally under the control of state jurisdiction.

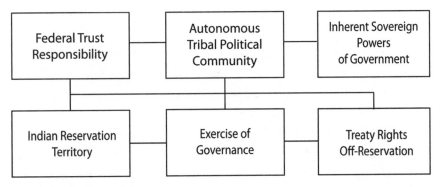

3. Pre-alienation model.

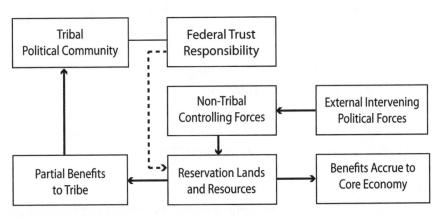

4. Post-alienation model.

dynamic and imbalanced tension among competing interests where reservation resources become expropriated to primarily benefit the core political economy.

The Process of Indian Incorporation

Indian incorporation theory explains the effects of the historic processes of expansion by the US political economy into tribal affairs. Prior to treaty relations with tribes, most Indian groups were isolated from the growing and incorporating US economy. Rather than incorporating these groups as minority parts of the broader society, tribes were forced, instead, to relocate to the territorial frontiers.[18] Only after treaty-making occurred, which resulted in the creation of separate and distinct Indian territorial areas, did the nature of contacts with Indian societies begin to constitute a basis for the incorporation by the dominant economy. Jorgensen (1972) provides one of the earliest analyses of Indian incorporation and dependency. He observed that the lack of development and the accompanying slow rate of acculturation of Indians into the US economy was not due to the isolation of Indians from the incorporating political economy, but was, rather, a direct result of exploitation by the incorporating state. The earliest form of resource expropriation is linked to the General Allotment Act of 1887, which, in seeking to assimilate Indian societies into the US political economy, permanently disrupted a formerly cohesive pattern of community ownership and provided for the eventual alienation of much of the reservation land base. This disruption resulted in the relocation of non-Indians to many reservations, followed by the interventions by state and local governments to assert jurisdiction over the newly alienated reservation lands.

The historic transformation of the political and economic status of tribal communities is described by Snipp (1986, 145) in terms of two distinct phases of development: *captive nations* and *internal colonies*. Captive nationhood describes the status of tribes following their subordination to the United States in the nineteenth century. The process of political subordination occurred in treaty-making periods, which permanently altered the political nature of the tribes and transformed their autonomy under the doctrine of *limited tribal sovereignty*. The state of "captive nations" expresses the transition from autonomous government status to a limited structure of self-government. Although the status of captive nations insured a significant measure of political, although bounded, autonomy, it also resulted in increased tribal dependency upon the federal government and served to further impoverish Indians by limiting their access to their

18. Resulting from the relocation period of US Indian policy that occurred between 1828 and 1887.

traditional economic pursuits of hunting, gathering, fishing, and trapping. With regards to the development of tribal natural resources, their dependence and economic vulnerability as captive nations paved the way for their emergence as internal colonies.

As internal colonies, Indian lands became developed primarily for the benefit of the non-Indian economy, thus exposing tribes to new forms of economic exploitation through political domination. Resource development of Indian lands served as the primary mechanism for transforming tribal communities from captive nations into internal colonies. The stages of internal colonization began with the economic penetration of Indian resources that occurred during the mid-to-late nineteenth century. Where treaty agreements and the subsequent removal of tribes from ceded territories initiated their status as captive nations, the federal government's sale of surplus land and the leasing of reservation resources established a firm control over Indian resources.[19] Leasing facilitated the economic penetration by granting non-Indian access to Indian resources through the Bureau of Indian Affairs' delegated trust responsibility. Indian resources primarily served as exported commodities, providing agricultural, forestry, and fisheries products, as well as mineral and energy resources. Both energy resources and land areas[20] became particularly desirable commodities. In the 1970s, to counter federal mismanagement of Indian resources,

19. Snipp (1990, 10) argues that reservations constitute "captive nations" because their sovereignty is subject to the higher political authority of the United States and their lands constitute "closed enclaves" within the American society. Thus, the "captive nations" nature of tribes can be equated with "subservient territorial groups captured and absorbed in a state of subordination." He observed that the period of transition from captive nation to internal colony occurred primarily during the 1950s when attempts to exploit natural resources were accelerated. The most notable of such expropriations occurred with the removal of energy resources provided to major US corporations by the Bureau of Indian Affairs under favorable leasing terms.

20. By 1960, in agricultural leasing alone, more than 25 percent of the six million acres administered by the BIA were leased to non-Indians. To further enhance the US economy's access to Indian resources, Congress in the 1960s liberalized leasing terms of up to ninety-nine years on certain reservations.

tribes began to challenge the BIA's role in the trust management of Indian resources and sought to advance their own ability to manage those trust resources.[21]

Incorporation theory views the process of incorporation as a continuum, beginning with initial contact and continuing to an eventual state of complete absorption. Tribes that were fully terminated during the federal termination era represent a terminal state of complete absorption.[22] While dependency theory views the assimilation of both the tribal territory and the tribal social group into the dominant US political economy as the logical end of incorporation, such assimilation rarely occurred. Few, if any, tribal communities approached a state of full termination, and those that were terminated have since become reinstated. The effects of incorporation among tribes range significantly, dependent to a large degree on the perceived value of a tribal resource. Energy resource exploitation, for example, frequently occurred in the larger, energy resource-rich Indian territories of the Southwest. Other variables influencing incorporation include the proximity of Indian lands to urbanized regions. In recent decades, many Indian reservations that are located in close proximity to growing urban regions

21. The Council of Energy Resource Tribes (CERT) was formed in 1975 by twenty-two energy resource tribes for the purpose of improving Indian control over reservation energy production. In 1977, CERT contemplated a management agreement with OPEC for technical assistance in management of its oil reserves. The federal government, concerned with the political implications of an OPEC-sponsored energy development program within the US, intervened with financial support to develop tribal management capacity and to avoid an alliance with OPEC. CERT later advised the Laguna Pueblo in New Mexico to decline a $191,000 pipeline right-of-way extension, and eventually settled for a $1.5 million agreement. In another case, the Atlantic Richfield Company offered the Navajos $280,000 for a pipeline easement that the BIA routinely approved. CERT advised the Navajos to renegotiate and a lease valued at $70 million over twenty years was later signed.

22. The effect of termination included the dismantling of the self-governance structure of those tribal communities and the absorption of former trust lands and reservation resources into the US economy. As first recognized in the Merriam Report of 1928, assimilation, and later, termination, served as a taking of tribal political, cultural, and territorial resources while leaving the individual members of the former tribes in a state of disintegration.

have attracted the attention of the real estate economy seeking access to largely undeveloped and undervalued reservation lands.

While it is useful to conceptualize incorporation as a continuum process, where varying conditions and circumstances contribute to the degree of incorporation experienced by individual tribes, it is important to emphasize that the process of incorporation can be interrupted, reversed, and, under certain circumstances, eliminated. The reconstitution of the terminated Menominee Tribe illustrates a process of reversal, although such reversal action was dependent upon the willingness of the incorporating society, through congressional plenary powers, to reverse its policies of termination.[23] Other means for reversing incorporation depend upon the ability of tribal governments to mobilize and assert the necessary persuasive power to induce such an outcome. The pan-Indian movements are responses by tribes to change their status as peripheral societies by strengthening Indian cultural and political identity. Cornell (1984) argues that the crisis in Indian and non-Indian relations during the past several decades has led to a shift from unilateral to bilateral administration in Indian affairs. The bilateral administration of Indian affairs plays an important role in current federal self-determination policy and represents an important step in reversing a prior system of unilateral federal control.

In view of new opportunities for tribal development in such areas as trade, economic development, gaming, and tourism, which are intended to foster stable tribal economies, Cornell points out that some tribes have willingly accepted the exchange of increased participation in the US political economy for a decreased level of autonomy as a condition of their participation. Increased participation in the economy often requires tribes to comply with the political economy's rules that govern an economic activity, such as in accepting the requirements of federal gaming legislation, which may represent new forms of tribal cooptation.[24]

---

23. See the Menominee Restoration Act of 1973, 25 U.S.C. § 903.

24. Tribes entering into gaming ventures are required to proceed through a tenuous process of incorporation because federal gaming legislation requires tribes to enter into

Representing a radical shift in federal self-determination policy, the federal Indian Gaming Regulatory Act created a situation that forced tribes to negotiate with states before gaming enterprises would be permitted. The coercive gaming policy obligated tribes into a relationship with states that was not based on the principles of tribal empowerment, but, rather, under the false presence of a government-to-government relationship. However, the relationship was imbalanced from the start as the tribes were placed in the untenable position of "asking" the state for permission to exercise their inherent right to regulate and operate gaming activities—activities that states have always enjoyed unrestrained access to (Rosser 2009). While acknowledging that tribes have had some success in negotiating compact agreements with states, Corntassel and Witmer (2008) emphasize that tribal jurisdiction should not be conceded lightly for short-term economic gain. While recognizing the benefits derived from gaming compacts with states, they caution against the potential for longer-term perils if their governing authority is compromised. However, the economic benefits derived through increased incorporation, especially for those tribes that have experienced significant economic growth in the gaming industry,[25] may offset the negative effects of incorporation through newly acquired forms of economic and political power.

---

compact agreements with states. This, in effect, forms a co-regulatory control mechanism over a reservation activity. The state-tribal gaming compacts provide for co-regulatory control over gaming activities in addition to imposing limitations on the forms of economic activities tribes are permitted. Many of the compact tribes view the negotiation process as a form of federal and state-imposed coercion. In addition, gaming tribes often become subjected to capital markets' unilateral conditions as they attempt to secure financing and access to specialized management expertise necessary for conducting the operations of gaming.

25. The Shakopee Indian Tribe of Minnesota and Mashantucket Pequot Indian Tribe of Connecticut have both experienced tremendous success in the gaming industry. Consequently, conditions for their members have shifted dramatically from those of severe poverty to financial independence and increased political influence.

Responses to Incorporation

The degree of incorporation within the US political economy varies tremendously among tribes, from relatively minor levels of involvement to more extensive forms of incorporation. Five forms of tribal responses to incorporation (Snipp 1990) are illustrated in table 3: (1) cultural revitalization movements, (2) pluralistic accommodation, (3) rebellion, (4) ethnic development, and (5) tribal sovereignty-building processes.

Because they represent social movements rather than political movements, *cultural revitalization movements* are distinguished from other responses. During the 1870s post-treaty period, this response was illustrated by many Indian groups to initial phases of incorporation through their re-participation in the "Ghost Dance."[26] Participation in the Ghost Dance movement represented an attempt to resist assimilation in order to reintegrate the community, increase its solidarity, and enhance its cultural survivability. This movement represented complete isolationism and rejection of the effects of incorporation by minimizing, or entirely eliminating, relations external to the tribal community.

Pluralistic accommodation refers to the preservation of tribal self-determination while concurrently integrating tribal economies into the broader political economy. Pluralistic accommodation produces a state of political and cultural plurality in the broader society by accepting the presence of quasi-independent tribal political enclaves. The response implies a more balanced reciprocity provided that the relations between the tribal enclave and the core political economy serve the interests of both communities, without the imbalances inherent in the core-periphery model. The approach requires a willingness by the dominant society to accommodate the independence of tribal enclaves by balancing political power-sharing arrangements similar to those shared among state-established jurisdictions. In this respect, a regional nesting is created containing

---

26. Hall (1987, 17) describes the participation in Ghost Dance as a response to "relative or absolute deprivation, to isolationism, to the allotment movements, and to demographic changes."

TABLE 3 Responses to Indian Incorporation

	Impact of Core on Tribal Periphery			
	None	*Weak*	*Moderate*	*Strong*
Tribal Condition	Relative Isolation	Initial Incorporation	Increased Incorporation	Fully Incorporated
Response by Tribes to Core's Intervention	No Response	Cultural Revitalization	Pluralistic Accommodation; Rebellion; Ethnic Development	Tribal Sovereignty-Building

Source: Nicholas C. Zaferatos.

semi-autonomous tribal political enclaves that are connected through mutually agreeable political, social, and economic arrangements.

Rebellion incorporates a range of tribal responses that challenge the increasing forces of incorporation. The actions by the American Indian Movement during the 1970s represent a rebellious response that was aimed at undermining the structure of federal Indian agencies rather than at merely protesting their control over Indian affairs. The significance of confrontation is in its ability to bring about a direct and active tribal role in shaping federal Indian policy outcomes. *Ethnic development* signifies a response to external forces that disrupt tribal community cohesiveness through new forms of Indian organizational development and mobilization. These activities include the establishment of supranational organizations such as the National Congress of American Indians and the National Association of Gaming Tribes. Such organizations encourage new political forums to more broadly support Indian self-determination movements.

Tribal sovereignty-building represents a response that seeks to maximize tribal control over specific aspects of the incorporation process. Under mild conditions of incorporation, where external forces are minor or gradual, the ability of tribal governments to adapt to external influences may outweigh the need to resist. When incorporation becomes increasingly threatening or disruptive, a more forceful tribal response in the form of political or legal action, may be required to assert the tribe's sovereignty or treaty rights. As illustrated in the Northwest treaty fisheries litigation cases, the defense of treaty rights through litigation proved to be a powerful response to the incorporation of treaty-guaranteed fishing rights as, at the time, the tribal share of the fisheries harvest had been reduced to about 5 percent of the harvestable catch.

Identifying Institutional Power Relations

In this final section, regarding institutions that act to repress tribal governance, the important work of Michel Foucault (1973, 1977) is introduced. The identification of the repressive forces that are imposed by the political economy upon tribal communities is necessary before effective planning strategies can be formulated. Foucault presents a discourse of investigative research that is particularly informative to this undertaking by focusing on the identification of controlling mechanisms that affect the nature of relations between communities. "Genealogical work,"[27] the structure of Foucault's research, gathers information about controlling mechanisms by closely examining their historical context. The research approach is based on critical historical inquiry that examines the nature of power relations and the institutions that serve as agents of subjugation. Genealogy research attempts to discover the effects and consequences of centralizing powers on individuals and communities.

Boyer (1987) extends Foucault's research approach to the apparatus of planning itself to consider how power is manifested in the work of planning. Boyer's premise is that once the state intervenes in the affairs of a community, it does so according to a predetermined program with the intent of controlling its relationship with the community. According to Foucault, the implications of institutional relationships are often represented as forms of repressive relationships in which a dominant power

27. Foucault's genealogical research begins with investigations of classical seventeenth century political economy institutions, where the birth of institutional power serves to justify the treatment of the individual as a commodity. See also Foucault 1973, 1977, 1979, 1988.

forces its *rationalization* upon others through a process of *normalization*,[28] or, when applied to the case of Indians, a process of assimilation and incorporation. The general intolerance by the dominant society's "reason" to any other form of "reason" creates what Foucault refers to as the "disciplined society." As a corollary, the prevailing US society's past repressive attitudes toward Indians, together with its imposition of authority over tribal affairs, serves as a mechanism of oppression that separates Indians from prevailing norms and creates a structure of social and political exile.

Foucault envisions a tolerant society in which each individual is able to fully participate in the freedoms intrinsic to that society. Friedmann (1987) also refers to such a tolerant society as "the good society," where individuals are neither controlled nor excluded. Such a tolerance encourages a society that would collectively participate in the execution of power. It is Foucault's view that the real political task of a society is to criticize the working institutions that appear to be both neutral and truth seeking and to criticize them in such a manner that all forms of repression, which he calls "political violence," are unmasked and confronted. In its transactions with non-Indian communities, tribal planning must develop a greater capacity to recognize the controlling mechanisms that have historically impeded tribal development and that have held their communities in a perpetual state of repression. The genealogical approach, with its potential for unmasking the hidden mechanisms that create imbalances in periphery societies, and for making the systems of subjugation more comprehensible, is an important element in the work of tribal planning.

Conclusion and Implications for Planning

The tribal economy's linkage to the broader US political economy has resulted in chronic underdevelopment on most Indian reservations. Political economy and development theory help to unveil the complex conditions that tribes face as they seek to advance their own development. Federal interventions have directly and indirectly altered the ownership

28. "Process of normalization" refers to the source from which norms arise and are applied as a system of control.

and control of the resources that were once exclusively held by tribes and have acted to diminish tribal autonomy. Early federal assimilation interventions have permanently altered the formerly independent state of tribes and have provided the US political economy access to Indian resources. As dependency theory argues, the reversal of tribal underdevelopment is inextricably linked with a tribe's ability to overcome the suppressive influences imposed by the core political economy.

Although these theories were first formulated to explain the structural dependency of macro-economic relations in international development, they have also been applied to describe the imbalanced relations between the reservation economy and the US political economy, in which tribes function as periphery economies and the US political economy functions as the core. The model presumes an underlying condition of equity imbalance, with a net outflow from the reservation economy benefiting the growth of the larger political economy.

Critical theory helps us understand the complex and historic conflicts that occur in the tribal setting by unveiling subjugating forms of relations. Additionally, it seeks to overcome the undemocratic tendencies within institutions through a humanizing process of expanding tolerance for social differences, which is especially important in multi-cultural contexts. Critical theory helps to inform Indian communities in order to overcome the pending paradox of a self-determination policy that is held captive due to the lack of an effective means with which to negotiate with the dominant mechanisms of the US political economy. The conditions contributing to Indian underdevelopment are directly correlated to the development processes of the US political economy. This view of Indian underdevelopment refutes earlier theories that claimed that the conditions of Indians had not improved because tribes remained isolated and unassimilated. According to Jorgensen (1972, 287), the American Indian "is, and has been for over one hundred years, fully integrated into the national political economy," albeit, as a subjugated community. Jorgensen emphasizes that the impoverished conditions of Indians can be directly attributed to their severely restricted access to their own resources. Modern Indians, Jorgensen (1972, 296) observed, are the progeny of the "super exploited Indians of the nineteenth century who were forced to relinquish their territory, their self-governance, and their self esteem" so that the political economy could grow.

Indian community development must be concerned with the nature and structure of the relations of power that create the "subjugation of Indians" and, in terms of dependency theory, the "dependent Indian periphery." Indian self-determination, as a political movement, has made tremendous gains since the proclamation of the federal policy in 1970. While the federal policies and actions of the assimilation and termination eras have been formally repudiated, the hidden and sublime controlling mechanisms borne from that period continue to exist and continue to interfere with the goals of Indian self-determination. Planning approaches that link the history of Indian subjugation to current forms of unequal exchange in the relationship between the tribes and the larger political economy help to reveal the persistent causes of tribal repression. It is those mechanisms that perpetuate the continued subjugation of tribes that must be exposed and addressed before tribal planning can successfully proceed.

6

Identifying Oppositional Forces
in Tribal Planning

IN THE PRACTICE OF PLANNING, complex obstacles inevitably are encountered that must be addressed through a cogent planning strategy. Many of the obstacles that operate within the tribal setting are exogenous: they emanate from past federal policies that produced the extraordinarily complex conditions found on many reservations. These outside forces impede the ability of tribes to function as self-governing communities. The oppositional forces and their effects on the tribal political community are identified in table 4 in a general framework of planning constraints.

The horizontal axis in table 4 depicts two primary types of external oppositional forces that, to varying degrees, operate in the tribal planning setting: (1) public policy forces, as reflected in the past and current actions imposed by non-tribal governments, and (2) private and institutional forces, as reflected by individuals and institutional interests. Together, they represent the forces of *incorporation* of the US political economy. The vertical axis in the framework represents the three components that constitute the endogenous tribal political community: tribal self-governance and sovereignty, the tribal territory and resources, and the tribal community's internal self-sufficiency and social cohesiveness. The matrix illustrates how oppositional forces create conditions that challenge and constrain a tribal community's self-governance and affect the management of tribal resources and other tribal interests. The framework attempts to generally represent the most pervasive examples of constraints that are encountered in tribal community development. A discussion of

TABLE 4 Matrix of Oppositional Forces in Indian Community Development

Attributes of the Tribal Political Community	Oppositional Forces of the Political Economy	
	Public Policy: Past and Current Non-Indian Government Interests	*Private Individual and Institutional Interests*
1. Self-Governance and Sovereignty	1.1. Government policy diminishing tribal self-governance; state and local powers	1.2. Private opposition to tribal governance
2. Territoriality and Natural Resources	2.1. Assimilation and incorporation of reservation resources	2.2. Non-Indian reservation occupancy and ownership of reservation assets
3. Tribal Sufficiency and Social Cohesiveness	3.1. Social fragmentation, cultural assimilation, and alienation	3.2. Restricted access to capital and reservation economic alienation

Source: Nicholas C. Zaferatos. © 2012 Taylor & Francis Ltd.

the effects of these oppositional forces to a tribe's sovereignty, its territory, and its self-sufficiency and social cohesiveness, follows.

Government Policy Diminishing Tribal Self-Governance

Two of the earliest actions that led to the diminishment of tribal powers of self-government occurred in treaty-making, which imposed limitations on tribal sovereignty, and in the establishment of bounded tribal territories. Subsequent action by both executive orders and congressional acts further reduced tribal territorial areas, resulting in boundary claims disputes that remain unresolved and subject to continuing litigation. As more fully described in chapter 2, the nation's policy history of assimilation and termination served to both diminish tribal authority and to make possible the intrusion of state and local policies in the management of reservation lands and resources. These political interventions created a complex composition of reservation land ownership and property rights, and a legacy of overlapping jurisdiction in many reservations. While the courts have long established that tribes retain inherent rights to control their territories, the allotment of the reservations, their occupancy by non-Indian fee landowners and the subsequent intrusion of state and local government regulations over non-trust reservation lands have combined to create a planning situation that defies a tribe's exclusive control of its homeland.

The conversion of reservation trust lands to fee simple title, coupled with the significant apportionment and removal of land areas from the originally defined reservations, has created a jurisdictional scheme that superimposes tribal, federal, state, and local, and special purpose governments with overlapping interests. The diminishment of tribal self-governance and the accompanying intrusion of the political economy onto the reservations present the greatest challenge to tribes as they struggle to advance their community's well-being. Tribal planning is constrained by lingering questions regarding the extent of a tribe's governing authority and its rights to resources that lie within and beyond the reservation boundaries. Further complicating tribal planning are the ensuing problems associated with sorting out the multiple layers of reservation laws and regulations that are imposed by non-tribal governments.

The current federal policy of self-determination has helped to reinstate many of the dormant tribal powers that had previously been diminished through congressional acts and executive orders. Further, the fiduciary role of the federal government as trustee over tribal resources has been clarified through the enactment of Indian self-determination legislation, amendments to statutes, court decisions, and the promulgation of trust agency policies and regulations. These recent events have helped to reinforce tribal self-governance, strengthen the governing capacity of tribes, and clarify many of the long-standing questions regarding the status of tribal authority.

As discussed in chapter 4, states do not possess jurisdiction over matters on reservations that only involve Indians, unless specifically delegated such jurisdiction by Congress. While states generally possess criminal jurisdiction over non-Indians within reservations, tribes also possess civil jurisdiction over non-Indians. In many cases, state, local, and tribal governments may all share concurrent civil jurisdiction over non-Indians on reservations. In cases where the situs, person, and subject matter create concurrent civil jurisdiction, the laws of the state, local, and tribal governments may each concurrently apply, and a non-Indian may be required to comply with multiple laws. Hence, a non-Indian may be subject to pay two sets of taxes and license fees, comply with two different land use regulations, and face two sets of civil proceedings before both non-Indian and Indian courts. In part, concurrent legislative jurisdiction over non-Indian lands and non-Indian persons has led to defiance and litigation by aggrieved non-Indian occupants of Indian country.[1]

Competitive jurisdiction also exists in areas affected by reservation economic development (Harvard Project on American Indian Economic Development 2008). Taxation of sales, business activities, severance taxation, non-Indian personal income taxation, and indirect taxation of Indian property have all been subject to controversy and legal challenge (Presidential Commission on Indian Reservation Economies 1984). Tribes have only recently begun to fully exercise their jurisdiction over non-Indian activities in an effort to expand their authority and to exercise greater influence over reservation development.

A concurrent concern regarding the management of reservation resources involves the balance between a tribe's inherent powers and the federal government's fiduciary role, particularly where trust natural resources, treaty rights, and explicit statutory regulations are involved.[2] For example, the location of Indian lands on or near major river systems and regional groundwater aquifers has created what is probably the most complex legal conflict in contemporary tribal-state-federal jurisdictional relations. Western states have relied on the "prior appropriations doctrine" to allocate water rights, which is based on the canon, "first in

1. Nationally, approximately 50 percent of all reservation residents are non-Indian.

2. *United States v. Mitchell*, 463 U.S. 206 (1983) upheld an allottee's claims for damages, due to BIA mismanagement of their timberland, and affirmed the federal fiduciary obligation to managing Indian natural resources for the benefit of Indian interests.

time, first in right." Historically, under state law in many western states, a water user obtains a right, senior and superior to all subsequent users, if the user appropriates water by diverting it from a watercourse or by putting it to a beneficial use. Once these conditions are met, the water user has established an appropriation date. In contrast, federal, rather than state law, defines Indian water rights. The landmark Supreme Court decision in *Winters v. United States* held that sufficient water was impliedly reserved to fulfill the purposes of the reservation. This doctrine of federal reserved rights establishes a vested right, whether or not the resource is actually put to use, and enables a tribe to expand its water use over time in response to changing reservation needs.[3] In the long-contested dispute involving both tribal water rights and treaty fishing rights, the courts in *United States v. Washington* have upheld the tribes' treaty rights to harvest fish, and the state was directed to end its system of unilateral control over fisheries resources and enter into co-management arrangements with affected tribal governments. Subsequent decisions affirmed that, as part of a treaty fisheries right, tribes also held a treaty right to a protected fisheries environment. The precondition of a protected fisheries environment further expanded tribal interests to off-reservation regional planning that included water quality and water quantity policy considerations. Toward that end, in a 2013 decision,[4] the courts ruled that the state must treat the water supply requirements of fish as a water right that is superior to those of competing junior water users. As a result, the implications to regional property owners who face the prospect of losing their development rights for lack of water availability has fueled further animosities towards tribes.

3. The Supreme Court has addressed the substantive content of Indian water rights in *Arizona v. California*, where federal reserved rights on the Colorado River were upheld for Indian reservations established by executive order. The amount of water reserved was sufficient to satisfy the present as well as the future needs of the tribe. The test was based upon the amount of water necessary to irrigate all the "practicably irrigable acreage" on the reservation.

4. *Swinomish Indian Tribal Community v. Department of Ecology*, No. 87672-0 (Wash. Sup. Ct. October 3, 2013).

In these examples, litigation represented a form of conflict resolution to protect tribal interests from the injurious effects that resulted from an imbalanced relationship between tribes and the US political economy. In each case, a demonstrable injury to tribal interests was overcome through the actions initiated by the tribes that sought to prevent the state's mismanagement or misappropriation of natural resources that primarily benefited non-tribal interests at the expense of tribal interests.

The power of tribes to regulate activities that may harm tribal lands, environmental quality, and natural resources is derived from their treaty proprietary rights, their inherent sovereignty, and their delegated authority to administer federal programs. By retaining all aspects of their sovereignty except those specifically withdrawn by Congress or those inconsistent with overriding federal interests, tribes are generally understood to possess sufficient powers to protect the health and welfare of their reservation population and their reservation environment. As the preservation of a reservation's environmental quality is a prerequisite for the continued survival of tribal communities, the assurance of clean water, air, and land on Indian reservations assumes a central priority in tribal planning. Past systems of control that usurped tribal authority over Indian lands and resources, and replaced that authority with state and local jurisdiction, are gradually becoming clarified through legislative actions, litigation, [5] negotiated settlements, and other measures.

Private Opposition to Tribal Self-Governance

While the federal self-determination policy served to strengthen the tribal capacity to govern reservation affairs, in response, local tensions began to emerge as non-Indian interests reacted to the exercise of previously dormant tribal powers and consequently formed organizations to formally

---

5. The exercise of state environmental jurisdiction over reservation lands has also been found to be preempted. In *State of Washington, Department of Ecology v. United States Environmental Protection Agency*, 752 F.2d 1465 (9th Cir. 1985), the courts affirmed the federal government's exclusive responsibility to manage the environmental quality of Indian reservations, clarifying that the state is restricted from applying its environmental laws upon reservation lands.

TABLE 5 Forms of Non-Indian Opposition to Tribal Governance

Interests	Effects on Tribal Governance
Non-Indian landowners	Occupants of reservation resist tribal civil regulation, taxation, tribal services
On-reservation economic interests	Businesses that operate on reservations resist tribal taxation and regulation
Off-reservation economic interests	Competition for treaty-based off-reservation fisheries resources, water rights

Source: Nicholas C. Zaferatos.

resist and challenge tribal authority. Reactive opposition particularly targeted the tribal powers of taxation, land use regulation, and treaty rights. Table 5 summarizes several forms of non-Indian opposition to the rise of tribal governance.

In the mid-1970s, non-Indian property owners who perceived tribal governments as a threat to their rights and interests formed the Interstate Congress for Equal Rights and Responsibilities (ICERR) on several Indian reservations. Following the landmark 1974 *Boldt* decision[6] in Washington State, non-Indian property owners joined forces with off-reservation fishers to launch the anti-Indian movement of the self-determination era. This movement expanded in the early 1980s, seeking popular support for public initiatives that would overturn Indian rights. At the same time, it spread to several other states where a network of property owners, agricultural interests, businesses, and conservative extremist groups was formed. Over the next two decades, the anti-Indian movement continued to grow predominately in rural areas, becoming more politically active with each stage of its development.

The anti-Indian movement challenged tribal asserted rights to natural resources off-reservation and reservation non-Indians became the core

6. *United States v. Washington*, 384 F. Supp. 312 (W.D. Wash., 1974), *aff'd*, 520 F.2d 676 (9th Cir.), *cert. denied*, 423 U.S. 1086, (1976).

organizers of what eventually became a highly structured anti-Indian movement (LaDuke 1999). The United Property Owners of Washington (UPOW) and Protect Americans' Rights and Resources (PARR) in Wisconsin emerged as the principal constituent organizations. The anti-Indian movement grew steadily from a half dozen non-Indian property owner groups in two states in 1976 to more than fifty organizations operating in fifteen states as well as in Canada by 2013. Many of these organizations are affiliated with the Citizens Equal Rights Alliance (CERA).[7] The first of these organized networks, ICERR,[8] formed in 1976 to provide a union between on-reservation property owners and non-Indian sport and commercial fishers who opposed tribal treaty protected fishing rights. The movement, which later merged with CERA, continues to be influential in several states that contain Indian reservations, and, in particular, in matters regarding off-reservation Indian treaty rights. In 1991, the number of persons participating in anti-Indian activities was estimated to be more than 10,000 nationwide, and persons who contributed funds or other manner of support to the anti-Indian groups was estimated to exceed 35,000 (Ryser 1992).

ICERR promoted the ideology of "white civil rights" and sought the protection of non-Indian property and the overturning of the *Boldt* decision. Former Attorney General Slade Gorton[9] represented Washington State before the US Supreme Court in a series of legal actions against Indian tribes that culminated in *United States v. Washington*. Gorton became a vocal critic of tribes and of federal Indian policy and argued that the US Constitution did not permit superior rights to any one group.

7. See Citizens Equal Rights Alliance website, http://www.citizensalliance.org.

8. At the founding meeting of the ICERR in 1976, its organizers adopted the following goals: "All state and local laws shall apply within all reservations; constitutional rights of all Americans shall supersede treaty rights; jurisdiction of tribal governments over non-tribal members shall be prohibited; Indian reservations shall not be enlarged; tribal members should have no right to participate in non-tribal governments unless subject to all laws of non-tribal governments; and the granting of public funds to any people based on race must be prohibited." See Hanna, Deloria, and Trimble (2011).

9. Slade Gorton later won election to the US Senate in 1992.

He subsequently coined the term "super-citizens," a derogatory reference to Indians. Gorton's condemnation of tribal actions tended to legitimize the growing demand for non-Indian rights on Indian reservations.[10] By 1983, ICERR formed a new organization with the express purpose of expanding popular support. Salmon-Steelhead Preservation Action for Washington Now (S/SPAWN) reinforced ICERR's goals with its promise "to promote passage of a public initiative to protect salmon." In 1985, S/SPAWN changed its name to Steelhead/Salmon Protection Association and Wildlife Network, incorporating as a national, non-profit scientific and public educational foundation. Its objective was to "promote the organization and establishment of a Presidential Commission to study the effects of federal Indian policies on non-tribal Indians and non-Indian citizens of the U.S." (Ryser 1992, 26). S/SPAWN was again transformed into a new organization, the United Property Owners of Washington (UPOW), retaining both the leadership and affiliations of S/SPAWN with on-reservation non-Indian property groups. UPOW organizers concentrated on organizing opposition to a 1989 lawsuit that was filed by sixteen Washington tribes in order to define their treaty rights for harvesting shellfish outside the reservations, as shellfish harvesting was excluded in the original *Boldt* decision. On December 20, 1994, the federal district court released its ruling regarding the harvesting of shellfish in *United States v. Washington*, deciding in favor of the tribes.

ICERR and CERA claim to be civil rights-type organizations for non-Indians with the stated objective of limiting or eliminating Indian tribes. The formation of these organizations produced the post-self-determination phase of the anti-Indian movement. The organizations are generally comprised of non-Indian members who purchased former tribal lands and

10. Washington's 456 Initiative ballot was originally co-authored in 1983 by State Senator Metcalf as Initiative Measure no. 84. Since the Washington State legislature earlier rejected a proposed bill to subvert treaty rights, the legislation was converted into the initiative that sought to challenge the "special legal status" of Indians and won passage in 1984. Passage of the initiative proved to be an empty victory, however. State officials chose to ignore the law, as the state was not empowered to reverse treaty obligations. Nevertheless, the initiative effectively fueled anti-Indian sentiment.

who call upon the federal government to remove all non-Indian owned reservation lands from reservation status.

The tribal response to the growing organization of anti-Indian movements that have focused on challenging the foundations of Indian sovereignty has been one of mobilization. At its 58th Annual Session in 2001, the National Congress of American Indians, whose members include more than 250 tribal governments, adopted a resolution condemning the actions of anti-Indian organizations and other hate groups, specifically calling attention to the activities of groups such as Citizens for Equal Rights Alliance, United Property Owners, and Upstate Citizens for Equality.

Assimilation and Incorporation of Reservation Resources

The intent of the General Allotment Act of 1887 was multifaceted, as it sought to break up commonly held reservation territories into individually owned trust parcels, to integrate those parcels into a system of fee title ownership that would later become subject to state taxation and control, and to declare, as surplus, other reservation lands that would become absorbed into the private economy. The act resulted in a large-scale movement of non-Indian settlement onto the reservations. By the late 1960s, it was evident that the resulting checkerboard land ownership pattern on the allotted reservations contributed to jurisdictional uncertainty with respect to whether state or tribal authority would prevail over those alienated lands. The allotted reservation territories became jurisdictionally splintered as states began to intrude onto the reservations by imposing taxation and regulations.

By the 1980s, one half million non-Indians held land title on Indian reservations and more than one half of the total Indian population resided off-reservation. While many non-Indians now reside permanently on Indian reservations, others are absentee landowners. By 2012, fifteen states contained more non-Indians living on reservations than tribal members. On certain Washington State Indian reservations, the non-Indian population exceeds the tribal population by a 4:1 ratio (2010 US Census).[11] Michigan

---

11. The Puyallup Reservation's non-Indian population in Washington State comprises 97 percent of the total reservation population.

contained the highest percentage of non-Indian reservation residency, averaging almost 90 percent of the total population on several reservations. As tribes continued to experience a weakened ability to control their territories, they faced growing interference from non-Indian interests. Since the 1970s, reservation non-Indian landowners have emerged as a powerful force challenging the stability and integrity of tribal governments by rejecting their authority and by pursuing political representation through local and state governments. Due to their inaccessibility to the tribal election process, non-Indian landowners tend to view tribal governments as illegitimate. The growing pressures placed on state governments has led to increased confrontation with tribes over a broad range of jurisdictional issues, which, in turn, has intensified the encroachment of state powers on many Indian reservations. This represents a de facto annexation of reservation lands and has become a primary obstacle confronting tribal reservation planning.

The principle of inherent Indian sovereignty, first acknowledged in *Worcester v. Georgia*,[12] recognized Indian nations as "distinct political communities." More recent Supreme Court rulings further clarified the extent of tribal authority in exercising criminal and civil jurisdiction over non-Indians within the reservations. A precedent established in the *Montana*[13] ruling found a tribe's authority did not extend "beyond what is necessary to protect tribal self-government or to control internal relations" absent congressional delegation (Goeppele 1990, 564). However, *Montana* also established two exceptions where tribal authority may apply to non-Indians. Tribal authority is recognized in the event of consensual relations between the tribe and non-Indians and over the conduct of non-Indians on fee lands when such conduct threatens the political integrity, economic security, or health and welfare of the tribe.

Following *Montana*, subsequent lower court decisions[14] affirmed tribal authority over non-Indians under the second *Montana* exception

---

12. 31 U.S. (6 Pet.) 515 (1832).

13. *Montana v. United States*, 450 U.S. 544 (1981).

14. The Tenth Circuit Court of Appeals in *Knight v. Shoshone and Arapaho Tribes*, 670 F. 2d 900 (1982), upheld tribal zoning authority over non-Indian fee land under

when non-Indian activity was found to threaten the integrity of a tribe and its resources. The *Brendale*[15] opinion challenged the basic tenets of land use planning by permitting uncoordinated and dual regulatory authority over reservation land use management. While the ruling also supported a tribe's right to sue to enjoin actions that would have a "demonstrably serious impact and imperil their political integrity, economic security, or their health and welfare," the *Brendale* solution to jurisdictional conflict resolution remains inconsistent with the principles of comprehensive planning.

In order for tribes to retain the ability to meaningfully "define the essential character" of the reservation, and thereby strengthen their right of self-government, the paradox that is presented in the *Brendale* argument must be reconciled. A strategy that balances the interests of both the tribal community and the non-Indian community may prove to be most successful in resolving conflicts in reservations that contain multiple ownership interests and solving problems associated with reservation planning under a bifurcated reservation jurisdiction. Such an approach argues for a broader definition of the reservation community in terms of a *plurality of interests* and departs from the *Brendale* view of the bifurcated community. Should the courts continue the process of dividing reservations into areas where tribes do and do not retain authority, there is little hope for achieving comprehensiveness and unity in planning reservation communities.

Non-Indian Reservation Occupancy and Ownership of Reservation Assets

Private property and business owners often view the tribe's authority to enact business, development, and taxing controls that restrict economic activity as a threat to their interests. A perception of mistrust toward tribal governments generally stems from an unfamiliarity with tribal governance

---

the second *Montana* exception where no competing local or county zoning ordinances existed to restrict land use on non-Indian fee lands on the reservation.

15. *Brendale v. Confederated Tribes and Bands of Yakima Indian Nation*, 492 U.S. 408 (1988).

structures and a concern that tribal political processes are not accessible to non-Indians. When tribal regulation is perceived to restrict the exercise of one's economic property rights, property owners tend to challenge that authority by seeking the intervention of the states or the courts.

As non-Indian resident populations and non-Indian owned businesses continue to grow on the reservations, the confluence of those interests pose increased threats to tribal governance to the point where a tribe may no longer be able to maintain, in reference to *Brendale*, the reservation's "essential character." Unless a tribe can demonstrate its primary governance over the entire reservation, a future court may find that state interests have supplanted its authority. This situation is demonstrated in a 2001 Supreme Court case, *Atkinson Trading Co. v. Shirley*,[16] which held that the Navajo Nation lacked the authority to apply its hotel occupancy tax on a non-Indian business located on fee simple land within the reservation despite the fact that it serviced the business with certain governmental services. The Court maintained that the tribe's authority to tax did not extend beyond tribal lands unless it could meet the *Montana* exceptions. The Court concluded that the tax was not based on any consensual relationship, nor was it essential to maintain the tribe's political integrity. The uneven application of *Montana*[17] makes it difficult to predict how far a tribe's regulatory power may extend. Hence, the ability of a tribe to demonstrate its capacity to provide for the well-being of all reservation interests may become a determining factor in deciding regulatory jurisdictional outcomes. Tribal planning, therefore, concerns not only how to provide general governmental services, but also how to describe those services, in light of the *Montana* and *Brendale* criteria, as essential components of the tribe's political, social, and economic integrity.

16. *Atkinson Trading Co. v. Shirley* 532 U.S. 645 (2001).

17. In other instances, the courts have applied the same *Montana* exemptions in support of a tribe's right to exercise authority over water resources within the borders of the reservation, including non-tribal land. See *Montana v. EPA* 137 F.3d 1135 (9th Cir. 1998), *cert. denied*, 521 U.S. 921 (1998).

Social Fragmentation and Cultural Assimilation

Intercultural tensions, experienced between Indian and non-Indian residents on and adjacent to reservations, invariably arise as a result of the discrepancy between mainstream American values and Indian values. Likewise, cultural preferences within a tribal community may lead to a diversity of social preferences. For example, traditional Indian values that may favor the conservation of resources over resource exploitation are highlighted in the Indian economic development literature (Cornell 1987; Harvard Project on American Indian Economic Development 2008; Social Investment Forum 2010) and conflict with other views that favor development. Historically, dominant societies have attempted to impose their own socioeconomic systems on tribal groups. Formerly, this was viewed as an inevitable by-product of development. However, the destruction of weakened societies by prevailing societies corresponds with a view of social de-evolution that threatens the cultural cohesiveness of tribal communities. Successful reservation community development is more likely to result when cultural values are intrinsically linked to economic development and the disparity of values among the broader political economy are first reconciled (Adamson and Klinger 2008; Jorgensen 2007).

Deloria and Lytle (1984) suggest that models for Indian community development should take into account the absorptive capacity of tribes for development, which may differ from and require a longer period than other segments of the US society. The process of arriving at consensus, which can be quite lengthy, but is extremely important in tribal decision-making, is not well understood by non-Indian culture. Failure to recognize the time element associated with consensus decision-making demonstrates the general failure to understand the process of the tribal political culture. In order to effectively deal with cultural plurality and cross-cultural communications, strategies are required to address the specific circumstances faced by each tribe. As Native American cultural values are integral to tribal decision-making, the development of tribal natural resources necessitates an assessment of the impact such development may have on traditional values (Adamson 2008). "Almost everything that can be recommended in terms of cultural revival and consolidation involves the fundamental problem of determining a contemporary expression of tribal identity. Inevitably, cultural self-government and cultural self-determination must precede their political and economic counterparts if developments in these latter areas are to have any substance and significance" (Deloria and Lytle 1984, 251).

The protection of Indian spiritual sovereignty, beliefs, religion, languages, and sacred sites are essential for the perpetuation of Indian culture and therefore are of central importance in tribal planning. After a long history of Indian religion and cultural resource exploitation, tribal rights to religious and cultural protection were affirmed in the American Indian Religious Freedom Act of 1978, which recognized the importance of Indian religious practices. The act further directed all federal agencies to insure that their policies do not interfere with the free exercise of Indian religious practices. Decades of struggle by Native American tribal governments to protect against grave desecration and to repatriate religious and cultural property to Indian tribes and Native owners culminated in the Native American Graves Protection and Repatriation Act of 1990. While supported under the federal trust responsibility, the successful attainment of tribal rights for cultural protection is also dependent upon the cooperation of state and local governments to diligently protect off-reservation religious, burial, and archaeological resources that are located within their jurisdictions. Many tribal communities have developed the capacity to effectively protect their cultural resources under tribal policies that are applied within reservation boundaries, and through agreements with non-tribal governments for the protection of off-reservation cultural resources located in off-reservation ancestral homelands. Several tribes have experienced effective partnerships with state and local government historic preservation agencies that provide for early and meaningful tribal involvement in reviewing development proposals that occur off-reservations. Such collaborative arrangements have helped to ensure that the potential impacts to cultural resources are addressed.

**Restricted Access to Capital
and Reservation Economic Alienation**

Financial institutions have historically been reluctant to provide loans to Indian individuals and tribal governments for the financing of housing, infrastructure, or economic development without the security of federal loan guarantees. Access to capital financing for reservation development continues to be limited as lenders and investors tend to regard the tribal political setting as unstable, where laws are subject to change by tribal governments (Cornell 1986). Further, lenders may unfairly perceive tribal courts as biased, failing to protect private property rights of non-Indians by according them due process of law. This perceived uncertainty tends to increase risk, which, as in the case of financing gaming business ventures,[18] increases the cost of financing on Indian reservations (Harvard 2008).

The trust status of tribal resources involves a complex framework of federal regulatory control over Indian assets, as authorized by treaties, statutes, and regulations that govern trust resources and trust funds. The trust status of Indian resources, by limiting a tribe's access to its assets

18. Gaming development illustrates how federal intervention can restrict tribes from readily accessing financing to support tribal economic development. While the courts have affirmed the inherent tribal right to conduct gaming activities, Congress intervened with passage of the Indian Regulatory Gaming Act of 1988. The act further regulates most forms of gaming activities and, most importantly, requires that an agreement with states must be reached prior to the conduct of certain forms of gaming activities. Access to capital financing to develop tribal gaming enterprises was severely restricted when, under pressure from the private gaming industry, the federal government imposed new restrictions to the federal loan guarantee program, eliminating its use in funding gaming developments. Without access to the loan guarantee program, conventional financing became virtually inaccessible. This placed a burden upon tribes to turn to private sources of capital. The private financing alternative often necessitated private arrangements by requiring equity "kickers," or a portion of the net revenues from the operations to offset the perceived risk. Tribal alienation from conventional forms of government financing thus created a situation where tribal revenues were forced to be shared with private investors. The net effect of the federal loan guarantee moratorium is twofold: it increased the tribal direct cost of capital financing and it delayed the development of tribal gaming operations.

for investment and collateralization purposes, is considered to be a major obstacle in financing tribal community development. State financial institutions are usually limited to approved forms of securities for loans. Since Indian property is held in trust and cannot be mortgaged, financial institutions are reluctant to provide loans without federal guarantees. Many tribes are now enacting their own uniform commercial codes in an effort to provide protection to financial institutions. Under the provisions of the Internal Revenue Code, the Indian Tribal Government Tax Status Act of 1982 enables tribes to be treated as states, or political subdivisions of states, and authorizes tribes to issue tax-exempt bonds to provide essential governmental services, including reservation infrastructure projects. However, the tribal tax-exemption remains imprecise and continues to impede tribal efforts to raise capital for economic development, capital that is generally available to most other forms of government.

Tribes are also further frustrated by the federal government's trusteeship of their assets, as BIA leasing policies, land services, appraisals, surveying, and delays with required approvals each contribute to the increased costs and uncertainty of reservation development. As a result, many tribes are now initiating their self-governance right to directly manage certain BIA trust services in order to develop greater efficiencies in the management of those resources. The federal trust of Indian lands and resources has inadvertently resulted in a challenging contradiction. While the trust responsibility serves to protect those resources from state and local regulations and taxation, it is difficult to attract capital to the reservation, as resources held in trust are not subject to foreclosure and other state security laws.

Problems may also arise as the economic goals of a tribe may differ from conventional goals of the private economy. When operated as public enterprises, many tribes tend to de-capitalize their businesses by redirecting retained earnings towards the support of essential community services, acquisition of lands lost through assimilation, cultural priorities, and community welfare programs, rather than reinvesting in business expansion. Tribal enterprises also tend to emphasize both employment and profitability goals concurrently. In the relatively short period of tribal governance rebuilding after the 1960s termination era, the private sector continues to view tribal governments as generally unstable, with a high turnover of elected officials and key administrative staff, and factionalism among constituencies, conditions that adversely affect perceptions about the tribal business environment. In spite of such perceptions, whether warranted or not, the tribal capacity for business development and investment has grown exponentially as the number of successful tribal business activities continue to increase. To support tribal business development and its access to capital, a growing number of professional tribal business associations have emerged. The Native American Financial Officers Association (NAFOA), in particular, provides support for the advancement of independent and culturally-vibrant tribal communities through assistance in financial management, economic and fiscal policy, and education and training programs.

Another variable that affects capital access for tribal economic development concerns the tribes' governmental immunities from suit. While more than 130 tribes have Indian Reorganization Act (IRA) corporate charters which permit them to sue and be sued, tribes are reluctant to conduct business under their corporate charters, preferring instead to retain their immunity structure. Suits against a tribal sovereign are only permitted under expressed tribal or congressional waivers of sovereign immunity where the remedy does not involve tribal property held in federal trust. Sovereign immunity to suit is perceived as a major risk to investors since it makes actions by the tribal governments immune from challenge and exposes investment to loss in cases where a tribe elects to deny a claim by raising its immunity protection.

The private investment sector may also consider tribal employment preferential laws a disincentive for investing on reservations. The Indian Reorganization Act first established the provision for Indian employment preference in the administration of federal services affecting Indian tribes. The "Buy Indian" and the Indian Self-Determination and Education Assistance acts further created Indian preference in contracting. The Supreme Court in *Morton v. Mancari*[19] held that Indian preference is based on the

19. 417 U.S. 535 (1974).

unique legal status of Indian tribes as politically recognized entities and therefore does not constitute racial discrimination. Many tribal governments now impose their own Indian preferential legislation, known as tribal employments rights ordinances (TERO), affecting all businesses located within reservations. Balancing tribal social needs in employment with investment capital needs requires reconciliation in order to remove barriers to tribal capital accumulation and reservation development.

Tribes can pursue economic development through a variety of structures (Grant and Taylor 2007). They can directly establish tribal business ventures and public corporations as business arms of the tribe; permit tribal members and non-Indians to charter private corporations under tribal law; encourage non-Indian businesses chartered under the state laws to conduct activities on their reservations; and regulate and tax individual businesses within reservation boundaries. These forms of economic development present choices regarding the type and extent of economic development that would be most appropriate and beneficial in meeting the needs of a tribe. As collective owners, public enterprises assure maximum control and benefit over the activity. Promoting individual member entrepreneurs fosters a private tribal economic base. Private non-Indian activities and joint ventures offer an alternative to stimulating reservation economic growth by reducing tribal financial exposure and associated investment risks. The determination of the appropriate form of enterprise development is largely dependent upon the community's economic, as well as social and cultural objectives (Grant and Taylor 2007).

Conclusion and Implications for Planning

In overcoming constraints to their own development, tribes must first clearly define their community's future development vision, while, simultaneously, strengthening their institutional structures and their capacity for managing the political economy of their reservations. A strategy for achieving these objectives involves the establishment of an inclusive definition of the reservation that is broad enough to consider the interests of the tribal community along with the interests of the non-Indian residents and business community that occupy the reservation. Although *Brendale* defers final judgment concerning tribal reservation jurisdiction to future court reviews, it has indicated that the primacy of tribal jurisdiction exists, and under certain circumstances, may comprehensively apply to all areas of the reservation. The success of tribal community development ultimately depends upon the reconciliation of the obstacles to tribal authority, such as those described in this chapter. The necessity for clarifying a tribe's authority over its reservation affairs is of paramount importance to tribal self-determination. If they are to come to terms with a history that has inflicted a patchwork of non-tribal interests into their affairs, tribes must be prepared to address the dynamic and complex reservation land tenure and demographic conditions in order to further advance their goals. The legitimacy of tribal policy is undoubtedly strengthened when those policies demonstrate a consideration for the multiplicity of interests that exist in the reservation setting.

The pathway toward the reconciliation of the oppositional forces that are present in tribal planning is dependent upon improving tribal relations with non-tribal governments as well as with the non-tribal resident and business community of the reservation. The objective should be one of attaining a balance among the various competing interests—an approach based on political plurality that seeks to reconcile the multi-dimensional interests of the reservations. Such an approach may help to finally resolve the persistent undermining of tribal political authority and to reinforce the defensibility of tribal jurisdiction.

Part THREE

The Dimensions of Tribal Planning

7

An Adaptive and Contingent
Model of Tribal Planning

THE EVOLUTION OF INDIAN POLICY and the associated history of jurisdictional conflict has produced the political setting within which tribal planning now occurs. In order for tribes to overcome the continued resistance to their own development, effective political action that emanates from the exercise of tribal sovereignty is essential. Because Native American Indian tribes are culturally, geographically, and politically diverse, any effective planning strategy must take into account the situational variables that are particular to each reservation. This chapter proposes a general model for Native American Indian reservation planning that aligns a tribe's community development objectives with its historic experiences and its political capacity. The approach emphasizes the consideration of external jurisdictional forces that interfere with a tribe's affairs, thereby creating a dynamic planning environment. Adaptive and contingent planning approaches are particularly effective in evaluating dynamic planning environments. These approaches provide a systematic process that enables a tribe to assess its political conflict situation prior to selecting strategies for confronting those conflicts in order to achieve its future-planning ends.

Theories are important to the practice of planning because they help to explain the variables that affect a community's development. The variables pertaining to the development of Native American Indian reservation communities are among the most complex found in American planning. As discussed in the preceding chapters, these variables result from of a long history of political and cultural subjugation, the forced subdivision and subsequent sale of reservation lands to non-Indians, the jurisdictional encroachment onto reservations by non-tribal governments, and the resulting marginality of reservation economies.

Overcoming jurisdictional conflict is largely dependent upon a tribe's capacity to sufficiently exert its own political actions in order to counteract and eliminate subjugating influences. Such actions, which include negotiation, cooperation, and litigation, may be employed as confrontational tactics, when appropriate, in order to resist the imposing subjugation. Tribal political action in these situations seeks to remove, or at least reduce, the effects of unilaterally imposed policies that impede tribal authority. The resolution of jurisdictional conflicts can sometimes be effectively mediated through cooperative agreements to mutually accommodate competing interests. Where tribal interests exist in off-reservation areas, the mediation of disputes allows for increased political pluralism whereby tribal interests may become acknowledged, rather than ignored, within a broader multi-jurisdictional region.

In order for tribes to advance their community development, they must not only engage in planning, but must also simultaneously consider the factors that impede their development. Planning can help tribes overcome obstacles to their development and help achieve their self-determined goals. As tribes encounter external conflict, their response should be guided by an informed planning approach that considers both the historic circumstances that gave rise to conflict as well as the tribe's capacity to exercise political action to respond to the conflict. Planning in reservation communities is fundamentally a political and strategic process that advances the interests of tribal nations through the exercise of their own political autonomy.[1]

A conceptual model for tribal planning is presented that emphasizes the consideration of the external factors that contribute to the disruption of a tribe's development. Planning's theories, as well as advances in Indian

1. Senghass (1988) equates a community's ability to act autonomously by first conceiving an appropriate set of implementation actions and then marshalling resources necessary to carry out the proposed action.

self-determination policy brought about by the Native American leadership and the nation-building experiences of tribes, inform the framework. To establish a general context for tribal planning, a typology is presented that expresses the general objectives of tribal self-determination that are common to many tribal nations and that are based on a shared history of subjugation and survival. These principles are integrated into a conceptual planning model that is both anticipatory and adaptive, simultaneously considering both past and present conditions as planning strategies are selected to overcome anticipated future conflicts.

Informing Tribal Planning through Planning's Theoretical Traditions

Theories in planning help make problems that occur in a planning situation understandable. Incorporation theory (chapter 5) explains the effects of the historic expansion of non-tribal interests into tribal affairs (Page 1985; Snipp 1986) and the resulting erosion to tribal sovereignty. Jorgensen (1972) observed that the lack of development and the accompanying slow rate of acculturation of Indians into the US economy were a direct result of exploitation by the incorporating economy. The General Allotment Act made possible reservation exploitation through the alienation of the reservation land base and the resulting non-Indian ownership and control of reservation lands (Deloria and Lytle 1984; Deloria 1985). The application of state and local jurisdiction often supplanted tribal authority over these alienated lands. Incorporation theory illustrates the imbalances that resulted between a tribal nation and the US political economy as tribal resources became controlled by and absorbed into the political economy. Therefore, reestablishing tribal authority over reservation affairs is a necessary first step toward reversing reservation incorporation.

Similarly, the characteristics of incorporation must also be identified by emphasizing the context within which tribal planning occurs. Phenomenological approaches in planning (Bolan 1980; Castells 1980, 1983) interpret the nature of the planning environment in terms of the underlying conditions that contribute to social and political conflict. The approach emphasizes an understanding of the events that are occurring in the tribal planning environment and their relationship to conflict. In this context, the tribal planning situation represents a dialectic tension between the interests of a tribe and those of opposing interests. As a phenomenological approach, tribal planning becomes primarily concerned with the dynamic conflicts that are present in the planning situation. Therefore, planning becomes chiefly oriented toward overcoming conflicts through its general planning methodology.

Methods that help to restore a community's self-governance are also important in tribal planning (Jojola 2008). An underlying assumption of self-help approaches to community development (Christenson and Robinson 1989) maintains that a community can achieve self-determination within the constraints imposed by the political economy in which a community is embedded. As a community-building strategy, it is directed toward increased community self-reliance and views a community's development as a social and political process capable of bringing about desired changes. Self-help approaches are reflected in federal Indian self-governance grants and contract programs that were initially introduced under the Indian Education and Self Determination Act of 1975 and have since expanded to include the eligibility of tribes for delegated program responsibility under the environmental statutes. These programs have been pivotal in developing the governance capacity of tribal nations to carry out their own planning and community development activities.

Use of Confrontational Tactics

Several forms of intervening strategies can be applied to offset jurisdictional subjugation. Confrontation tactics can be an effective strategy for challenging the imposition of external jurisdictions in tribal affairs. However, the use of confrontational tactics, alone, serves principally as a stopgap measure when a tribe's political authority is asserted to confront a non-tribal government's presumed jurisdiction in reservation affairs. Confrontation may lead either to further conflict, usually involving litigation, or to negotiated solutions.

Several outcomes are identified under the confrontational approach in figure 5: (1) the intruding jurisdiction may defer to the tribe's jurisdiction under a negotiated agreement; (2) an agreement may be reached for mutual governmental cooperation, representing an outcome of regional pluralism; (3) the confrontation may result in litigation leading to the further outcomes of; (4) a court order mandating the governments to cooperate; (5) a ruling in support of exclusive of non-tribal jurisdiction; or (6) a ruling in support of exclusive tribal jurisdiction. The latter two outcomes do not necessarily resolve the conflict, however, as a tribe is either faced with the conditions of continued incorporation, as it is subjected to further non-tribal jurisdictional intrusion, or, in the case where its jurisdiction is affirmed, may face isolation from the region. In some cases, such as in the *Brendale* "closed area" of the Yakima Reservation, isolation may be a preferred outcome. Yet, in other situations, political isolation of a tribe may impair its ability to participate in regional governance and thus reduce its influence in regional policy-making. The successful negotiation of disputes through cooperation represents an outcome where tribal interests are both affirmed and integrated within the regional policy landscape. Negotiated outcomes become formalized in agreements that can lead to further intergovernmental cooperation in other areas of mutual interest.

The confrontation approach emphasizes social and political justice considerations by polarizing a community's objectives into well-defined

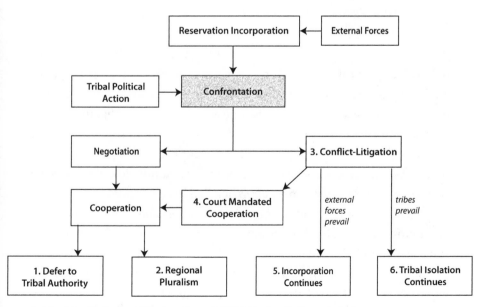

5. Model of tribal political action. © 2012 Taylor & Francis Ltd.

issues and emphasizes the identification of strategies to produce change in the situation (Forester 1980; Hoch 1994; Kemmis 1990). Advocacy planning, which emerged in the 1960s, illustrates how political change can effectively be brought about through the use of confrontational tactics (Alinsky 1972). The approach has been used as a short-term strategy by tribal nations to assert their interests in situations where tribes are largely underrepresented. Roberts (1979) recognized the confrontational approach as an effective tactic in tribal planning to persuade non-tribal governments to consider tribal concerns when confronted with litigation or other actions intended to disrupt the political status quo. The advocacy approach may also be effective in advancing tribal interests in off-reservation areas, where tribes do not possess governance rights. However, the approach alone does not adequately resolve long-standing problems when on-reservation tribal jurisdiction is challenged. A longer-term strategy is needed in order to bring about permanent conditions that are favorable, rather than oppositional, to tribal objectives.

Community Self-Sufficiency:
Strategic and Adaptive Approaches

Etzioni's (1968, 2001) classic model of the self-sufficient political community is particularly pertinent to the tribal context because it emphasizes the necessity for a community to control its territory through its own political and administrative processes, independent of external influences. The self-sufficiency strategy emphasizes the importance of a community breaking away from controlling external linkages that disrupt the community (Senghass 1988; Etzioni 2001). As planning seeks to mediate relations that stand between the self-sufficient community and its external forces, the self-sufficiency model provides a foundation from which a tribal community development approach can be developed.

The nature of the relationship between tribes and their surrounding communities, which has historically been viewed in terms of coercive relations, has significant importance as the history of Indian litigation clearly exemplifies. Social learning approaches (Dunn 1971; Korten 1980, 1984; Faludi 1973) seek to achieve utilitarian outcomes by emphasizing accommodating solutions among the competing interests that are present in reservation affairs.[2] However, a prerequisite condition for the successful mediation of conflict is that a level playing field be established whereby a tribe's community objectives and the principles of tribal sovereignty are clarified and affirmed. In order for historic conflicts rooted in normative differences to be reconciled, as typified by Native and non-Native community relations, there must also be a mutual acceptance of each community's respective social values. Tribal planning, therefore, should simultaneously be concerned with the resolution of normative as well as political conflicts that exist in the tribal planning situation.

To assess the threats to tribal self-governance, strategic and adaptive approaches warrant particular attention. Strategic planning (Steiner 1979; So 1984) provides a methodology for systematically identifying opportunities and threats to a community's self-determination.[3] The process also assesses the community's capacity to adapt necessary measures for overcoming conflicts by identifying the inherent strengths and weaknesses of the organization from which political actions are derived. As weaknesses within the political organization, itself, that must be strengthened are addressed, the approach is pragmatic. Insofar as the methodology is concerned with the organization's primary instinct for political survival, central to the concept of tribal self-determination, it is particularly well suited to the tribal-planning situation.

Adaptive planning provides a structure for selecting the most appropriate responses to a given situation. The preferred action should be

---

2. Etzioni (1968) describes three forms of social relations as normative relations, utilitarian relations, and coercive relations. Normative relations contribute to cooperation when participants share similar norms and seek common outcomes in the planning process. Utilitarian relations seek to avoid or contain conflict and focus on achieving complementary interests and mutually acceptable outcomes. Coercive relations often result in conflict when the opposing goals of the participants remain unresolved.

3. Strategic planning's application to public policy evolved in the 1960s from its development as a corporate decision-making tool during the preceding decade. The approach assesses a community's strengths and weakness as it prepares to adapt strategies in response to identified opportunities and threats that lie within an organization's planning environment.

contingent upon the characteristics of the situation (Bryson and Delbecq 1979; Bryson and Einsweiller 1988; Kemp 1992), and alternative actions considered against criteria that maximize goal achievement. The tribal planning approach, therefore, should be both anticipatory and reactive. The selection of planning strategies is guided by the anticipation of future consequences and requires the ability to continuously adapt new strategies as new situations arise, based on the strategy's effectiveness in reducing threats to a community's interest (Alexander 1985, 1995). Strategic planning actions usually involve a multiple set of approaches (Bunnell 1997; Riffle 2000), including organizational capacity-building measures, mediation, negotiation, and the use of confrontational measures.

Sovereignty, Self-Determination, and the Scope of Tribal Planning

The scope of tribal planning is broad and complex, encompassing comprehensive planning, land use regulation, natural resources management, environmental protection, public safety, health and welfare protection, and the provision of capital facilities and infrastructure to support the overall development of the tribal reservation community. As with planning activities carried out by local governments, tribal planning activities are similarly supported by police powers, authorized under a tribe's own constitution. A tribe's regulatory authority is also concurrently exercised through the express congressional delegation of tribal authority. Additionally, tribal planning emphasizes the promotion of economic development in which the tribal government itself functions as the primary focal point for establishing rules and directing resources to create and maintain a reservation economy. Hence, in the absence of a developed private tribal economy, tribal governments perform a regulatory as well as an entrepreneurial role to stimulate capital formation and economic development. Tribal planning is also intrinsically concerned with the preservation of the community's cultural identity. Therefore, an essential aspect of tribal planning involves the adaptation of programs and activities that serve the economic, environmental, and cultural priorities of the community.

The process of defining a tribe's community goals is one that reflects the distinct needs and social values of each tribal community. However, many tribal nations share a common set of concerns that are derived from a collective past. Namely, they each strive for cultural survival, political independence, and economic betterment (Cornell 1987; Cornell and Kalt 1992; Jojola 1998; Harvard Project on American Indian Economic Development 2008). Forming the foundation for a general tribal planning model, these collective concerns emphasize the defense of tribal sovereignty, the maintenance of social cohesiveness and the control of territorial resources. Figure 6 illustrates the three dimensions that constitute these primary considerations in tribal planning.

With the understanding that a tribal nation's well-being is inevitably linked to its political, cultural, and economic sustainability, the tribal planning approach, then, has two primary objectives. The first concerns the exercise of political autonomy as a means of preserving its social and political cohesiveness. The second concerns the exercise of control over reservation resources. Since the control of reservation resources is paramount to the attainment of tribal economic self-sufficiency, the conditions that supplant a tribe's control over its reservation affairs impairs its advancement. An effective tribal planning approach requires a capacity to simultaneously assess the nature of conflict situations while evaluating actions that can overcome such conflicts.

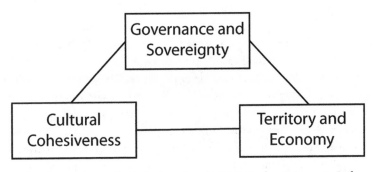

6. The dimensions of tribal planning. © 2012 Taylor & Francis Ltd.

The Principles of Tribal Self-Determination

Over the last several decades, through the reawakening of many aspects of their formerly dormant inherent sovereignty, tribes have achieved renewed powers with which to attain their goals. Since the early 1970s, primarily as a consequence of Indian political action by Native American leadership, the organizing principle of federal Indian policy has been framed to emphasize the restoration of tribal sovereignty and self-determination. This ideal advocates that tribes, themselves, should make the decisions that affect their communities. The federal courts have affirmed the rights of tribal nations to shape the future of their communities under the tribal sovereignty doctrine.[4] In addition to being a philosophical ideal, tribal self-determination also applies to federal programs that enable tribes to self-administer government activities. Since the enactment of the Indian Self-Determination and Education Assistance Act of 1975,[5] the federal government has consistently supported the transference of federal services administration directly to the tribes. The policy is now well established in federal legislation and furthered through the enactment of the Tribal Self-Governance Act of 1994.[6] Despite these important policy advances, the most important variable facing many tribes as they chart their futures continues to be their ability to exert control over their affairs.

Since the introduction of the Indian policy of self-determination, Indian policy has been firmly based on four organizing principles as developed by a coalition of representative tribal leaders and the National Congress of American Indians (National Indian Policy Center 1993).[7]

---

4. See *California v. Cabazon Band of Mission Indians*, 480 U.S. 202 (1987).

5. Pub. L. No. 93-638 (codified at 25 U.S.C. § 450 et seq.).

6. H.R. 4842, Title II. The preamble to the act reaffirms Congress's findings that "the tribal right of self-government flows from the inherent sovereignty of Indian tribes as nations, and the special government-to-government relationship" between the federal government and the tribes. The act provides for the direct transference of federal trust programs guaranteed to them in treaties, statutes, and other agreements to tribal governments and acknowledges the continuing trust responsibility of the federal government.

7. The "Tribal-Federal Government-to-Government Proposal" of June 10, 1993, American Indian Policy Center. Washington, D.C.

These principles consist of the affirmation of the federal trust responsibility, the right to tribal self-governance, the right to a permanent tribally controlled reservation homeland, and the federal protection of tribal sovereignty and treaty rights. A typology is presented in table 6 associating the four organizing principles of self-determination with the three imperatives that comprise the tribal political community: political sovereignty, cultural cohesiveness, and territoriality. The typology reflects a general framework for guiding the development of tribal communities and Indian policy within the multi-governmental structure of American government.

Based on these self-determination principles, tribal planning should, within a general tribal planning framework, systematically evaluate how its strategic actions would advance the political, territorial, and cultural imperatives that constitute the tribal community:

The Political Imperative. Although inherent tribal sovereignty has never been extinguished, tribal political authority has been historically eroded, enabling the political encroachment by non-tribal governments, principally by state, local, and special purpose governments. The political imperative of tribal planning requires the strengthening of tribal self-governance in order to enable the fullest exercise of tribal powers. This is accomplished by strengthening the powers of tribal governance, enhancing the tribe's administrative capacities, and removing non-tribal jurisdictional authority from the reservation thereby eliminating political subjugation and the conditions of reservation incorporation.

The Cultural Imperative. Native American culture and religion are inseparable from tribal policy development. Tribal cultural norms often assign to reservation lands and natural resources a social use value that emphasizes the sustainability of the reservation homeland and the prevention of developmental impacts that may negatively affect the social community. In addressing the cultural imperative, tribal planning should emphasize the protection of the community's cultural stability, ensure the sustainability of reservation natural resources, and take special care to foster the abatement of cultural alienation.

The Territorial Imperative. Of paramount importance to tribal community development is the improvement of the community's physical, social, and economic conditions. Tribal nations can overcome the problems posed

TABLE 6 Principles and Imperatives of Tribal Self-Determination

Guiding Principle	Imperatives in Tribal Planning		
	Political Governance	*Cultural Cohesiveness*	*Reservation Territory*
1. Federal Trust Responsibility	Tribes hold governments to honoring treaty promises	Uses of trust resources support tribal well-being as determined by tribes	Tribes hold federal trustee accountable to defend tribal authority and to preempt political intrusion
2. Tribal Self-Governance	Federal-tribal relationship based on the recognition of tribal sovereignty	Tribal right to determine community priorities and futures	Federal support of tribal capacity building to achieve economic self-sufficiency
3. Permanent Homelands	Tribes affirm their right to exclusive reservation governance	Tribal authority asserted to prevent reservation cultural alienation	Federal-tribal partnership protecting reservation homelands
4. Sovereignty and Treaty Rights	Federal-tribal partnership strengthening the capacity of tribal self-governance	Federal-tribal partnership ensures protection of Indian health, welfare, spiritual, and cultural resources	Tribes hold federal trustee accountable for protection of treaty rights

Source: Nicholas C. Zaferatos. © 2012 Taylor & Francis Ltd.

by underdevelopment by regaining control over their territorial resources. Tribes that employ approaches analogous to Friedmann's (1982, 1987) self-reliant development can selectively reduce dependency relationships with the surrounding political economy. As tribal governments assume the primary role for managing reservation assets, this approach becomes increasingly important in tribal planning. To advance the tribal territorial imperative, tribes should explicitly define their future vision and their reservation development objectives, while developing their administrative capacity to effectively manage their lands and natural resources.

Constructing the Tribal Planning Model

Two dimensions comprise the activity of tribal planning—an internal dimension and an external dimension. The internal dimension concerns the determination of a tribe's future as an expression of its sovereignty and its social and cultural priorities. Planning begins by first defining the tribal nation's visions and goals and the assessment of its capacity to achieve those goals (figure 7). This process incorporates community-visioning processes to articulate its interests and priorities[8] and should clearly identify the tribe's governing role in guiding the community's development.

The external dimension concerns the tribe's interface with outside interests, particularly those of state and local governments, as well as the private economy (Altshuler and Behn 1997; Bardach 1998). Because these external influences have often preempted tribal jurisdiction and the attainment of tribal goals, an approach is needed to equate tribal decision-making to the anticipation of conflicts that may arise during the implementation of the community's development programs. These exogenous variables in tribal planning are the most difficult to control, as they represent independent political forces. The external dimension in tribal planning, therefore,

8. Notwithstanding that among some tribal nations social and political fragmentation may persist, and communities should carefully resolve their internal disputes through a process that provides for the fullest participation of its membership in community decision-making.

addresses the political threats to a tribe's self-determination and the actions that are necessary to eliminate political subjugation. To advance tribal goals, new forms of relationships with these external variables are required in order to support, rather than preclude, the advancement of tribal interests.

Parameters of the Tribal Planning Model

The tribal planning model is designed to anticipate opposition from outside forces that may arise in the future-planning environment. The model combines methods from phenomenology and adaptive approaches in planning to emphasize the consideration of the dynamics in the planning environment. As an adaptive approach, it emphasizes the selection of strategies that are most responsive to the conditions that are identified in the tribal-planning environment. The approach utilizes strategic decision-making in order to link the tribe's empirical knowledge about its planning situation to the selection of alternative actions that are deemed to be most effective in those situations.

Figure 7 depicts four phases in tribal planning. In phase I, the tribal nation articulates its community objectives and strategic programs are prepared. Goal setting (stage 1) establishes the priorities for the long-term development of the reservation community and identifies the organizational and administrative capacities that are needed to carry out its programs. The strategic plan (stage 2) translates the selection of goals into specific programs and actions, and allocates resources for the administration of reservation development programs. The strategic plan should be an integrated strategy that simultaneously advances the community's political, social, economic and environmental objectives for reservation development. Phase II activities involve the expansion of the tribe's political capacity (stage 3) to administer its programs and to effectively exercise political action. Here, the tribal political infrastructure may be expanded to include the enactment of tribal laws, regulations, standards, and administrative and enforcement procedures, as well as the authorization to enter into intergovernmental agreements, where appropriate, to overcome jurisdictional conflicts through cooperative means.

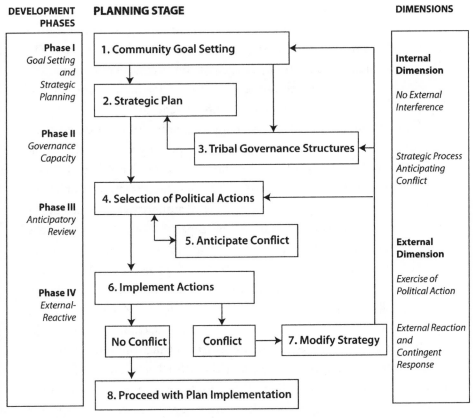

7. Tribal community development planning framework. © 2012 Taylor & Francis Ltd.

Under phase III, actions are selected contingent upon the likelihood of their success based upon the tribe's capacity to carry out its programs and the anticipated resistance from external variables. As a strategic activity, it is at this stage that potential conflicts that may arise during the plan's implementation are identified. Actions that may result in potential conflict (with external variables) are identified (stage 5) and contingent actions are evaluated to enhance the tribe's preparedness. In evaluating the tribe's political vulnerability, the approach guides the selection of contingent actions based on the perceived threats that may occur in the future planning situation. Alternative actions may include modifications to the tribal program, strengthening of self-governance powers, identification of confrontational tactics, or other approaches aimed at resolving pending disputes through negotiation. Emphasized here is the iterative feature in the process of selecting actions, as each action is considered against the anticipation of a conflict response during implementation. The process represents an anticipatory approach to circumventing conflict.

Tribal planning requires a clear understanding of the extent of the authority that a tribe is believed to possess, especially in allotted reservations that are heavily populated with non-Indian residents and that have experienced a history of non-tribal jurisdictional encroachment upon the reservation. In light of the limitations to tribal authority as provided under the *Montana* and *Brendale* rulings, the capacities of tribal governance should be carefully evaluated as strategic plans are prepared.[9] The development of tribal legislative and regulatory systems necessitates a legal analysis of the courts' rulings to ensure that contemplated actions conform to the scope of tribal powers believed valid, especially when such powers are applied to activities affecting non-Indian interests (Goeppele 1990).

In phase IV tribal actions are implemented (stage 6). If no opposition is encountered, the action proceeds without further alteration (stage 8). Resistance to tribal actions that are encountered during implementation results in two possible responses. If the form of opposition was anticipated earlier (stage 5), then pre-selected contingent actions can be employed to counter the resistance (stage 4). If the condition was not anticipated, the situation is then treated as a new variable (stage 7) that requires further consideration. The decision process for newly encountered variables includes the reconsideration of the tribal goals and strategic plan (stage 2) as well as the adequacy of the tribe's political capacity (stage 3). During this stage, the tribal action may be deferred until an appropriate response can be identified. The objective of this final phase is to carefully monitor

---

9. In general, tribes that can clearly establish a reservation policy that maintains both the "essential character" of the reservation and the tribe's political integrity, economic security, or the community's health and welfare, as defined in the *Montana* test, may have the strongest defense in a future jurisdictional dispute.

the responses that result from the implementation of a tribal action, and to employ a contingent response.

Conclusion and Implications for Planning

This chapter presents a model for tribal community planning that combines the consideration of a tribal nation's historic experience with its community development aims. The approach emphasizes the identification of conflicts that arise from a tribe's historic and current relationship with its surrounding region. The planning approach is phenomenological as it emphasizes the dynamics of the tribal planning setting and calls for the continuous assessment of adverse conditions that operate in that environment during the development and implementation of a tribe's planning system. Mutual learning is an especially important technique for overcoming adversity so that the normative goals, as well as the political interests of a tribe, can be effectively communicated. Forming mutually beneficial relationships between tribes and their surrounding communities is a necessary first step in the acceptance of dissimilar and often conflicting community priorities, and in achieving regional plurality.

The tribal planning model emphasizes the strategic features in tribal decision-making, as it anticipates the likelihood of obstacles in its future-planning situation. In the process of advancing tribal objectives, strategies are selected that are determined to be best suited to the dynamics of that future-planning situation. The model integrates a feedback loop to assess whether planned actions should be modified in the face of unanticipated resistance. The assessment of a tribe's planning situation is dependent upon both accurate feedback information and the capacity to interpret that information before contingent strategies are selected. As conflicts arise during plan implementation, contingent actions may involve further enhancement to a tribe's political structure and administrative capacity, the reconsideration of community goals, priorities, and strategies, or the application of other approaches necessary to reconcile the conflict such as cooperation, negotiation, or confrontational tactics.

The planning model is not intended as a prescriptive blueprint for how to perform tribal planning, but rather as a framework for understanding the dynamic relationships that exist within a tribe's planning situation.

Its aim is to empower tribal communities by anticipating and responding to the multiple variables that operate in tribal affairs. As a conceptual approach, it provides a process for aligning tribal planning strategies with historical considerations. As a strategic approach, it strengthens the capacity of tribal nations to directly confront political opposition when encountered. As a cognitive process, it involves a long-term and continuous view of the business of tribal planning and development. As Cornell and Kalt (2007) observe, what doesn't work for tribal planning and development is a short-term view; a long-term view is indispensable if it is to be successful. The effectiveness of tribal planning depends upon a tribe's capacity to exercise its political resolve while simultaneously assessing its planning environment. A great deal of patience must be exercised as the process continuously navigates a strategic course through the changing circumstances that inevitably arise in the tribal planning setting.

Part FOUR

Case Studies in Mediating
Tribal Planning Relationships

8

Mediating Tribal-State Conflicts

Experiences from Washington State

NATIVE AMERICANS, like other indigenous peoples throughout the world, are asserting and gaining recognition of their aboriginal rights to land, natural and cultural resources, and self-governance (Barry and Porter 2012). While their approach to claiming their rights depends upon their particular political circumstances, they have primarily relied on the judicial system. The legal process has often resulted in shifting the balance of power in the political landscape when Native interests are affirmed (Burayidi 2003). Over the past several decades, the emerging recognition of Native American Indian rights has challenged what had predominantly been an exclusive state planning system, resulting in tensions as Indian interests became more fully integrated within newly formed systems of mutual governance (Dyck 1985; Harwood 2005). The accommodation of emerging tribal interests within the broader political landscape of natural resource management and land use planning, in particular, has affected planning systems that were once presumed to be free of tribal authority (Jorgensen 2007).

Intergovernmental relationships provide a way for tribes to have their voices heard and to influence decisions beyond their reservation boundaries (Hicks 2007). The comparatively new approach to multi-jurisdictional planning has been viewed with varying degrees of success (Hibbard, Lane, and Rasmussenet 2008; Jentoft, Minde, and Nilsen 2003; Yiftachel 1998). The presumed status of state control over the management of natural resources, environmental quality, and land use planning are inevitably shaken whenever a court affirms the validity of a tribal claim of injury to property rights or to a tribe's assertion of political authority, especially when a court mandates new forms of management that include tribal interests along with those of the state. As with any process of change that disrupts the political status quo, opportunities can also arise to enhance the management of resources under the new and evolving systems of co-management (Tully 2000, 2004). Such precedents have been well established in Washington State.

The recent development of tribal-state planning systems that accommodate Native American Indian interests is a response to the often-forced recognition of those rights by intervening parties. Barry and Porter (2012) identify two forms of recognition, referring to one as "territorial recognition" that links traditional culture with place and the other as "political structures recognition," referring to the rights of Native peoples to self-govern territories and resources where treaty rights have been established. The result has been an expansion of state planning approaches that include co-management (Howitt and Bromling 1996; Jentoft, Minde, and Nilsen 2003; Lane and Williams 2008); increased consultation and accommodation of tribal stakeholders (Sandercock 1998, 2003, 2011); and the state's incorporation of Native traditional knowledge in environmental management (Daniels and Vencatesan 1995). In the US policy context, where regional planning has had a mixed record of success since reaching its high point during the era of the New Deal in the mid-1930s, coordinated planning processes recently reemerged based on the government-to-government model that reflects the federal Indian self-determination and self-governance policy. The mutual governance approach has been especially supported as a tribally preferred planning model for the management of off-reservation treaty-based resources (Barry and Porter 2012; Jojola 2008). These new forms of planning help avoid further conflict while simultaneously advancing tribal cultural, natural resources, and community development objectives (Lane and Hibbard 2005). However, the successful attainment of mutual governance necessitates difficult negotiations in the transition from state-dominated planning systems to pluralistic regional systems that integrate tribal interests in land and natural resources management decision-making (Forester 2009; Yiftachel and Huxley 2000).

This chapter uses a case study approach to examine the mutual interests of the state and the tribes in Washington State and the negotiation processes that ultimately led to new forms of agreement for the co-management of governmental services. The policy shift is largely the result of the mandates of the federal courts that required Washington State to fully accommodate tribal rights in fisheries management decisions. The chapter examines one particular approach in the negotiation process that assisted the state and the tribes to reach agreements for the mutual accommodation of interests. The consensus-based model pioneered in Washington State by the tribes, natural resource-based industries, environmental organizations, and the state's natural resources agencies represents an innovation in public policy mediation that resulted in a series of landmark agreements. For more than a decade, the model, facilitated under the auspices of the Northwest Renewable Resources Center,[1] whose membership included the affected parties, served as the principal mediation method in Washington State.

Tribal Governments and the Native American Population in Washington State

The 2010 US census recognized 103,869 Indian people residing within the state of Washington. While many Indians reside on one of the twenty-nine Indian reservations within the state, the majority of the Indian population resides off reservation, yet maintains strong and continuing relations with their associated tribes. Of the reservation populations, 78 percent of all reservation residents are non-Indians. The sixteen tribes located within the densely populated Puget Sound region of western Washington State have reservation populations of about 60,000, of which 8,870 or 15 percent are Indians and the majority (85 percent) are non-Indians.

Important political differences exist among the Puget Sound tribes, with most tribes being established under federal treaties and others by

---

1. A group representing the corporate, tribal, environmental, and government sectors in Washington State established the Northwest Renewable Resources Center in 1984. Services included conflict assessment, dialogue facilitation, mediation, and training in cross-cultural communications. The organization mediated natural resource and environmental policy disputes in Washington, Idaho, Alaska and Oregon. It was disbanded in January 1998.

executive order. Some tribes were organized under the provisions of the Indian Reorganization Act of 1934, while others retained their aboriginal form of government. The Puget Sound region of Washington State includes those lands ceded in the Stevens Treaties,[2] under the Treaty of Point Elliott, the Treaty of Medicine Creek, and the Treaty of Point No Point. Figure 8 illustrates the ceded territories of western Washington State. Each of the treaties was signed by a group of tribes and bands residing in the ceded territories. The successor tribes of those treaties are each federally recognized. Table 7 shows reservation land areas for the sixteen tribes located in the Puget Sound region. The table depicts the approximate Indian and non-Indian resident population and the approximate distribution of trust and fee title lands in each of these territories.

The sixteen tribes of the Puget Sound region posses varying degrees of incorporation as reflected by their reservation land tenure characteristics. Highly incorporated reservations contain fee lands held in private, non-Indian ownership, as well as a larger proportion of non-Indian residents within the reservation boundaries. Table 7 shows a correlation between reservation alienated land holdings and the type of reservation formation. Alienated lands occur in all reservations that were created under treaties and subjected to the General Allotment Act. In contrast, reservation alienation is essentially absent in reservations established in the years following the act. The presence of land use conflict exists where the alienation of trust territories is present. Table 7 also indicates the presence of state and local jurisdictional intrusion upon reservation lands. Direct forms of jurisdictional conflict occur where non-tribal government authority is imposed upon alienated reservation lands. For all alienated reservations subjected to the General Allotment Act, some degree of territorial alienation was found to occur, representing a form of incorporation by the

---

2. The Stevens Treaties included a series of similar treaties negotiated between Washington Territorial Governor Isaac Stevens and area tribes. As a result of all of the executed Stevens Treaties in Washington, Idaho, and Montana, approximately 64 million acres of land were relinquished.

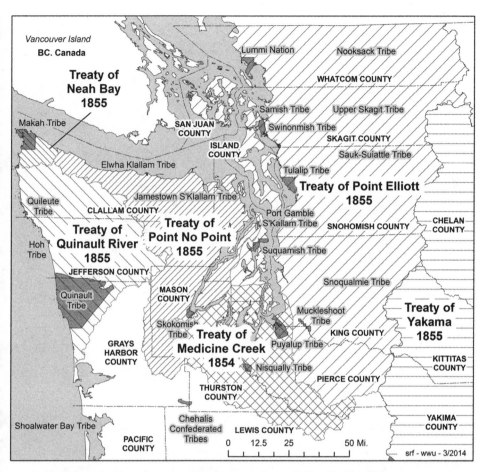

8. Ceded territories of western Washington State. Stefan Freelan, Western Washington University, 2014.

US political economy. Incorporation is manifested through non-Indian ownership and occupancy of reservation land, and by the encroachment upon the reservation by non-tribal interests. In such situations, state or local policies often conflict with tribal policies, and impede a tribe's ability to effectively manage its reservation environment. Of central concern to tribal planning is the mediation of conflicts that occur among tribes, the state, and local governments in reservation affairs, as well as in off-reservation areas where tribal proprietary rights are at stake.

TABLE 7 Puget Sound Area Indian Reservation Characteristics

Tribe	Reservation Formation and Land Tenure Characteristics						Resident Population		
	Form of Creation	Date Established	Total Acres	Alienated Acres	Percent Alienated Acres	Territorial Conflict	Native	Total	Percent Non-Indian
Jamestown S'Klallam	Recognition	1980	210	0	0%	Indirect	3	16	81.3%
Lower Elwha	Recognition	1968	443	0	0%	Indirect	274	315	13.0%
Lummi	Treaty / E. O.	1855	12,504	5,181	41%	Direct	2,114	4,193	49.6%
Muckleshoot	Treaty / E. O.	1857	3,850	2,270	59%	Direct	1,033	2,205	53.2%
Nisqually	Treaty / E. O.	1857	4,700	3,693	78%	Direct	392	588	33.3%
Nooksack	Recognition	1973	10	0	0%	Indirect	337	547	38.4%
Port Gamble S'Klallam	Recognition	1936	1,341	0	0%	Indirect	514	699	25.5%
Puyallup	Treaty / E. O.	1855	18,062	17,446	95%	Direct	1,327	41,341	96.8%
Sauk Suiattle	Recognition	1973	23	0	0%	Indirect	37	45	17.8%
Suquamish	Treaty / E. O.	1855	8,012	4,449	56%	Direct	388	4,834	92.0%

TABLE 7 Puget Sound Area Indian Reservation Characteristics (*cont.*)

Tribe	Reservation Formation and Land Tenure Characteristics						Resident Population		
	Form of Creation	*Date Established*	*Total Acres*	*Alienated Acres*	*Percent Alienated Acres*	*Territorial Conflict*	*Native*	*Total*	*Percent Non-Indian*
Skokomish	Treaty / E. O.	1855	4,987	1,996	40%	Direct	519	730	28.9%
Squaxin Island	Treaty	1854	2,175	668	30%	Direct	327	405	19.3%
Stillaguamish	Recognition	1984	21	0	0%	Indirect	76	102	25.5%
Swinomish	Treaty / E. O.	1855	7,169	3,317	46%	Direct	655	2,664	75.4%
Tulalip	Treaty / E. O.	1855	22,490	11,920	53%	Direct	2,265	9,246	75.5%
Upper Skagit	Recognition	1982	130	0	0%	Indirect	192	238	19.3%
Total			86,127	50,940	59%		10,453	68,168	84.7%

Note: "Treaty / E. O." stands for "treaty or executive order."

Sources: Adapted from the 2000 US Census: Selected Population Characteristics for American Indian and Alaska Native Areas; 2000 US Census: Profile of General Demographic Characteristics, Summary File 1, 100-Percent Data, for American Indian Reservation Areas; Washington State Department of Transportation, "Transportation Guide for Indian Tribal Governments"; and personal communications (1995, 2005).

The Evolution of Indian Policy in Washington State

The historic conflicts between the state of Washington and the twenty-nine tribal governments are multifaceted and, in certain cases, associated with decades of continuing litigation. Table 8 provides a summary of state-tribal issues and depicts the state's general interests in tribal affairs. Since statehood, Washington State's Indian policy has reflected a history of contentious relations and conflict. The state has participated in shaping federal Indian law through its direct or amicus curiae participation in litigation. While some of this past litigation has been involuntary in defense of suits brought against the state or its agencies, other litigation has been initiated by the state. The focus of recent Indian litigation in Washington State has expanded from treaty fishing rights of the 1970s to concerns of tribal land claims, natural resource management, water rights, and the assumption of tribal civil jurisdiction over non-Indians. Tribal-state conflicts have occurred in the regulation and appropriation of water resources, the application of taxes, and the enactment of land use controls within the exterior boundaries of the reservations. While disputes continue in other areas of tribal-state relations, including continued fisheries litigation, these current issues pose complex challenges that affect the interests of the tribes as well as the state, local and special purpose governments, and non-Indian reservation residents and property owners.

Since 1985, negotiation and mediation were emphasized as alternatives to litigation, broadening the state's approach to resolving conflicts with the tribes. This trend towards negotiation evolved further, in 1989, when Washington State's governor proclaimed a new precedent to guide relations with federally recognized Indian tribes. The precedent sought to reverse one hundred years of hostile relations with tribes by recognizing the legitimacy of tribal sovereignty. The policy established a government-to-government relationship with tribal governments, making it consistent with the federal self-governance policy. This approach of cooperative relations with tribes, endorsed in the historic tribal-state Centennial Accord (State of Washington 1989a, 1989b), has led to several notable successes in resolving historic conflicts. The nature of the state's conflicts with tribes and the new policy directives supporting their resolution are discussed below.

Washington State's Historic Policy Position

The state's historic response to Indian conflicts has been characterized as a piecemeal approach. During the 1980s, the attorney general established an Indian Litigation Coordinating Committee within the Office of the Attorney General and charged the committee[3] with the task of establishing a comprehensive approach for assessing conflicts with the tribes. The history of conflict leading to litigation between the state and the tribes was largely due to the confusion about the political status of tribes within the federal system. While tribes possess certain governmental powers, it has historically been the position of the state that such powers are not equivalent to state powers. A unique characteristic of tribal governments, that has been pivotal in the conflictive relationship, is that non-Indians residing within the boundaries of reservations are not entitled to participate in the election of tribal governments that are empowered to enact tribal laws. The situation becomes particularly acute when, as in the Puget Sound region, non-member residents constitute a large majority of the reservation population. It has been the contention of the state that the lack of direct representation in government conflicts with the American democratic principle of "consent of the governed."[4] The unique status differentiating tribal member residents from non-member residents has thus emerged as an important source of conflict between tribes and non-Indian residents and has led to the state's intervention in tribal self-governance. Throughout history, Congress has contributed to the confusion by reversing its Indian policies regarding the nature and extent of tribal sovereignty. The vacillations in federal policy, ranging from termination of tribal political authority to the fostering of tribal

---

3. The committee was chaired by then Deputy Attorney General Christine Gregoire, who has since served as the director of the Washington Department of Ecology, Attorney General, and between 2005 and 2013, as governor of Washington State.

4. While ballot box participation in general elections is limited to the membership of a tribe, participation in other areas of tribal governance does not preclude a tribe from appointing non-members to governmental committees and commissions in order to foster effective resident participation in the affairs of the reservation.

political self-determination, has often resulted in the state being reactive to federal policy shifts rather than developing a cogent state-tribal policy. Disputes arising between the state and tribal governments have primarily been addressed through the three approaches of negotiation, legislation, and litigation.

The principal means for resolving tribal-state conflicts in Washington State has been through the courts. This approach, however, further aggravated the already tentative relationship between the parties and has often led to additional litigation. The Puyallup "test case," filed in the 1960s to settle the fishing rights controversy, illustrates this anomaly. The decision of the lower court was appealed to the United States Supreme Court on three separate occasions.[5] Rather than ending the controversy, the litigation evolved into the even more complex *United States v. Washington*[6] "test case." The emotional and often violent confrontations between fishers affected by the case contributed to cultural tensions between the Indian and the non-Indian communities.

Congress's plenary power provides a second approach for clarifying the balance of tribal and state authority through the preemption of state laws over tribes. Once Congress enacts laws, legal conflicts between state and tribal law may be evaluated in the light of legislative intent, especially with respect to preemption, as a guide to judicial decisions. While this approach can be effective in resolving state-tribal disputes, practical limitations may result, as Congress is often reluctant to limit either state power or tribal rights without the agreement of the affected parties. Further, legislative solutions do not always achieve satisfactory resolution of those

---

5. While that case resolved most of the allocation issues in the 1979 Passenger Fishing Vessel decision, a number of related issues still remained unresolved or in various stages of litigation. See *Puyallup Tribe v. Department of Game*, 433 U.S. 165 (1977); *Washington Game Department v. Puyallup Tribe*, 414 U.S. 44 (1973); *Puyallup Tribe v. Department of Game*, 391 U.S. 392 (1968); *Swinomish Indian Tribal Community v. Department of Ecology*, No. 87672-0 (Wash. Sup. Ct. October 3, 2013).

6. *United States v. Washington*, 384 F. Supp. 312 (W.D. Wash. 1974), *aff'd*, 520 F.2d 676 (9th Cir. 1975), *cert. denied*, 423 U.S. 1086 (1976).

problems and often lack permanence. The history of tribal-state disputes in Washington suggests that many of the disputes are a result of shifting federal legislative policy.

Dispute resolution through negotiation was identified by both the state and the tribes as the most preferable means for reconciling state-tribal conflict[7] in order to avoid costly litigation and confrontational outcomes. While negotiation under some circumstances may be preferable to litigation, other circumstances may preclude the parties from accepting compromised outcomes through the negotiated approach. When disputes arise over the assertion of sovereign control over a resource or territorial area, a compromised solution is often untenable as the state may be prohibited from contracting away its sovereign plenary powers. Tribes similarly defend their sovereignty as fundamental to their continued existence. In such situations, neither the state nor a tribe may willingly concede its sovereign control over resource ownership or rights to control land where such a concession constitutes a legal precedent leading to the diminishment of its rights. Negotiation is further complicated when uncertainty exists in interpreting questions of property rights. Such a situation occurred in the Washington fisheries litigation. While negotiation resulted in co-management of the fisheries resource by the state and tribes, this outcome was reached only after the court mandated cooperation after establishing a general allocation standard.[8] Prior to that decision, the opposing and entrenched positions of the parties precluded a negotiated settlement involving the allocation of the resource. In this case, litigation directly provided an opportunity for subsequent negotiation of the tribal-state dispute by narrowing the context of the negotiation to the means of managing the allocated resource. The three approaches to

---

7. In Washington State, tribes are considered a "public agency" for purposes of application of the Inter-Local Government Cooperative Act, Wash. Rev. Code 39.34. The law allows public agencies to enter into agreements for cooperative efforts where necessary to promote "mutual advantage," including the provision of services and facilities.

8. In *Washington v. Washington State Commercial Passenger Fishing Vessel Ass'n*, 443 U.S. 658 (1979).

conflict resolution experienced in Washington State can be summarized, pursuant to the state's perspective,[9] as follows:

• Negotiation is preferred when the problem is limited in scope and does not involve issues of sovereignty.

• Litigation is preferred when negotiation appears unworkable or when resolution requires a definitive determination.

• Legislation is preferred if it is limited in scope and does not create a need for further clarification through litigation.

Current Disputes in Washington's State-Tribal Relations

Prior to the release of Governor Gardner's historic Indian policy statement in 1989, and the subsequent signing of the Centennial Accord, cooperation based on a government-to-government basis between the state and the tribes had been limited. The types of conflicts between the state and the tribes varied greatly, depending upon the circumstances and the nature of the dispute. The history of tribal-state legal conflicts reveals a diversity of contexts and issues, with the state identifying varying interests in these situations. One major area of state concern involves the proprietary interests of state agencies regarding land ownership. When tribal activities impact these proprietary interests, the state may object in order to protect the value of the property. The other major area of state interest concerns the uniform application of its laws. The state's interests include the collection of revenue, the management of natural resources, and the regulation of business and individual activities. In an attempt to universally apply its laws to all citizens residing within its jurisdiction, the state has resisted the demands of tribal governments to be recognized as separate and independent sovereigns. In addition, the state also represents *parens patriae* interests on behalf of its citizens that often require it to choose between representing the interests of one group over those of another. In some circumstances, the state may not have an explicit interest in how a tribal issue is resolved, only that it be resolved to clarify the uncertainty of

9. State of Washington (1985, 15).

TABLE 8 Summary of State-Tribal Conflicts

Conflict Issue	State's Position
Land Claims	State and private property rights; clarification of property title, public rights of way, and easements
Water Resources	Universal application of laws; liability in granting water rights
Environmental Management	Universal application of laws; "environmental" treaty right
Fish and Game	Natural resource allocation; tribal access across private and state lands
Civil Regulatory	Regulation of non-Indian reservation lands; lack of representation in tribal governance; consistency with statewide land use policies
Taxation	State tax revenue; precedent for tribal civil jurisdiction over non-Indians
Gaming	Regulatory control; revenue competition

Source: Nicholas C. Zaferatos.

a situation. The state's interests in defending its sovereignty and property rights are represented in table 8 in seven major categories of disputes that are common in many tribal-state relationships.

1. Land Claims

Several land claim cases were filed during the past three decades involving claims of tribal ownership to the tidelands adjacent to reservations and to aboriginal land title. The state has expressed the opinion that if these claims are upheld, affected land areas previously thought to be free of Indian title would become encumbered, complicating the current understanding of land title and raising further questions concerning the state's liability in transferring original title to those lands. Many of the land claims instituted by tribes involve lands underlying "navigable waters," including tidelands. In *Montana v. United States*,[10] the Crow Tribe claimed that portions of the Big Horn River located within the Crow Reservation were held in trust for the tribe. The US Supreme Court rejected the claim, holding that the state owned the riverbed, having acquired it under the "equal footing doctrine"[11] upon its admission to the Union in 1889. The court, however, established a general exception to the equal footing doctrine in ruling that when a "public exigency" exists at treaty execution, Congress may depart from its general policy of reserving the ownership of the riverbeds to future states.

In three cases,[12] the Ninth Circuit court, recognizing the tribes' historic dependency upon fishing, held that submerged lands are vested in a tribe rather than the state. This dependency proved to be the basis in supporting the tribes' claims, even though the related treaties lacked an expressed intent to convey the submerged lands to tribal ownership. Several land claims cases are pending or have recently been concluded in the federal courts in Washington.[13] In *Swinomish*,[14] six different cases were consolidated, with the United States and the Swinomish Indian Tribal Community as plaintiffs and the state and various private entities as

---

10. *Montana v. United States*, 450 U.S. 544, 556–57 (1981).

11. The "equal footing doctrine" applies to those states that entered the Union on an "equal footing" with the same rights and powers as the original thirteen. Since the original thirteen states owned the lands beneath navigable waters, subsequent states likewise owned those lands.

12. *Confederated Salish and Kootenai Tribes v. Namen*, 665 F.2d 951 (9th Cir. 1982), involved the south end of Flathead Lake in Montana; *Muckleshoot Indian Tribe v. Trans-Canada Enterprises, Ltd.*, 713 F.2d 455 (9th Cir. 1983), involved the White River in Washington; and *Puyallup Indian Tribe v. Port of Tacoma*, 717 F.2d 1251 (9th Cir. 1983), involved part of a river bed of the Puyallup River in Washington.

13. These cases included the *Suquamish Tribe v. AAM*, No. C82-1549V (W.D. Wash. May 20, 1986); *United States v. Cascade Natural Gas Corp.*, No. C76-550V (W.D. Wash. August 29, 1996), known as the "*Swinomish*" case; and *United States v. Pend Oreille County Public Utility District No. 1*, No. C-80-116-RMB (E.D. Wash. May 25, 1984), known as the "*Kalispel*" case.

14. *United States v. Cascade Natural Gas Corp.*, No. C76-550V (W.D. Wash. August 26, 1996).

defendants.[15] *Swinomish* reached settlement through successful negotiations between the parties,[16] resulting in a right-of-way lease to the pipeline companies and railroad and an option to purchase all remaining properties adjoining the claimed tribal tideland properties, which the tribe subsequently exercised. In the *Swinomish* case, the willingness of the parties to seek amicable settlement was largely motivated by the tribe's interest in securing the properties in question for its long-term security. The tribe believed that even with a favorable court ruling, such long-term objectives remained tenuous, as litigation often results in estranged relations between the parties.

In these and similar cases, the state's interest in land claims reflects its concern with preserving the status quo in private property ownership rights since those rights were previously granted and protected by the state. Further, decisions favoring tribal claims raise liability questions to both the state, which conveyed original title to such lands, and to private title insurance companies that insure the validity of the title, free of encumbrance. Tribal claims to aboriginal and treaty title also include claims to lands whose titles have been conveyed by the state to non-tribal individuals and those treaty-reserved lands subsequently excluded from a reservation by executive order.

2. Water Resources

An ongoing focus in state-tribal discourse is the state's authority in managing the allocation of water rights. At the time reservations were created, the treaties implied sufficient water would be reserved to satisfy the primary purposes of the reservations. The priority date of this federally reserved water right corresponds with the date when the federal reservation was first established. The quantity of the federally reserved water

---

15. Included among the defendants are Burlington Northern, Inc., Cascade Natural Gas, and Transmountain Pipeline Co. Additional defendants included individuals who own alienated reservation lands.

16. The state voluntarily withdrew its participation in the *Swinomish* case in 1986 and did not elect to participate in any of the settlement negotiations, which were left to the tribe and the upland property owners.

right, however, has not been determined for the reservations within the state. The US Supreme Court developed a "reserved rights" doctrine in *Winters v. United States*,[17] referred to as the Winters doctrine, which held that when the United States reserved lands for special purposes, "it impliedly reserved water in sufficient quantities to satisfy the primary purposes for which the lands were set aside, with priority dating back to the establishment of the federal reservation."[18]

Further complicating the water rights dialogue is the tribes' demand to have its proprietary fisheries resources protected from environmental degradation under phase II of the *Boldt* decision.[19] Should the courts uphold tribal claims of insufficient water flows to sustain treaty protected fisheries habitat, fisheries water rights would have a priority date senior to other water rights granted by the state. In a related case, in *Swinomish Indian Tribal Community v. Department of Ecology*, the Washington State Supreme Court ruled that the state's current groundwater exemption standard represented a form of water allocation, which was junior to a water right necessary for sustaining fisheries resources.[20] The history of tribal-state water conflict involves two principal issues: the application of the state's codes within the boundaries of the Indian reservations and the applicability of the state adjudication system to Indian reserved water rights.

Application of State Water Codes within Reservations. Washington State has enacted comprehensive codes covering all phases of water resource management. The surface water code[21] and the groundwater code[22] created permit systems for the right to withdraw and use water to provide certainty in water resource management. These codes also provide

---

17. 207 U.S. 564 (1908).

18. See *Cappaert v. United States*, 426 U.S. 128, 138–42 (1976).

19. *United States v. Washington*, 506 F. Supp. 187 (W.D. Wash. 1980), *en banc* appeal dismissed, No. 91-3111 (9th Cir. Dec. 17, 1984).

20. The ruling is significant as it affects future urban development in the county, which relies on the groundwater exemption to meet the state's requirement for water availability before a development permit can be issued.

21. Wash. Rev. Code 90.03.

22. Wash. Rev. Code 90.44.

for a *general adjudication*[23] of existing water rights granted under common law. The state's water code permit system has been applied to waters within Indian reservations since 1917. The first tribal challenge raised objection to the state's allocation of waters flowing through non-Indian owned lands within the Tulalip Indian Reservation. In 1962, the administrator of the state's code asked the attorney general to clarify the state's policy. This request was made in response to the tribe's assertion that the state had no authority to approve an application for a water right permit within the reservation. In an informal opinion, the attorney general opined that Washington's water right permit system "allowed a non-Indian to divert waters, located on non-Indian lands within an Indian reservation, if those waters exceeded the amounts needed to satisfy prior rights, including the reserved rights of Indians."[24] This analysis of the state's jurisdiction[25] was later upheld in *Tulalip Tribes of Washington v. Walker.*[26]

Several tribes, along with the United States, initiated litigation in the 1970s against individual water users that used water from streams or other watercourses located entirely within or passing through Indian reservations.[27] The state was both a defendant, as a user of water in these actions, and a party, through its regulatory interests. In these cases, the state asserted its jurisdiction to regulate "surplus" or "excess" waters reserved to the tribe under the Winters doctrine. The Ninth Circuit ruled in *Colville* that the state held no jurisdiction because what was involved was a situation "where the watershed was entirely within the boundaries of the Colville Indian Reservation and, therefore, under those facts, the

23. See Wash. Rev. Code 90.03.110–245 and 90.44.220–230.

24. State of Washington (1985, 39).

25. The opinion contradicted an earlier 1928 Attorney General's Office opinion that concluded the state's water rights laws could not be applied within the Colville Indian Reservation because of the preemptive impact of 25 U.S.C. § 381 (Letter of February 28, 1928).

26. No. 71421 (Snohomish Co. Sup. Ct. Feb. 7, 1963).

27. *Colville Confederated Tribes v. Walton*, 647 F.2d 42 (9th Cir. 1981), *aff'g* in part and *rev'g* in part 460 F. Supp. 1320 (E.D. Wash. 1979), *cert. denied*, 454 U.S. 1092 (1981); *United States v. Anderson*, 738 F.2d 1358 (9th Cir. 1984).

state's regulatory jurisdiction was preempted." However, in *Anderson*,[28] the Ninth Circuit held that state water rights may be applied to excess or surplus waters abutting non-Indian lands within an Indian reservation, but the state water rights law does not apply to reservation-restricted streams such as those that arise, flow, and terminate entirely within a reservation.

State Water Rights Adjudications. Having waived its immunity to suit under the McCarran Amendment,[29] the United States has been joined as a defendant in several state general adjudication proceedings. These cases have resulted in quantifying all claims for water rights of the United States, including claims for reserved rights of Indians. These cases have provided a more clear understanding of the complex area of water rights. Three key points follow:

• Washington courts are delegated jurisdiction in determining the validity of reserved rights claimed by the United States in a general adjudication for an Indian tribe or an Indian;[30]

• The United States representation in a general adjudication proceeding, as trustee for a tribe, is binding upon Indian tribes as to the scope and extent of rights quantified for them in such proceedings;[31]

• The disclaimer provisions of the Washington State Constitution and its related federal "enabling act"[32] do not prohibit states from joining the United States, as trustee for an Indian tribe, in a general adjudication proceeding.

28. *United States v. Anderson*, 736 F.2d 1358 (9th Cir. 1984).

29. 43 U.S.C. § 666 (1982).

30. See Yakima river system water rights related decisions in *Dept. of Ecology v. Acquavella*, 131 Wash.2d 746 (Wash. 1997); *Dept. of Ecology v. Yakima Reservation Irrigation District*, 121 Wash.2d 257 (Wash. 1993); *Dept. of Ecology v. Acquavella*, 100 Wash.2d 651 (Wash. 1983).

31. See also *Nevada v. United States*, 463 U.S. 110 (1983); *Arizona v. California*, 460 U.S. 605 (1983).

32. Wash. Const. art. 26, § 2; Enabling Act of 1889, 25 Stat. 676, chs. 180, 276–84 (1889).

Federal Indian reserved rights are established independently from the state water rights system and are generally recognized by the state. These rights have an early date of priority since many reservations were created in the 1850s. The Washington Attorney General's Office (State of Washington 1985, 43) has acknowledged an important distinction in Indian water rights since, unlike state-based rights, they are not lost by nonuse. Therefore, both dormant and unexercised rights remain existent in the state. While several courts have affirmed a *Winters* right for in-stream uses, including fisheries, the quantification and scope of these rights remain unsettled. The question has been advanced in terms of an "environmental treaty right" in the *United States v. Washington* fisheries litigation. The state has maintained that, while it may be possible to reserve a right for fisheries purposes, that right may be limited by a number of factors. These factors take into account the fact that many fisheries have been destroyed by federal dam construction and the exercise of a fishery in-stream right might conflict with the exercise of an irrigation right, which also may have been a constituted purpose of the reservation. Therefore, the state has maintained that an in-stream fishery right must be determined and quantified in conjunction with the overall scope and purpose of the reservation. The state's position reflects an attempt to balance the recognized treaty reserved water rights among the water rights subsequently conveyed to other users under the state's common law. A further complication arises in the transfer of water rights to non-Indian ownership. The ability of a tribe to alter the purposeful use of a reserved right to another use remains problematic. In *Walton*,[33] the Ninth Circuit court ruled, "no change to another use may be made until the reserved right is first exercised for the use for which it was reserved."

In recent decades, tribes in Washington have identified the development of comprehensive resource use and environmental protection policies as important components of their self-governance. Tribal water codes enacted on several reservations generally rely on the tribe's inherent

---

33. *Colville Confederated Tribes v. Walton*, 647 F.2d 42, 46–49 (9th Cir. 1981).

sovereign authority to manage their impliedly reserved water rights. These codes deny the validity of state issued permits relating to any excess waters since quantification of the resource has not yet been adjudicated.

3. Environmental Management

The state of Washington administers comprehensive pollution control programs for air and water pollution, and hazardous waste disposal.[34] Each relevant federal statute requires a comprehensive federal program unless an approved state program is developed and the US Environment Protection Agency (EPA) defers the subsequent delegation of program responsibility. In each program, the EPA has excepted Indian land from the state program. Prior to and following the enactment of these federal statutes, the state has administered its state pollution control laws within the boundaries of Indian reservations. At the time of the adoption of the federal-state comprehensive program, EPA acknowledged such state jurisdiction by approving state water quality standards applicable within a reservation and issuing waste discharge permits to industries within a reservation. It was not until the late 1970s that questions of state authority were challenged, which led to the formulation of the EPA Indian policy. The question of environmental control first arose with a challenge to state jurisdiction on the Muckleshoot and Tulalip Indian reservations. A similar issue was presented to the Ninth Circuit in a jurisdiction challenge by the state against an EPA regulation that denied state jurisdiction over Indian lands in its hazardous waste program. The state had argued that the hazardous waste program, like other pollution control programs, must be administered by a single agency to avoid a situation of "checkerboard jurisdiction." In 1985, the Ninth Circuit issued its landmark decision,[35] holding that the state lacked jurisdiction over Indians on Indian lands.

On November 8, 1984, EPA Administrator William A. Ruckleshaus issued the EPA Indian policy, the first explicit statement of a federal agency

34. Wash. Rev. Code 70.94, 90.48, and 70.105, respectively.

35. *State of Washington v. Environmental Protection Agency*, 752 F.2d 1465 (9th Cir. 1985).

supporting its trust responsibilities under the federal self-determination policy. Since 1984, agency programs and several federal statutes have been amended to support tribal self-determination by providing a procedure for the delegation of those programs to the tribes. The core principle of the policy is its commitment to working with federally recognized tribes on a government-to-government basis in order to enhance environmental protection. In carrying out the EPA's responsibilities on Indian reservations, the policy emphasizes the involvement of tribal governments in making decisions and managing environmental programs that affect reservation lands. The agency's Indian policy is furthered by the adoption of the following guiding principles:[36]

• The agency stands ready to work directly with Indian tribal governments in a "government-to-government" relationship;

• The agency will recognize tribal governments as the primary parties for setting standards, making environmental policy decisions, and managing programs for reservations;

• The agency will take affirmative steps to encourage and assist tribes in assuming regulatory and program management responsibilities for reservation lands;

• The agency will take appropriate steps to remove existing legal and procedural impediments to working directly and effectively with tribal governments on reservation programs;

• The agency will assure that tribal concerns and interests are considered whenever the EPA's actions and/or decisions may affect reservation environments;

• The agency will encourage cooperation between tribal, state and local governments to resolve environmental problems;

• The agency will work with other federal agencies that have responsibilities on Indian reservations in cooperative efforts to help tribes assume environmental program responsibilities for reservations;

36. US Environmental Protection Agency. 1984. "EPA Policy for the Administration of Environmental Programs on Indian Reservations." Washington, DC: US Environmental Protection Agency.

• The agency will strive to assure compliance with environmental statutes and regulations on Indian reservations; and

• The agency will incorporate these Indian policy goals into its planning and management activities and ongoing policy and regulation development processes.

Following the clarification of the EPA policy and subsequent provisions in federal environmental legislation, tribal governance has focused on the development of tribal environmental protection programs and legislation. Several tribes have since been designated "treatment as a state" status, enabling them to proceed with the formulation of reservation environmental protection programs under federal rules. While it is the intent of many tribal programs to operate independent of state program authority, others have sought cooperative agreements with state programs to improve environmental protection on a regional basis.

4. Fish and Game

Washington's fishing dispute involves the three-decade interpretation and implementation of the fishing rights clause contained in the Stevens treaties, which reads: "The right of taking fish, at all usual and accustomed grounds and stations, is further secured to said Indians, in common with all citizens of the territory. . . ." The state issued its first opinion on this clause in 1899,[37] providing an interpretation that emphasized equal access to—rather than a guarantee of an equal apportionment of—the fishery:

> Indians were not discriminated against by the license laws of the state, but they have today all rights that are guaranteed them by the treaty. That is, they have the right to fish at usual and accustomed grounds and stations in common with all citizens of this state. No more, no less.

During the 1950s and 1960s, confrontations arose as Indian fishers engaged in off-reservation net fishing on traditional freshwater fishing

---

37. 1897–1900 Op. Att'y Gen. 102, 103 (Nov. 10, 1899).

grounds, areas that had become prohibited to fishing under state law. To resolve the dispute, the attorney general initiated a "test case"[38] against the Puyallup Tribe and its individual members. The Supreme Court ultimately upheld the exercise of some state authority over treaty Indians, particularly with regards to the state's authority to regulate fishing where "reasonable and necessary for conservation." However, the test case did not conclude the dispute as the litigation and controversy continued. In 1971, the United States filed a declaratory judgment action in the US District Court for the Western District of Washington. The United States argued that the "in common" language mandated the equal division of the harvestable number of salmon and steelhead between Indian and non-Indian fishermen. The intervening tribes claimed an exclusive treaty right to take fish without any restrictions. The state alleged that the treaties did not guarantee an equal allocation right, but rather, provided only for equal access to the fishery. The district court in 1974[39] construed the fishing clause of the treaties to require an allocation of the fishing resource between treaty Indians and other citizens. The allocation was interpreted as "50 percent plus" of the harvestable resource.[40] The district court, however, rejected the tribe's claim to an unrestricted tribal fishery by reaffirming the state authority to regulate for conservation. The court also agreed to retain continuing jurisdiction of the case "to grant such further relief as may be found to be appropriate on motion of any party—and to assure compliance with the judgment entered herein."[41] Following a number of appeals to the Ninth Circuit and the Washington Supreme Court, in 1978

---

38. *Puyallup Tribe v. Department of Game*, 391 U.S. 392 (1968).

39. *United States v. Washington*, 384 F. Supp. 312 (W.D. Wash. 1974).

40. The court-ordered division of fish worked as follows: first, the treaty tribes designated a reservation catch; second, the tribes specified the number of salmon and steelhead that they would take for ceremonial and subsistence fisheries; third, after the reservation, ceremonial and subsistence harvest was subtracted from the total fish available for harvest, the remainder was then divided equally between the treaty Indian fishermen and all other citizens.

41. 384 F. Supp. at 405.

the US Supreme Court agreed to review the major issue of construction of the "in common" fishing language.[42]

In 1979, the Supreme Court decided *Passenger Fishing Vessel*,[43] ruling that the fishing clause required a division of the fishery resource. The allocation previously prescribed was modified to entitle the tribes to less than the "50 percent plus" formula created by the District Court.[44] In addition, 50 percent of the Indian allocation was construed as a maximum allocation subject to further reduction if a lesser amount provided for a "moderate living" for Indians. Since the 1979 opinion, fisheries litigation has been limited to questions about the proper management of the resource. Although litigation in the fisheries area has been highly publicized, the importance of negotiation and cooperation in resolving disputes should be emphasized. The US District Court in *United States v. Washington* required a salmon management plan and established a fisheries advisory board to facilitate the resolution of disputes between the state fishery management agencies and the Indian tribes.

The Environmental Right Dispute. Phase II—In *United States v. Washington*,[45] the intervener tribes contended that they not only had a right to unrestricted fishing, but they also had a right to have the fishery protected from environmental degradation. This issue was reserved by the district court for later resolution. The tribes sought the court's implementation of an environmental impact process that would be triggered whenever a state agency contemplated a state or a private action that could impact the size or quality of a fish run. In *Passenger Fishing Vessel*,

42. *United States v. Washington*, 520 F.2d 676 (9th Cir. 1975), *cert. denied*, 423 U.S. 1086 (1976).

43. *Washington v. Washington State Commercial Passenger Fishing Vessel Ass'n*, 443 U.S. 658 (1979).

44. Ceremonial and subsistence catch were ordered to be included, and harvests by non-residents of Washington taken from Washington State fish runs will not be included as part of the non-Indian share.

45. *United States v. Washington*, 506 F. Supp. 187 (W.D. Wash. 1980), *en banc* appeal dismissed, No. 91-3111 (9th Cir. Dec. 17, 1984).

the district court ruled that such a treaty right exists, but on appeal, the Ninth Circuit modified and withdrew the district court opinion.[46] Since 1984, the environmental right question has continued to be of serious concern to the state and its threat has prompted greater cooperation toward achieving a mediated solution in a variety of habitat protection matters.

Shellfish. While *United States v. Washington* addressed the allocation of the salmon fishery, it did not address the allocation of shellfish. The federal district court[47] did, however, provide:

> In order to be entitled to exercise off-reservation treaty fishing rights to nonanadromous fish and shellfish, any tribe party to this case shall, prior to any attempt to exercise such rights, present prima facie evidence and arguments supporting its claim to treaty entitlement to such nonanadromous fish and shellfish upon which the court may make a preliminary determination as to the tribe's entitlement of such species, pending final determination of tribal treaty-right entitlement to nonanadromous fish and shellfish.

Settlement discussions intended to avoid litigating the shellfish allocation question were entered into by the state, sixteen tribes, and other affected parties in the early 1990s in an attempt to negotiate an acceptable management and allocation plan for the shellfish resource. As the parties were unable to reach agreement, the litigation proceeded in 1994. On December 20, 1994, the district court released its ruling,[48] confirming that treaty tribes have a right to harvest 50 percent of the natural production of shellfish. Two controversial elements of the decision concerned tribal access to commercially cultivated shellfish beds and the tribal right to cross private property to exercise harvest rights. The state had argued that the commercial beds were intended to be excluded from the treaty

---

46. *United States v. Washington*, 694 F.2d 1374 (9th Cir. 1983).

47. *United States v. Washington*, 459 F. Supp. 1020, 1037 (W.D. Wash. 1978).

48. *United States v. Washington*, No. CV-9213, subproceeding no. 89-3 (W.D. Wash. December 20, 1994).

guarantee of equal access to harvestable areas. The court ruled that, while the private harvest of artificial production was not subject to the tribal harvest share, the underlying beds were. Fear that the court would allow tribal access across private properties prompted private property interests to become involved, organizing under the United Property Owners of Washington (UPOW).[49] The court ordered the parties to negotiate and to submit either a jointly agreed upon implementation plan or separate proposals provided that agreement could not be reached.

The outcomes of the long history of natural resources litigation in Washington State illustrate how the mechanism of litigation often mandates effective state-tribal cooperation in natural resource management. Once the pivotal question regarding the extent of proprietary rights becomes established, attention then shifts to concerns for the resource itself, and to ways of cooperatively achieving resource sustainability through best harvest management practices.

5. Tribal Civil Regulation of Non-Indians

The application of tribal civil regulatory authority over non-Indians and fee lands located within the boundaries of a reservation has presented ongoing conflicts in the state-tribal relationship. Since 1970, advancement in tribal organizational capacity has accelerated the exercise of civil jurisdiction over non-Indians by the enactment of laws governing the conduct of businesses on fee land, and the application of zoning and other land use restrictions. The tribes have maintained that their jurisdiction over non-Indians preempts state and local jurisdiction. The state's position has traditionally opposed the assertion of tribal jurisdiction that displaces state regulatory authority.

---

49. UPOW sought to join the litigation and participated in earlier settlement negotiations seeking to prohibit Indians from gaining rights of access across privately held shoreline properties. The organization's membership was originally comprised of on-reservation non-Indian property owners. The shellfish litigation expanded UPOW membership to include off-reservation coastal property owners not previously engaged in issues involving treaty-claimed rights.

The US Supreme Court analyzed tribal-state jurisdictional disputes by applying a preemption test from *McClanahan v. Arizona State Tax Comm'n*,[50] based on the application of tribal regulation to its own members. The test has been broadly interpreted to encompass "the right of reservation Indians to make their laws and be ruled by them"[51] and serves to affirm tribal territorial sovereignty.[52] The Supreme Court has liberally construed the preemption test to favor the federal Indian policy for the expansion of tribal jurisdiction in a number of opinions.[53] However, it has also affirmed concurrent state jurisdiction over certain reservation activities by non-Indians unless expressly preempted by federal law. Because of the origins of tribal sovereignty, the preemption analysis is based on the principle of balancing the competing state, federal, and tribal interests rather than relying merely on congressional intent to preempt state law. This further clarification, referred to as the *particularized inquiry* test, provides for preemption to occur without an express congressional statement. In addition, the courts have ruled that federal approval of tribal ordinances exercising exclusive jurisdiction does not alone confer a delegation of power by Congress.[54] The *particularized inquiry* test, then, requires the courts to balance the interests of each party. If tribal regulation is consistent with prior federal policy and traditional notions of Indian sovereignty, the courts may favor exclusive application of tribal law. The Ninth Circuit Court of Appeals in *Snow v. Quinault Tribe*[55] upheld tribal civil jurisdictional authority over non-Indians on their own lands. Conversely, in *United States v. Anderson*,[56] the court ruled that state regulation applied

---

50. 411 U.S.164 (1973).

51. *Williams v. Lee*, 358 U.S. 217, 219–20 (1958).

52. *New Mexico v. Mescalero Apache Tribe*, 462 U.S. 324 (1983).

53. For example, see *Rice v. Rehner*, 463 U.S. 713 (1983); *White Mountain Apache Tribe v. Bracker*, 448 U.S. 136 (1982); *Montana v. United States*, 450 U.S. 544 (1981).

54. *Washington v. Confederated Tribes of the Colville Indian Reservation*, 447 U.S. 134, 156 (1980).

55. 709 F.2d 1319 (9th Cir. 1983), *cert. denied* 104 S. Ct. 2655 (1984).

56. 736 F.2d 1358 (9th Cir. 1984).

to excess water located on non-Indian lands situated within the Spokane Indian Reservation. The problem in determining the extent of tribal jurisdiction over non-Indians is one of defining the tribal interest in exercising jurisdiction over non-Indians. The subjective nature of the *particularized inquiry* test clouds the extent of state or tribal regulatory power. In general, the federal district courts and the Ninth Circuit Court of Appeals have displayed a tendency to uphold tribal assertions of jurisdiction.

The states' arguments have stressed two principal concerns with regards to the assertion of tribal civil jurisdiction. The first relates to the principle of representation without the right to participate in tribal elections, resulting in non-Indians being subjected to regulation without participating in the electoral process.[57] The second concern deals with the nature of tribal sovereignty itself, which is not subject to the constitutional restrictions and safeguards common to other forms of government. The Indian Civil Rights Act of 1968,[58] however, overcomes many of these concerns by imposing certain statutory restrictions upon tribal governments, including the constitutional guarantees of due process and equal protection. The antagonistic position of the state in challenging virtually every attempt by tribal governments to exercise powers of self-government has contributed to a general sense of distrust in the relationship between these governments.

6. Taxation

State taxation over property owned by Indians on Indian lands has been the subject of conflict since statehood. The earliest Washington Attorney General opinion, issued in 1898, generally recognized that United States laws protect a tribal Indian from taxation, but remained tentative in that position. The state's opinions paralleled this position when a framework to more fully analyze Indian tax questions began to develop

---

57. This exclusionary condition is not dissimilar to the exclusion of resident aliens residing within the United States who also are prevented from certain citizenship privileges.

58. Act of April 11, 1968, Pub. L. 90–284, Title II, 82 Stat. 77 (codified at 25 U.S.C. §§ 1301–03 (1983)).

in the 1900s.[59] In 1906 Attorney General John Atkinson provided a more forceful opinion in advising that Indian lands, together with permanent improvements and personal property, should be subject to state taxation during the trust period of an allotment. This developed into a position that asserted state taxing authority unless expressly preempted by federal law or treaty, an approach that many states generally rely upon to this day.

While the Supreme Court's decision in *Moe v. Confederated Salish and Kootenai Tribes*[60] affirmed the exclusion of state taxation of Indian personal property within a reservation, it raised further questions regarding the state's authority to impose a tax on non-Indians within reservations where a tribal tax on the same transaction already exists. This decision also addressed the state's authority to impose a collection requirement on the tribe. These questions were later addressed in 1980 in *Washington v. Confederated Tribes of the Colville Indian Reservation*,[61] where the court ruled in favor of the state's right to impose its tax, in addition to the tribe's tax, on non-Indians purchasing cigarettes from an Indian vendor within the reservation.

With the concurrent development of tribal government capability and reservation economies, tribes have increasingly relied upon taxation as a means of raising revenues, thereby introducing new forms of conflict between tribal and state taxing systems. The Washington Attorney General's Office has participated as amicus curiae in several cases, asserting that state citizens are immune from the controls of tribal government. In *Merrion v. Jicarilla Apache Tribe*,[62] Washington State's amicus argument did not challenge the power of a tribe to impose a tax on non-Indians, since that power was recognized in *Colville*, but, rather, challenged that

59. For example, in 1901 Attorney General Stratton opined that off-reservation personal property belonging to Indians who have severed tribal relations was subject to tax. The opinion emphasized that there was "no law which exempts from taxation" such property (1901–1902 Op. Att'y Gen. 185 (Sept. 6, 1901)).

60. 425 U.S. 463 (1976).

61. 447 U.S. 134 (1980).

62. Brief of State of Washington as Amicus Curiae in Support of Petition for Writ of Certiorari at 3, *Merrion v. Jicarilla Apache Tribe*, 455 U.S. 130 (1982).

this power was based on the concept of inherent tribal sovereignty.[63] By so arguing, the state asserted a broader interest:

> If this inherent tribal sovereignty argument is accepted, non-members would be subject to the general regulatory power of a tribal government in which they cannot participate. For what is at stake is not just taxing power over non-members, but a broad range of regulatory power including land use controls over non-Indian lands located within a reservation boundary, control over non-Indians fishing and hunting on such lands, and a whole host of other types of regulations.

In the *Merrion* case, the state also argued that adopting the tribe's inherent sovereignty argument would damage the state's proprietary interests in lands within a reservation since a tribe could expel for non-payment of taxes and would have unlimited taxing power. In 1992, the Supreme Court ruled[64] that the state of Washington can impose an ad valorem tax on reservation fee patent land owned by reservation Indians or the tribe itself. Following the *Colville* case, questions involving the state power to tax have been substantially resolved. The major remaining policy issue is the extent to which the state should involve itself in disputes between non-Indians and tribal taxing authorities. The position of the state demonstrates a concern for the imposition of general state civil regulatory authority, which extends beyond matters of tax revenues to questions regarding the control over the use of the reservation land base itself.

7. Gaming

Indian tribes have expanded their reservation economies through gaming activities during the past two decades, resulting in a new arena of state-tribal conflict and a series of complex litigation. The gambling cases largely rely on the distinction in the state gambling statutes between activities

---

63. This interest also was expressed in the amicus brief to the court in *Snow v. Quinault Indian Nation*, 709 F.2d 1319 (9th Cir. 1983), *cert. denied*, 104 S. Ct. 2655 (1984).

64. *County of Yakima et al. v. Confederated Tribes and Bands of the Yakima Indian Reservation*, 502 U.S. 251 (1992).

that are generally permitted under a *civil/regulatory* test, and activities prohibited under a *criminal/prohibitory* test. Early litigation involved the state's challenge to tribal operation of bingo games where the courts concluded that a state's gaming laws constituted *civil/regulatory* laws. Under such distinction, the court concluded[65] that since the state's public policy permits certain forms of gambling such as bingo, the states were merely in disagreement with the tribes over the range of restrictions imposed on gaming regulations rather than over the permissibility of the activity.

In 1988, Congress intervened in tribal gaming activities in order to provide a framework by which tribes and states could negotiate agreements governing the conduct of certain types of gaming that might encourage economic development in Indian country. The Indian Gaming Regulatory Act of 1988 (IGRA) established three separate classes of gaming. Class I include traditional gaming activities that have historically been practiced by the tribes. These were permitted to continue without any interference by federal or state laws. Class II defines non-pari-mutuel and non-house banking wagering such as bingo and pull tabs, which require compliance with federal laws, but preclude the imposition of state laws. Class III includes all other games, including house betting casino table games and electronic betting devices, such as slot machines. Under the IGRA, tribes are required to negotiate a class III compact with the state, which, as occurred in Washington State, establishes limitations on the scope, number, and types of allowable games, hours of operation, and wagering limits. A feature of the legislation is its provision to foster cooperation by both the state and the tribes in regulatory oversight of the gaming activity.

Tribal-State Mediating Structures

Negotiation can be a successful approach for conflict resolution when all parties are able and willing to negotiate, particularly when the number of parties and range of issues are limited. Negotiations become increasingly complex and difficult when a number of parties and diverse interests are involved. The divided nature of the individual parties presents a further

---

65. *California v. Cabazon Band of Indians*, 480 U.S. 202 (1987).

problem in negotiation. The United States, represented by several agencies, may represent varied interests. When the state of Washington negotiates an issue, it similarly represents several interests as a landowner, a sovereign, and a representative for private individuals. The state's recent position has largely been one of balancing the dual approaches of litigation and negotiation. While past litigation has served to clarify some issues, often at great expense and by incurring animosity among the parties, litigation has also led to court rulings that have essentially required states to cooperate with tribes. The following section examines the effectiveness of recent experiences under the state's current Indian policy that promotes cooperation as the preferred approach for resolving state-tribal conflicts. As established in the 1989 Centennial Accord, the approach calls for an equal footing between the two governments.

Mediating structures are important for fostering resolution of tensions between institutions and, particularly, in dynamic social settings that are characterized by social and cultural plurality. The search for effective forms of conflict resolution to the historic divisions that exist in tribal and non-tribal relations, as alternatives to litigation, begins with finding ways to encourage meaningful dialogue among the participants. The term *mediating structures* (Ackoff 1984) describes the mechanisms that are necessary for fostering communication with the purpose of resolving conflict. As a way of mediating differences between tribal communities and the interests that are external to those communities, a commitment to effective dialogue, that promotes mutual understanding of the conflict, must first be established.

The formulation of Washington State's Indian policy emerged following the landmark Supreme Court decision in *United States v. Washington*. In an attempt to reach agreement for the implementation of the fisheries decision, the Court mandated that the state and the tribes cooperate. New forms of dialogue were urged by the Court, which launched the parties into a newfound method of dispute resolution to resolve the question of fisheries co-management. The approach used in fisheries co-management formed the basis for cooperation in other areas of public policy management and governmental relations with the tribes. Eventually, the cooperative process became institutionalized through a formal process of agreement making.

The dramatic shift in intergovernmental relations between the state and Washington Indian tribes began in the early 1980s with the mutual acceptance of the Comprehensive Cooperative Resource Management principles (CCRM). The principles are based on the recognition that natural resources cannot be managed in isolation from other resource management approaches. This method has resulted in institutional changes that affect the nature of the political, social, and economic relationships between the various interests in resource management, including the tribes, state, and federal governments, industry, the environmental community, and the general public. CCRM operates on the view that cooperation, not litigation, is the best way to resolve management resource issues (NWIFC 1991, B189), where emphasis is placed on discovering common ground upon which to build agreement. The process emphasizes a separation between participant group needs from entrenched group positions, and problems and opportunities are collectively identified in order to form a unified basis for agreement. CCRM was successfully extended to many areas of resource dispute resolution, as follows:

Cooperative Fisheries Management

Seeking to redress and implement the provisions of the Stevens Treaties guaranteeing the tribes' reserved rights to fish, *United States v. Washington* established the tribes as co-managers of the resource. Because of the continued resistance by both the state and tribes to overcome adversary positions, the federal court assumed direct management of the fishery resource. In 1984, a tribal-state plan for cooperative management of fisheries in Puget Sound was finally jointly developed and approved by the federal court, which effectively replaced the role of the court with the direct participation of the tribes. The successful CCRM approach first applied to fishers co-management quickly spread to include other areas of state-tribal resource cooperation.

The Pacific Salmon Treaty

CCRM was expanded to include tribal-state negotiations with Canada over the mutual interception of fish stocks. In 1985, through the cooperation of the tribes, the state, sport and commercial fishing groups, federal fisheries agencies, and others, the Pacific Salmon Treaty was established. The Pacific Salmon Commission was formed by the United States and Canadian governments to implement the treaty and to provide regulatory recommendations to each country. The Commission includes direct representation by tribal leaders.

Watershed Planning

In 1986, the CCRM approach was extended by the tribes and the state to the management and enhancement of salmon fisheries using a watershed-by-watershed approach. Watershed planning began through a joint intergovernmental educational effort to involve broad fisheries interests. The process, which included a participant list of more than 10,000 individuals, resulted in recommendations for an enhancement program. The enhancement projects sought to resolve key problems that were identified as contributing to the depressed natural salmon stocks. Sub-regional planning teams were organized to develop comprehensive resource production and management plans for each drainage area in an effort to advance the watershed planning approach.

Timber Fish and Wildlife Agreement

No effort has embodied the principles of CCRM more than the landmark 1987 Timber, Fish and Wildlife Agreement[66] (TFW). Following more than a decade of litigation among timber landowners, tribes, environmental organizations and state natural resource agencies, the TFW has been referred to as "a historical New Deal for Washington forests."[67] The agreement introduced an inclusive process for public policy management of state and privately held forestlands and a new institutional culture in natural resources policy (Halbert and Lee 1990). The TFW process represented a policy shift toward government-to-government cooperation with tribes

66. Washington State Department of Natural Resources. *Timber, Fish and Wildlife Agreement: A Better Future in our Woods and Streams, Final Report.* 1987. Olympia: Washington State Department of Natural Resources (hereafter cited in text as *TFW*).

67. *Seattle Times.* 1986. "Timber Fish Wildlife Agreement Offers New Way to Manage State Forests." August 22, A22.

in an effort to end the history of conflict. After identifying the central controversial issues, a consensus-based mediation was sought, predicated on the willingness of the participants to attempt face-to-face negotiations. These negotiations, which occurred during a six-month period, involved approximately sixty meetings (TFW, 1). The meetings resulted in the Timber, Fish and Wildlife Agreement of 1987, entered into by representatives of twenty-four separate parties, including treaty tribes, state agencies, the timber industry, environmental groups, and the mediators. Of concern to the tribes were issues that included the protection of fisheries habitats by extending the tribes' property rights interests under phase II of the *Boldt* decision and the protection of tribal cultural resources from timber harvest practices. The TFW process addressed tribal concerns by providing greater access by the tribes to forest practices review and approval procedures and through the recognition of the importance to protect cultural and archaeological resources in off-reservation areas.

The politics supporting the TFW negotiations are referred to as *pluralistic* in that the initially deadlocked position of the parties served to equalize the power of each party. McFarland (1987) suggests that the TFW process resembled aspects of pluralistic theory where the participants represented three distinct sets of actors: a "governmental agency," represented by the Washington State Department of Natural Resources; an economic producer, represented by the timber industry; and "countervailing groups," which expressed opposition to certain goals of the economic producers. The latter group was comprised of the tribes, the environmental community, and non-timber state agencies. According to pluralistic theory, controversy tends to result in a sequence of conflicts that then prompts a cycle of reform. Similarly, the successes of the TFW emerged from a history of litigation and the responsive intervention by the governor, the state legislature, tribal governmental leaders, and the leadership from the business community.[68]

---

68. In the cycle of reform, according to pluralist theory, the rising power of countervailing groups enhances the autonomy of the governmental agency. Before the TFW, the Washington State Department of Natural Resources was widely viewed as the representative

Sustainable Forestry Roundtable

In the late 1980s, the State Department of Natural Resources sought the assistance of tribal governments and other participants of the TFW process to establish a cooperative effort known as the Sustainable Forestry Roundtable. It was intended as an extension of the TFW process to address issues brought by the Forest Practices Board, local governments, and other interest groups in the state. Following eighteen months of discussions, a draft legislative and regulatory proposal was developed that provided for direct tribal participation in the implementation of the agreement. The legislature, however, declined to enact the proposal.

Environmental Memorandum of Understanding

To further the commitment of the state and the tribes to cooperative approaches to resource and environmental problem solving, in 1989 an environmental memorandum of understanding (MOU) was developed. The MOU outlined the general tribal objectives relating to the enhancement and net gain in the productive capacity of fish and wildlife habitats. The protection and conservation of the productive capacity of habitats, and the restoration and enhancement of damaged habitats, as well as mitigation techniques, were identified by the tribes as the principal means of achieving this goal. The state's commitment in the MOU acknowledges the sovereignty of the tribes and pledges to work under the government-to-government basis. The approach, based on the principles of CCRM, is another example of the commitment to cooperation for solving intergovernmental resource-based issues in Washington State.

Water Resource Planning: Chelan Agreement

In 1990, a water resources planning retreat was held at Rosario Resort on Washington's Orcas Island and was attended by 175 leaders who

---

of the timber companies (Halbert and Lee 1990, 143). As a result of the process, the agency regained an autonomous position balanced by the interests and participation of the countervailing groups. McFarland (1987) observed how the institutionalization of countervailing power in the TFW process provided an effective substitute for judicial conflict.

represented various constituencies in water resources. After three days of initial negotiation, an interim team, consisting of representatives of seven caucuses, was created to outline a framework for a cooperative water resources planning process to balance the competing statewide interests in water resources. In a following retreat held at Lake Chelan, the Chelan Agreement was produced that outlined the basic goals and principles for cooperative water resource planning. The goals incorporated the primary concern of the tribes regarding their long-term policy objective of achieving an overall net gain in the productive capacity of fish and wildlife habitats. The process, which provided for demonstration projects involving two watersheds continues to address the complex issues relating to the allocation of water resources in Washington State.

Puget Sound Water Quality Management

Treaty tribes were further recognized as important participants in the efforts to protect and enhance the water quality of Puget Sound. In 1985, in recognition of tribal interests, the Washington State legislature created the Puget Sound Water Quality Authority (PSWQA) and designated a seat on the authority for tribal representation. This provided for direct tribal involvement and decision-making regarding the broad programs and policy recommendations that affect state water quality public policy.

The Centennial and Millennium Accords

On August 4, 1989, Governor Gardner and the federally recognized tribes signed the 1989 Centennial Accord outlining the implementation of the government-to-government relationship. Based on the cooperative intergovernmental approach that was successful in fisheries and natural resources management, the intent of the accord was to formalize the cooperative relationship and encourage its use in other areas. As part of a new philosophy based on mutual respect, the resulting policy established a government-to-government relationship to address complex problems. Natural resource management, social welfare concerns, economic development, and issues of governmental jurisdictional cooperation that had not previously been addressed were incorporated into this new approach. The accord required the state and the tribes to periodically establish goals for improved services and to identify obstacles in achieving those goals. The accord committed both the state and tribal governments to a process of accountability. The accord also required each state agency to initiate a procedure to implement the government-to-government policy and a plan of accountability. The parties later entered into the Millennium Accord in 1999. Its intent was to institutionalize the government-to-government relationship by establishing a compact to implement the terms of the Centennial Accord on a day-to-day basis.

DNR Tribal Policy

Consistent with the Centennial Accord, in 1991 the Department of Natural Resources issued its independent tribal policy recognizing the sovereign status of the state's federally recognized Indian tribes. The policy commits the department to conducting relations with tribes as one government to another. The policy also establishes a procedure for resolving mutual issues and concerns with the tribes at the lowest organizational level of governmental authority and directs department executives and managers to meet regularly with their respective tribal counterparts for the purposes of discussing mutual concerns that require priority attention and staffing by the department. The policy further states that the department is committed to "more fully understand and appreciate the unique values and cultures represented by the tribes" (Washington State Department of Natural Resources 1991).

Institutions for Mediation:
The NRRC and Regional Cooperation

The Northwest Renewable Resources Center (NRRC) emerged in 1984 to assist various Washington State interests in resolving disputes regarding renewable resource management. The NRRC was formed by the tribes and business leaders to help resource users, managers, and conservationists resolve disputes over renewable resources through the negotiation process. The catalyst leading to the creation of the NRRC was phase II of the *Boldt* decision. The tribes held the view that treaty fishing rights become meaningless if the habitat supporting fisheries is diminished.

The affected tribes had therefore interpreted their fishing rights to extend also to the right of habitat protection. In 1987 the courts concurred that government has a "duty to prevent the degradation of the habitat to an extent that will deprive the tribes of their moderate living needs."[69] The ruling also prevented the state from subordinating the tribal fishing right to other purposes. As a political strategy for resolving concerns relating to the effect of a phase II ruling, the Northwest Water Resources Committee[70] identified four options. The first two options considered judicial action and legislative and congressional intervention, both of which, it was concluded, were too risky and expensive to pursue. The third option, that of maintaining the status quo, risked subjecting future resource questions to the court's further test on impacts to fisheries habitats, and was likewise regarded as being too risky. The fourth and preferred option outlined a comprehensive political strategy containing four stages:

• The creation of a new arrangement providing for tribal participation in current governmental decision-making;

• A series of negotiations aimed at resolving specific issues related to natural resource policy;

• The development of fisheries protection and development programs to broaden the responsibility for fisheries enhancement; and

• Assurance that governmental fisheries agencies manage salmon harvest to provide a safe margin of allocation to meet the tribe's expectation for increased harvest.

The NRRC was founded on the belief that deadlocks over natural resources policy can be constructively addressed through direct communication between adversaries to facilitate their search for common

---

69. *United States v. Washington.*

70. The Washington State business community formed the Northwest Water Resources Committee as a party in *United States v. Washington.* The recommendations prepared for the committee were contained in the report "*U.S. v. Washington,* Phase II: Analysis and Recommendations" (Gordon, Thomas, Honeywell, Malanca, Peterson, and O'Hern 1981).

ground. The need for a neutral convener in such deliberations defined the NRRC's principal role. NRRC's formation resulted from the problem-solving approach sought by the Northwest Water Resources Committee and the tribes in discussions exploring alternative ways to resolve long-standing natural resources disputes. Unlike traditional forms of mediation, the NRRC was formed as a coalition of members from the business, environmental, and tribal communities to help resolve disputes in the renewable resource arena. By focusing on broad problems and within a process for generating legislative objectives, the NRRC acted as a body for generating policy. The NRRC's neutral forum was also recognized by the Washington Department of Fisheries when it requested its facilitation in breaking the fisheries management deadlock with the tribes. That dispute had created a litigation free-for-all that threatened to involve other resource policy issues in an endless series of litigation.

The first high profile project undertaken by the NRRC dispute resolution approach focused on the management of Indian and non-Indian salmon harvest in the state. As a result of the NRRC mediation, the Washington Department of Fisheries and the treaty tribes have since successfully co-managed the state's salmon runs. Under co-management, both the state and the tribes share the responsibility for conservation. Another project of the NRRC, The Long Live the Kings Project, responded to the decline of king (or chinook) salmon by constructing a series of short-term enhancement projects to rebuild the degraded runs of wild salmon. The approach focused on building broad consensus about the need for wild salmon enhancement. The successes of these two early projects prompted the NRRC involvement in other environmental policy and land use mediations involving the tribes.

Extending the principles of intergovernmental cooperation to the local level, several important efforts aimed at establishing cooperative institutional relationships between tribal and local governments have also occurred. The three-year "Tribes and Counties: Intergovernmental Cooperation Project" assisted tribal, county, and regional governments in establishing a number of cooperative problem-solving processes that have addressed a spectrum of complex jurisdictional issues ranging from land use and environmental regulation to taxation and service delivery. Table

9[71] summarizes several of the efforts undertaken in developing intergovernmental cooperation among local and tribal governments and agencies in Washington State[72] and illustrates the growing trend that emphasizes cooperative approaches in intergovernmental dispute resolution.

Conclusion and Implications for Planning

The negotiated approach to natural resources conflict resolution between tribes and the state of Washington necessitated a broader public policy response that opened avenues for tribal participation in many new areas of state-tribal interaction. The experiences depicted illustrate the process of tribal political development that began with the assertions of treaty rights and evolved into utilitarian and cooperative relations for resolving long-standing disputes related to fisheries management and environmental protection. The experiences are illustrated in figure 9, demonstrating the application of the tribal planning model presented in chapter 7.

While these experiences were motivated by the tribes' interests to protect off-reservation tribal treaty rights under the regulatory authority of the state, the process was later expanded under the Comprehensive Cooperative Resource Management model to demonstrate its effectiveness in forging agreements for the resolution of both on-reservation and off-reservation issues involving state and local governments. The approach is particularly prevalent in reservations that exhibit a high degree of incorporation, as exemplified by most of the Puget Sound area tribes that contain alienated land holdings and which elect to participate in the intergovernmental negotiation process. The ensuing dialogues, fostered by the negotiated approach, encourage the development of social learning among its participants. The examples illustrated in these cooperative agreements represent a progression in state-tribal organizational development that reached an institutional pinnacle when tribes and the state approved the

71. Adapted from Northwest Renewable Resources Center (NRRC), 1992, "A Short Course on Tribal-County Intergovernmental Coordination," NRRC Tribes and Counties: Intergovernmental Cooperation Project, Seattle, WA: NRRC.

72. Several of these cooperative projects also involved the participation of federal, state, and regional governments, and private and public groups.

TABLE 9 Tribal-Local Government Cooperation since 1980

Project	Tribal-Local Participants	Purpose
West Point Secondary Treatment Upgrade Project	Suquamish and Muckleshoot Indian Tribes; Seattle Metro	Effort to identify project impacts, design, and implementation of mitigation relating to marine habitat issues
Columbia River Gorge National Scenic Area Management Plan	Yakima Indian Nation, Nez Perce Tribe, Warm Springs Tribe; USDA Forest Service; counties	The Columbia River Gorge Commission charged to protect cultural resources and treaty rights in the Columbia River Gorge National Scenic Area
Puyallup Lands Settlement Agreement	Puyallup Indian Tribe; Port of Tacoma; Pierce County; the Cities of Tacoma, Fife, and Puyallup	Agreement resolving a long-standing land claim by the tribe and established a trust fund for environmental enhancement, economic development, and training programs
Snohomish County Aquatic Resource Protection Program	Tulalip Tribes; Snohomish County	Program to develop wetlands protection measures
Seattle Water Department relations with Muckleshoot Indian Tribe	Muckleshoot Indian Tribe; the city of Seattle; Seattle Water Department	Development of long-term agreements supporting tribal fisheries protection objectives
Lake Roosevelt Forum	Colville Confederated Tribes; Spokane Tribe; county, state, and federal agencies	Established mutual approaches to cooperative regional planning in the Lake Roosevelt region

TABLE 9 Tribal-Local Government Cooperation since 1980 (*cont.*)

Project	Tribal-Local Participants	Purpose
Skokomish Tribe-Mason County Government-to-Government Agreement	Skokomish Indian Tribe; Mason County	Memorandum of understanding (MOU) approving a cooperative government-to-government relationship to minimize jurisdictional conflict
Seattle City Light; Skagit River Agreement	Upper Skagit; Sauk-Suiattle; Swinomish Indian Tribal Community; Seattle City Light	Agreement providing $100 million for mitigation as a condition to the Federal Energy Regulatory Commission relicensing of three dams on the Skagit River
The Swinomish-Skagit Joint Comprehensive Plan	Swinomish Indian Tribal Community; Skagit County	MOUs guiding a process for joint land use planning—hailed as a landmark in tribal-county coordination
Indian Land Tenure and Economic Development Project	Swinomish Indian Tribal Community; Quinault Indian Nation; Skagit County; Clallam County	Two MOUs approved for tribal-local government cooperation in land use and timber management
Hood Canal Coordinating Council	Port Gamble S'Klallam and Skokomish Indian Tribes; Kitsap, Mason, and Jefferson counties	Process of policy coordination for protection and restoration of Hood Canal waterways

Source: Nicholas C. Zaferatos.

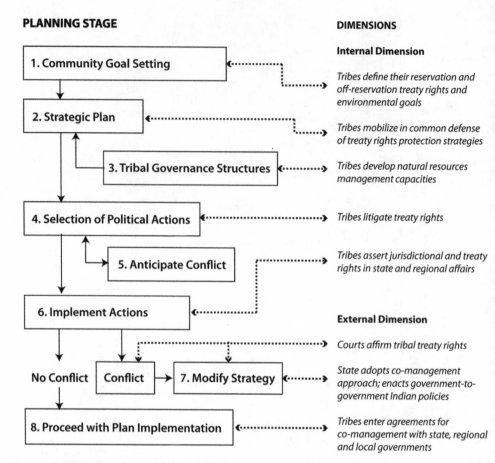

9. Tribal planning model depicting the negotiative approach.

Centennial Accord. The agreement formally brought to a close a 100-year period of adversity and conflict with the state's acknowledgment of the political sovereignty of tribal governments. These experiences also serve to illustrate the process of institutionalizing the cooperative approach through its horizontal application across agencies of state government, as well as its vertical application to involve federal, state, and local government relationship-building with tribal governments. The precedent favoring negotiated solutions through expanded and inclusive dialogue may offer a pathway to the long-sought reconciliation of other types of historic conflict posed by the external forces of the political economy.

9

Regional Pluralism

The Skagit Valley Experience

COOPERATION BETWEEN LOCAL GOVERNMENTS can produce greater efficiencies in the provision of local government services (Bardach 1994; Nye, Zelikow, and King 1997; Zegans 1990). Coordination of government policies can also reduce jurisdictional conflicts and help attain a unified regional development policy that is especially necessary for the achievement of a community's goals (Altshuler and Behn 1997; Bardach 1998; Bunnell 1997; Howitt and Bromling 1998; Riffle 2000). Many states encourage local governments to voluntarily create joint plans for economic growth, land use, transportation, and other aspects of regional planning.[1] In 1990, Washington State mandated local government cooperation when it enacted the Growth Management Act (Wash. Rev. Code § 26.70A). The act requires local land use plans to be consistent with adjoining local jurisdictions, creating a requisite for intergovernmental cooperation. While cooperation among counties and municipalities has progressed in Washington State during the past two decades, less progress has been made in improving the coordination of planning with Washington's tribal governments.

One of the most perplexing problems facing regional cooperation in Washington State lies in the relationship between local governments,

---

1. Wisconsin's intergovernmental cooperation law requires local governments within metropolitan areas to sign compact agreements with neighboring municipalities or counties for the provision of joint public services (Wisconsin Statutes ch. 66, subch. III: Intergovernmental Cooperation, §§ 66.0301–66.0315).

which derive their authority to plan from the state, and tribal nations, whose authority emerges from their own inherent sovereignty and who are not subject to state planning laws (Cornell and Kalt 1992; Frizzel 1974; Sutton 1991). Further complicating the situation is the fact that local governments have historically applied their own policies within tribal reservations, policies that have often conflicted with tribal policies (Cornell 1984; Deloria 1985; Johnson 1988). Adding to the confusion is the absence of a clear directive in Washington's planning legislation that requires or even encourages local governments to coordinate their plans with neighboring tribes. The differences that exist between tribal and non-tribal community goals can often result in regional conflict.[2] Litigation is often the result of such conflicts, further frustrating efforts towards a consistent and unified regional planning vision (Gardner 1980; O'Connell 1983; Scott 1982; Zaferatos 2004b). This chapter examines the case of one Washington tribe, the Swinomish Indian Tribal Community, whose reservation is located in western Washington on the Salish Sea.[3] Figure 10 shows the location of the Swinomish Indian Reservation and its surrounding local jurisdictions. A brief history of regional conflict is followed by a discussion of the approaches used by the tribe to achieve inter-jurisdictional coordination in the Skagit region.

Origins of Regional Conflict

The causes of regional conflicts between Washington's tribes and state and local governments arose more than a century ago when events occurred that permanently altered the character of many Indian reservations. As discussed more fully in previous chapters, the General Allotment Act of 1887, which allowed for the subdivision and sale of Indian lands, made both the occupancy of reservation lands by non-Indians and

---

2. Conflicts among tribes also exist, especially regarding treaty fishing rights (Olson 1990; Cohen 1986; Deloria 1973).

3. The Salish Sea consists of a network of coastal waterways located between southern British Columbia, Canada, and northwestern Washington State. Its major water bodies include the Strait of Georgia, the Strait of Juan de Fuca, and Puget Sound.

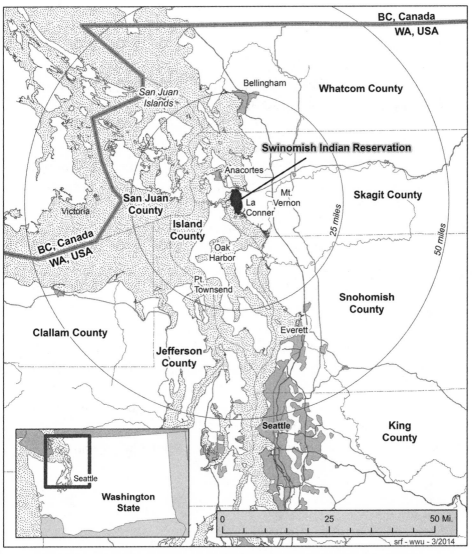

10. Swinomish Indian Reservation and surrounding region. Stefan Freelan, Western Washington University, 2014.

the imposition of non-tribal government authority over those lands possible. The tribes of the Salish Sea region each depict varying forms of "incorporation"[4] as reflected in their reservation land tenure conditions (Sutton 1975, 1991). Highly incorporated reservations contain "alienated" fee lands that were sold out of federal trust ownership and a large population of non-Indian residents. The Puget Sound area tribes' combined reservation population of approximately 68,000 is composed of about 15 percent Indians and 85 percent non-Indians.[5] The need to address questions concerning a tribe's ability to maintain its political authority in reservations whose demographics exhibit such a large proportion of non-tribal members is evident.

Conflicts between tribal and non-tribal governments in Washington State are complex and have led to decades of continuing litigation, as was previously described. Recently, the focus of Indian litigation in Washington State has shifted away from treaty fishing rights that were dominant in the 1970s to concerns of tribal land claims, land use regulation, water rights, and the management of natural resources. Civil jurisdictional disputes have occurred in the regulation and appropriation of reservation water resources (Dufford 1979), the application of tax laws (Clow 1991), and the imposition of state and local government land use and environmental regulations within the exterior boundaries of the reservations (Weaver 1990; Williams 1992a, 1992b).[6] These issues pose new challenges that affect the interests of the tribes, the state and local governments, as

---

4. "Incorporation" refers to the history of state and the political economy's infringement upon tribal sovereignty and reservation lands and natural resources. See chapter 5.

5. US Census, 2000. See chapter 8.

6. On September 18, 2002, the US Court of Appeals for the Ninth Circuit upheld tribal land use jurisdiction over reservation fee simple lands held by an individual Indian person. See *Gobin and Madison v. Snohomish County v. The Tulalip Tribes of Washington*, 304 F.3d 909 (9th Cir. 2002). The court affirmed that by making this person's fee lands freely alienable and encumberable, Congress did not expressly authorize county jurisdiction over those lands, nor did exceptional circumstances warrant that county jurisdiction would apply.

well as non-Indian owners of reservation property. A unique characteristic of reservation governance is that non-Indians residing within reservations are not entitled to participate in the election of the tribal governments that enact reservation laws. The situation becomes particularly problematic when non-members constitute a majority of the reservation population. Reservation land tenure conditions, therefore, have served as a catalyst for the imposition of state and county jurisdiction in reservation affairs.

Resolution of the historic divisions in the relationships between tribes and non-tribal governments requires new ways of forming meaningful working relationships. In order to mediate jurisdictional disputes, and as a procedure for developing intergovernmental policy reform, a meaningful dialogue is first needed in order to learn about the divergent interests and values that exist in tribal and surrounding non-Indian communities (Ambler 1992; Kauger, Du Bey, and Mankiller 1990; National Conference of State Legislatures 1989; Northwest Renewable Resources Center 1993, 1997). By the early 1980s, the state's approach to resolving conflicts with tribes had shifted to emphasize negotiation[7] as an alternative to litigation.[8] The trend toward negotiated solutions evolved further under the 1989 Centennial Accord agreement, which proclaimed a government-to-government relationship as the basis of the state's tribal policy (State of Washington 1989a, 1989b). Although the new policy relationship was motivated by the need to address Indian interests in the management of fisheries resources, the process was also suitable for resolving local and regional conflicts ranging from inconsistencies in regional planning and public service delivery to the long-sought after reconciliation of on-reservation land use conflicts.

7. See chapter 8. The formation of the new approach in tribal-non-tribal relations in Washington State emerged following the landmark Supreme Court decision in *United States v. Washington* in which the court essentially mandated that Washington State and the tribes cooperate in natural resources management.

8. While the benefits of negotiation often outweigh the costs of litigation, other circumstances may preclude the parties from accepting compromises, such as in cases where neither the state nor a tribe may concede its sovereign rights to control land.

Forming an Intergovernmental Working Relationship

According to a survey of tribal and country planning departments in Washington State,[9] several obstacles impede the coordination of land use planning by tribes and local governments. The survey identified three categories of obstacles that needed to be overcome before improved coordination could occur (Doering 1992): (1) differences in planning approaches, (2) differences in community cultures, and (3) jurisdictional obstacles. The survey found differences in the manner in which county and tribal planning priorities were established. The survey respondents acknowledged that fundamental cultural differences were manifested in county and tribal policies and agreed that these differences needed to be better understood in order to avoid misrepresentations that would most likely result if they were ignored. Tribal respondents emphasized the importance of recognizing the legitimacy of tribal sovereignty as the most important problem that required reconciliation before intergovernmental coordination could successfully proceed. County respondents expressed frustration over the tribal tendency to emphasize issues of sovereignty and rights guaranteed by treaty, while it was important to tribes to establish a relationship based on the Centennial Accord's government-to-government principles and were therefore frustrated by the tendency of counties to treat tribes as special-interest groups.

The survey also identified an important difference in the interpretation of the *Brendale* decision.[10] Most county planners interpreted the decision as an affirmation of county jurisdiction over non-Indian owned fee lands on the reservation. Respondents from tribes conversely interpreted the decision as a general affirmation of a tribe's reservation authority unless reversed by the courts, as happened in one section of the Yakima

9. The survey was conducted in 1992 by the Northwest Renewable Resources Center and included all eighteen Washington counties that contained Indian reservation and twenty-five federally recognized tribes in Washington State.

10. *Brendale v. Confederated Tribes and Bands of Yakima Indian Nation*, 492 U.S. 408 (1988).

case[11] due to reservation-specific circumstances. County planners also indicated a concern for the growing political pressure from non-Indian constituents living on reservations who demanded that the county apply its full jurisdictional authority, as they felt underrepresented in tribal decision-making processes. County planners also indicated frustration when attempting to involve formal tribal participation in the review of their planning proposals that were subject to mandated deadlines. Frustration resulted when tribal input was either received after the public comment period was closed or was not received at all. Since a tribe exercises its planning authority under its own inherent powers, tribal planning priorities, schedules, and procedures differ from those of local planning agencies operating under state rules. Tribal planners were equally frustrated by the county's presumption of jurisdiction within reservation boundaries, given the establishment of legal precedent that precludes a state's general preemption of tribal authority. Although both groups of planners indicated support for improved coordination with their counterpart planning agencies, they felt powerless to overcome the pervasive disparities of their respective planning systems. The survey suggested several measures to help overcome the barriers in tribal-county relationships:

Regular Meetings. Tribal and county planners identified the importance of establishing regular meetings among planning staff. Regular meetings would help planners stay informed about current issues affecting their jurisdictions and build trust by learning more about each agency's priorities.

Continuing Education. Tribal and county planners recognized the need for mutually gaining knowledge about county and tribal governing systems, Indian policy history, cultural and community development priorities, and new approaches for establishing intergovernmental cooperation for addressing inconsistencies in land use policies.

---

11. In *Brendale*, the courts affirmed the tribe's jurisdiction over non-members in the Brendale section of the case, but affirmed the county's jurisdiction in the Wilkinson section of the case.

Meetings of Elected Officials. Regular meetings between elected officials were noted as a necessary first step for establishing long-term cooperative relationships. Without the explicit support of elected officials, it was felt that staff level relationships would be limited.

Formal and Informal Agreements. Agreements, it was noted, are important steps for institutionalizing a continuing working relationship between tribal and county planning agencies. Memoranda of understanding and interagency procedures were determined to be necessary for guiding a coordination process.

The survey of planning professionals provided useful insights into the problems experienced by government planning agencies, especially as planners are often called upon to recommend strategies for overcoming policy and jurisdictional conflict. There was overwhelming support for increased cooperation by county and tribal planners and a willingness to

11. Aerial view, Swinomish Indian Reservation. With permission of the Swinomish Indian Tribal Community Archive.

establish a government-to-government relationship as a way to overcome historic conflict.

The Case of the Swinomish Indian Tribal Community

One of the most noteworthy differences between tribal and non-tribal cultures concerns long-standing attitudes toward land stewardship and land ownership. Where non-Indian society generally views land as a commodity, and incorporates this view within a general system of individual ownership and property rights operating under free market economies, Native Americans almost uniformly emphasize the importance of communal ownership and uses of land (Roberts 1975). The 1855 Treaty of Point Elliott set aside the Swinomish Indian Reservation as a permanent homeland for exclusive and collective tribal use. Like most other reservations, the Swinomish tribe was severely impacted by the effects of the 1887 General Allotment Act, which ignored the important cultural value of collective land ownership and use. Over time, as Indians on the reservation were granted individual allotments of land, the allotments eventually became sold to non-Indians as a result of non-use or were lost, due to nonpayment of state imposed taxes, which many Indian families could not afford to pay. The process of reservation land division and alienation occurred over a relatively short period of a few decades and produced the current checkerboard pattern of reservation land ownership, which is currently comprised of approximately 45 percent alienated, fee simple land holdings.

Despite recent social, political, and economic development gains that have partially been attributed to supportive federal Indian self-determination policies and programs, the economic conditions on the Swinomish Indian Reservation continue to be depressed. Consequently, establishing a viable, self-sustaining reservation economy has become a primary objective of the tribe—a challenge that continues to be complicated by historic patterns of land ownership and jurisdictional obstacles (Endreson 1991; Zaferatos 1998, 2003). Land tenure patterns on the reservation have emerged as a central cause of jurisdictional conflict as local governments have imposed their own set of regulatory policies that have impeded the ability of the tribe to effectively use its reservation resources to benefit its community (Northwest Renewable Resources Center 1997).

Non-tribal interests operating within the boundaries of the Swinomish Indian Reservation include the presence of the state and local governments in civil and criminal jurisdiction, regulation of hunting, fishing, and natural resources, provision of roads and utilities, taxation, and the zoning of fee-simple reservation land use. The inherent right of the tribe to exercise exclusive jurisdiction over its reservation had been preempted through a series of long term intrusions by the state and local governments. Hence, the tribe recognized that in order to influence its own reservation development, it was first necessary to reawaken its still-dormant powers of self-government so that its own reservation vision could be advanced and its political authority throughout the reservation landscape could be asserted.

Swinomish Self-Determination

Regaining control of the reservation was believed to be the first step toward achieving tribal self-determination. Beginning in the late 1970s and early 1980s, the tribe focused on overcoming the imposition of state and local jurisdictional encroachment on its reservation through a two-phase strategy, first, by enacting sufficient self-governance powers to preempt county-asserted jurisdiction and, second, by negotiating interlocal cooperative agreements (Page 1985; Swinomish Indian Tribal Community 1989). The first approach sought to expand the tribe's authority to regulate land use, public utility services, management of water resources and timber harvest practices by establishing comprehensive land use and environmental protection policies and regulations. The tribe adopted a comprehensive land use plan and exercised its inherent powers by enacting a zoning ordinance in 1978 that applied to all lands within the exterior boundaries of the reservation, regardless of ownership type. Although the tribe had exercised its zoning authority since 1978, an obstacle was created when Skagit County concurrently exercised its zoning authority over reservation fee lands through delegated powers presumed valid under Washington State's Planning Enabling Act.

In the 1980s, following years of frustration that were the result of the application of a dual set of conflicting land use policies on the reservation, along with continued conflicts regarding the protection of off-reservation treaty fisheries interests, the tribe began a concerted effort to overcome discord by developing improved working relationships with both the state and local governments. It became increasingly aware that political tension would continue unless a dramatic shift occurred in the way regional decisions were made (Hall 1987, 1990; Page 1985). A change was needed to ensure that tribal interests were fully considered in regional planning (Winchell 1995). Moreover, the tribe also recognized that improved government relations would be needed if it were to reconcile the encroachment by non-tribal jurisdictions onto the reservation. By declaring a policy that asserted its own political authority in matters concerning reservation development, the tribe sought to effectively disrupt the political status quo of non-tribal government rules on the reservation. No longer would those jurisdictions presume to have unchallenged authority over the affairs of the reservation. By pursuing a strategy of cooperation (Cornell 1987; Cornell and Kalt 1990; Endreson 1991), the tribe hoped to overcome the inconsistencies in reservation development policies, as well as to increase its influence in off-reservation decisions that affected its treaty-based interests.

Since 1984, an extensive set of historic inter-local agreements have been entered into with Skagit County regarding land use cooperation, as well as other agreements that fostered inter-local cooperation with regional, municipal, special purpose governments, and state and federal agencies. Together, these agreements have effectively bolstered the tribe's interests both on the reservation and throughout the Skagit Valley region. The approach to regional cooperation replaced the previous unilateral system of county and local jurisdiction with a cooperative planning system that was inclusive of tribal priorities. These agreements, detailed in table 10, address land use, public safety, utilities, public health, and environmental protection. The strategy of establishing a form of mutual governance, both on and off the reservation, proved decisive in reducing many policy conflicts and in realigning regional policies to achieve greater consistency with tribal interests.

TABLE 10 Swinomish Intergovernmental Cooperative Agreements

Nature of Agreement	Date	Agreement	Affected Parties
Land Use	1987	Memorandum of understanding (MOU) for cooperative land use planning and administration	Skagit County
	1996	MOU for co-administration of land use policy	Skagit County
	1989	Transportation planning and development	US Department of the Interior, Washington Department of Transportation, Skagit County
Public Safety	1994	Cross-deputization agreement	Skagit County Sheriff
	1990	Mutual aid agreements	Skagit County municipalities of Burlington, LaConner, Anacortes, Sedro Woolley, Concrete, and Coupleville (Island County)
Utilties, Public Health, and Parks	1984 1997	Regional wastewater facility sharing and plant expansion agreement	Town of LaConner
	1984	Skagit County coordinated water supply systems planning	City of Anacortes, Skagit Public Utility District, Skagit County, Washington Department of Health, local water associations
	1987	Agreement to incorporate private reservation water associations under the tribal utility laws	State-created reservation water associations

TABLE 10 Swinomish Intergovernmental Cooperative Agreements (*cont.*)

Nature of Agreement	Date	Agreement	Affected Parties
	1993	Agreement to incorporate sewer discrict under tribal utility laws	Shelter Bay community sewer commission
	2010	Joint purchase and management of regional park	Washington Parks and Recreation Commission, Trust for Public Land
Environmental Protection	1996	Skagit River water rights agreement	City of Anacortes, Skagit Public Utility District, Skagit River Tribes, Skagit County, Washington Department of Ecology
	1989	Approval for "treatment as a state" under US Environmental Protection Agency (EPA) regulations	US EPA
	1996	Tri-Party agreement for CWA NPDES permit administration	US EPA, Washington Department of Ecology
	1996	Tribal environmental agreement	US EPA
	1996	Air quality technical assistance	Northwest Air Pollution Authority
	1997	Protocols and draft MOU for coordinated forest practices	Washington State Department of Natural Resources

Source: Nicholas C. Zaferatos. © 2012 Taylor & Francis Ltd.

Cooperative Strategies in Reservation Land Use Planning

The checkerboard land tenure conditions on the reservation created jurisdictional overlap in the application of two separate and different regulatory schemes, resulting in urban development patterns on reservation fee lands that conflicted with tribal policies. In 1986, rather than litigate questions regarding the validity of Skagit County's jurisdiction over reservation fee lands, the governments agreed to resolve policy conflicts by embarking on a collaborative planning program. The philosophy that guided the effort advocated resolving the inconsistencies through a mutually agreeable land use policy. The effort also aimed to address cooperation in the administration of the jurisdictionally separate, but consistent, dual zoning ordinances.

As the planning director and general manager for the tribe, I played an active role in developing the 1987 memorandum of understanding between the tribe and the county, the intent of which was to participate in a process of cooperative land use planning. The process began many years earlier, in 1983, when I attended several informal meetings with the county planning director. Our discussions focused on exploring ways of transcending our jurisdictional quandary by overcoming the inconsistencies within our respective land use policies. We shared a common view that, if the tribe and county could arrive at a consistent land use policy, matters regarding which government ultimately possessed jurisdiction would become secondary to our respective governments' primary interests. We not only imagined developing consistent language in our respective plans and regulations, but also a system for cooperating in permits review and administration. A sort of *mirroring policy process* was conceived that would allow tribal and county planners to work together closely with the expectation that future land use conflicts could be overcome through collaboration.

Since we shared a common professional language, as well as a set of professional planning ethics that called for providing leadership in reconciling problems faced by local communities, we agreed to encourage our respective governing councils to consider this new approach that held promise for circumventing the jurisdictional confrontation that appeared inevitable (Northwest Renewable Resources Center 1997). Initially, the tribe was concerned that entering into an agreement with the county might be viewed as a weakening of its jurisdictional position, which, at that point, was very firm. While the tribe was willing to acknowledge that the county did indeed have legitimate interests in the affairs of the reservation, it would not acknowledge the county's jurisdiction. To determine the validity of the county's jurisdictional claim would require a decision by the courts, which, at the time, neither government wanted. The goal of the cooperative approach was, instead, based on the belief that local communities should be able to resolve their differences through mutual dialogue in order to avoid litigation. The idea of a formal agreement between the two governments eventually gained political support, and the timing was right for beginning the process of cooperatively addressing the land use policy discrepancies.

Tribal and county elected officials met on several occasions to discuss issues of mutual concern, acknowledging that historic events had created a situation whereby Indian and non-Indian interests were both present on the reservation. They further acknowledged that neither government could successfully act unilaterally without incurring objections from the other party and the threat of litigation. They agreed that it would be advantageous to avoid costly litigation by resolving differences under a formal government-to-government relationship. They also recognized that an accommodation would facilitate the development of a long term working relationship that could help address other mutual concerns both on and off the reservation.

In 1987, following six months of discussions, the Swinomish Indian Senate and the Skagit County Board of Commissioners entered into a memorandum of understanding[12] agreeing to pursue a process leading to

---

12. The nationally acclaimed agreement and subsequent joint plan received commendation from the Washington State governor in 1990 and awards from Harvard University's Honoring Nations Project, the Washington Chapter of the American Planning Association, the Planning Association of Washington, and the Washington State Office of Historic Preservation.

the coordination of land use planning and the regulation of fee lands on the reservation. A comprehensive land use plan would jointly be developed along with implementing ordinances and administrative procedures. The plan would be developed on the basis of sound planning principles reflecting the priorities of each community, with questions of jurisdiction taking a secondary position. The governments also agreed that consensus would be their preferred means for reaching decisions.

The tribe's motivation to enter into the formal agreement was based upon two primary considerations. First, as an important cultural norm, the tribe had traditionally sought non-confrontational relationships with its neighbors and fully supported the prospect of improved relations with a former adversary. Second, in the event of an unfavorable decision, litigation risked the possibility of diminishing the tribe's sovereignty, which could also adversely affect other tribal governments. In addition, the tribe was interested in avoiding the costs associated with litigation and the potential of furthering non-Indian animosity and anti-tribal sentiment, particularly in light of the controversial effects of the treaty fisheries decision.

As specified in the MOU, a nine-member Advisory Planning Board composed of four tribal appointees, four county appointees, and a neutral facilitator[13] was established to oversee the planning effort. Before addressing substantive issues, the board attended a series of educational work sessions on federal Indian policy and law, functions of tribal and county governments, regional histories of tribal and non-tribal communities, and consensus-based negotiating and problem solving techniques. The work sessions served as a form of social learning intended to broaden understanding and appreciation for cultural and political differences between the two communities and to prevent misrepresentations of each party's interests. In 1987, after convening for a period of nine months, the board developed a draft comprehensive land use plan for the reservation and forwarded it to each respective government for review.

13. The Northwest Renewable Resources Center's Land Tenure Project, a Washington nonprofit mediation service, provided a facilitator for the project.

The draft Swinomish Joint Comprehensive Plan was the first national planning effort between a tribe and a county (Larsen 1989; Northwest Renewable Resources Center 1997). The plan articulated goals and established policies to guide the stewardship of reservation lands and natural resources and outlined a framework for cooperative implementation that was later agreed upon by the governments. Each government relied on its own perceived authority, agreeing to defer questions about jurisdiction, if necessary, to a future time. While the tribe continued to assert its exclusive jurisdiction to all reservation lands, the approach provided for the active participation by the county in reservation decision-making, recognizing that successful coordinated regional planning is a desired outcome not otherwise achievable under the conditions of unilateral governance and conflicting policies. The plan expressed the cultural significance of the reservation as a tribal homeland and sought to ensure that future development would be responsive to tribal community goals while concurrently addressing the broader interests of all reservation residents. By providing for the consideration of a plurality of reservation interests, the plan was also mindful of prior federal court precedents[14] concerning questions of a government's rightful authority over reservation fee lands (Scott 1982; Goeppele 1990; Kauger, Du Bey, and Mankiller 1990; Weaver 1990).

Testing the Cooperative Spirit

Although either government was free to end its participation in the joint planning program at any time, intergovernmental cooperation persisted, having survived changes in tribal and county leadership as well as in professional planning staff. The agreement has provided a written record of a process that has been successfully employed for more than a quarter of a century in the hopes of reaching mutual understanding on difficult issues.

---

14. As established in the second exception in *Montana v. United States*, 450 U.S. 544 (1988) and *Brendale v. Confederated Tribes and Bands of Yakima Indian Nation*, 492 U.S. 408 (1988).

In 1996, a second agreement was signed to jointly administer the land use policy. The agreement provided a procedure for reviewing land use applications and established a process for dispute resolution to ensure future consistency in land use matters mutually administered by the two governments. Under the procedure, either planning agency may accept and transmit to the other agency applications for land use permits on reservation fee lands. In the event of a disagreement under the two-agency review process, staff members from both agencies would meet to further discuss and resolve differences. If they are unable to reach agreement, the matter is then forwarded to a five-member advisory board appointed jointly by the governments to help mediate an acceptable outcome. If resolution is still not reached, the matter is then referred to the two governing bodies for final resolution. Further, while the county does not assert an interest over tribal trust lands, in the spirit of regional cooperation, the tribe also forwards trust land use permit applications to the county for their comment.

Despite the long-term success of the program, conflicts between the governments still persist. The agreement has survived administrative appeals, filed in the 1990s, by both the county and the tribe. The tribe appealed the county's Critical Areas Ordinance for failing to adequately protect fisheries resources in the region. The county appealed the federal government's decision to accept a 350-acre reservation fee parcel into tribal trust ownership for a tribal economic development project.[15] Even though the governments have worked tirelessly to maintain consistency in their mutual land use policy, these separate appeal actions illustrate

---

15. In 1998, the tribe filed an appeal before the Washington State Growth Management Hearings Board (*Skagit Audubon Society, et al. v. Skagit County and Agriculture for Skagit County et al.*, No. 00-2-0018c) claiming that the county inadequately protected critical resources areas for fisheries resources. The Board affirmed the tribe's claim and remanded back to the county. In 1999, the county sought to reverse a Bureau of Indian Affairs decision (*United States Department of the Interior, Office of Hearings and Appeals, Interior Board of Indian Appeals*, No. IBIA 02-1002-A) to accept 350 acres of fee land owned by the tribe into trust ownership for tribal economic development. The major issues that were raised concerned the conversion of farmland to urban uses.

that consistency is not always attainable.[16] Both legal actions followed failed attempts to negotiate a compromise solution, yet illustrate how the institutionalized relationship in the land use arena can endure even when other conflicts cannot amicably be settled through negotiation. As the 1987 MOU had anticipated and provided for, and as these legal appeal proceedings demonstrate, deference to a third-party mediator is sometimes necessary.

Despite such instances of disagreement, the cooperative approach was instrumental in resolving several other land use conflicts. A unified position was taken in 1997 when a concurrent county and tribal "stop work" order was issued that required a fee property owner to comply with tribal cultural resources protection policies. In the late 1980s, the county supported a property owner's petition to the tribe to approve a residential subdivision that had been approved by the county a decade earlier, but had been inconsistent with prior tribal policies. The tribe agreed to classify the project as a "non-conforming" use, subject to several new conditions. The collaborative process established under the MOU helped the governments reconcile these, as well as other, past land use inconsistencies.

Extending the Cooperative Model to Regional Governance

Just as the cooperative process was successful in accommodating broader non-tribal interests in on-reservation affairs, it also contributed to changing attitudes and behaviors by promoting the education of, and appreciation for, the diverse values reflected in the broader Indian and non-Indian regional community. Though the plural planning construct was initially intended to address on-reservation land use conflicts, it was later expanded to other areas of public policy to encourage regional approaches

16. The tribe unilaterally amended its comprehensive land use plan and zoning ordinance in 1998, designating the property for "tribal economic development" for a marina, mixed-use commercial development, and a wetland restoration project. The county objected to the land title transfer as well as to the issuance of federal and tribal marina development permits in 1997. The site remains designated as "agriculture" in the county's comprehensive plan, while a portion of the site is designated for "tribal economic development" in the tribe's plan.

in transportation planning, public safety, the provision of public utilities, and environmental protection, as summarized earlier in table 10.

Transportation Planning

As with land use, transportation planning within the reservation also involves interests beyond just those of the tribes, as tribal, state, county, and federal agencies each maintain transportation systems on the reservation. Successful transportation improvements are not always possible without a coordinated effort involving all affected parties. The State Highway 20 intersection on the reservation illustrates this concern. The dangerous intersection experienced a high occurrence of traffic accidents and fatalities and was recognized by each government as a major public safety problem. Improvements to the intersection were necessary. In the mid-1990s, the tribe conducted a study to identify cost-effective solutions and assumed the lead agency role for coordinating project planning. The Washington Department of Transportation, Skagit County, and the Skagit Council of Governments, the regional transportation planning authority, supported the tribe's highway improvement project. Funding through the Federal Highway Administration was matched by state and regional funds, and the highway improvements were successfully completed in 2003.

Regional Public Safety

Whether a state, tribe, or local law enforcement agency has jurisdiction on the reservation depends on whether an offense has occurred on non-Indian fee land or trust land, and whether the offense was caused by a tribal member, an Indian person enrolled with another tribe, or a non-Indian person. To overcome the complexity of law enforcement jurisdiction and to reduce duplicative public safety programs, the tribe, county, and other regional municipalities established cross-deputization commissions. These commissions authorize tribal and non-tribal police officers to act, in limited circumstances, under dual state and tribal authority. Before the commissions could be authorized, however, standards and procedures for law enforcement had to become consistent. The tribe's law enforcement agency provides first response for emergency calls on the reservation, reducing the average response time from more than forty-five minutes for the more distant county sheriff's response, to less than five minutes for the tribe's on-reservation police response. Since 1990, mutual aid agreements have provided a system of coordinated law enforcement throughout Skagit County.

Utilities, Public Health, and Parks

Funded by federal, tribal, and municipal town governments, a regional wastewater treatment facility was constructed and then expanded, serving a region that included the reservation and the adjacent Town of LaConner. In 1984 and 1997, agreements were entered into to provide for sufficient wastewater treatment capacity to meet the future projected growth demands within the reservation's urban growth boundaries. Extensions of tribal utility service hookups required compliance with tribal land use policies, furthering the tribe's control over reservation land use development. Tribal representatives continue to share governance with the town on the regional wastewater sewer commission that oversees the operation of the system.

In 1983, when Skagit County declared western Skagit County's Fidalgo Island a "critical water supply area" under Washington State laws, local water purveyors joined together to solve the region's water supply and coordination problems. In 1984, the Washington Department of Health, the county, the tribe and other regional water purveyors participated in the state's first water supply planning program that included an Indian tribe under the state's water supply coordination laws.[17] In carrying out its responsibilities as the reservation's designated utility service provider, the tribe constructed a public water supply system that serves the majority of the reservation's urban population under a common set of regional utility standards. More than 50 percent of the tribe's utility service population is composed of non-Indian reservation customers. Further, evidence of an available public water supply is required under Washington's Growth Management Act before new urban development can occur. The Skagit

17. In Washington State, tribes are considered public agencies, and state and local agencies are permitted to enter into agreements with tribes for joint or cooperative efforts where necessary to promote "mutual advantage" (Wash. Rev. Code § 39.34.010).

Coordinated Water Supply Plan designates the tribe as the public water supply authority for the reservation, further strengthening the tribe's land use authority since the extension of tribal utilities requires consistency with tribal land use policies.[18]

In order to overcome the inefficiencies associated with operating small, isolated private water associations within the reservation,[19] and at the request of several water associations, the tribe agreed to directly supply water service to the associations' residential customers. After an adequate tribal water supply was secured, the agreement resulted in lifting a county-imposed building moratorium within the associations' service boundaries. Further, the incorporation of the water associations under tribal utility laws reduced the number of independent water associations and removed the presumption of a valid state authority that had originally created the reservation associations. In addition, a private, 950-unit reservation residential community petitioned the tribe in 1993 to reconstitute its private wastewater treatment utility as a tribal sewer utility district. After the sewer district was authorized as a "satellite utility district" under tribal laws, the residential community was able to expand its wastewater treatment plant capacity to meet applicable federal Clean Water Act standards, as well as tribal land use and environmental regulations. Similar to the private water association agreements, the incorporation of the sewer district served to further reduce the state's jurisdictional presence on the reservation and fostered consistency between the provision of utility services and tribal land use policy on the reservation.

18. The Skagit County Coordinated Water Systems Plan (Skagit County 1984, IB-3) requires "applications for new development are presented either to the incorporated cities if the development lies within the incorporated boundaries, to the Swinomish Tribal Community within the Reservation, or to Skagit County if it is in unincorporated areas outside the reservation."

19. Under the terms of the Skagit County Coordinated Water Supply Plan and the Swinomish Water Plan, the tribe acknowledged the historic existence of several state-created private water associations on the reservation and agreed to allow their continued operation as enclaves within the tribal utility system.

On June 23, 2010, a joint ownership agreement was signed by the Washington State Parks and Recreation Commission and the tribe for the purchase of Kiket Island, which is located on the reservation. The marine waterfront island, on Skagit Bay, had been a long-term acquisition priority for the tribe. Kiket Island is the first cooperatively owned and managed tribal-state public park established in Washington State's history. The park, named the "Kukutali Preserve," has more than two miles of intact shoreline and an environmentally vital lagoon surrounded by the eighty-four upland acres of mixed deciduous and old growth conifer forests. The Kukutali Preserve and its surrounding tidelands are home to numerous endangered and threatened species. The tribe, state, and the Trust for Public Land worked together to secure grants and donations for the purchase of the property.

Environmental Protection

Several agreements were entered into with the US Environmental Protection Agency (EPA) to further the tribe's capacity to protect the reservation environment. In 1996, a Tribal Environmental Agreement was signed to implement EPA's government-to-government Indian policy (US Environmental Protection Agency 1984) and the agency's commitment to intergovernmental partnerships for reservation environmental protection. The agreement assists the tribe in assessing reservation environmental protection needs and provides funding and federal technical assistance for establishing reservation environmental programs.

An historic intergovernmental agreement was also reached in 1996, when the tribe, the Washington State Department of Ecology, and the EPA agreed to cooperate in the administration of federal water quality permits. The agreement followed litigation between the EPA and the state's environmental agency that ruled that Washington State's environmental statutes do not apply on Indian reservations.[20] Under the agree-

20. See *State of Washington, Department of Ecology v. United States Environmental Protection Agency*, 752 F.2d 1465 (9th Cir. 1985).

ment, the tribe contracted with the state to perform technical studies for National Pollution Discharge Elimination Systems (NPDES) permit applications on the reservation. After consideration of the state's technical recommendations and issuance of a tribal shorelines management permit, a tribal recommendation was then forwarded to the EPA for a final decision regarding the issuance of the NPDES permit. The agreement provided for the state's involvement in regional environmental management by redefining its role as a consultative agency under tribal and federal authority.

The tribe further extended its intergovernmental cooperative approach to obtain state and federal assistance to carry out air quality protection and timber harvest management programs. A 1996 agreement with Washington's Northwest Air Pollution Authority helped the tribe develop and administer its reservation air quality program. The agreement produced government efficiencies by incorporating the technical resources of the state to attain mutual tribal, federal, and state air quality standards. In 1997, interagency procedures were also agreed upon with the Washington State Department of Natural Resources to jointly review and manage proposed timber harvests on reservation fee lands.

Finally, in 1996 the Swinomish tribe joined two other Skagit River tribes, several regional water purveyors, the state, and the county to establish a collaborative process for securing water rights from the Skagit River in order to meet future water supply demands and conservation requirements. The resulting agreement provided funding to conduct biological studies to establish optimal in-stream flow rates necessary to protect treaty fisheries (City of Anacortes et al. 1996). The agreement represented the first successful program in the state for resolving complex water rights issues by fully incorporating tribal interests. The recommendations regarding optimal in-stream flows to protect threatened and endangered salmon resources, one of several outcomes from the process, were later enacted as rules under Washington State laws. However, several years after adopting the in-stream flow rules, the state withdrew the standard. After lengthy attempts to negotiate a reasonable solution to the state's failure to protect fisheries resources, the tribe sought legal remedy. A judgment supporting the tribe's position was issued in 2013,[21] directing the state to take sufficient actions necessary for ensuring the protection of the fisheries resource.

Conclusion and Implications for Planning

The Swinomish tribe had acknowledged that effective reservation planning could not occur in isolation from its surrounding political region. Tribal initiatives fostering cooperation with state, regional, local, and special purpose governments resulted in effective outcomes that have helped to reconcile a long history of regional conflict and to develop a more inclusive regional public policy.

Several important lessons emerge from the Skagit Valley experience. First, regional cooperation in land use between tribes and counties becomes possible when they employ a multiparty, government-to-government approach, cognizant of the historic circumstances that first created conflicts. Second, the process requires the capacity to address emerging issues through continuous consultation, including a forum for dispute resolution. Third, the longstanding barriers to institutional communication must be continuously broken, although they may never entirely disappear. Fourth, successful cooperation cannot be forced or artificially accelerated; the commitment to regional cooperation requires personal and professional commitments by elected officials and, especially, by planning staff tasked with resolving complex and often contentious issues. Fifth, time and resources must be dedicated to education, orientation, and the development of skills among both policy-makers and staff involved in the relationship. Finally, unforeseen events and problems that arise require constant monitoring in order to protect the relationship. The new tribal-local government relationships that were formed are tenuous, fragile, and continually tested and require ongoing effort to ensure their sustainability. The willingness of the parties to cooperate invariably boils

---

21. See chapter 8, discussion of the ruling in *Swinomish Indian Tribal Community v. Department of Ecology.*

down to the willingness of individual leaders to form and maintain long-term relationships.

The experiences on the Swinomish Indian Reservation demonstrate that by incorporating multiple interests in public policy development, effective utilitarian relationships can result. The method employed a multi-jurisdictional, co-regulatory approach to regional governance, in which both tribal and non-tribal interests were simultaneously engaged in public policy formulation. This approach avoids conflict by focusing on solutions to the most pressing issues facing each community, rather than on the question of which government has ultimate jurisdiction. The cooperative planning approach represents a way forward by reversing a history of jurisdictional uncertainty and conflicts in public policy and by promoting the interests of both tribal and non-tribal communities. As a strategic approach for tribal empowerment, the Swinomish cooperative model is illustrated in figure 12, with reference to the general tribal planning model that was presented in chapter 7. The key dimensions to the model include the tribe's internal planning process that began with an evaluation of community goals and its social preference in supporting cooperation over conflict with respect to how it engages with neighboring communities. That value was reflected in its strategic plan for pursuing cooperating relationships, first with Skagit County and then by forming new relationships with other jurisdictions. Concurrent with its strategic plan formulation, the tribe simultaneously began to develop its governing infrastructure to expand its land use authority over the entire reservation. The selection of political actions included the dual acts of applying its inherent political authority to regulate reservation activities and employing the cooperative planning approach. The external dimension in the model involved the negotiation of agreements to support inter-jurisdictional planning with county, municipal, regional, special purpose governments, as well as with state and federal agencies. With agreements reached in each of the successive planning undertakings, the tribe's political empowerment was significantly expanded as it emerged as the primary governance authority on the reservation.

Over the past two decades, tribes in Washington State have experienced a transformation in their relationships with the state. The new

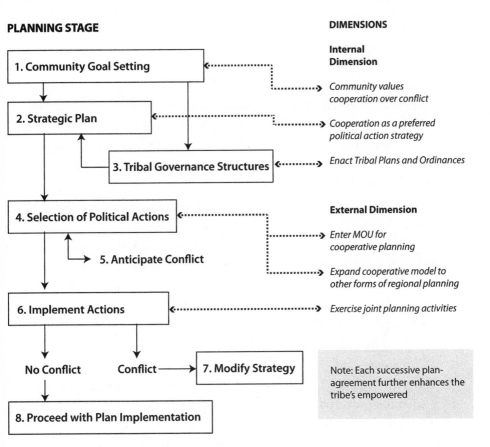

PLANNING STAGE

DIMENSIONS

1. Community Goal Setting

2. Strategic Plan

3. Tribal Governance Structures

4. Selection of Political Actions

5. Anticipate Conflict

6. Implement Actions

No Conflict Conflict → **7. Modify Strategy**

8. Proceed with Plan Implementation

Internal Dimension

Community values cooperation over conflict

Cooperation as a preferred political action strategy

Enact Tribal Plans and Ordinances

External Dimension

Enter MOU for cooperative planning

Expand cooperative model to other forms of regional planning

Exercise joint planning activities

Note: Each successive plan-agreement further enhances the tribe's empowered

12. Tribal planning model illustrating the Swinomish tribe's strategic approach.

precedent favoring negotiated solutions first applied in the late 1970s to resolve fisheries management conflicts has led to the reconciliation of other policy conflicts among state, local, and tribal governments. The Skagit Valley approach encourages social learning and cooperation among government participants, creating political plurality in the region. The case study illustrates how the principles of the Centennial Accord can be applied to promote cooperation across agencies of state government, as well as to improve local and regional planning with tribal governments.

From the perspective of the region, the experiences represent a new path forward in the promotion of regionalism and pluralism in planning that is inclusive of the interests, and respectful of the authority, of Native

American nations. From the perspective of the tribe, the approach represents a strategic shift away from continued conflict within its planning situation. The tribe's willingness to consider the plurality of interests on the reservation, in addition to its internal community interests, enabled it to construct a sufficiently broad reservation planning strategy that served the entire reservation community. It is a response to the lessons learned from *Montana* and *Brendale*, as well. In light of the situation that tribes face today, the defense of a tribe's governance is growing increasingly dependent on its ability to demonstrate a capacity to govern on behalf of all of the interests within the reservation community, including those of the non-Indian community.

The Swinomish tribe's cooperative experiences illustrate the effectiveness of employing an adaptive and strategic approach to reservation planning. As an adaptive approach, it begins by clarifying a future vision for its reservation community that is inclusive, rather than exclusive, of non-Indian interests. That vision is manifested through a series of capacity building steps that enabled the tribe to reawaken its dormant powers of self-government and to assert its claim as the primary reservation authority. As a strategic approach, in choosing cooperation over confrontation, the tribe not only avoided the inevitable risks associated with challenging the county's authority in reservation affairs, but found a resolution to its jurisdictional standoff, which later led to other conflict-avoidance outcomes both on the reservation and throughout the larger region. In the end, the process served to broaden the tribe's influence both on and off the reservation, greatly enhancing the tribe's empowerment.

10

Appropriate Technologies and the Native American Smokehouse

THE HISTORIC SUPPRESSION of traditional Indian spiritual practice was, in part, overcome when the Swinomish tribe opened its long anticipated ceremonial smokehouse. The celebrated resumption of smokehouse activities, however, presented new environmental health threats that were not adequately anticipated during the building's planning and construction phase, and that required remediation. This chapter examines how the tribe was able to eliminate a public health risk by forming partnerships with technical experts and government agencies, while simultaneously modifying its own development regulations in order to protect the culturally important practice of open fire burning in traditional spiritual ceremonies.

In contrast to past federal policies that disrupted the fabric of Native American communities, current federal policies encourage tribal governments to reconstruct their political, economic, and cultural communities with the goal of achieving sustainable community improvement. Beginning in the late 1960s and early 1970s, tribes began programs focused on political and community reconstruction. As a result, their spiritualism, which had been suppressed as a result of federal assimilation policies that sought to diminish Indian identity by prohibiting the use of traditional languages and spiritual practice, began to reemerge.[1] For many Coast Sal-

---

1. Non-Indian society used institutional mechanisms, including the passage of laws prohibiting religious practices, to disrupt tribal cultural cohesion (LeVine and Campbell

13. Exterior view, Swinomish Indian smokehouse.

ish Indians, the reconstruction of the traditional smokehouse, the ceremonial place of worship, became the centerpiece of their community redevelopment. The Swinomish tribe sought to reestablish its ceremonial smokehouse in order to support the revival of its cultural and traditional spiritualism, known as *Seowyn*.

In the early 1990s, construction of the traditional smokehouse on the Swinomish Indian Reservation finally commenced. Adhering to stringent traditional design criteria while simultaneously complying with newly adopted tribal sanitary, public safety, and structural building codes, the smokehouse design provided for two large open fire pits, which are vitally important in Seowyn ceremonial practice. While the new building embodied the promise of helping to revive the community's spiritual tradition, it also raised new concerns—it was anticipated that the burning

---

1972). During the late 1800s it was declared illegal for Indians to practice any aspect of traditional religion. The suppression of Indian religion eventually led to a diminished knowledge of valuable traditions (Castile 1982). While the legal persecution of traditional religion abated following the passage of the Indian Reorganization Act of 1934, prohibition of the practice was not repudiated until passage of the Indian Freedom of Religion Act in 1978 (Pub. L. No. 95-341, 92 Stat. 469 (1978), codified in part at 42 U.S.C. § 1996 (1994)).

fires within the enclosed structure might contribute to airborne pollution that could pose a public health threat to the smokehouse occupants.

Tribal Community Development and the Priority of Culture

Tribes have been engaged in reestablishing their reservation governing role since the introduction of the tribal community development programs under the federal Great Society initiatives of the 1960s. The early period in tribal community development emphasized political reorganization as well as the provision of basic governmental services and social programs, public housing, reservation infrastructure development, and the defense of treaty rights. The self-determination era fostered important advances in tribal political sovereignty development. The effects of the federal strategy, however, also promoted new forms of dependencies, including dependencies on non-tribal forms of development that met federal, but not necessarily tribal, community development standards and objectives. These development standards were often required as a condition of federal construction funding and were often inconsiderate of tribal cultural preferences. As the development of the reservation community progressed, greater attention returned to a focus on the priorities of the cultural community in order to more meaningfully ensure that tribal traditional and spiritual values were integrated within the tribes' overall community development approach.

Traditional culture and religion are viewed as inseparable from tribal identity. For the Swinomish people, reservation lands and natural resources are viewed as elements of the larger cultural community rather than as ends to themselves. The community often emphasizes a natural resource social use value over its economic exchange value to highlight the importance of cultivating personal relationships with the natural environment, as evidenced in both past and current spiritual and ceremonial practices.

In the process of building tribal governance capacity, tribes often adopt or adapt rules and standards commonly used by other jurisdictions. This approach is not only efficient as it avoids having to reinvent the wheel, but more importantly, it helps foster consistency in the application of uniform standards both on the reservations and throughout a region. This was the case with the Swinomish tribe when, in its efforts to expand its capacity to manage building construction activities on its reservation, it adopted the Uniform Building Code as a technical appendix to its tribal building and development code. Universality of building standards is important as it helps to facilitate common usage among architects, engineers, contractors, and government building inspectors. Buildings constructed under commonly accepted standards also meet the conditions required for obtaining property insurance, as well as for other beneficial purposes. As tribes expand their political authority by enacting laws and regulations that mirror federal or state standards, rather than reflecting their own particular community development preferences, they should carefully consider how those standards might impede their cultural development.

The Swinomish Indian Homeland and Seowyn Ceremonial Practice

Promised to four related Indian bands, the Swinomish Indian Reservation was set aside by the 1855 Treaty of Point Elliott and further redefined by executive order in 1873. Swinomish ancestors have inhabited the reservation area for several thousands of years. Numerous known archaeological sites are located within the reservation boundaries, and several historic villages and shell-midden sites have been identified along the reservation coastline. At the site of the current Swinomish Indian Village (the location of tribal governmental services, tribal housing, and several religious buildings) was Twiwok, an Indian settlement believed to have been continuously inhabited for more than 3,500 years.

Members of the Swinomish Indian Tribal Community are descendants of the Swinomish, Kikiallus, Samish, and Lower Skagit tribes. The ancestors of these groups lived in the Skagit River valley and on the coastline and islands near the river's mouth and spoke the Coast Salish language. The culture and economy of the inhabitants of the Skagit region was centered around natural resources, including salmon, shellfish, and upland resources such as cedar, camus, berries, and wildlife. Resource gathering activities, in response to seasonal availability of the various resources, resulted in a fluctuation of village demography where families dispersed to seasonal locations. During aboriginal times, the most significant unit

14. Ceremonial room interior and
upper bleacher seating area.

of social organization was the winter village community (Roberts 1975; Smith 1941).

The social component of the Skagit Region villages primarily involved marriages, summer exchange visits, and winter ceremonials. The winter ceremonials included both invitational feasts and the "spirit dance." The spirit dance was usually held in the house of a young person who had recently acquired a guardian spirit following spiritual questing, fasting, bathing in the solitude of the wilderness, and years of training. The spirit provided protection and special knowledge. In return, the individual was expected to perform a spirit dance that involved ceremonial costuming and the singing of a particular song to which members of different village communities were invited to witness. The other winter ceremonial, the invitational feast, was a larger affair that included bathing and fasting in order to attract spiritual guardians. The feast, occurring in large smoke-house structures, included games, gambling, trading, singing, dancing, and masked performances (Suttles 1951). Also called "potlatches," these feasts were important economic institutions, allowing wealthy communities to convert accumulated food and other wealth into higher social status and prestige.

Smokehouse practices were abruptly interrupted in the late eighteenth century. The devastating smallpox epidemics of 1782 and 1783 reduced the Native population by almost one half and resulted in the destruction of many of the infected smokehouses throughout the area (Guilmet 1991). The current Swinomish reservation village, in fact, contained a large smokehouse that burned down during a subsequent smallpox epidemic prior to 1900. Furthermore, one of the most devastating rules imposed by the Bureau of Indian Affairs (BIA) during the early reservation period of the nineteenth century outlawed the practice of traditional spirit dancing, as well as the practice of Indian medicine, encompassing holistic approaches to physical, emotional, and spiritual healing. The federal government viewed the elimination of Native religion as a politically important strategy since traditional religion served to strengthen tribal cohesiveness, which, in turn encouraged resistance to federal intrusion.

As a response to the oppressive policies, the Swinomish decided to take their spirit dance and feasts underground, operating a large smokehouse off the reservation on nearby Guemes Island, which at the time was still isolated from the Anglo community. Between 1906 and 1912, the Swinomish, along with other tribes, appealed to the BIA to lift the ban on traditional Indian spiritual practices. The BIA consented on the condition that the ceremonies would be limited only to a public display of dance. Hence, the revived dances were referred to as *show dances* and were open to the public. After the public left, however, traditional spiritual dances would occur in private. Between 1912 and 1913, a large smokehouse, more than 100 feet long and 40 feet wide, was built on the northern end of the reservation to house the event. The traditional smokehouse building contained bleacher seating along the interior walls that surrounded an area of open fires. Two or more fires would be constructed during ceremonies with an opening in the roof that permitted exhaust smoke to escape the building. The building, however, was later lost in a fire (Roberts 1975). Despite the restrictions to their ceremonial practices, the Swinomish people have retained many aspects of their traditional culture. A growing number of the current tribal membership now practices Seowyn. The importance of spiritual practice and its members' continuous connection to it are integral parts of the tribe's cultural identity.[2]

Rebuilding the Tribal Ceremonial Smokehouse

Funds to construct the ceremonial smokehouse were secured during the late 1980s when the tribe entered into a cultural mitigation agreement with the city of Seattle. The city sought to renew its Federal Energy Resources Commission (FERC) license in order to continue to operate hydroelectric facilities on the Skagit River. During the application process, the city agreed to address environmental impacts to tribal fisheries and cultural resources that would result from the continued operation of its dams on the river. The settlement agreement provided for a sum of money to be allocated to the Swinomish and the two other tribes of the Skagit River for purposes of mitigating the impacts to cultural resources.

With funding in place under the terms of the agreement, the Swinomish Indian Senate, the tribe's governing body, authorized project planning to commence for the construction of the smokehouse. An oversight committee was established that included representation from the Swinomish Smokehouse Organization, an independent nonprofit religious organization that was separate and distinct from the tribal government. A site was selected and dedicated within the Swinomish Village, and proposals were solicited for architectural services. Project design objectives sought to incorporate the architectural principles of the Northwest longhouse, emphasizing the use of traditional building materials and construction techniques, and the employment of tribal members in each phase of project construction.

The design process revealed several potential problems that required reconciliation. Under the tribe's building standards, it would be difficult, if not impossible, for the traditional smokehouse to meet strict building

2. Larry, Campbell (member of the Swinomish Smokehouse Organization and cultural resources planner with the Swinomish Planning Office). 1999. Personal conversation with Nicholas Zaferatos.

regulations. Because the building was intended to serve traditional spiritual practices, the design required, among other considerations, that the ceremonial floor be composed of earthen clay material with open fire pits. The tribe was determined to achieve its traditional design goals while complying, within reason, with building codes and safety requirements adapted from standard state building regulations, which were written without consideration of traditional Native American ceremonial activities.

Project architects were sensitive to designing the structure in a manner that cloaked many of the code-compliant structural features, including the installation of a system of lateral bracing hidden between the building's rough-sawn cedar planked interior and exterior walls. Tribal permit variances were issued to permit the structure to be constructed with an earthen floor that was necessary for the ceremonial dances. While the facility's public restrooms, kitchen, and dining areas were designed to comply with standard plumbing, electrical, structural and health regulations, the provision of two large open fire pits in the main ceremonial room presented a more difficult design challenge. After considering and rejecting an imposing chimney exhaust system, it was determined that fire protection could be adequately addressed by providing water standpipes and pressure hoses, fire extinguishers, and fire suppression training for the smokehouse firemen, who are responsible for maintaining the spiritually important burning of the fires.

A related concern was the potential health risks associated with the open burning of wood fires in the center of the ceremonial room that would accommodate more than 600 individuals. To address this concern, the project architects examined the design of other operable smokehouse structures in the region and consulted the literature on historic smokehouse structures in order to anticipate the probable air movement characteristics from the open flame and the resulting exhaust smoke. The structure was designed with a large overhead roof-opening that would permit venting of smoke from the building. Several small openings were constructed beneath the bleacher seating to provide an exterior air supply source to the open fires. Since the building shell was not enclosed in an airtight vapor barrier, air intake through the building's walls was also

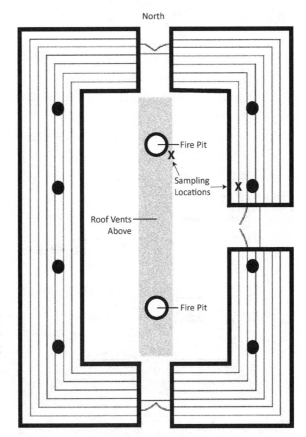

15. Floor plan of main ceremonial room showing air quality test sampling locations.

thought to be sufficient for providing an adequate source of fresh air to the building's occupants.

Features of the Swinomish Smokehouse

The Swinomish Smokehouse is a 200-foot long by 70-foot wide cedar-planked frame structure and is divided into two sections by an open breezeway. The northern section contains the main ceremonial room. The southern section contains a kitchen, dining area, restrooms, and a *local room*, used for private ceremonial activity. The main ceremonial area consists of a 70-foot by 100-foot open meeting room with seven rows of bleachers around all four sides. There are exterior exit doors on the north, south, and east walls (figure 15). Smoke from the fires is vented at the roof peak. The roof is designed with a second, higher peak, which is situated three feet above the lower peak. The three-foot-high east and west vertical walls of the second peak are open to the outside and provide 400 square feet of roof ventilation area for fire combustion products (figure 16).

The open fires play a vital role in the ceremony and provide the sole source of heat for the winter gatherings. Two open fires are burned on the main floor during a ceremony. Traditionally, the fires had been built on the clay dirt floor. The wood burned is usually Douglas fir and is sometimes seasoned, depending on availability and cutting schedules. Approximately three cords of wood are burned for each ceremony, and ceremonies typically last about twelve hours. Wind direction is usually from the southeast during the winter ceremonial season.

16. Interior roof in ceremonial room showing smoke hole.

Assessing the Health Risks of Fire Combustion
in Smokehouse Ceremonies

The smokehouse construction commenced during the spring of 1991 and was substantially completed in 1992. The building was informally conveyed to the Swinomish Smokehouse Organization for community use during the winter ceremonial season of 1993. During the first two winters of ceremonial events, several tribal Seowyn members indicated the presence of a large amount of visible smoke that remained present throughout the evening's ceremony. Members complained of burning irritation in their eyes and expressed concern for the health of occupants, particularly for tribal elders suffering from respiratory health problems.

Recognizing that air quality data would be needed in order to determine whether a health risk existed, the tribe's planning department requested technical assistance to evaluate the risk potential from open fire emissions. The tribe called upon the resources of several agencies and the University of Washington to address the concern with smoke and carbon monoxide emissions from fires during smokehouse ceremonies. To assess whether there was a basis for health concern, tribal staff obtained assistance from the Northwest Air Pollution Agency (a regional air pollution agency) and the Washington State Department of Labor and Industries (a state OSHA agency) to sample indoor air for carbon monoxide, particulate, and polynuclear aromatic hydrocarbons (PAHs) during a ceremony in March 1997. Over a four-hour period, carbon monoxide was measured at 67 parts per million (ppm) parts of air. Respirable particulate was measured in three locations over the course of a twelve-hour ceremony at 3.9, 3.4, and 2.8 milligrams per cubic meter (mg/m^3) of air. No PAHs were detected. These measurements indicated that there was reason for concern regarding carbon monoxide and particulate exposure.

Potential adverse health effects from carbon monoxide exposure include reduced exercise tolerance, recurring heart pain, headache, dizziness, light-headedness, and concentration, memory, and vision problems (Morris 1990). During pregnancy, carbon monoxide poses a greater risk for the fetus than to the mother. With exposure to wood smoke particulates, health studies have found evidence of shortness of breath, reduced lung capacity and a greater chance of respiratory diseases such as bronchitis, pneumonia, and asthma. Adverse health effects from wood smoke can be more severe for children (Larson and Koenig 1994).

Concerned that the strict application of air quality standards might disrupt the traditional Seowyn practices, the tribe requested further technical assistance to assess the public and occupational health risk and to devise solutions that would not visibly interfere with the building's traditional features. The University of Washington Environmental Health Department provided advice for improving air quality and for testing the effectiveness of implemented solutions. The tribe's priorities were to improve air quality and reduce health risks, to make the best use from heat generated from the fires, and to provide a safe and comfortable ceremonial environment. A criterion for any smoke control alteration to the building required that the appearance of the fire not be altered and that the installation of any mechanical equipment not be visible or audible in the ceremonial space. The evaluation began by examining how wood combustion is likely to behave inside an enclosed building. This led to the development of a smoke emissions and air movement model, which was later tested within the Swinomish Smokehouse. The successful simulation test of the concept led to the design and permanent installation of smokehouse improvements, which were then tested for effectiveness in reducing harmful exposures to occupants.

Wood Combustion and Smoke Control in Simulation Tests

A fire that achieves complete combustion will produce less harmful combustion products. Combustion is dependent upon the availability of oxygen to feed the chemical reaction and the type and water content of the fuel source (Butcher and Parnell 1979). When adequate oxygen is available, the chemical reaction produces carbon dioxide (CO_2). The absence of sufficient oxygen produces more carbon monoxide (CO). In low concentrations, carbon dioxide is a non-toxic compound. Carbon monoxide, on the other hand, may pose serious detrimental health effects (National Fire Protection Association 1981; Hazardous Substances Data Bank 1997).

The temperature of the fire is dependent on oxygen supply and water content of the wood. A fire with adequate oxygen will burn hot. Wet wood will burn at a lower temperature because energy is expended to evaporate the water before the wood can burn. A fire burning at a lower temperature will smolder, producing more smoke. Complete combustion from a hotter fire will result in smaller amounts and sizes of particles. Different wood species have different chemical composition depending upon their resin content. A wood with high resin content will produce more smoke. Alder has considerably lower resin content than Douglas fir, the two most available firewood types, and would therefore burn with less smoke than would fir (National Fire Protection Association 1981).

The movement characteristics of the combustion products within the smoke plume as well as the movement that occurs when the plume reaches the roof are both important considerations for effective smoke removal. As the smoke column rises, it expands as it mixes with the cooler ambient air of the larger room (Butcher and Parnell 1979; National Fire Protection Association 1981). As it reaches the roof, it will exit through the vent openings if there are no disruptive air or temperature patterns to interfere with that movement. Interfering air patterns can be caused by several factors, including wind entering at the roof vent openings, mixing of the plume with colder room air, and air currents produced by replacement air entering the building at the roof vents.

If additional oxygen is provided to a fire, it will burn more efficiently. One way to add oxygen could be to feed air to the fire by installing a duct below the fire. The heat from the fire would create suction within the duct to pull air from outside of the building. This concept was independently suggested by University of Washington staff and by tribal community members, who were aware that this approach had been used in other smokehouses.

To test this concept, a temporary fire pit was built on the clay floor using a concrete block base covered by a metal grate and located at the northernmost fire pit location. A one-foot diameter duct ran from the base of the pit to the north building entrance. Plastic sheeting covered the north entrance, blocking outside air from entering the building except through the duct.

A series of tests were conducted to determine the concentrations of smoke and CO produced by the single open fire with the air supply duct in place and without the duct in place. The testing was next conducted with two fires burning without the duct. The fourth test monitored emissions with the duct in place to one of the two fires. Area samples for respirable particulate and carbon monoxide were collected using data logging instrumentation. Air velocity within the duct was measured to determine the volume of air that was naturally pulled through the duct. The wood burned for this test was seasoned, dry Douglas fir. The fire was smaller than what is typically burned during ceremonies, containing two and occasionally three layers of four-foot-long split logs, whereas a typical ceremonial fire contains three to four layers of split logs.

Carbon Monoxide Measurements

All carbon monoxide concentrations measured were markedly lower than concentrations measured during the March 1997 ceremony when a four-hour time-weighted average of 67 ppm was recorded. Test results were compared to the allowable EPA air concentration of 9 ppm averaged over eight hours. Concentrations varied over the course of each test. Carbon monoxide concentrations close to the fire remained relatively stable, and the lowest concentrations were measured at ten feet above the bleacher area on the building's posts (figure 15). With one fire connected to the air supply duct, carbon monoxide concentration was found to be low and stable. When one fire was burned without connection to the air supply duct, the concentration began to rise, particularly at the bleacher location. When a second fire without connection to the duct was added, CO levels rose at both the bleachers and at the high post locations. When the duct was re-introduced to the north fire, levels immediately began to drop. CO concentrations averaged over the testing period were 2.6 ppm at the fire and 1.1 ppm high on the post. Both were well below the EPA standard of 9 ppm.[3]

Particulate Measurements

Respirable particulate samples were collected at six locations on the west, north, and east bleachers and on four individuals who participated in the

3. 40 C.F.R. § 50.6 "Particulate Matter" and § 50.8 "Carbon Monoxide" (1997).

TABLE 11 Respirable Particulate Concentration, September 1997 Concept Tests

Location	Concentration in mg/m³ without Duct	Concentration in mg/m³ with Duct
West area—top bleacher	1.1	0.6
East area—top bleacher	0.04	0.02

Source: Nicholas C. Zaferatos. © 1996 Regents of the University of California.

testing. Some samples were below the EPA respirable particulate (PM10) standard of 0.15 mg/m³. Table 11 shows a comparison of samples taken at two different locations for a ducted and non-ducted fire. When the air supply duct was not used, particulate levels were two times higher. There was a marked difference in concentrations between the east and west bleachers that might have been due to wind through the vents blowing smoke into the northwest corner of the building. The particulate samples collected during concept testing were reduced by an average of ten times compared to samples collected during the March ceremony where the mean concentration was 3.4 mg/m³.

Observation of Smoke Plume and Make-Up Airflow

Smoke emanating from the fire and its rise to the peak of the roof was visually observed. The fire connected to the air supply duct burned clear and hot. Very little smoke could be seen coming from the edges of the flame. The combustion product column moved quickly to the roof peak. At the peak, the smoke became turbulent and swirled at the peak rather than exiting immediately. Initially, a small vent hole at the north end of the roof peak was open. There was a particularly turbulent area at the north end of the peak. When the north vent hole was covered, the turbulence disappeared.

Without the air duct, the fire did not burn as clearly. More smoke could be observed at the edges of the flame. The smoke column moved more slowly toward the peak, and there appeared to be a turbulent area at the peak, extending at times below the second peak. The observed difference between fires was dramatic when two fires were burning at once, with only one of the fires connected to the air supply duct. The fire that was connected to the air supply duct burned hotter and its smoke column appeared to maintain enough heat to move directly upward toward the roof vents. This condition contrasted with the fire that was not connected to the air supply duct whose smoke column tended to mix with ambient room air and was carried back down along the cool exterior walls along the bleachers (figure 17). As a result of the observation of the turbulent area at the peak and the tribe's concern about the effect of wind blowing through the vents, it was concluded that operable shutters should be installed and tested.

On the day of testing, airflow was also measured during typical fire burning. An average airflow to support each fire was calculated at approximately 1,000 cubic feet per minute (cfm) from these measurements. It was also observed that the airflow tended to significantly increase during the period when wood was added to the fire when the fire was raging. As the fire burned hotter, more ambient room air was pulled into the very hot smoke column and drawn out of the building at the roof vent. The phenomenon of drawing ambient room air into the smoke column is known as

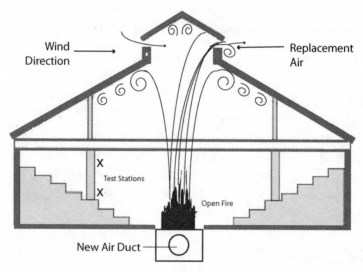

17. Smoke dispersion from a cooler fire mixed with ambient room air.

entrainment. Entrained air must also be factored into the airflow calculations, since air will otherwise be drawn into the building from open cracks or crevices and doors to replace the air exiting through the smoke vents.

Post-Construction Fire Pit Test

The fire pit simulation test results were presented to the tribe and to members of the Swinomish Smokehouse Organization. Organization members understood the potential health risks from continued exposure and urged the tribe to install permanent air supply ducts at both fire pits. With funding secured from an EPA air quality demonstration grant, fire pits with permanent air supply ducts to the exterior of the building were constructed at both the north and south fire pit locations. Fire pits are six-foot diameter pre-cast concrete vaults and extend three feet below ground level in order to accommodate falling ash and a two-foot diameter concrete air duct. A six-foot diameter metal grate placed at floor level over the concrete vault provides a surface for firewood while allowing direct air feed to the fire from the duct extending outside the building. Each fire's duct extends to the exterior of the building below the floor and is protected from rainfall by existing roof extensions. An exterior metal grate covers each duct's air intake vault. The sunken fire pits and ducting infrastructure are invisible from public view, except for the grates over the pits and the exterior air supply vaults.

Upward swinging shutters were also installed on all opening roof openings for the east roof vents and on two of the six openings for west roof vents. Some roof vents on the west side were left opened to ensure that a minimum amount of venting would occur. The shutters can be opened or closed by the firemen via a rope-and-pulley system.

After completion of construction during the autumn of 1998, a second air-monitoring test was conducted to evaluate the effect of the new fire pits and shutter system on reducing air pollutants in the smokehouse. Carbon monoxide and respirable particulate levels and air velocity at the duct entrances were measured. The shutter system was evaluated by visual observation of smoke movement at the roof peak. The wood used for the fire on this day was wet, but cured. Over the test period of approximately four hours, one cord of wood was burned at both fires. This would be

18. Installation of air inflow pipe and fire pit vault.

equivalent to the size of a typical fire during a twelve-hour ceremony when three cords are normally consumed.

Carbon Monoxide Measurement

Carbon monoxide was measured in two of the same locations that were measured during the September tests. Carbon monoxide direct-reading instruments with data loggers were used. Carbon monoxide airborne concentrations at the two sample locations measured an average of 12.4 parts per thousand (ppt) nearest to the fire and 16.5 ppt at the bleach next to the pole. Early in the test period, an incident occurred that demonstrated the effectiveness of the ducting in reducing CO. Air testing began when the north fire was burning and the duct grate outside the north door was open, allowing airflow to the fire. At 11:15, staff conducting the test went outside and found that the wind had blown a plywood board over the duct grate blocking the air supply to the north fire. The plywood was removed. The blocking of the air supply to the north fire caused the high peak of 37 ppt early in the test. When the air supply duct was unblocked, CO concentrations quickly dropped to an average of about 10 ppt.

Another noteworthy observation was that the addition of new wood affected CO concentrations. When wood was first added to the fire, the testing staff observed that the smoke seemed to clear immediately. Because of this observation, the time when wood was added to the fire was noted to see if there was a correlation to carbon monoxide levels. When wood was added, the fire burned vigorously, fire temperature rose and the smoke column rushed to the roof. One explanation may be that more ambient room air became entrained in the hotter smoke column thereby pulling more of the smoky air out of the building as the hotter air plume sought the cooler, lower pressure air outside the roof vents. The carbon monoxide concentrations gradually rose at the end of the test. Without the addition of more wood, the fire smoldered, possibly producing more CO. To understand how the carbon monoxide dispersed within the smokehouse, a direct reading CO monitor was carried throughout the bleachers to identify areas where the CO concentration had built up. In the upper portion of the bleachers, the concentration was higher than at lower portions of the bleachers, and the northwest corner and north end generally showed higher concentrations. This spatial dispersion was observed several times throughout the post-construction test and helped determine how best to balance the openings of the shutters.

Particulate Measurement

Respirable particulate was measured on the bleachers and at eight feet above the bleachers at three different support posts so that results could be compared to the March ceremonial test. Several of the respirable particulate samples exceeded the EPA respirable particulate limit of 0.15 mg/m^3. Samples eight feet up on the support posts had higher particulate concentrations than samples taken on the bleachers during the same time period (table 12). The bleacher samples would be more representative of

TABLE 12 Respirable Particulate Mean Concentration (mg/m^3)

Test	Concentration at Bleacher	Concentration at Support Post
March—ceremony	No sample	3.4
September—concept test	0.4	No sample
October—installation test	1.3	2.6

Source: Nicholas C. Zaferatos. © 1996 Regents of the University of California.

the exposure received by persons sitting in the bleachers. Samples collected during September concept tests were considerably lower than the initial March or post-construction October tests. In September, dry, seasoned wood was used and smaller fires were burned. Although it is not possible to conclude whether dry wood or small fires were more important in reducing the exposure concentration, it was observed that the dry wood used in September appeared to burn cleaner than the wetter wood used during the October test.

Observation of Smoke Plume

For the October tests, the outside temperature was cooler and the prevailing wind stronger than during the September tests. The wind was from the southeast, the typical wind direction for the winter season. The air seemed smokier during the October test than during the September test. Firemen, and other observers who had not seen the September test, reported reduced smoke over typical ceremonial conditions. The smoke plume did not appear to move with as much speed as it did during the September test. The wet wood probably caused a cooler fire, producing smoke that would not rise as quickly. At the beginning of the October test, the same turbulent smoke pattern was seen at the roof as during the September test. All shutters were open. The wind from the southeast appeared to be blowing some of the smoke plume below the second peak and into the northwest corner of the building. Various shutters were closed to determine which shutters should be closed to remove the turbulent smoke at the roof and therefore reduce the CO levels in the bleachers. The shutter configuration most effective in eliminating the turbulent pattern and movement of smoke into the northwest corner consisted of closing all but the middle two shutters on the east wall and leaving all of the west roof vents open.

Recommended Action

The air ducting to the fire pit notably reduced carbon monoxide concentrations in the smokehouse by providing more oxygen to feed the fire chemical reaction. With dry, well-seasoned wood, CO levels were below the EPA standard for CO. Airborne particulate levels were also reduced with the introduction of additional air supply through the ducting system, although the reduction was not as great as the carbon monoxide reduction. Better control of particulate might be achieved by warming the air above the bleachers to discourage the hot air plume from mixing with the cold air above the bleachers, along with the use of dry, seasoned wood.

The shutters were effective in eliminating turbulent air patterns at the peak, which interfere with movement of the smoke plume out of the roof vents. Great improvements were achieved in air quality with the combined addition of the ducting system and shutters. Two areas where additional improvements would enhance air quality and comfort in the smokehouse are through the consistent use of dry, well-seasoned wood and through the introduction of a heated makeup air supply to replace the air volume exiting the building with the smoke plume. The difference in air quality measurements between the September and October tests is partially due to the difference in dryness of the wood used on those two test days.

Conclusions and Implications for Planning

Tribal governments are advancing their community development by constructing new facilities to meet vital community needs and by enacting regulations to improve the overall quality of reservation development. While frequently relying on building codes and environmental standards adapted from federal or state agencies, tribes should carefully anticipate the potential for conflict when those standards are applied to traditional cultural activities. In the Swinomish example, the construction of the cultural smokehouse not only resulted in the successful resurgence of

19. Ceremonial
room showing
test fire.

important cultural traditions but also brought about new concerns regarding public health risks. Successful tribal development can be measured by a tribe's ability to meet its community's needs without compromising its environmental health or its cultural priorities.

Once it became aware of the public health risk, the tribe sought technical assistance from outside experts that included the University of Washington and federal and state agencies. The successful outcome from the interagency partnership is attributed to the willingness of each participant to respect the necessity for a culturally appropriate solution, one that did not interfere with traditional ceremonial practices. The use of air quality monitoring equipment and air movement theory helped the tribe and members of the Smokehouse Organization to better understand the health risks associated with the operation of open fires during the winter ceremonies. Technical advisors and community members jointly developed corrective improvements based on acceptable low-technology solutions. The process resulted in building stronger community self-reliance by involving tribal Smokehouse Organization members in each phase of the project.

The Swinomish Smokehouse experience demonstrates how a community can successfully undertake corrective actions to protect its cultural and environmental conditions. Provided with new information about the risks associated with traditional ceremonial practice, the Swinomish Smokehouse Organization mobilized its members to participate in the project. Their extensive understanding about fire burning dynamics fostered a strong working relationship with both tribal officials and technical partners that resulted in a culturally and technically acceptable solution. Tribal members participated in monitoring air quality during the testing periods, evaluated and agreed upon corrective measures, and comprised the work crew that constructed the permanent improvements. Smokehouse members responsible for the ceremonial fires also instituted new procedures for managing the open fires and the air current dynamics to correspond to conditions inside and outside the smokehouse. Understanding the importance of a well-seasoned, dry firewood supply prompted smokehouse members to construct an exterior wood storage facility and to secure a long-term supply of suitable fuel material.

The Swinomish Smokehouse experience is an example of tribal self-reliance, cultural revival, and environmental health risk mitigation. Correlated with the general planning model presented in chapter 7, figure 20 illustrates the internal and external dimensions of the community's smokehouse development experience. Internally, the tribe prioritized the importance of tribal cultural revival by securing funds for the design and construction of the smokehouse. As part of its political building process, it had enacted, and then amended, its building code to ensure that construction activities on the reservation protected the public health

PLANNING STAGE   **DIMENSIONS**

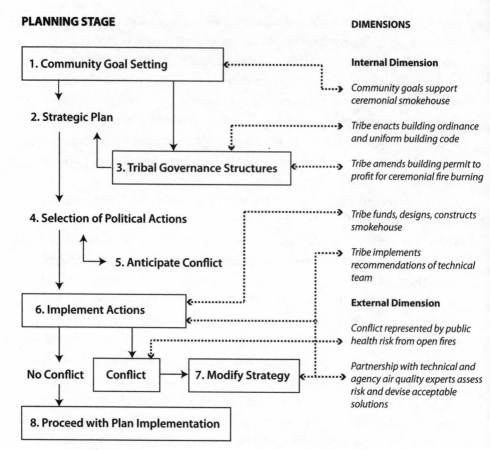

20. Relating the smokehouse experience to the tribal planning model.

and safety, as well as the community's cultural priorities. The case study demonstrates the importance of relationship-building as the tribe sought technical assistance from a university and state and federal agencies. Each partner, in communicating technical testing results to the tribe and its Swinomish Smokehouse Organization members, respected the culturally sensitive nature of the investigation. Recommendations for low-technology remedies illustrated the team's respect for honoring the traditions of ceremonial practice. The experience represented a community-based learning approach as the project commenced with the construction of a cultural priority, followed by the recognition of a potential health risk, the enlisting of a technical support team, and the formulation of corrective actions. The learning experience culminated in the adoption of technical recommendations, installation of improvements, and behavioral adjustments instituted regarding the operation of open fires during winter ceremonies. The project's outcome included reducing risks to the community's health while protecting spiritual practices. Unlike the case study experiences in previous chapters, the smokehouse experience did not concern questions of jurisdiction. Instead, it serves to demonstrate the importance of inter-agency collaborative partnerships in helping to augment a tribe's governing capacity.

11

Environmental Justice on the Swinomish Indian Reservation

ON THE MORNING OF DECEMBER 4, 2002, a blessing ceremony occurred on the Swinomish Indian Reservation to heal the land that once contained a seven-acre hazardous waste dump. Spiritual leaders from the tribe prayed over the site of a recently completed $4.5 million cleanup remediation. Members of the tribe extended words of thanks and offered gifts of blankets and cedar boughs to those who helped heal their reservation homeland. It was a humbling ceremony because the Swinomish people, despite years of actively pursuing environmental justice on this now blessed site, only had words of appreciation for all who were present. The rain that fell on the site during the ceremony filtered through a layer of clean soil that replaced the excavated hazardous material and once again replenished the Swinomish aquifer that had been perilously close to becoming contaminated. It was a reminder of the risks that the tribe would have faced had it not been successful in its two-decade effort to convince the federal government of the necessity for cleaning up the site. Had the aquifer become contaminated, the 1855 Point Elliott Treaty promise of a sustainable homeland for the future generations of Swinomish People might not have been attainable.

Before the enactment of laws regulating the disposal of petroleum by-products, the Texaco and Shell corporations had hired a local contractor to dispose of refinery wastes in a disposal pit on the reservation. Located on privately owned reservation fee land, neither the federal government nor the tribe had a role in reviewing or approving the dumpsite. In the 1950s and 1960s, such practices were common on Indian reservations.

Congress enacted the Comprehensive Environmental Response, Compensation, and Liability Act (CERCLA), commonly known as Superfund, on December 11, 1980. The law provided broad federal authority to respond to releases or threatened releases of hazardous substances that might endanger public health or the environment. CERCLA established requirements concerning closed and abandoned hazardous waste sites, provided for liability of persons responsible for releases of hazardous waste at these sites, and established a trust fund to provide for cleanup when no responsible party could be identified. The law authorized two kinds of response actions: actions to address releases or threatened releases requiring prompt response and actions that reduce the dangers associated with releases or threats of releases of hazardous substances that are serious, but not immediately life threatening. Response actions under CERCLA can only be conducted at sites listed on the US Environmental Protection Agency's (EPA) National Priorities List (NPL).

Despite an initial federal study conducted in the 1980s to assess the site's eligibility under the Superfund national priority criteria, the site was not deemed eligible. The EPA presumed the dumpsite would be exempt under CERCLA because the law did not address releases of petroleum, including crude oil or any fraction thereof that is not otherwise specifically listed as a hazardous substance under the Superfund law. The on-site assessment also failed to notify or to solicit any input from the tribe. During the following two decades, the tribe struggled to convince the EPA (via formal and informal petitions) that the site should be made a federal priority for cleanup, as it threatened the very existence of the Swinomish people. Under an agreement that was later signed, the petroleum refineries agreed to finance the cleanup costs and remove 58,760 tons of petroleum waste product and contaminated soil from four disposal ponds on the Swinomish reservation site.

Environmental Justice and the
Indian Reservation Environment

Over the past decades, recognition that the nation's minority populations and lowest-income communities face a disproportionate amount of adverse health and environmental risk (Slade and Cowart 2000; Stephens

2000) has resulted in serious concern. In 1994, this concern led President Clinton to issue Executive Order 12898 (Clinton 1994a) that focused federal action on environmental justice concerns. EPA responded by developing the Environmental Justice Strategy, which sought to promote justice and equal protection under the law for all environmental statutes and regulations without discrimination based on race, ethnicity, or socioeconomic status (Bryant and Mohai 1992; Bryant 1995; Hines 2001; Ringquist 1998; Towers 2000). Environmental justice implies that potentially harmed communities would have an opportunity to participate in decisions that affect their environment and that their concerns would be fully considered in the decision-making process (Ferris 1993; Harris 1997; Harris and Harper 1997; Helfand and Peyton 1999). Environmental justice is achieved when all people enjoy the same degree of protection from environmental and health hazards, as well as equitable access to decision-making (Newton 1996; Faber 1998). The predominant concern with regards to environmental justice, as well as environmental justice scholarship, focuses on the inequitable distribution of hazards in low-income minority communities (Bullard 1993; Ishiyama 2003).

Environmental justice for tribes involves a different set of concerns than those of other communities, namely, that tribes are sovereign nations and enjoy a unique legal and political status that differentiates them from other environmental justice communities (Suagee 1999; Walker et al. 2002; Wood 1994, 1995a, 1995b). The essential identity of tribes, including their histories, beliefs, physical and spiritual subsistence, is often dependent on particular places, resources, and environmental conditions—conditions that tribes, themselves, have the inherent right to determine (LaVelle 2001; National Environmental Justice Advisory Council 2000). Because Indian tribes and their reservation communities are distinct from other American minority communities, issues of environmental justice are not limited to procedural and distributive justice concerns; they are also intertwined with their unique sovereignty status (Goldtooth 1995; Kuehn 2000). Moreover, much of the environmental justice literature does not adequately address the particularly complex political and historic tribal context. When viewed as an element in tribal self-determination, environmental justice also concerns the procedural redistribution of power in decision-making (Ishiyama 2003; Pulido 1996), whereby procedural justice becomes a central theme in Indian environmental justice (Shrader-Frechette 1996; Suagee 1994).

Tribes as Political Communities

In 1832, Chief Justice Marshall declared that Indian tribes are "distinct political communities having territorial boundaries, within which their authority is exclusive, and having a right to all the lands within those boundaries, which is not only acknowledged, but guaranteed by the United States."[1] The Court acknowledged that the necessity for a tribe to exercise control over its territory was a fundamental and necessary attribute of tribal self-government. In almost all of the treaties entered into between 1787 and 1871, Indians ceded their lands in exchange for promises, including the guarantee of permanent reservations for the tribes and the federal protection of their safety and well-being. The Supreme Court has held that such promises establish a special trust relationship. The relationship brought with it the continued promise to create "a duty of protection" toward Indians. Furthermore, in *United States v. White Mt. Apache*[2] *and United States v. Navajo,*[3] the Court applied previous case law regarding which circumstances warrant a claim by a tribe against the United States for damages of trust. As a trustee of tribal lands and resources, the United States has a duty to ensure that tribes are able to fulfill the original purposes for which their reservations were first established—as tribal homelands—and to take all reasonable steps necessary for protecting trust resources. Under its fiduciary duties as a trustee for Indian resources, the United States can be held liable for failing to protect a tribe's resources (Cohen 1942; Cohen 1986; Royster and Fausett 1989). Thus, the federal trust obligation is broad; it requires the United States to aid tribes in their efforts to protect reservation resources from damage or degradation (Wood 1994). Moreover, it also provides federal assistance in order to

1. *Worcester v. Georgia*, 31 U.S. (6 Pet.) 515 (1832).
2. *United States V. White Mt. Apache Tribe*, 537 U.S. 465 (2003).
3. *United States v. Navaho Nation*, 537 U.S. 488 (2003).

develop tribal self-governing capacities to effectively manage reservation resources (Wood 1995b).

Native American Indian cultures have always had a unique interdependent relationship with the natural environment that supports their existence (Roberts 1975; Harmon 1998). The lands, waters and all living things that comprise the environment of Indian lands are integral components of the social, cultural, and spiritual life of Indian people. Natural resources management has traditionally been a central responsibility of tribal governments (Deloria and Lytle 1984; Lester 1986). Tribal governments have been adamant in protecting the integrity of their environment through the exercise of their sovereign powers to assert management control over resources contained within their reservation boundaries (Deloria 1985; Cornell and Kalt 1992). This is accomplished by setting standards for the environmental integrity of their territories and by regulating activities that might affect that environment.

In the 1970s, when many federal environmental laws were enacted, Congress, for the most part, overlooked the sovereign status of tribal governments and did not provide for direct tribal government involvement in the environmental management of their reservations. As a result, most tribes were severely delayed in developing their environmental infrastructure (Goldtooth 1995). Through a series of congressional acts, policy statements, and executive orders, between 1970 and 2000, the legislative and executive branches of the federal government recognized the federal trust responsibility to tribes and their resources, acknowledged the governmental status of Indian tribes and established a "government-to-government" relationship policy with the tribes (American Indian Lawyer Training Program 1988; Ayer 1991; Clinton 1994b, 1998, 2000; Native American Rights Fund 1988; Nixon 1970; Wood 1995a). In 1984, EPA published its agency policy for the development and implementation of tribal environmental protection programs (US Environmental Protection Agency 1983, 1984a, 1984b). The EPA Indian policy provides the necessary guidance for the administration of environmental programs on Indian lands by promising to work with tribes on a government-to-government basis and to recognize tribal governments as the *primary* authority for implementing federal environmental programs on tribal lands. The policy commits the agency to take steps to assist the tribes in assuming regulatory responsibility for reservation lands and encourages cooperation between the tribes and the state and local governments in the implementation of federal environmental programs.

The EPA policy has also resisted the application of state regulatory jurisdiction by affirming its trust responsibility on Indian lands. In defending against Washington State's application of environmental jurisdiction on Indian lands, the Ninth Circuit Court of Appeals affirmed that EPA properly denied Washington State's assertion of hazardous waste regulatory jurisdiction over reservation environments.[4] Similar reasoning was applied in other cases where the Court of Appeals for the Tenth Circuit affirmed EPA's authority to implement the Underground Injection Control (UIC) program on Indian lands even before Congress specifically authorized EPA to do so under the 1986 Amendments to the Safe Drinking Act. In *Nance*,[5] the court supported EPA's approval of the Northern Cheyenne Tribe's redesignation of the reservation air shed from class II to class I, even though no express authorization for such action was mentioned in the federal Clean Air Act.

During the past two decades, tribes have made significant progress in ensuring that the protections under the nation's environmental laws extend to Indian country (Tsosie 1996; Suagee 1991, 2002a). The EPA's 1984 Indian policy has led to the amendment of several of the nation's environmental laws, authorizing Indian tribes to assume the primary role for managing their environmental resources (Coursen 1993; Harris and Harper 1997; Lewis 1986). The authority of tribes to assume the primary role as managers of their environmental resources affords them the opportunity to implement environmental protection programs that are consistent with their traditional values. It is more difficult, however, for the tribes alone to accomplish these goals when faced with the environmental degradation caused by non-Indian persons on non-Indian reservation lands (Sanders and Otsea 1982; Weaver 1990). While Indian tribes, as

4. *State of Washington, Department of Ecology v. EPA*, 752 F.2d 1465 (9th Cir. 1985).
5. *Nance v. EPA*, 645 F.2d 701 (9th Cir. 1981), *cert. denied*, 102. S. Ct. 976 (1982).

sovereign nations, retain the right to manage and control their reservation affairs, their authority to extend tribal laws to non-Indians has been, at times, unclear or contested (Zaferatos 2004a). Tribal authority is based on the dual power of inherent authority and authority delegated by Congress under the environmental statutes. Subject to the overriding legislative power of the federal government and the Supreme Court's rule of judicial divestiture (Suagee 2002b), a tribe has the power of self-government to "make its own laws and be ruled by them" (National Indian Policy Center 1993; Goeppele 1990). For example, under the Clean Water Act, tribes may exercise their authority under their inherent sovereignty. In addition, in several instances, Congress has also delegated civil regulatory authority to Indian tribes. Under the Clean Air Act, EPA interpreted Congress's intent in the "treatment as a state" (TAS) provision as a delegation of authority to tribes (Suagee 2002b).

Several federal environmental statutes authorize tribes to apply to EPA for TAS, similar to the procedure afforded to the states (EPA 1984b, 1995). TAS statutes allow certain federal powers to be directly exercised by a tribe and provide grant assistance to help build the prerequisite tribal technical and administrative capacity necessary for exercising delegated federal authority under environmental statutes. TAS programs transfer primary administrative duties to tribes, allowing them to act with authority equal to that of states over their reservation territories. Delegated federal power under TAS can be especially important in addressing environmental violations involving non-Indians on non-Indian lands within the reservation, where the reach of tribal authority, alone, may not be sufficient to enforce compliance with tribal laws (Zaferatos 1998). Tribal governments, thus, have access to substantial powers to protect the health and welfare of the reservation population and to preserve the quality of the reservation environment.

Although the EPA has a responsibility to protect the reservation's environmental quality, it often does not exercise its obligations within reservations. Despite EPA's adopted Indian policy, the authority to delegate programs to the tribes occurred approximately two decades after the initial enactment of the environmental laws. Because of the exclusion of tribes in the early period of environmental management capacity development, tribal lands were often ignored, the tribal role in the implementation of federal programs was ill defined, and tribal capacity to operate regulatory programs remained largely underdeveloped.

The Swinomish Tribe's Environmental Authority and Tribal Capacity Building

The Swinomish tribe is a federally recognized Indian tribe that was organized pursuant to the Indian Reorganization Act (1934) and whose inherent authority is pursuant to its constitution and bylaws. Like other reservations that were formed under treaties and that were later subject to the General Allotment Act of 1887, much of the Swinomish Indian Reservation became substantially alienated. This condition led non-tribal governments, including state and local governments, to ignore tribal jurisdiction on non-trust reservation lands, and often impose their own authority, instead. Even though the tribe had asserted its governing powers over all reservation lands and resources and had claimed the right to protect, conserve and restore the total environment of the lands, air, waters, flora and fauna, and other resources traditional to its culture, prior to the 1970s, its authority was largely ignored.

Since the late 1970s, when the tribe enacted its first land use laws and environmental protection ordinances, the level of environmental management capacity was only in its initial stage of development. As a natural resource trustee under both tribal and applicable federal laws, the tribe's environmental management capacity slowly emerged in the 1980s. With funding provided under the Bureau of Indian Affairs' (BIA) Public Law 638 program, Department of Health and Human Services, Indian Health Services, and various EPA grant programs, the tribe's technical capacity eventually grew into a comprehensive environmental management program comprised of scientists, planners, managers, attorneys, and consultants that oversaw the development of a reservation-wide environmental policy infrastructure. The formation of a tribal environmental commission, the Swinomish Culture and Environmental Protection Agency in 1989 led to the negotiation of agreements with EPA, under TAS, that provided for the cooperative management of tribal environmental resources; the development of tribal standards for land use, air quality, surface and groundwater quality; and eventually the tribe's oversight of the PM Northwest (PMNW) dumpsite remediation project.

As part of a strategy to expand its technical capacity and its jurisdiction on the reservation, the tribe also supported initiatives, more fully detailed in chapter 9, that led to improved inter-governmental cooperation with federal, state, and local governments in an effort to better address long standing land use and natural resource management problems, both on and off the reservation. Beginning in 1989, several environmental agreements were entered into with EPA and state agencies to further strengthen the tribe's capacity for protecting the reservation environment (table 13). In 1996, a Tribal Environmental Agreement (TEA) was signed, implementing EPA's government-to-government Indian policy and the agency's commitment to integrated partnerships for reservation environmental protection. The agreement helped the tribe to comprehensively assess reservation environmental problems and provided funding and technical assistance for establishing several reservation environmental programs. In 1996, an historic tri-lateral agreement was also reached with EPA and the Washington Department of Ecology (WDOE) for cooperation in the administration of federal water quality permits. Under the agreement, the tribe contracted with the state to perform technical studies for National Pollution Discharge Elimination Systems Program (NPDES) permit applications until such time that the tribe was able to enact its own water quality standards and formally apply for EPA program delegation. The tribe's intergovernmental cooperative approach also led to developing collaborative air quality, timber management, and water resources management programs, both on and off the reservation. The tribe's environmental management capacity expanded over a two-decade period to address several complex and historic environmental problems on the reservation, one of the priorities being the threat posed to reservation groundwater associated with the historic PMNW petroleum dumpsite.

Stemming from its awareness of several historic disposal practices that had occurred on the reservation since the late 1950s, the tribe prioritized the investigation and assessment of potentially hazardous threats to its

TABLE 13 Swinomish Environmental Management Agreements

Date	Agreement	Affected Parties
1989	Approval for "treatment as a state" under EPA regulations	US EPA
1996	Tri-Party Agreement for CWA NPDES Permit Administration	US EPA; Washington Department of Ecology
1996	Tribal Environmental Agreement	US EPA
1996	Air quality technical assistance	Northwest Air Pollution Authority
1997	Protocols for Coordinated Forest Practices Regulation; Draft Memorandum of Understanding	Washington State Department of Natural Resources

Source: Nicholas C. Zaferatos. © Springer Science+Business Media: Environmental Management.

reservation. The following account summarizes the events that occurred between 1981 and 2000 chronicling the tribe's attempt to assess the environmental threat to groundwater resources from the PMNW dumpsite, one of several disposal sites on the reservation which operated without permits. The case study traces the tribe's decades-long appeal for federal action to remove the potential threat to the reservation environment.

History of the PMNW Dump Site and the Tribe's Exclusion in EPA Environmental Assessment

Section 103 of CERCLA requires industries that were engaged in the transport and disposal of hazardous waste material to submit a disclosure report on disposal practices on or before June 9, 1981. Three industries reported the disposal of materials on the Swinomish Indian Reservation. The Texaco and Shell Petroleum refineries are located immediately adjacent to the reservation on Fidalgo Island in Skagit County, Washington. On June 11, 1981, the Texaco Corporation reported the disposal of 126,000 gallons of waste to a reservation landfill between 1958 and 1961, and indicated that there were "no likely suspected releases to the environment."

The Shell Oil Company reported on June 8, 1981, that its waste disposal between 1960 and 1968 included refinery wastes that were not tested prior to disposal at the same reservation site.

On May 29, 1981, PM Northwest Inc. reported its activities in handling waste materials, collected from the Shell and Texaco refineries since 1958, and listed a variety of waste materials, including spent catalyst, oil sludge, and spent caustic materials that were disposed of in a non-trust, fee title landfill site it owned and operated on the northern end of the reservation, in close proximity to the petroleum refineries. It reported a disposal quantity of 13,000 cubic feet of material within its 21.9-acre reservation facility. The site was not permitted to operate as a hazardous waste disposal site by federal, state, or tribal governments. In fact, these agencies had no knowledge about the operations of the site until the years following its closure. PMNW, a non-Indian company, operated its disposal site since 1958 and reported closing the dumpsite in 1967. The disposal pits were covered over with clean soil. In the disclosure report, PMNW indicated that "at the present time there was approximately one acre where some oil has surfaced." It also reported that there were no homes or wells in the area for at least a mile in any direction.

In investigating the potential types of toxicants in the Shell and Texaco reports of waste materials disposed of on the reservation, WDOE, working with the EPA CERCLA inquiry, identified several potential types of pollutants, including aluminum oxide, hydrochloric acid, fluorides, and other hazardous materials, that were commonly associated with refinery products. EPA reviewed the disclosure reports and in a correspondence to WDOE found that "there was not enough information to make judgment," recommending that a site visit be scheduled for further review. An EPA site assessment contractor conducted a site investigation in June 1981, without notifying the tribe of its investigation. The contractor determined that the PMNW site score under CERCLA criteria would likely be " . . . low, and it is likely that the quantities of heavy metals involved is small," an opinion based largely on the Shell and Texaco disclosure reports. EPA findings later revealed a copy of an invoice dated January 6, 1970 (several years following the reported closure of the dumpsite), from PMNW to Shell listing 939 barrels of waste material and 295 drums that had not been previously reported in the CERCLA Section 103 disclosure. On October 23, 1985, EPA sent a letter to PMNW announcing that additional information was required to accurately profile the nature and extent of past waste disposal activities at the site.

In November 1985, following discussions between EPA, BIA, WDOE and PMNW, a subsequent EPA on-site investigation took place, again, without notifying the tribe. The investigation reports concluded that large quantities of uncharacterized petroleum refinery wastes were disposed of at the site. In 1986, having been first notified about the inspection by the BIA, the tribe sent a letter to EPA stating it had not been contacted regarding investigations conducted by the EPA site assessment contractor and that, unknown to EPA or to its contractor, the tribe's public water supply was located within one mile of the site. The tribe outlined several of its concerns: (1) the PMNW site was located in close proximity to the tribe's groundwater source, a sole source reservation aquifer; (2) disposal quantities remained unknown; (3) tribal members working for both companies in the 1960s informed the tribe that the companies disposed of large quantities of caustic liquids in 55-gallon drums into PMNW pits; (4) the potential existed for groundwater seepage contamination to the reservation aquifer as well as to adjacent marine wetlands; and (5) the assurance that EPA would afford the tribe the opportunity to directly and substantially participate in subsequent investigations.

Although the EPA site investigation report identified the existence of three surface ponds, there was limited information regarding the ponds' contents. This prompted the tribe to request EPA to conduct soils and groundwater testing. In response, EPA conducted a limited soils and groundwater sampling investigation, in June 1986, and concluded that measurable amounts of several petroleum products existed in the soils. However, the potential for groundwater contamination remained unknown. The EPA report, made available to the tribe, concluded that it was not necessary for any further actions under CERCLA to be taken and that no further Superfund actions should be considered. In fact, EPA refused to consider the site as a candidate for the Superfund program due to its interpretation of the "exemption rule," which excluded oilfield waste under both the Resource and Recovery Act (RCRA) and CERCLA.

In 1987, in response to EPA's decision, and continuing through 1990, the tribe repeatedly attempted to persuade EPA that additional hazardous site analysis should be conducted in order to fully evaluate the potential threats to the reservation environment.

The tribe's persistence resulted in EPA agreeing to pursue a further inquiry, and on November 23, 1990, EPA informed the tribe that it had sent a letter to PMNW requesting additional information pursuant to CERCLA and RCRA. The letter requested PMNW to identify the chemical characterization of all hazardous substances disposed at the site, and, for each hazardous substance, to identify how it was handled by providing a shipping manifest along with any environmental investigations that may have been conducted. The PMNW response failed to disclose any additional information concerning the potential for hazardous risk at the site. On January 4, 1991, the tribe formally notified EPA that it had failed to properly inform and involve the tribe in early site investigations, which resulted in the exclusion of crucial tribal testimony. The tribe emphasized that by excluding the tribe in the investigations EPA ignored both tribal jurisdiction and its interests regarding reservation public health matters. The tribe urged EPA to acknowledge its fiduciary responsibility pursuant to the federal trust doctrine and demanded that EPA undertake a comprehensive site investigation under CERCLA. However, on February 1, 1991, the EPA regional director again reaffirmed its position that since it appeared the PMNW dumpsite was not eligible for NPL listing, Superfund resources would not be available for funding any further investigation or for the remediation of the site.

The Tribe's Continuing Efforts to Persuade EPA to Honor Its Trust Responsibility

Between 1991 and 1995, the tribe continued to reiterate its concerns regarding the potential threat to the reservation groundwater supply and demanded that measures be taken to guarantee that reservation groundwater be fit for human consumption. In response to the tribe's continued persistence, EPA sent a letter to Texaco in 1995 stating that "USEPA obtained information indicating the presence of hazardous substances within the material disposed at the PMNW site, as defined by Section 101 of CERCLA," which provided the long awaited formal notification to the refinery of its potential liability as defined under CERCLA.[6] The notification requested additional information concerning materials disposed of at the site, including materials contained in the drums that were reported by the tribe to have been buried at the site.

In late 1996, EPA finally agreed to conduct a further study and authorized its site contractor to perform yet another site investigation. Site characterization was further defined in May 1997, when EPA conducted an emergency removal assessment, which included subsurface sampling in twelve test pits within the approximate boundaries of the disposal ponds. The samples were analyzed for volatile organic compounds (VOCs), semi-volatile organic compounds (SVOCs), metals, and total petroleum hydrocarbons (TPHs). Numerous contaminants were detected with several exceeding the Washington State Model Toxics Control Act (MTCA) cleanup standards. However, after reviewing the consultant's technical report released on July 16, 1997—which found that benzene exceeded the cleanup standard level for protection of groundwater in three samples; xylene exceeded the cleanup standard for groundwater in one sample; TPHs exceeded the cleanup standard in six samples; and TPH (diesel) exceeded the cleanup standard in nine samples—EPA again dismissed the site's eligibility based on the CERCLA petroleum exclusion provision.

To assist the tribe in analyzing the EPA technical reports, an environmental consultant was retained to advise the tribe's council and planning staff about the potential risks to the reservation environment and to design a further investigation suitable for assessing the reservation environmental risk. On July 29, 1997, based upon its consultant's recommendations, the tribe requested that EPA conduct a new analysis for the detection of solvents not previously tested for, including tecnol, cyanide, zinc, nickel, and cadmium, metals that are often associated with refinery wastes. The tribe also noted that, while EPA's preliminary data showed very

6. See section 107(a).

high levels of diesel petroleum hydrocarbons and benzene, xylene, and other volatiles, the limited excavation that was conducted in the May 1997 test failed to uncover the drums, which had been reported by the tribe to be buried at the site. Based on its preliminary review of the consultant's data, EPA responded that it did not see further work warranted because "the primary contaminant is oil related product" and "no surface waters are affected or directly threatened" by the site.

Unable to convince EPA to proceed with further investigations, in the summer of 1997, the tribe hired its own contractor to conduct a magnetic survey to detect evidence of buried drums. The tribe's research included a review of aerial photographs of the site taken between 1960 and 1975, which revealed the existence of a fourth disposal pit that was previously unreported. The aerials provided clear evidence of the location of the disposal ponds. Using global positioning and geographic information systems (GIS) mapping, tribal staff were able to pinpoint the coordinate locations for the ponds and establish a survey grid on the site. The magnetic survey conducted in October 1997 detected the presence of several clusters of magnetic anomalies over the buried disposal ponds. The findings provided persuasive evidence of the probable existence of buried drums. In a subsequent meeting with the EPA Regional Director, the tribe presented its research findings and again urged an additional EPA investigation in order to recover the buried drums in the disposal ponds and to test the contents of the drums.

EPA-Tribal Cooperation in Environmental Remediation

In a meeting with the tribe in February 1998, EPA agreed to locate and uncover the buried drums, sample for toxic materials, and further investigate the possibility of contamination of groundwater in the site vicinity. This proved to be a pivotal meeting between the tribe and EPA, as the regional director, persuaded by the evidence presented in the tribe's magnetic survey study, finally agreed to reassess the site under CERCLA rules. EPA also agreed to conduct its relationship with the tribe pursuant to the EPA government-to-government policy and to expand the sampling investigation in order to detect the presence of PCBs, chlorinated organics, and other compounds in the groundwater system.

The decision to proceed with the investigation in full cooperation with the tribe was formalized in an agreement that was drafted by tribal attorneys. Between 1998 and 1999, EPA conducted an integrated site assessment (ISA) to determine the need for a site clean-up response action. The site assessment involved the collection of samples from the former disposal ponds and from surrounding areas that were potentially impacted from contaminant migration. Samples collected from the disposal ponds, in June 1998, included aliquots from eleven excavated drums and from sludge material surrounding the drums. A total of thirty-six soil, sludge, or product samples and six infiltrated groundwater samples were collected. In 1999, subsequent samples were collected from on-site monitoring wells, the tribe's municipal well, the perimeter of the dump site, and from a wetland area located immediately to the east of the dump site. A total of twenty-two groundwater, five surface water, twenty-two sediment and twenty-four wetland samples were collected in the subsequent investigation.

The ISA also recovered several buried drums and documented the release of hazardous substances at the site, which led the regional director to reach a pivotal conclusion—that a federal response to the site containing hazardous substances was not limited by the petroleum exclusion provision under CERCLA. This consequential opinion modified EPA's earlier position and led to a decision supportive of federal remediation action. Future response activities for the site included the removal of hazardous substances for off-site disposal at an RCRA-approved hazardous waste management facility, additional characterization of groundwater contamination, implementation of a response action to address potential groundwater problems, and the investigation and implementation of response actions for hazardous substances that had migrated away from the PMNW property. EPA agreed to further evaluate the site for placement on the National Priorities List (NPL) pursuant to section 105 of CERCLA. Results from the ISA activities are presented in table 14.

On April 25, 2000, EPA urged the responsible parties, including PMNW and the oil refineries, to voluntarily enter into negotiations for the performance and financing of a cleanup response action under CERCLA.

TABLE 14 Integrated Site Assessment Findings

Sample Location	Federal or State Standards	Sampling Results
Disposal pond surfaces and subsurface soils, sludge, and drum contents	Region 9 soil PRGs,* EPA MCLs,** or MTCA Method A Soil Cleanup Levels***	benzene (94,000 ug/kg), benzo[a]-anthracene (100,0000 ug/kg), carbon tetrachloride (2200 ug/kg), mercury (7900 ug/kg), naphthalene (1,300,000 ug/kg), 1,3,5-trimethyl-benzene (540,000 ug/kg), benzo[b]-fluoranthene (5,700 ug/kg), benzo[a]-pyrene (200,000 ug/kg), carbazole (200,000 ug/kg), chrysene (300,000 ug/kg), 1,2,4-trimethyl-benzene (950,000 ug/kg),1,3,5-trimethyl-benzene (540,000 ug/kg), 1,2-dibromo-3-chloropropane (25,000 ug/kg), 2,6-dinitrotoluene (300,000 ug/kg), n-nitrosodium-phenylamine (1,000,000 ug/kg), tetrachloroethene (28,000 ug/kg), arsenic (26,000 ug/kg), cadmium (3,800 ug/kg), chromium (2,700,000 ug/kg), lead (330,000 ug/kg). Total petroleum hydrocarbon (TPH) standard was exceeded in 33 of 37 samples collected from the identified source areas.
Groundwater samples from monitoring wells	Region 9 PRGs (tap water), EPA MCLs or MTCA A Protection of Groundwater Cleanup Levels	benzene (650 ug/l), benzo[b]-flouranthene (5 ug/l), bis(2-ethylhexyl)-phthlate (20 ug/l), naphthalene (45.4 ug/l), 1,3,5-trimethyl-benzene (280 ug/l), dibenzofuran (43 ug/l), chrysene (23 ug/l), ethylbenzene (140 ug/l), 1,2,4-trimethyl-

TABLE 14 Integrated Site Assessment Findings (*cont.*)

Sample Location	Federal or State Standards	Sampling Results
		benzene (570 ug/l), methylene chloride (23 ug/l), toluene (910 ug/l), vinyl chloride (2 ug/l), antimony (20.6 ug/l), barium (2,200 ug/l), chromium (410 ug/l), lead (7.51 ug/l)
Surface water samples collected from locations in and near the adjacent wetland area	Ambient Water Quality Criteria, or MTCA B Surface Water Cleanup Levels	arsenic (13.7 ug/l), aluminum (6790 ug/l), copper (47.9 ug/l), iron (53,900 ug/l), lead (130 ug/l), mercury (0.14 ug/l), nickel (31 ug/l)
Sediment samples collected from locations in and near the adjacent wetlands area	MTCA Sediment Quality Standards	cadmium (8.85 ug/kg)
Other volatile organic compounds, semi-volatile organic compounds, and metals detected in the media sampled at the site	Detected substances below screening or regulatory levels	VOCs and SCOVs are not naturally occurring chemicals and should not be present. Detected metals exceeded background concentrations.

* Primary Remediation Goals (PRGs)

** Maximum Contaminant Levels (MCLs)

*** MTCA Method A Soil Cleanup Levels

Source: Nicholas C. Zaferatos. © Springer Science+Business Media: Environmental Management.

The Cleanup Agreement

EPA negotiated a Memorandum of Agreement (MOA) with the tribe that established the working relationship, roles and responsibilities between EPA and the tribe (US Environmental Protection Agency 2000b). EPA would act as the lead agency for site cleanup activities, working in close consultation with the tribe. The tribe would be a signatory to an administrative order on consent (AOC) for the cleanup activities at the PMNW site (US Environmental Protection Agency 2002a). The mutual commitments made by the tribe and EPA to work together to satisfy the goals of the agreement are summarized in paragraph IV.2 of the MOA as follows:

> EPA will consult with the tribe with respect to (1) all major decision points, broad issues, and overall results regarding the Site and (2) other matters regarding the Superfund process concerning the Site which the parties may agree are of significance to the tribe as discussed during their periodic meetings or other communications.

As used in the MOA, the term "consult" was defined as the "process of seeking, discussing, and considering the views of the tribe at the earliest time in EPA Region 10's decision making." Consultation would mean more than simply providing notification and allowing tribal comment on agency decisions. Rather, consultation would involve ongoing, two-way communication with the goal of attaining a consensus that would effectively address the concerns of the tribe. Equally important, the AOC provided that the tribe would be "treated as a state" under section 126 of CERCLA with respect to implementation of response actions. The tribe's role as a state, together with EPA's obligations to deal with the tribe on a government-to-government basis, were controlling under the agreement. The tribe was directly involved in all aspects of the site cleanup work, including overseeing field work and reviewing and commenting on work products and deliverables. Equally important, the agreement provided that tribally established cleanup standards would be enforced, which exceeded state of Washington cleanup standards for residual soil by 30 percent. The agreement enabled the tribe to further expand its environmental management staff by reimbursing the tribe for its staffing and technical consultant costs in conducting AOC activities. EPA primarily relied on the on-site expertise of the tribal staff and the tribe's consultants to oversee the site remediation.

The agreement between EPA, the tribe, and the responsible parties provided for the entire cleanup of the site. The response was conducted in two phases. Phase 1 involved contaminant source removal as a "time-critical removal action" (TCR). Phase 2, a "non-time critical removal action" (NTCR), assessed the potential risk to off-site properties and evaluated further EPA response actions. The phase 2 investigation would be conducted following completion of the phase 1 TCR action.

Conclusions and Implications for Planning

What differentiates the Swinomish experience from non-tribal environmental justice cases, and qualifies the experience as an example of Indian environmental justice, was EPA's dual responsibility to advance national environmental policy and laws, including environmental justice, while concurrently advancing its special trust responsibility to correct past damages to reservation resources. It is critical that Indian environmental justice acknowledge tribal sovereignty and the fundamental tribal interest in reservation environmental management. From 1981 to 1986, site investigation activities conducted by EPA and its consultants occurred in the complete absence of any involvement by the tribe. In 1986, after EPA announced that no cleanup actions were required, the tribe was finally notified of the unilateral decision. When the tribe protested EPA's findings and decisions, the potential of risk to tribal resources was repeatedly minimized. The tribe, however, was diligent in its efforts to protect its reservation resources. To establish that an environmental risk was present, it relied upon its own authority to conduct investigations that showed the existence of buried drums on the site, along with other evidence that was brought forth. Beginning in 1987, tribal leaders lobbied continuously on a government-to-government basis, until 2000, when the agreement providing for site cleanup was finally negotiated. The remediation effort resulted in several environmental and political outcomes:

• The protection of human health and the environment through the excavation and off-site disposal of 58,790 tons of hazardous materials;

- The attainment of tribally determined environmental standards for residual soil cleanup that exceeded the state's requirements;
- Federal assurances that potential off-site contaminant migration would not present a risk to human health and to the environment;
- The negotiation of the MOA and AOC defining the government-to-government relationship governing the cleanup program;
- The reimbursement of costs related to ongoing tribal efforts to implement cleanup of the site; and
- The expansion of the tribe's environmental management capacity to collaborate on a technically equal basis with EPA during the cleanup process.[7]

In addition to the prerequisite condition for establishing an environmental management authority based on inherent tribal powers of self-government, in order for tribes to fully achieve their goals for ensuring a safe reservation environment, cooperation and support from the federal government, pursuant to the federal trust responsibility, is also needed. The type of support that is required varies among tribes, including funding to acquire and develop technical environmental capacity, federal technical assistance to jointly solve environmental problems, and political support to mutually carry out the EPA Indian trust policy. From the Swinomish perspective, reservation homeland security required the removal of environmental threats from the reservation pursuant to its own established policies, which recognize a sacred obligation to care for and minister to the lands and resources of the reservation and to ensure a homeland that does not pose a risk to human health and to the environment. Because the reservation is essentially an island surrounded by saltwater, the reservation's sole-source groundwater aquifer and adjoining wetlands and tidal areas could have significantly been degraded by migration of contaminants from the disposal site had the cleanup action not occurred.

---

7. That capacity later enabled the tribe to successfully manage the closure of a large reservation solid waste landfill site, clean up other abandoned reservation waste sites, manage several aquatic habitat restoration projects, and to more fully participate in other regional environmental management activities.

21. Superfund excavation of PM Northwest site in progress. With permission of the Swinomish Indian Tribal Community Archive.

The Swinomish experience occurred during a decade prior to the framing of "environmental justice." Although the long-pursued Superfund action had not been characterized as an "environmental justice" case, per se, I believe it, nevertheless, serves as an exemplar of Indian environmental justice as it reflects a tribe's enduring struggle to remedy an environmental injustice. In this case, environmental injustice was caused through a long history of events that led to the political subjugation of the reservation in which tribal jurisdiction was ignored and suppressed, allowing for tribal lands and resources not only to be occupied, but, as this case study demonstrates, also polluted by non-tribal interests. Through its own initiative, the tribe was able to bring sufficient federal attention to finally remove a serious environmental risk. Environmental justice was accomplished through the concurrent tribal actions of political assertiveness, of acquiring technical knowledge to assess environmental risk, and of implementing an effective strategy to achieve remedial action.

In the case of the Swinomish Indian reservation, the tribe's persistence over a period of two decades proved instrumental in the eventual removal of a threat to the reservation environment. The PMNW case illustrates a progression of events that systematically led to the tribe's attainment of its reservation environmental protection goals. Equally important, the experience also helped to inform EPA's own understanding of its responsibilities as a trustee for the reservation environment, as EPA (1) initially minimized the potential threat to the very existence of the Swinomish people by neglecting to fully consider the threats to tribal resources and tribal members' health; (2) neglected to consult with the tribe on a government-to-government basis, thereby failing to ensure procedural environmental justice and to uphold its trust responsibility; and (3) eventually came to respect the crucial contributions of the tribe, whose experience, growing expertise, and traditional knowledge proved instrumental to the cleanup, restoration, and healing of the PMNW dumpsite and the Swinomish homeland. Ultimately, EPA availed itself of an important opportunity to facilitate tribal self-determination and to support effective tribal environmental management.

The MOA that was executed with the tribe represented a framework for structuring a good faith government-to-government procedure for the CERCLA response action and fulfilled EPA's trust responsibilities to effectively consult with the tribe regarding the protection of reservation environmental resources. The MOA identified each government's role and responsibility in relation to the remedial actions and provided for financial and technical assistance that enabled the tribe to effectively manage the remediation work. The MOA further created a consultative relationship between EPA and the tribe consistent with the EPA Indian policy. In accordance with that policy, EPA recognized the tribe as the primary party for setting standards, making environmental decisions, and managing programs affecting the reservation environment.

The project demonstrates the importance of expanding a tribe's environmental governance capacity in order to fully enable the tribe to directly participate in the environmental cleanup process. Following an almost twenty-year effort, the cleanup investigations and cooperative management activities became a model of both technical and political collaboration between the federal and tribal environmental agencies. The environmental remediation experience on the Swinomish Indian reservation demonstrates how tribal self-governance and environmental management capacity building are two integral elements in tribal planning, as well as necessary conditions before effective environmental justice can occur in Indian country. The Swinomish experience is summarized in figure 22, which correlates the experience to the general planning model introduced in chapter 7. The experience not only removed the environmental risk that threatened the long term survival of the Swinomish People, but it also helped to foster a meaningful partnership, illustrating how

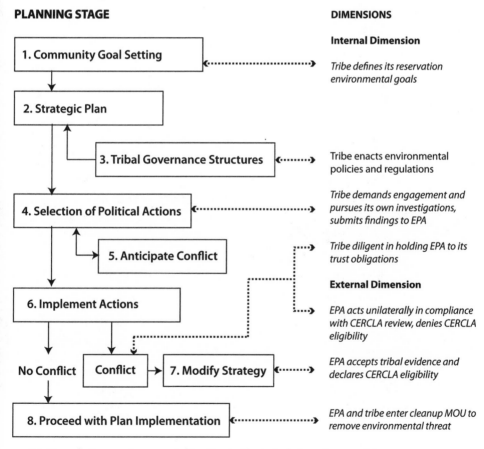

22. Correlating environmental justice to the tribal planning model.

a tribe and the federal trustee can effectively work together to manage the reservation environment.

In keeping with tribal cultural traditions, the project concluded with a "Blessing of the Land" ceremony—a cultural sharing, healing, and recognition process that included individuals from the tribe, EPA, the refineries, the property owner, contractors, and media. Hosted by the tribal chairman and Swinomish spiritual leaders and held under a tent in the woods during a Pacific Northwest rain, the ceremony closed with the remembrance of why everyone was brought together. One of the oil company representatives present expressed his gratitude to all of those who took an active part in the cleanup and healing process and particularly thanked the tribe for helping to remind everyone involved about the sacredness of the land.

12

Conclusion

IF PLANNERS working in Indian country are to be effective, they must understand both the opportunities and the risks inherent in a tribe's limited political sovereignty, from which the powers to plan their tribal homelands are derived. Their planning approach should, as much as possible, be aligned with the process of tribal governance capacity building. This book is written from the perspective of tribal planning as a process that is linked to tribal empowerment, and therefore, those activities are inseparably intertwined. Planners working in the service of tribal communities must become competent in the dual aspects of substantive planning, which concerns planning subject matter, and procedural planning, which concerns implementation, particularly when conflicts are involved. Understanding the procedural constraints that are implicit in the work of tribal planning is the principal focus of this book.

Throughout this book, I have argued that tribal planners must not accept what may appear to be insurmountable obstacles as static boundaries to their work. Obstacles are not static, but rather, dynamic, malleable, and subject to change. Neither federal constraints, nor state constraints, nor the entrenched influences of the larger political economy should limit a tribe's vision-making ability. The unraveling of obstructions that stand between a tribe and its vision of a sustainable future community is a necessary step in freeing the tribe from suppression. Planning is an indispensable mechanism and a methodical procedure for altering the variables that block a tribe's community development. Possessing the capacity for understanding past and current circumstances, planning represents a cognitive process for mapping the strategic steps that are necessary for moving the tribal community forward.

I have also attempted to elucidate a way of thinking about how to approach the difficult conditions that separate tribal planning from planning that is occurring outside of Indian country. The approach is one that builds tribal empowerment while simultaneously integrating, rather than isolating, tribes from their political surroundings. In order for tribes to excel in their community development, their political resolve must be strong and relentless, but it must also have the capacity to address two important prerequisite conditions: it must expand its capacity to perform the broad functions associated with governance, and it must be willing to interact within its political landscape. Tribal planning strategies must take into account the balance of interests that are active within the tribal planning situation and must be genuinely considerate of those interests.

As illustrated through case study experiences, tribal interests can be advanced when tribes effectively assert their position in situations where they were once isolated, which historically resulted in political subjugation. The rebalancing of the political landscape, where tribal interests are infused into mainstream planning, is not easy to achieve. Ultimately, as tribes emerge as the primary drivers of planning rather than as planning objects, the work of tribal planning achieves a transformational quality, as it releases tribes from their subjugated past.

This book presents the idea of tribal sovereignty as an ever-evolving political concept that has been shaped and reshaped by past federal policies and legal doctrine. In contrast, the continued reshaping of tribal sovereignty in the twenty-first century has expanded to emphasize the essential interests of tribes. The reshaping of the idea of sovereignty is propelled primarily through the mobilizing efforts of tribal nations, themselves, and considerably aided by a stable federal Indian self-governance policy and the emerging recognition of tribal sovereignty rights by state governments. The newfound dimension of tribal sovereignty provides important innovative pathways for tribes to further advance their development.

I have emphasized that the control of the reservation territory is of paramount importance to the sustainability of tribal communities. By better understanding how to negotiate the jurisdictional boundaries that define tribal governance, tribes are finding new avenues for re-delineating the balance of powers that operate within their tribal planning situations.

The lessons learned from court rulings are important considerations in tribal planning and should serve to guide the reframing of tribal sovereignty as a formative power. As planning advances a tribal community's political integrity, its economic security, and its cultural well-being, its formative power is being exercised in ways that also contribute to contemporary American planning principles that call for more equitable forms of community development and multicultural diversity in regional planning.

Moreover, the definition of the tribal community's *essential character*, as emphasized in *Brendale*, is becoming reimagined, as tribes have begun the process of expanding reservation planning to incorporate the diversity of interests that are present within the broader reservation community. By defining the *essential character* of a reservation to include a broad community of interests, tribes become better positioned as the principal government in advancing the well-being of the entire reservation community. The redefined essential character of the reservation can be accomplished through such planning strategies as involving non-tribal residents in the formulation of reservation policies and extending essential governmental services to benefit all reservation residents. Under this inclusive approach to reservation planning, tribal governments begin to assume their rightful place as the principal government in reservation affairs. The ability to foster effective dialogue with which to communicate a tribe's priorities can result in improved relationships between tribal and non-tribal communities and in the eventual acceptance of a more pluralistic community. Furthermore, a reservation plan that addresses the holistic needs of the diverse reservation community presents the strongest argument in the defense of a tribe's political authority.

The case studies illustrate how the operation of co-management can be a workable alternative in meeting the dual concerns of tribal and non-tribal interests. Co-management is not intended as a weakening of tribal governance, provided that the content of concurrent policies are in agreement, as the case of Skagit County and Swinomish planning has shown. When overlapping policies are consistent, a condition of jurisdictional concurrency is created as two separate governments simultaneously apply their individual, but compatible policies to achieve mutual goals. In the case of the Skagit Valley region, this approach represented an alternative to a jurisdictional showdown and helped to circumvent continued conflict. As a step toward achieving consistency in regional planning, it has significantly reduced both jurisdictional uncertainty and policy disagreements for more than a quarter of a century.

This book also emphasizes the importance of tribal planning in addressing the relations of power structures that create the *subjugation of Indians* and the *dependent Indian periphery*. As a political movement, Indian self-determination has made considerable gains since the 1970 federal policy proclamation. The assimilation and termination policies of the past have been repudiated, and the hidden and sublime controlling mechanisms born from those policies are gradually becoming unveiled through tribal planning approaches that link the history of Indian subjugation to conditions of unequal exchange in relations with the political economy. By revealing these imbalanced relations, tribes are beginning to overcome many of the causes of their repression.

The pathway toward the reconciliation of oppositional forces that are present in tribal planning is ultimately dependent upon improved relations with non-tribal "others." Strategic tribal actions that aim to achieve an accord among "other" competing interests induce outcomes that lead to political plurality and help to overcome competition among the different interests in tribal affairs. Such approaches may finally lead to a permanent resolution to the persistent undermining of tribal authority.

The planning approach argued throughout this book is phenomenological, as it emphasizes the dynamics within the tribal planning setting and calls for a planning mentality that continuously assesses the adverse conditions that operate in that dynamic planning environment. The tribal planning model, presented in chapter 7, emphasizes the strategic features in tribal decision-making in order to anticipate obstacles in future-planning situations before planning actions are selected. In the process of advancing tribal objectives, strategies are selected that best suit the dynamics of that future-planning environment. The model integrates a feedback loop to assess whether planned actions should be modified in the face of resistance. As conflicts arise during plan implementation, contingent actions are selected to further enhance the tribe's political structure and its administrative capacity; to reconsider community goals, priorities, and strategies; and to consider additional strategic responses necessary for reconciling conflict.

The planning model provides a framework for understanding the dynamic relationships that exist within a tribe's planning situation. Its aim is to empower tribal communities by both anticipating and responding to the variables that operate in tribal affairs. As a cognitive operation, it provides a process for aligning tribal planning strategies with historical considerations. As a strategic operation, it strengthens the capacity of tribal nations to confront political opposition when encountered. As a conceptual operation, it involves a long-term, intuitive view of the business of tribal planning and reservation community development. As a purposeful operation, it endeavors to free Indians from their isolation and subjugation by fully integrating tribal visions within the broader political landscape. The effectiveness of tribal planning depends upon a tribe's ability to exercise its political resolve as it navigates a strategic course through the ever-changing circumstances that shape its future.

The experiences of tribes in Washington State demonstrate how, by incorporating multiple interests in public policy formulation, effective utilitarian relationships can result. The planning methods employ a multi-jurisdictional, co-regulatory approach to regional governance, where both tribal and non-tribal interests are simultaneously engaged in public policy making. The approach defers conflict by focusing on solutions to the pressing issues facing each government. Rather than arguing about which government has ultimate jurisdiction, efforts were devoted to garnering a better understanding of the multiplicity of visions that are reflected in multicultural communities. By validating the interests and values of both tribal and non-tribal communities, cooperative planning approaches can represent a way forward in reversing a history of jurisdictional uncertainty and conflicts in public policy. The cooperative planning approach broadens a tribe's influence, both on and off the reservation, ultimately enhancing its empowerment.

Acknowledgments | Appendixes | References | Index

Acknowledgments

I WISH TO EXPRESS my most sincere gratitude to the many friends, family, and mentors who have inspired me during my career. Prior to joining the academe, I spent the previous two and one half decades in professional planning practice, primarily as the general manager and director of planning with the Swinomish Indian Tribal Community. My circle of colleagues was influential in helping me form my notions about tribal planning and in carrying out many successful planning endeavors, some of which are reflected in these pages. I am particularly grateful to Allan Olson, the former tribal attorney and current tribal general manager. We worked closely together to formulate the strategies that helped our tribe overcome its long history of subjugation and to achieve many of its development objectives. My circle of trusted colleagues also included Brian Deveau, John Stephens, John Petrich, Larry Campbell, Lauren Rich, Stewart Jones, Rusty Kuntze, Rick Ballam, Alissa Kalla, and Larry Wasserman. My gratitude is extended to both past and current tribal leaders: Swinomish Chairman Brian Cladoosby, former chairman Robert Joe Sr., Lorraine Loomis, Barbara James, Diane Edwards, Liddie Grossglass, Laura Wilbur, Susan Wilbur, Pete Fornsby, George McCloud, Ivan Willup, Dewey Mitchell, Helen Ross, Landy James, Francis Peters, Chester Cayou Sr., as well as to Father Pat Twohy, Billy Frank Jr., Terry Williams, Darrell Hillaire, and Ron Allen for their wisdom and inspiration.

Much of the work in building regional institutional bridges would not have been possible without the dedication and professionalism of my colleagues in the Skagit County region, including Shirley Solomon, who facilitated much of our intergovernmental work; former Skagit County planning directors Bob Schofield, Scott Kirkpatrick, Dave Hough, and

Gary Christensen; former Skagit County commissioners Bill Vaux and Bob Hart; City of Anacortes Planning Director Ian Muntz; and other Skagit leaders. My special thanks is also extended to my doctorate dissertation chair, Professor Donald Miller at the University of Washington, for his invaluable guidance as I began to form concepts about the application of planning's theories to the conditions facing Native American communities. My appreciation is also extended to the editorial staff at Syracuse University Press—including Deanna McCay, acquisitions editor; Bruce Volbeda, copyeditor; Victoria Lane, senior designer; and Kay Steinmetz, managing editor—for their support throughout the manuscript review and production process.

Finally, my gratitude is extended to my family, who continue to encourage me in my life's work. To my wife, Cynthia, who not only inspires me every day, but has also devoted countless hours reviewing and editing the series of manuscript drafts; to my daughter, Tamara, who is a continuous source of inspiration; to my mother, Peggy, and to my sister, Olga, who have always encouraged me in all that I do. Finally, a special word of appreciation to Bocelli Cat, who has been my constant companion these past two years, observing patiently from his vantage point on the piano, his tail gently wagging to the motion of my keystrokes, never once disturbing my concentration as I made my way through the manuscript.

Federal Court Decisions

Alaska v. Native Village of Venetie Tribal Government, 522 U.S. 520 (1998).

Arizona v. California, 460 U.S. 605 (1983).

Arizona Public Service Co. v. EPA, 211 F.3d 1280 (D.C. Cir. 2000).

Atkinson v. Haldane, 569 P.2d. 151 (Alaska 1977).

Atkinson Trading Co. v. Shirley, 532 U.S. 645 (2001).

Blue Legs v. United States Environmental Protection Agency, 668 F. Supp. 1329 (D.S.D. 1987).

Blue Legs v. BIA, 867 F.2d 1094 (8th Cir. 1989).

Brendale v. Confederated Tribes and Bands of Yakima Indian Nation, 492 U.S. 408 (1988).

Braxton v. United States, 500 U.S. 344 (1991).

Bryan v. Itasca County, 426 U.S. 376 (1976).

Bugenig v. Hoopa Valley Tribe, 266 F.3d 1201 (9th Cir. 2001).

California v. Cabazon Band of Indians, 480 U.S. 202 (1987)

Cappaert v. United States, 426 U.S. 128 (1976).

Cardin v. DeLaCruz, 671 F.2d 363 (9th Cir. 1982), *cert. denied*, 459 U.S. 967 (1982).

Cherokee Nation v. Georgia, 30 U.S. 1 (1831).

Colorado River Indian Tribes v. Marsh, 605 F. Supp. 1425 (C.D. Cal. 1985).

Colville Confederated Tribes v. Walton, 647 F.2d 42 (9th Cir. 1981).

Confederated Salish and Kootenai Tribes v. Namen, 665 F.2d 951 (9th Cir. 1982).

Confederated Tribes of the Yakima Indian Nation v. Whiteside, 825 F.2d 529 (9th Cir. 1987).

Cotton Petroleum v. State of New Mexico, 490 U.S. 163 (1988).

County of Oneida v. Oneida Indian Nation, 470 U.S. 226 (1985).

County of Yakima v. Confederated Tribes and Bands of the Yakima Indian Nation, 492 U.S. 408 (1988).

Dept. of Ecology v. Acquavella, 131 Wash.2d 746 (Wash. 1997).

Dept. of Ecology v. Yakima Reservation Irrigation District, 121 Wash.2d 257 (Wash. 1993).

Dept. of Ecology v. Acquavella, 100 Wash.2d 651 (Wash. 1983).

Drysdale v. Prudden, 195 N.C. 722, 143 S.E. 530 (1928).

Duro v. Reina, 495 U.S. 676 (1990).

Euclid v. Ambler Realty Co., 272 U.S. 365 (1926).

Evans v. Shoshone-Bannock Land Use Policy Commission, No. 4:12-CV-417-BLW (D. Idaho December 20, 2012).

Frontenelle v. Omaha Tribe, 430 F.2d 143 (8th Cir. 1986), *cert. denied,* 107 S. Ct. 2461 (1987).

Gobin, Kim; Guy Madison v. Snohomish County; v. The Tulalip Tribes of Washington, 304 F.3d 909 (9th Cir. 2002).

Governing Council of Pinoleville Indian Community v. Mendocino County, 684 F. Supp. 1042 (N.D. Cal. 1988).

Hagen v. Utah, 510 U.S. 399 (1994).

Holly v. Totus, No. C-78-2-JLQ (E.D. Wash. 1983).

Johnson v. M'Intosh, 21 U.S. (8 Wheat.) 543 (1823).

Knight v. Shoshone and Arapahoe Indian Tribes, 670 F.2d 900 (10th Cir. 1982).

Match-E-Be-Nash-She-Wish Band of Pottawatomi Indians v. Patchak and *Salazar v. Patchak,* Nos. 11-246 and 11-247, 567 U.S. ___ (June 18, 2012).

McClanahan v. Arizona State Tax Commission, 441 U.S. 164 (1973).

Merrion v. Jicarilla Apache Tribe, 455 U.S. 130 (1982).

Moe v. Confederated Salish and Kootenai Tribes, 425 U.S. 463 (1976).

Montana v. EPA, 137 F.3d 1135 (9th Cir. 1998), *cert. denied,* 521 U.S. 921 (1998).

Montana v. United States, 450 U.S. 544 (1981).

Morton v. Mancari, 417 U.S. 535 (1974).

Muckelshoot Indian Tribe v. Trans-Canada Enterprises, Ltd., 713 F.2d (9th Cir. 1983).

Nance v. EPA, 645 F.2d 701 (9th Cir. 1981).

National Farmers Union Ins. Co. v. Crow Tribe, 471 U.S. 845 (1985).

Nevada v. Hicks, 533 U.S. 353 (2001).

Nevada v. United States, 103 S. Ct. 2906 (1983).

New Mexico v. Mescalero Apache Tribe, 462 U.S. 324 (1983).

Oliphant v. Suquamish Indian Tribe, 435 U.S. 191 (1978).

Puyallup Tribe v. Department of Game, 391 U.S. 392 (1968).

Puyallup Tribe v. Department of Game, 443 U.S. 165 (1977).

Puyallup Indian Tribe v. Port of Tacoma, 717 F.2d 1251 (9th Cir. 1983).

Rice v. Rehner, 463 U.S. 713 (1983).

Santa Clara Pueblo v. Martinez, 436 U.S. 49 (1978).

Santa Rosa Band of Indians v. Kings County, 532 F.2d 655 (9th Cir. 1975), *cert. denied*, 429 U.S. 1038 (1978).

Seminole Nation v. United States, 316 U.S. 286 (1942).

Skagit Audubon Society, et al. v. Skagit County and Agriculture for Skagit County et al., No. 00-2-0018c (W. Wash. Growth Management Hearings Board 2000).

Snohomish County v. Seattle Disposal Company, 70 Wash.2d 668 (Wash. 1961), *cert. denied*, 389 U.S. 1016 (1967).

Snow v. Quinault, 709 F.2d 1319 (9th Cir. 1983), *cert. denied*, 104 S. Ct. 2655 (1984).

Solem v. Bartlett, 465 U.S. 463 (1984).

South Dakota v. Bourland, 508 U.S. 679 (1993).

South Dakota v. Yankton Sioux Tribe, 118 S. Ct. 789 (1998).

State of Washington, Department of Ecology v. United States Environmental Protection Agency, 752 F.2d 1465 (9th Cir. 1985).

Strate v. A-1 Contractors, 520 U.S. 438 (1997).

United States v. AAM, Nos. C82-1522V and C82-1549V, 670 F. Supp. 306 (W.D. Wash. 1986).

Swinomish Indian Tribal Comm'y v. Dep't of Ecology, No. 87672-0 (Wash. October 3, 2013).

Tulalip Tribes of Washington v. Walker, No. 71421 (Snohomish Co. Super. Ct. Feb. 7 1963).

Tyndall v. United States, No. 77-0004 (D.C. Cir. April 22, 1977).

United States v. Anderson, 738 F.2d 1358 (9th Cir. 1984).

United States v. Cascade Natural Gas Corp., No. C76-550V (W.D. Wash.).

United States v. Kagama, 118 U.S. 375 (1886).

United States v. Mitchell, 463 U.S. 206 (1983).

U.S. v. Navaho Nation, 537 U.S. 488 (2003).

United States v. Payne, 264 U.S. 446 (1924).

United States v. Pend Oreille Cty. Pub. Util. Dist. No. 1, 585 F. Supp. 606 (E.D. Wash. 1984).

United States v. Washington, 506 F. Supp. 187 (W.D. Wash. 1980), *en banc* appeal dismissed, No. 91-3111 (9th Cir. Dec. 17, 1984).

Unites States v. Washington, No. C70-9213, Subproceeding No. 89-3, Dkt. 14331 (April 8, 2002), 873 F. Supp. 1422 (W.D. Wash. December 20, 1994).

United States v. Washington, 641 F.2d 1368 (9th Cir. 1981) *cert. denied*, 454 U.S. 1143 (1982).

United States v. Washington, 384 F. Supp. 312 (W.D. Wash. 1974), *aff'd*, 520 F.2d 676 (9th Cir. 1975), *cert. denied*, 423 U.S. 1086 (1976).

United States v. Wheeler, 435 U.S. 313 (1978).

United States v. Winnebago Tribe, 542 F.2d 1002 (8th Cir. 1976).

United States v. Winters, 207 U.S. 563 (1908).

United States v. Yakima Tribal Court, 806 F.2d 853 (9th Cir. 1986), *cert. denied*, 107 S. Ct. 2461 (1987).

Washington v. Confederated Tribes of the Colville Indian Reservation, 447 U.S. 134 (1980).

Washington Game Department v. Puyallup Tribe, 414 U.S. 44 (1973).

Washington v. Washington State Commercial Passenger Fishing Vessel Association, 443 U.S. 658 (1979).

White Mountain Apache Tribe v. Bracker, 448 U.S. 136 (1980).

Williams v. Lee, 358 U.S. 217 (1958).

Worcester v. Georgia, 31 U.S. (6 Pet.) 515 (1832).

Federal Statutes

Major Crimes Act
18 U.S.C. § 1153

This act provides for offenses committed within Indian country as follows: (a) Any Indian who commits against the person or property of another Indian or other person any of the following offenses, namely murder, manslaughter, kidnapping, maiming, a felony, sexual offenses, assault with intent to commit murder, assault with a dangerous weapon, arson, burglary, robbery, and a felony under section 661 of this title within Indian country, shall be subject to the same law and penalties as all other persons committing any of the above offenses, within the exclusive jurisdiction of the United States. (b) Any offense referred to in subsection (a) of this section that is not defined and punished by federal law in force within the exclusive jurisdiction of the United States shall be defined and punished in accordance with the laws of the state in which such offense was committed as are in force at the time of such offense.

Northwest Ordinance of 1787
Act of August 7, 1787, 1 Stat. 50.

This act, ratified by Congress in 1789, establishes the US government's relationship to tribes as having a similar status to that of a foreign nation and declared a policy of "utmost good faith" toward Indians, their lands, and their properties.

Nonintercourse Act of 1790 and 1834
25 U.S.C. § 177, 1 Stat. 137, 1790; and 4 Stat. 729, 1834.

This act established that no purchase, grant, lease, or other conveyance of lands, or of any title or claim thereto, from any Indian nation or tribe of Indians, shall be of any validity in law or equity, unless the same be made by treaty or convention entered into pursuant to the Constitution.

Treaties Statute of 1871
25 U.S.C. § 71

In 1871, Congress prohibited further treaty-making with Indian tribes by declaring that "No Indian Nation or tribe within the territory of the United States shall be acknowledged or recognized as an independent nation, tribe, or power with whom the United States may contract by treaty; but no obligation of any treaty lawfully made and ratified with any such Indian nation or tribe prior to March 3, 1871, shall be hereby invalidated or impaired."

General Allotment (or Dawes) Act of 1887
25 U.S.C. §§ 331–34, 339, 341, 348, 349, 354, and 381

The act authorized the allotting of tribal lands to individual tribal members, the land to remain in trust for twenty-five years. The stated reason for allotment was to provide for tribal members to become self-supporting members of their communities. The result was that after the twenty-five year trust period, the land became eligible for state taxation resulting in over 17.5 million acres of land lost to non-Indian ownership.

Dead and Down Timber Act: Act of February 16, 1889
25 U.S.C. 196

This act provided for the allotment of lands in severalty to Indians on reservations.

Indian Appropriations Act of March 3, 1909
35 Stat. 783

This act provided for the first directed appropriation of funds for Indian forestry programs as an exercise of federal trust responsibility over Indian resources.

Indian Reorganization Act of 1934 (Wheeler-Howard Act)
25 U.S.C. §§ 461–79.

This act represented a new approach to tribal sovereignty and a commitment to protect Indian culture. Tribes had the opportunity to vote to accept or reject the restructured form of tribal government mandated by the act. The form of government drawn up by this act was based on a written constitution mandating open elections and has frequently been compared to a municipal government. Additional provisions in the act include the following: section 461, "Allotment of land on Indian Reservations," prohibited further allotment of land after June

18, 1934; section 463, "Restoration of Lands to Tribal Ownership," provided for the protection of existing rights; and section 476, "Organization of Indian Tribes; Constitutions and Bylaws; Special Election," established rights of any tribe to organize for its common welfare, and adopt an appropriate constitution and bylaws, effective when ratified by a majority vote of the adult members of the tribe. The constitution also vested the following rights and powers: to employ legal counsel, the choice of counsel and fixing of fees to be subject to the approval of the Secretary of the Interior; to prevent the sale, disposition, lease, or encumbrance of tribal lands, interests in lands, or other tribal assets without the consent of the tribe; and to negotiate with the federal, state and local governments; section 477, "Incorporation of Indian Tribes . . . ; Ratification by Election," authorized the secretary of the interior, upon petition by at least one-third of the adult Indians, to issue a charter of incorporation to such tribe.

Johnson-O'Malley Act

The Johnson-O'Malley Act of 1934 permitted the federal government to contract for various reservation services with state and local governments and private contractors. Indian people on the reservations thus became entitled for the first time to some state welfare services and Indian children entered the public school system.

Indian Claims Commission Act of 1946

25 U.S.C. § 70a (omitted, upon termination of the Commission in 1978).

The Indian Claims Commission was established in 1946 and granted blanket permission for suits for compensation for land or other resources taken from Indian tribes.

Indian Country Statute

18 U.S.C. § 1151

This statute defined the term "Indian country" to mean "(a) all land within the limits of any Indian reservation under the jurisdiction of the US Government, notwithstanding the issuance of any patent, and including the right-of-way running through the reservation, (b) all dependent Indian communities within the borders of the United States whether within the original or subsequently acquired territory thereof, and whether within or without the limits of a state, and (c) all Indian allotments, the Indian titles to which have not been extinguished, including rights-of-way running through the same."

House Concurrent Resolution 108 of 1953
67 Stat. B132 (1953)

This document included the recommendation that all Indian tribes and individual members thereof should be freed from federal supervision and control, and from all disabilities and limitations specifically applicable to Indians. It further declared that the secretary of the interior should examine all existing legislation and treaties dealing with such Indians and report to Congress his recommendations on such legislation, to accomplish the purposes of this resolution.

Public Law Number 83-280 of 1953
67 Stat. 588 (1953) as amended, 18 U.S.C. § 1162, 25 U.S.C. §§ 1321–26, 28 U.S.C. § 1360

18 U.S.C. § 1162—"State jurisdiction over offenses committed by or against Indians in the Indian country." This section of the act made possible the termination of a tribe. Tribes that were deemed ready for termination were paid a per-acre fee and the unique relationship between the tribe and the federal government was then terminated. What tribes soon discovered was that the termination of the reservation meant the termination of federal benefits and services and also the termination of the tribe as a sovereign institution.

25 U.S.C. § 1321 and 1322. Enacted as part of the Indian Civil rights Act of 1968, these two statutes modified Public Law 280 to require, before any other state may assume civil or criminal jurisdiction over Indian country, "the consent of the Indian Tribe . . . affected by such assumption."

25 U.S.C. § 1323—"Retrocession of jurisdiction by State." This section authorized the United States to accept a retrocession by any state of all or any measure of the criminal or civil jurisdiction, or both, acquired by a state pursuant to the provisions of the title.

Menominee Termination Act of 1954
Ch. 303, 68 Stat. 250 (1954) (repealed 1973)

The purpose of this act is to provide for orderly termination of Federal supervision over the property and members of the Menominee Indian Tribe of Wisconsin.

Menominee Restoration Act of 1973
25 U.S.C. §§ 903–903f.

Federal recognition was extended to the Menominee Indian Tribe of Wisconsin and tribal rights and privileges were reinstated.

Indian Civil Rights Act of 1968
82 Stat. 25 U.S.C. §§ 1301–41.

The purpose of this act was to protect individual Indians from their own tribal governments and presents a limitation on tribal sovereignty. The act mandates that tribal governments must provide many of the same protections provided by the US Constitution. Congress did recognize the sovereignty issue by omitting from the act some rights recognized in the Constitution which would have clearly conflicted with traditional Indian practices.

National Environmental Policy Act of 1969
83 Stat. 852-856, Pub. L. No. 91-190.

This legislation requires federal agencies, including the Bureau of Indian Affairs, to consider the effects of its undertakings on natural and cultural resources.

Alaska Native Claims Settlement Act of 1971
85 Stat. 688, Pub. L. No. 92-203.

This act provided for the settlement of certain land claims of Alaska Natives. The act revoked reservations and Indian allotment authority in Alaska. Under this act, the role of the BIA was diminished.

Indian Finance Act of 1974 (Act of April 12, 1974)
25 U.S.C. § 1451

This act established the policy of Congress to help develop and utilize Indian resources whereas Indians would fully exercise responsibility for the utilization of management of their own resources in order to enjoy a standard of living from their own productive efforts comparable "to that enjoyed by non-Indians in neighboring communities."

Indian Self-Determination and Education Assistance Act of 1975
25 U.S.C. § 450, Pub. L. No. 93-638

This act provided for (1) maximum Indian participation in the government and education of Indian people; (2) full participation of Indian tribes in programs and services for Indians conducted by the federal government; (3) encouraged the development of Indian human resources; (4) educational assistance; (5) support rights of Indian citizens to control their own resources.

Civil Rights Attorneys Fees Act of 1976
Act of October 10, 1976, Pub. L. No. 89-635, 80 Stat., codified at 28 U.S.C. § 1362 (1976)

This act provided the tribes the right to obtain attorneys fees if they prevailed in certain types of litigation, increasing the incentive of the tribes to litigate.

Indian Child Welfare Act of 1978
25 U.S.C. §§ 1901–63

This act addressed the long-standing problem of large numbers of Indian children being transferred from their natural parents to non-Indian parents pursuant to state adoption and guardianship proceedings.

American Indian Religious Freedom Act of 1978
92 Stat. 469 (1978), codified in part at 42 U.S.C. § (1996)

This act was passed in 1978 and explicitly recognizes the importance of traditional Indian religious practices and directs all federal agencies to insure that their policies will not abridge the free exercise of Indian religions.

Indian Gaming Regulatory Act of 1988
25 U.S.C. § 2703

This act establishes the statutory basis for the operation, regulation, and protection of Indian tribal gaming activities.

Native American Graves Protection and Repatriation Act (NAGPRA)
25 U.S.C. § 3001

NAGPRA was enacted in November 1990 as a sweeping federal human rights law to provide four important protections over Native American Cultural Resources: (1) it increases protections for Indian graves located on federal and tribal lands and provides for Native control over cultural items obtained from such lands in the future; (2) it outlaws commercial traffic in Native American human remains; (3) it requires all federal agencies and federally funded museums and universities to inventory their collections of dead Native Americans and associated funerary objects and repatriate them to culturally affiliated tribes or descendants on request; and (4) it requires all federal agencies and federally funded museums to repatriate Native American sacred objects and cultural patrimony under procedures and standards specified in the act.

Tribal Self-Governance Act of 1994
H.R. 4842, Title II

This act establishes that the tribal right of self-government flows from the inherent sovereignty of Indian tribes and nations; recognizes the special government to government relationship with Indian tribes, including the right to self-governance; finds that although progress has been made, the federal bureaucracy has eroded tribal self-governance and dominates tribal affairs. The act transfers control to tribal governments, upon tribal government request, regarding funding and decision-making for federal programs, services, functions, and activities, or portions thereof, in an effective way to implement the federal policy of government-to-government relations with Indian tribes, and strengthens the federal policy of self-determination.

References

Ackerman, Francis E. 1981. "A Conflict Over Land." *American Indian Law Review* 8 (2): 259–98.

Ackoff, Russell L. 1984. "On the Nature and Development of Planning." In *People Centered Development: Contributions Toward Theory and Planning Frameworks*, edited by David C. Korten and Rudi Klauss, 195–99. West Hartford, CT: Kumarian.

Adamson, Rebecca, and Scott Klinger. 2008. *The Histories of Social Investing and Indigenous Peoples: Using the Tools of Diverse Cultures to Restore Balance to a Fractured World*. Fredericksburg, VA: First Peoples Worldwide.

Alexander, Ernst R. 1985. "From Idea to Action: Notes for a Contingency Theory of the Policy Implementation Process." *Administration and Society* 16 (4): 403–26.

———. 1995. *How Organizations Act Together: Intergovernmental Coordination in Theory and Practice*. Trenton, NJ: Gordon and Breach.

Alinsky, Saul D. 1972. *Rules for Radical: A Pragmatic Primer for Realistic Radicals*. New York: Vintage.

Altshuler, Alan, and Robert D. Behn, eds. 1997. *Innovation in American Government: Challenges, Opportunities and Dilemmas*. Washington, DC: Brookings Institution Press.

Altshuler, Alan, and Marc Zegans. 1990. "Innovation and Creativity: Comparisons between Public Management and Private Enterprise." *Cities* 7 (1): 16–24.

Ambler, Marjane. 1992. "Reservations Face Broad Range of Environmental Threats and Misconceptions." *Business Alert* 7:5 (Falmouth, VA: First Nations Development Institute).

American Friends Service Committee. 1970. *An Uncommon Controversy: Fishing Rights of the Muckelshoot, Puyallup and Nisqually Indians*. Seattle: Univ. of Washington Press.

American Indian Lawyer Training Program. 1988. *Indian Tribes as Sovereign Governments*. Oakland, CA: American Indian Resources Institute.

American Indian Policy Review Commission. 1976. *Report on Trust Responsibilities and the Federal-Indian Relationship; Including Treaty Review*. Washington, DC: American Indian Policy Review Commission.

Amin, Samir. 1976. *Unequal Development*. Translated by Brian Pearce. New York: Monthly Review Press.

Amoss, Pamela Thorsen. 1972. "The Persistence of Aboriginal Beliefs and Practices among the Nooksack Coast Salish." PhD diss., Univ. of Washington.

Anderson, T. L., and D. P. Parker. 2008. "Sovereignty, Credible Commitments, and Economic Prosperity on American Indian Reservations." *Journal of Law and Economics* 15:641–66.

Ashley, J. S., and S. J. Hubbard. 2004. *Negotiated Sovereignty: Working to Improve Tribal-State Relations*. New York: Praeger.

Ausherman, Larry P. 1989. "Characteristics of an Effective Tribal Environmental Regulatory Program: The Perspective of the Regulated Community." *Rocky Mountain Mineral Law Foundation* 4B:1.

Ayer, M. Francis. 1991. "Meaningful Implementation of the Government-to-Government Relationship between Each Indian Tribe and the United States: A Concept Paper." Washington, DC: National Indian Policy Center.

Baker, Donald G. 1986. "Native Americans in the Twentieth Century." *American Indian Culture and Research Journal* 10 (4): 101–58.

Baran, Paul A. 1988. "On the Political Economy of Backwardness." In *The Political Economy of Development and Underdevelopment*, edited by Charles K. Wilber, part 2, ch. 7. 4th ed. New York: Random House.

Bardach, Eugene. 1994. "Turf Barriers to Interagency Collaboration in Human Services Delivery." (Working paper, Cambridge, MA: Harvard University, Kennedy School of Government, Innovations in American Government Program).

———. 1998. *Getting Agencies to Work Together: The Practice and Theory of Managerial Craftsmanship*. Washington, DC: Brookings Institution Press.

Barry, Janice, and Libby Porter. 2012. "Indigenous Recognition in State-Based Planning Systems: Understanding Textual Mediation in the Contact Zone." *Planning Theory* 11 (2): 170–87.

Barth, Frederick. 1969. *Ethnic Groups and Boundaries*. Boston: Little, Brown.

Barzelay, Michael, and Robert A. Leone. 1987. "Creating an Innovative Managerial Culture: The Minnesota 'STEP' Strategy." *Journal of State Government* (July–August): 166–70.

Benveniste, Guy. 1989. *Mastering the Politics of Planning: Crafting Credible Plans and Policies That Make a Difference.* San Francisco: Jossey-Bass.

Bolan, Richard S. 1980. "The Practitioner as Theorist: The Phenomenology of the Professional Episode." *Journal of the American Planning Association* 46 (2): 261–74.

Bond, Sophie. 2011. "Negotiating a 'Democratic Ethos' Moving beyond the Agonistic-Communicative Divide." *Planning Theory* 10 (2): 161–86.

Boyer, Christine M. 1987. *Dreaming the Rational City: The Myth of American City Planning 1890–1945.* Cambridge, MA: MIT Press.

———. 1994. *The City of Collective Memory.* Cambridge, MA: MIT Press.

Brand, Ralf, and Frank Gaffikin. 2007. "Collaborative Planning in an Uncollaborative World." *Planning Theory* 6 (3): 282–313.

Bryant, B., ed. 1995. *Environmental Justice: Issues, Policies, and Solutions.* Washington, DC: Island.

Bryant, B., and P. Mohai, eds. 1992. *Race and the Incidence of Environmental Hazards: A Time for Discourse.* Boulder, CO: Westview.

Bryson, John M., and Andre L. Delbecq. 1979. "A Contingent Approach to Strategic and Tactics in Project Planning." *Journal of the American Planning Association* 45 (2): 167–79.

Bryson, John M., and Robert C. Einsweiler, eds. 1988. *Strategic Planning: Threats and Opportunities for Planners.* Chicago: Planners' Press of the American Planning Association.

Bullard, R. D., ed. 1993. *Confronting Environmental Racism: Voices from the Grassroots.* Boston: South End.

Bunnell, Gene. 1997. "Ways Counties Can Improve Inter-Governmental Cooperation in Land Use Planning and Growth Management." *Wisconsin Counties* 37–40.

Burayidi, Michael. 2003 "The Multicultural City as Planners' Enigma." *Planning Theory and Practice* 4:259–73.

Butcher, E. G., and A. C. Parnell. 1979. *Smoke Control in Fire Safety Design.* London: E & F N Spon.

Canby, William C., Jr. 2009. *American Indian Law in a Nutshell.* 5th ed. St. Paul, MN: West.

Castells, Manuel. 1980. "Cities and Regions beyond the Crisis: Invitation to a Debate." *International Journal of Urban and Regional Research* 4 (1): 127–29.

———. 1983. *The City and the Grass Roots: A Cross-Cultural Theory of Urban Movements.* Berkeley, CA. Univ. of California Press.

Castile, G. P. 1982. "The Half-Catholic Movement: Edwin and Myron Eells and the Rise of the Indian Shaker Church." *Pacific Northwest Quarterly* 73:165–74.

Center for Applied Research. 1993. "The Economic and Fiscal Importance of Indian Tribes in Arizona." Technical report. Denver, CO: Arizona Commission of Indian Affairs.

Champagne, Duane, and Carol Goldberg. 2012. *Captured Justice: Native Nations under Public Law 280*. Durham, NC: Carolina Academic.

Christenson, James A., and Jerry W. Robinson Jr., eds. 1989. *Community Development in Perspective*. Ames: Iowa State Univ. Press.

Churchill, Ward. 1991. "American Indian Self Governance: Fact, Fantasy, and Prospects." *Z Magazine* 4 (10): 86–90.

City of Anacortes, Skagit County, Skagit Public Utility District, Swinomish Indian Tribe, Sauk Suiattle Indian Tribe, Upper Skagit Indian Tribe, and the Washington Department of Ecology. 1996. "Skagit River Water Rights Agreement." Intergovernmental agreement. Mount Vernon, WA: Skagit County Board of Commissioners.

Cline, Sarah N. 2013. "Sovereignty under Arrest? Public Law 280 and Its Discontents." Masters thesis, Oregon State University, Corvallis, OR, May 20.

Clinton, William J. 1994a. Executive Order 12898, February 11. Fed. Reg. 59:32, 7629.

———. 1994b. "Memorandum on Government Relations with Native American Tribal Governments. Communications to Federal Agencies." *Weekly Compilation of Presidential Documents* 30 (17): 936–37.

———. 1998. Executive Order No. 13084, 63 Fed. Reg. 96 (May 19).

———. 2000. Executive Order No. 13175, "Consultation and Coordination with Indian Tribal Governments." 65 Fed. Reg. 218: 67249–52 (November 6). *Weekly Compilation of Presidential Documents* 36 (45): 2806–9.

Clow, Richmond L. 1991. "Taxation and the Preservation of Tribal Political and Geographical Autonomy." *American Indian Culture and Research Journal* 15 (2): 37–62.

Cohen, Fay G. 1986. *Treaties on Trial: The Continuing Controversy over Northwest Indian Rights*. Seattle: Univ. of Washington Press.

Cohen, Felix S. 1942. *Felix S. Cohen's Handbook of Federal Indian Law*. Washington, DC: US Government Printing Office.

Collins, June McCormack. 1974. *Valley of the Spirits: The Upper Skagit Indians of Western Washington*. Seattle: Univ. of Washington Press.

Comprehensive Environmental Response, Compensation and Liability Act (CERCLA / Superfund), 42 U.S.C. 9610 et seq.

Cookson, J. A. 2010. "Institutions and Casinos on American Indian Reservations: An Empirical Analysis of the Location of Indian Casinos." *Journal of Law and Economics* 53:1–23.

Cornell, Stephen. 1984. "Crisis and Response in Indian-White Relations: 1960–1984." *Social Problems* 32 (1): 44–59.

———. 1987. "American Indians, American Dreams, and the Meaning of Success." *American Indian Culture and Research Journal* 11 (4): 59–70.

———. 2007. "Remaking the Tools of Governance: Colonial Legacies Indigenous Solutions." In *Rebuilding Native Nations: Strategies for Governance and Development*, edited by Miriam Jorgensen, 57–77. Tucson: Univ. of Arizona Press.

Cornell, Stephen, and Joseph P. Kalt. 1990. "Pathways from Poverty: Economic Development and Institution Building on American Indian Reservations." *American Indian Culture and Research Journal* 14 (1): 89–125.

———. 1992. *What Can Tribes Do? Strategies and Institutions in American Indian Economic Development*. Los Angeles: Univ. of California, Los Angeles, American Indian Studies Center.

———. 2007. "Two Approaches to the Development of Native Nations: One Works, the Other Doesn't." In *Rebuilding Native Nations: Strategies for Governance and Development*, edited by Miriam Jorgensen, 3–33. Tucson: Univ. of Arizona Press.

Corntassel, Jeff, and Richard C. Witmer II. 2008. *Forced Federalism: Contemporary Challenges to Indigenous Nationhood*. Norman: Univ. of Oklahoma Press.

Coursen, David F. 1993. "Tribes as States: Indian Tribal Authority to Regulate and Enforce Federal Environmental Laws and Regulations." 23 *Environmental Law Reporter* 10579.

Daniels, R., and J. Vencatesan. 1995. "Traditional Ecological Knowledge and Sustainable Use of Natural Resources." *Current Science* 69 (7): 569–70.

Davidoff, Paul. 1965. "Advocacy and Pluralism in Planning." *Journal of the American Planning Association* 31 (4): 331–38.

Deloria, Vine, Jr. 1973. *The Lummi Indian Community: The Fishermen of the Pacific Northwest*. Washington, DC: Smithsonian Institute.

———. 1985. *American Indian Policy in the Twentieth Century*. Norman: Univ. of Oklahoma Press.

Deloria, Vine, Jr., and Clifford M. Lytle. 1984. *The Nations within: The Past and Future of American Indian Sovereignty.* New York: Pantheon.

Doering, Karen. 1992. "Cooperation and Coordination between Tribes and Counties in Washington: A Survey of Planning Department Staffs." Report. Seattle: Northwest Renewable Resources Center.

Dufford, Philip W. 1979. "Water for Non-Indians on the Reservation: Checkerboard Ownership and Checkerboard Jurisdiction." *Gonzaga Law Review* 15 (1): 95–132.

Dunn, Edgar S. 1971. *Economic and Social Development: A Process of Social Learning.* Baltimore: John Hopkins Univ. Press.

Dyck, Noel, ed. 1985. *Indigenous Peoples and the Nation-State: 'Fourth World' Politics in Canada, Australia and Norway.* St. Johns: Institute for Social and Economic Research 14, Memorial University of Newfoundland.

Dyckman, John W. 1983. "Reflections on Planning Practice in an Age of Reaction." *Journal of Planning Education and Research* 3:5–12.

Endreson, Douglas B. L. 1991. "Resolving Tribal-State Conflicts." Policy report. Washington, DC: National Indian Policy Center.

———. 1993. "A Summary of the Case Law Interpreting the Indian Gaming Regulatory Act." Policy Report. Washington, DC: National Indian Policy Center.

Etzioni, Amitai. 1968. *The Active Society: A Theory of Societal and Political Processes.* New York: Free Press.

———. 2001. *Next: The Road to the Good Society.* New York: Basic Books.

Faber, D., ed. 1998. *The Struggle for Ecological Democracy: Environmental Justice Movements in the United States.* New York: Guilford Press.

Faludi, Andreas. 1973. *Planning Theory.* Urban and Regional Planning Series, vol. 7. Oxford, UK: Pergamon.

Ferris, D. 1993. "A Broad Environmental Justice Agenda: Mandating Change Begins at the Federal Level." *Maryland Journal of Contemporary Legal Issues* 5:115–27.

Forester, John. 1980. "Critical Theory and Planning Practice." *Journal of the American Planning Association* 46 (3): 261–74.

———. 2007. "Planning in the Face of Conflict." In *The City Reader,* edited by Richard T. LeGates and Frederic Stout, 387–99. 4th ed. New York: Routledge.

———. 2009. *Dealing with Difference: Dramas of Mediating Public Disputes.* New York: Oxford Univ. Press.

Foucault, Michel. 1973. *The Birth of the Clinic: An Archaeology of Medical Perception*. New York: Vintage.

———. 1977. *Power/Knowledge: Selected Interviews and Other Writings, 1972–1977*. New York: Pantheon.

———. 1979. *Discipline and Punish: The Birth of the Prison*. New York: Vintage.

———. 1988. *Madness and Civilization: A History of Insanity in the Age of Reason*. New York: Vintage.

Frank, Andre Gunder. 1969. *Latin America: Underdevelopment or Revolution*. New York: Monthly Review.

———. 1988. "The Development of Underdevelopment." In *The Political Economy of Development and Underdevelopment*, edited by Charles K. Wilber, 109–20. 4th ed. New York: Random House.

Fredericks, John. 1989. "State Regulation in Indian Country: The Supreme Court's Marketing Exemptions Concept, A Judicial Sword through the Heart of Tribal Self-Determination." *Montana Law Review* 50:49.

Friedmann, John. 1982. "Urban Communities: Self Management and the Reconstruction of the Local State." *Journal of Planning Education and Research* 2 (1): 37–53.

———. 1987. *Planning in the Public Domain: From Knowledge to Action*. Princeton, NJ: Princeton Univ. Press.

Frizzel, Kent. 1974. "Evolution of Jurisdiction in Indian Country." *Kansas Law Review* 22:341.

Gallay, Allan. 2002. *The Indian Slave Trade: The Rise of the English Empire in the American South, 1670–1717*. New Haven, CT: Yale Univ. Press.

Gardner, John W. 1980. *Towards a Pluralistic but Coherent Society*. New York: Aspen Institute for Humanistic Studies.

General Allotment Act ("Dawes Act"). 1887. 25 U.S.C. §§ 332–34, 339, 341, 348, 349, 354, 381.

Goeppele, Craighton. 1990. "Solutions for Uneasy Neighbors: Regulating the Reservation Environment after *Brendale v. Confederated Tribes* and *Bands of Yakima Indian Nation*, 109 S. Ct. 2994 (1989)." *Washington Law Review* 65 (2): 417–36.

Goldberg, Carole. 2009. "Public Law 280 Isn't the Proper Economic Stimulus for Indian Country." *Indian Country Today*, March 20.

———. 2010. "In Theory, In Practice: Judging State Jurisdiction in Indian Country." *University of Colorado Law Review* 81:1–28.

Goldtooth, T. B. K. 1995. "Indigenous Nations: Summary of Sovereignty and Its Implications for Environmental Protection." In *Environmental Justice: Issues, Policies, and Solutions*, edited by B. Bryant, 138–48. Washington, DC: Island.

Gordon, Thomas, Honeywell, Malanca, Peterson, and O'Hern (GTH) [law firm]. 1981. "U.S. v. Washington, Phase II: Analysis and Recommendations." Report prepared for the Northwest Water Resources Committee. Seattle: GTH.

Grant, Kenneth, and Jonathan Taylor. 2007. "Managing the Boundary between Business and Politics: Strategies for Improving the Chances for Success in Tribally Owned Enterprises." In *Rebuilding Native Nations: Strategies for Governance and Development*, edited by Miriam Jorgensen, 175–96. Tucson: Univ. of Arizona Press.

Greig, A., D. Hulme, and M. Turner. 2007. *Challenging Global Inequality: Development Theory and Practice in the 21st century*. New York: Palgrave Macmillan.

Growth Management Act. Wash. Rev. Code § 36.70A.

Guilmet, George M. 1991. "The Legacy of Introduced Disease: The Southern Coast Salish." *American Indian Culture and Research Journal* 15 (4): 1–32.

Habermas, Jurgen. 1973. *Theory and Practice*. Boston: Beacon.

———. 1979. *Communication and the Evolution of Society*. Boston: Beacon.

Halbert, Cindy L., and Kai N. Lee. 1990. "The Timber, Fish and Wildlife Agreement: Implementing Alternative Dispute Resolution in Washington State." *Northwest Environmental Journal* 6:139–75.

Hall, Thomas D. 1987. "Native Americans and Incorporation: Patterns and Problems." *American Indian Culture and Research Journal* 11 (2): 1–30.

———. 1990. "Patterns of Native American Incorporation into State Societies." In *Public Policy Impacts on American Indian Economic Development*, edited by Matthew C. Snipp, 23–38. Albuquerque: University of New Mexico.

Hanna, Tassie, Sam Deloria, and Charles E. Trimble. 2011. "The Commission on State-Tribal Relations: Enduring Lessons in the Modern State-Tribal Relationship," *Tulsa Law Review* 47 (3): 553. Available at http://digitalcommons .law.utulsa.edu/tlr/vol47/iss3/4.

Hardt, Michael, and Antonio Negri. 2000. *Empire*. Cambridge, MA: Harvard Univ. Press.

Harmon, Alexandra. 1998. *Indians in the Making: Ethnic Relations and Indian Identities around Puget Sound*. Los Angeles: Univ. of California Press.

Harris, G. R. 1997. "A Social Critique of Environmental Justice." *Journal of the American Planning Association* 63 (1): 149.

Harris, S. G., and B. L. Harper. 1997. "A Native American Exposure Scenario." *Risk Analysis* 17 (6): 789–96.

Harvard Project on American Indian Economic Development. 2008. *The State of the Native Nations: Conditions under U.S. Policies of Self-Determination.* New York: Oxford Univ. Press.

Harwood, S. A. 2005. "Struggling to Embrace Difference in Land-Use Decision Making in Multicultural Communities." *Planning Practice and Research* 20:355–71.

Hazardous Substances Data Bank (HSDB). 1997. "Carbon Monoxide," HSDB Ref. No. 903. Bethesda, MD: National Institutes of Health, US National Library of Medicine.

Helfand, G. E., and L. J. Peyton. 1999. "A Conceptual Model of Environmental Justice." *Social Science Quarterly* 80 (1): 68–83.

Hibbard, Michael, Heloisa Costa, and Anthony Gar-On Yeh, eds. 2008. *Dialogues in Urban and Regional Planning.* Vol. 4. Abingdon, UK: Routledge.

Hibbard, Michael, Marcus B. Lane, and Kathleen Rasmussenet. 2008. "The Split Personality of Planning: Indigenous Peoples and Planning for Land and Resource Management." *Journal of Planning Literature* 23:136–51.

Hicks, Sarah. 2007. "Intergovernmental Relationships: Expressions of Tribal Sovereignty." In *Rebuilding Native Nations: Strategies for Governance and Development,* edited by Miriam Jorgensen, 246–74. Tucson: Univ. of Arizona Press.

Hines, Revathi I. 2001. "African Americans' Struggle for Environmental Justice and the Case of the Shintech Plant: Lessons Learned from a War Waged. *Journal of Black Studies* 31 (6): 777–89.

Hobbes, Thomas. 1651. *Philosophical Rudiments Concerning Government and Society.* London: Royston.

Hoch, Charles. 1994. *What Planners Do: Power, Politics, and Persuasion.* Chicago: American Planning Association Planners Press.

Howitt, Arnold M., and Clifflyn Bromling. 1998. "Empirical Research on Innovation in State and Local Government: Prospects and Problems." (Working paper, Cambridge, MA: Harvard University, Kennedy School of Government, Innovations in American Government Program).

Indian Reorganization Act of 1934, 25 U.S.C. 476 et. seq.

Indian Self-Determination and Education Assistance Act of 1975. 1975. Pub. L. No. 93-638, 25 U.S.C. § 450.

Inter-Local Government Cooperation Act. Wash. Rev. Code § 39.34.010.

Ishiyama, Noriko. 2003. "Environmental Justice and American Indian Tribal Sovereignty: Case Study of a Land Use Conflict in Skull Valley, Utah." *Antipode* 35 (1): 119–39.

Jentoft, Svein, Henry Minde, and Ragnar Nilsen, eds. 2003. *Indigenous Peoples: Resource Management and Global Rights.* Delft, Netherlands: Eburon.

Johnson, Lyndon B. 1968. "Special Message to the Congress on the Problems of the American Indian: 'The Forgotten American.'" March 6. *Published Papers*, part I, p. 335, Washington, DC, Library of Congress. Text available online at *The American Presidency Project*, edited by Gerhard Peters and John T. Woolley. http://www.presidency.ucsb.edu/ws/?pid=28709.

Johnson, Ralph. 1988. "Zoning for Environmental Protection on Indian Reservations." In *Proceedings of the Second Annual Western Regional Law Symposium: Indian Tribes and the Environment.* Seattle: Univ. of Washington.

Jojola, Theodore S. 1998. "Indigenous Planning: Clans, Intertribal Confederations, and the History of the All Indian Pueblo Council." In *Making the Invisible Visible: A Multicultural Planning History,* edited by Leonie Sandercock 100–19. Berkeley: Univ. of California Press.

———. 2008. "Indigenous Planning: An Emerging Context." *Canadian Journal of Urban Research* 17 (1): 37–47.

Jorgensen, Joseph G. 1972. "Indians and the Metropolis." In *The American Indian in Urban Society,* edited by Jack O. Waddell and O. Michael Watson, 66–113. Boston: Univ. Press of America.

———. 1986. "Sovereignty and the Structure of Dependency at Northern Ute." *American Indian Culture and Research Journal* 10 (2): 75–94.

Jorgensen, Miriam, ed. 2007. *Rebuilding Native Nations: Strategies for Governance and Development.* Tucson: Univ. of Arizona Press.

Josephy, Alvin M., Jr. 1971. *Red Power—The American Indians' Fight for Freedom.* 2nd ed. Winter Park, FL: American Heritage.

Kauger, Yvonne, Richard Du Bey, and Wilma Pearl Mankiller; edited by Judy A. Zelio. 1990. "Promoting Effective State-Tribal Relations: A Dialogue." Proceedings of a session held at the National Conference of State Legislatures, Tulsa, OK, August 1989. Washington, DC: National Conference of State Legislatures.

Kemmis, Daniel. 1990. *Community and the Politics of Place*. Norman: Univ. of Oklahoma Press.

Kemp, Roger, ed. 1992. *Strategic Planning in Local Government*. Chicago: American Planning Association Planners Press.

Korten, David C. 1980. "Community Organization and Rural Development: A Learning Process Approach." *Public Administration Review* 40 (5): 480–511.

———. 1984. *People Centered Development: Contributions towards Theory and Planning Frameworks*. West Hartford, CT: Kumarian.

Kuehn, Robert R. 2000. "A Taxonomy of Environmental Justice." *Environmental Law Reporter* 30:10681–98.

LaDuke, Winona. 1999. *All Our Relations: Native Struggles for Land and Life*. Cambridge, MA: South End.

Lane, Marcus Benjamin, and Michael Hibbard. 2005. "Doing It for Themselves: Transformative Planning by Indigenous Peoples." *Journal of Planning Education and Research* 25:172–84.

Lane, Marcus Benjamin, and L. J. Williams. 2008. "Color Blind: Indigenous Peoples and Regional Environmental Management." *Journal of Planning Education and Research* 28:38–49.

Larsen, Richard W. 1989. "Skagit Summit: A Bridge of Understanding." *Seattle Times*, December 17, A21.

Larson, Timothy V., and Jane Q. Koenig. 1994. "Wood Smoke Emissions and Noncancer Respiratory Effects." *Annual Review of Public Health* 15:133–56.

LaVelle, John P. 2001. "Rescuing Paha Sapa: Achieving Environmental Justice by Restoring the Great Grasslands and Returning the Sacred Black Hills to the Great Sioux Nation." *Great Plains Natural Resources Journal* 5:43–101.

Lester, David. 1986. "The Environment from an Indian Perspective." *Environmental Protection Agency Journal* 12 (1): 27–28.

LeVine, Robert A., and Donald T. Campbell. 1972. *Ethnocentrism: Theories of Conflict, Ethnic Attitudes and Group Behavior*. New York: John Wiley and Sons.

Lewis, Jack. 1986. "An Indian Policy at EPA." *EPA Journal* 12:23–26.

Marx, Karl, and Friedrich Engels. 1978. "The Communist Manifesto." In *The Marx-Engels Reader*, edited by Robert C. Turker, 469–500. 2nd. ed. New York: W. W. Norton. First published 1848.

Marx, Werner. 1975. *Hegel's Phenomenology of Spirit*. Chicago: Harper and Row.

McFarland, Andrew W. 1987. "Interest Groups and Theories of Power in America." *British Journal of Political Science* 17:129–47.

Meszaros, Istvan. 1970. *Marx's Theory of Alienation*. New York: Harper and Row.

Miller, Bruce. 1993. "The Press, the Boldt Decision, and Indian-White Relations." *American Indian Culture and Research Journal* 17 (2): 75–98.

Moore, Jason W. 2003. "The Modern World-System as Environmental History? Ecology and the Rise of Capitalism." *Theory and Society* 32 (3): 307–77.

Morris, K. 1990. "Wood-Burning Stoves and Lower Respiratory Tract Infection in American Indian Children." *American Journal of Diseases of Children* 144:105–8.

National Conference of State Legislatures (NCSL). 1989. "Promoting Effective State-Tribal Relations: A Dialogue." Proceedings of a national issues seminar hosted by NCSL. Denver, CO: NCSL.

National Environmental Justice Advisory Council. 2000. *Guide on Consultation and Collaboration with Indian Tribal Governments and the Public Participation of Indigenous Groups and Tribal Members in Environmental Decision Making*. Washington, DC: National Environmental Justice Advisory Council, Indigenous Peoples Subcommittee, a federal advisory committee to the US Environmental Protection Agency. http://www.epa.gov/environmental justice/resources/publications/nejac/ips-consultation-guide.pdf.

National Fire Protection Association (NFPA). 1981. *Fire Protection Handbook*. 15th ed. Quincy, MA: NFPA.

National Indian Gaming Commission. 2010. "National Record of Tribal Casino Operations." *National Indian Gaming Commission* (website). http://www .nigc.gov.

National Indian Policy Center. 1993. *Tribal Participation in the Making of Federal Indian Law and Policy under the Proposed National Commission of Native American Governments' Recognition Act*. Edited by Douglas B. Anderson. Washington, DC: National Indian Policy Center.

Native American Rights Fund. 1988. "Draft Concept Paper for the Consideration of the Establishment of an Indian Environmental Entity." Boulder, CO: Native American Rights Fund.

Newton, David E. 1996. *Environmental Justice: A Reference Handbook*. Denver, CO: ABC-CLIO.

Newton, Nell Jessup, ed. 2012. *Cohen's Handbook of Federal Indian Law*. Albuqueruque, NM: LexisNexis.

Nixon, Richard M. 1970. "Special Message on Indian Affairs." *Public Papers of the Presidents of the United States: Richard Nixon*, 564–67.

Northwest Renewable Resources Center. 1990. "The Northwest Renewable Resources Center Responds to 'the New Politics of Natural Resources.'" *Northwest Environmental Journal* 6 (1): 8–18.

———. 1993. "Working Effectively at the Local Level: Tribal/County Cooperation and Coordination." In *Proceedings of Conference on Tribal/County Relations.* Conference held June 16–17. Seattle: Northwest Renewable Resources Center.

———. 1997. *Building Bridges: A Resource Guide for Tribal-County Intergovernmental Cooperation.* Seattle: Northwest Renewable Resources Center.

Nye, Joseph S., Jr., Philip D. Zelikow, and David C. King. 1997. *Why People Don't Trust Government.* Cambridge, MA: Harvard Univ. Press.

O'Brien, Sharon. 1986. "The Government to Government and Trust Relationship: Conflicts and Inconsistencies." *American Indian Culture and Research Journal* 10 (4): 57–80.

O'Connell, Michael P. 1983. "The Application of Tribal and State Laws such as Zoning, Water Management, and Hunting and Fishing Regulations on Indian Reservations in Washington." In *Law Conference Proceedings*, proceedings of a continuing legal education seminar, University of Washington School of Law, October 29; pp. 1–38. Seattle: Washington Law School Foundation.

Olson, Mary B. 1990. "The Legal Road to Economic Development: Fishing Rights in Western Washington." In *Public Policy Impacts on American Indian Economic Development*, edited by Matthew C. Snipp, 77–112. Albuquerque, NM: Institute for Native American Development, Univ. of New Mexico.

Owens, Nancy. 1978. "Can Tribes Control Energy Development." In *Native Americans and Energy Development*, edited by J. Jorgensen, 49–62. Boston: Anthropology Resource Center.

Paddock, Susan. 1998. "The Changing World of Wisconsin Local Government." In *The State of Wisconsin Blue Book, 1997–1998*, 99–172. Madison: Wisconsin Legislative Reference Bureau.

Paden, John N. 1970. "Urban Pluralism, Integration, and Adaptation of Communal Identities in Kano, Nigeria." In *From Tribe to Nation in Africa: Studies in Incorporation Processes*, edited by Ronald Cohen and John Middleton, 242–70. San Francisco: Chandler.

Page, Vicki. 1985. "Reservation Development in the United States: Peripherality in the Core." *American Indian Culture and Research Journal* 9 (3): 21–35.

Parman, Donald L. 1986. Review of *Treaties on Trial: The Continuing Controversy over Northwest Indian Rights*, by Fay G. Cohen. *American Indian Culture and Research Journal* 10 (4): 101–58.

Peet, Richard, and Elaine Hartwick. 1999. *Theories of Development*. New York: Guilford.

Pevar, Stephen L. 2012. *The Rights of Indians and Tribes*. 4th ed. New York: Oxford Univ. Press.

Pirtle, Robert, Mason D. Morisset, Frances M. Ayer, and Thomas P. Schlosser. 1992. "Implications of the Brendale Opinion: The Yakima Zoning Case." White paper. Seattle: Pirtle, Morisset, Ayer, and Schlosser [law firm].

Portes, Alejandro. 1976. "On the Sociology of National Development: Theories and Issues." *American Journal of Sociology* 82 (1): 55.

Presidential Commission on Indian Reservation Economies. 1984. *Report and Recommendations to the President of the United States*. Part 2. Washington, DC: Presidential Commission on Indian Reservation Economies.

Preston, Peter W. 1988. *Rethinking Development*. London: Routledge & Kegan Paul.

Prucha, Francis Paul. 1970. *American Indian Policy in the Formative Years: The Indian Trade and Intercourse Acts, 1790–1834*. Lincoln: Univ. of Nebraska Press.

Pulido, L. 1996. "A Critical Review of the Methodology of Environmental Racism Research." *Antipode* 28:142–59.

Rapley, John. 2007. *Understanding Development*. London: Lynne Rienner.

Riffle, Stanley. 2000. "Top Ten Strategies for Negotiating Successful Border Agreements." Oshkosh: Wisconsin City Managers Seminar.

Ringquist, E. J. 1998. "A Question of Justice: Equity in Environmental Litigation." *Journal of Politics* 60 (4): 1148–65.

Roberts, Hayden. 1979. *Community Development: Learning and Action*. Toronto, ON: Univ. of Toronto Press.

Roberts, Natalie Andrea. 1975. "A History of the Swinomish Tribal Community." PhD diss., Univ. of Washington.

Rosen, D. A. 2007. *American Indians and State Law*. Lincoln: Univ. of Nebraska Press.

Rosser, Ezra. 2009. Review of *Forced Federalism: Contemporary Challenges to Indigenous Nationhood*, by Jeff Corntassel and Richard C. Witmer II. *Great Plains Research* 19 (1): 136.

Rostow, Walt W. 1960. *The Stages of Economic Growth: A Non-Communist Manifesto*. London: Cambridge Univ. Press.

Royster, Judith V. 1991. "Environmental Protection and Native American Rights: Controlling Land Use through Environmental Regulation." *Kansas Journal of Law and Public Policy* 1:89–100.

Royster, Judith V., and Rory Snow Arrow Fausett. 1989. "Control of the Reservation Environment: Tribal Primacy, Federal Delegation, and the Limits of State Intrusion." *Washington Law Review* 64:581–96.

Ryser, Rudolph C. 1992. "Anti-Indian Movement on the Tribal Frontier: Right Wing Extremism Reaching for the Mainstream." Occasional Paper No. 16. Olympia, WA: Center for World Indigenous Studies.

Sachs, Wolfgang, and Tilman Santarius, eds. 2007. *Fair Future: Resource Conflicts, Security, and Global Justice*. London: Zed.

Sandbrook, Richard. 2000. "Globalization and the Limits of Neoliberal Development Doctrine." *Third World Quarterly* 21 (6): 1071–80.

Sandercock, Leonie, ed. 1998. *Making the Invisible Visible: A Multicultural Planning History*. Berkeley: Univ. of California Press.

———. 2003. *Cosmopolis II: Mongrel Cities in the 21st Century*. London: Continuum.

———. 2011. "Towards Cosmopolitan Urbanism: From Theory to Practice." In *Dialogues in Urban and Regional Planning Volume 4*, edited by T. L. Harper, M. Hibbard, H. Costa, and A. Yeh, 38–57. New York: Routledge.

Sanders, Allen H., and Robert L. Otsea Jr. 1982. *Protecting Indian Natural Resources: A Manual for Lawyers Representing Indian Tribes or Tribal Members*. Boulder, CO: Native American Rights Fund.

Scott, Jane E. 1982. "Zoning: Controlling Land Use on the Checkerboard: The Zoning Powers of Indian Tribes after *Montana v. United States*." *American Indian Law Review* 10:187–209.

Sen, Amartya. 1999. *Development as Freedom*. Oxford: Oxford Univ. Press.

Senghass, Dieter. 1988. "The Case for Autarchy." In *The Political Economy of Development and Underdevelopment*, edited by Charles K. Wilber. New York: Random House.

Shrader-Frechette, K. 1996. "Environmental Justice and Native Americans: The Mescalero Apache and Monitored Retrievable Storage." *Natural Resources Journal* 36 (4): 703–14.

Skagit County. 1984. *Skagit County Coordinated Water Systems Plan*. Mount Vernon, WA: Skagit County Health Department.

Slade, B. A., and L. Cowart. 2000. "Are Minority Neighborhoods Exposed to More Environmental Hazards? Allegations of Environmental Racism." *Real Estate Review* 30 (2): 50–57.

Smith, Adam. 1976. *An Inquiry into the Nature and Causes of the Wealth of Nations.* R. H. Campbell and A. S. Skinner, eds. Oxford: Oxford Univ. Press. First published 1776.

Smith, Marian W. 1941. "The Coast Salish of Puget Sound." *American Anthropologist* 43:197–211.

Snipp, Matthew C. 1986. "The Changing Political and Economic Status of American Indians: From Captive Nations to Internal Colonies." *American Journal of Economics and Sociology* 45 (2): 145–57.

———. 1990. *Public Policy Impacts on American Indian Economic Development.* Albuquerque: Univ. of New Mexico.

So, Frank S. 1984. "Strategic Planning: Reinventing the Wheel?" *Planning* 50 (2): 16–24.

Social Investment Forum. 2010. *Creating a Sustainable World: A Guide to Responsible Stewardship of American Indian Assets.* Washington, DC: Social Investment Forum Foundation.

Solomon, Shirley. 1995. "Tribal-County Cooperation: Making It Work at the Local Level." *Cultural Survival* 19 (3): 1.

State of Washington. 1971. *Are You Listening Neighbor?* Olympia: State of Washington, Indian Affairs Task Force.

———. 1978. *Transportation Guide for Indian Tribal Governments.* Olympia: Washington Department of Transportation.

———. 1985. *The State of Washington and Indian Tribes.* Olympia: State of Washington, Office of the Attorney General, Indian Litigation Coordinating Committee.

———. 1987. "Timber, Fish and Wildlife Agreement: A Better Future in our Woods and Streams." Final Report. Olympia: Washington Department of Natural Resources, Forest Regulation and Assistance Division.

———. 1989a. "Governor's Proclamation on Tribal Relations." January 3. Olympia: Office of the Governor.

———. 1989b. "Centennial Accord," August 4, 1989. Olympia: Office of the Governor.

———. 1990. *State Tribal Relations Training Manual.* Olympia: Governor's Office of Indian Affairs.

———. 1991. "Department of Natural Resources Tribal Policy." Olympia: Washington Department of Natural Resources, Brian Boyle, Commissioner of Public Lands.

Steiner, George A. 1979. *Strategic Planning: What Every Manager Must Know.* New York: Free Press.

Stephens, P. H. G. 2000. "Andrew Dobson, Justice and the Environment: Conceptions of Environmental Sustainability and Dimensions of Social Justice." *Environmental Politics* 9 (4): 174–75.

Suagee, Dean B. 1991. "The Application of the National Environmental Policy Act to Development in Indian Country." *American Indian Law Review* 16:377.

———. 1994. "Turtle's War Party: An Indian Allegory on Environmental Justice." *Journal of Environmental Law and Litigation* 9:461–97.

———. 1999. "The Indian Country Environmental Justice Clinic: From Vision to Reality." *Vermont Law Review* 23:567–604.

———. 2002a. "Dimensions of Environmental Justice in Indian Country and Native Alaska." *Environmental Justice Resource Center* (website). http://www.cjrc.cau.edu/summit2/IndianCountry.pdf.

———. 2002b. "The Supreme Court's 'Whack-a-Mole' Game Theory in Federal Indian Law, a Theory That Has No Place in the Realm of Environmental Law." *Great Plains Natural Resources Journal* 7 (90): 1–74.

Suttles, Wayne 1951. "Post-Contact Culture Changes among the Lummi Indians." *British Columbia Historical Quarterly* 18:29–103.

Sutton, Imre. 1975. *Indian Land Tenure: Bibliographical Essays and a Guide to the Literature.* New York: Clearwater.

———. 1991. "The Political Geography of Indian Country: An Introduction." *American Indian Culture and Research Journal* 15 (2): 1–2.

Swinomish Indian Tribal Community. 1989. *Draft Swinomish Comprehensive Plan.* LaConner, WA: Swinomish Office of Planning and Community Development.

Swinomish Indian Tribal Community and Skagit County, Washington. 1987. "Memorandum of Understanding for Establishing Tribal-County Regional Planning Program." LaConner, WA: Swinomish Office of Planning and Community Development.

———. 1998. "Memorandum of Understanding for Implementing a Coordinated Land Use Policy." LaConner, WA: Swinomish Office of Planning and Community Development.

Swinomish Tribal Mental Health Project. 1991. *A Gathering of Wisdoms. Tribal Mental Health: A Cultural Perspective*. Mount Vernon, WA: Swinomish Indian Tribal Community.

Swinomish Water Code, Title 22. 1995. Swinomish Indian Tribal Community, Swinomish Office of Planning and Community Development.

Towers, G. 2000. "Applying the Political Geography of Scale: Grassroots Strategies and Environmental Justice." *Professional Geographer* 51 (1): 23–36.

Tsosie, Rebecca. 1996. "Tribal Environmental Policy in an Era of Self-Determination: The Role of Ethics, Economics, and Traditional Ecological Knowledge." *Vermont Law Review* 21:225–333.

Tully, J. 2000. "The Struggles of Indigenous People for and of Freedom." In *Political Theory and the Rights of Indigenous People*, edited by D. Ivison, P. Patton, and W. Sanders, 36–59. Cambridge: Cambridge Univ. Press.

———. 2004. "Recognition and Dialogue: The Emergence of a New Field." *Critical Review of International Social and Political Philosophy* 7 (3): 84–106.

United States v. State of Washington, 384 F. Supp. 312 (W.D. Wash. 1974) (sometimes referred to as the "Boldt Fishing Case"), *aff'd*, 520 F.2d 676 (9th Cir. 1975), *aff'd*, *Washington v. Fishing Vessel Ass'n*, 443 U.S. 658 (1979).

United States v. State of Washington, 641 F.2d 1368 (9th Cir. 1981), *cert. denied*, 454 U.S. 1143 (1982).

US Census. 2000. Profile of General Demographic Characteristics. [Summary File 1, 100-Percent Data, for American Indian Reservation areas]. Washington, DC: US Bureau of the Census.

———. 2010. "Selected Population Characteristics for American Indian and Alaska Native Areas. Summary Population and Housing Characteristics." Washington, DC: US Bureau of the Census.

US Environmental Protection Agency. 1983. "Administration of Environmental Programs on Indian Lands." Washington, DC: US Environmental Protection Agency.

———. 1984a. "EPA Policy for the Administration of Environmental Programs on Indian Reservations." *US Environmental Protection Agency* (website). http://www.epa.gov/indian/policyintitvs.htm.

———. 1984b. "Indian Policy Implementation Guidance." November 8. Washington, DC: US Environmental Protection Agency.

———. 1995. "Final EPA/Tribal Agreements Template." *US Environmental Protection Agency* (website). http://www.epa.gov/indian/agree.htm.

———. 2000a. "Administrative Order on Consent," EPA Docket No. CERCLA-10-2000-0186.

———. 2000b. "Superfund Memorandum of Agreement between the Swinomish Indian Tribal Community and the USEPA Regarding Tribal Consultation during Implementation of the Superfund Program." Seattle: US Environmental Protection Agency, District 10.

Veblen, Thorstein. 1919. *The Vested Interests and the Common Man.* New York: Viking.

Walker, Jana L., Jennifer L. Bradley, and Timothy J. Humphrey Sr. 2002. "A Closer Look at Environmental Justice in Indian Country." *Seattle Journal for Social Justice*, 1 (2): 379–401.

Wallerstein, Immanuel. 1979. *The Capitalist World Economy.* London: Cambridge Univ. Press.

———. 1992. "The West, Capitalism, and the Modern World-System." *Review* 15 (4): 561–619.

Washington State Department of Natural Resources. 1991. "Department of Natural Resources Tribal Policy." Policy statement. Olympia: Washington State Department of Natural Resources.

Washington State Water Coordinating Act. Wash. Rev. Code § 70.116.

Weaver, Tim. 1990. "*Brendale*: Checkerboards, Land and Civil Authority: Managing the Reservation Environment." White paper. Seattle: Washington State Bar Association, Indian Law Section.

Wilber, Charles K., ed. 1988. *The Political Economy of Development and Underdevelopment.* 4th ed. New York: Random House.

Wilkinson, C. F. 2005. *Blood Struggle: The Rise of Modern Indian Nations.* New York: W. W. Norton.

Williams, Kristine M. 1992a. "*Brendale* and Its Relationship to Zoning on Indian Reservation Lands." *Planning and Zoning News* 10 (12): 1–4.

———. 1992b. "Coordinating Jurisdiction on Indian Reservations." *Planning and Zoning News* 10 (12): 5–10.

Winchell, Dick G. 1995. "Tribal Sovereignty as the Basis for Tribal Planning." *Indigenous Planners* 1.

Wood, Mary Christina. 1994. "Indian Land and the Promise of Native Sovereignty: The Trust Doctrine Revisited." *Utah Law Review* 1471–1569.

———. 1995a. "Fulfilling the Executive's Trust Responsibility toward the Native Nations on Environmental Issues: A Partial Critique of the Clinton Administration's Promises and Performance." *Environmental Law* 25:733–800.

———. 1995b. "Protecting the Attributes of Native Sovereignty: A New Trust Paradigm for Federal Actions Affecting Tribal Lands and Resources." *Utah Law Review* (1995): 109–37.

Yiftachel, Oren. 1998. "Planning and Social Control: Exploring the Dark Side." *Journal of Planning Literature* 12 (4): 395–406.

Yiftachel, Oren, and Margo Huxley. 2000. "Debating Dominance and Relevance: Notes on the 'Communicative Turn' in Planning Theory." *International Journal of Urban and Regional Research* 24:907–13.

Zaferatos, Nicholas C. 1998. "Planning the Native American Tribal Community: Understanding the Basis of Power Controlling the Reservation Territory." *Journal of the American Planning Association* 64 (4): 395–410.

———. 2003. "Planning for Sustainable Reservation Economic Development: A Case Study of the Swinomish Marina and Mixed Use Commercial Development." *American Indian Culture and Research Journal* 27 (3): 31–52.

———. 2004a. "Toward a Theory of Tribal Community Development: Overcoming Conflict in Native American Indian Reservation Planning." *Space and Polity* 8 (1): 87–104.

———. 2004b. "Tribal Nations, Local Governments, and Regional Pluralism in Washington State: The Swinomish Approach in the Skagit Valley." *Journal of the American Planning Association* 70 (1): 81–96.

———. 2006. "Environmental Justice in Indian Country: Dumpsite Remediation on the Swinomish Indian Reservation." *Environmental Management* 38 (6): 896–909.

Zaferatos, Nicholas C., and Mary Ellen Flanagan. 2001. "Appropriate Technologies in the Traditional Native American Smokehouse: Public Health Considerations in Tribal Community Development." *American Indian Culture and Research Journal* 24 (4): 69–93.

Zegans, Marc. 1990. "Innovations and the Municipal Attorney: Managing the Tension between Service and Control." (Working Paper, Cambridge, MA: Harvard University, Kennedy School of Government, Innovations in American Government Program).

Index

Italic page number denotes illustration.

aboriginal rights, 33–34, 165
acculturation, 76, 103, 105, 147–48
adaptive planning, 151–52, 158
agreements: awards for, 223n12; Centennial Accord, 172, 176, 196, 201–2, 213, 214, 235; Chelan Agreement, 200–201; early federal (1787–1828), *17*, 18–19; environmental protection and, 61, 200, 231–33, 270–71, 280–81, 284; fishing and gaming, 197–98, 199, 232–33; inter-local, 219–21; Millennium Accord, 201–2; parks and recreation, 231; PM Northwest remediation project, 280–81; public health and safety, 228–29; Skagit River Agreement, *207*, 232–33; Skokomish Tribe-Mason County Government-to-Government Agreement, *207*; as step in institutionalizing working relationships, 216; Swinomish Joint Comprehensive Plan, 222–27; Timber, Fish and Wildlife Agreement (TFW), 197–98, 199; transportation, 228; Tribal Environmental Agreement, 231, 270; tribes as agencies to enter into, 229n17; water resources and rights, 200–201, 229–33. *See also* treaties and treaty-making

agricultural leasing, 113–14, 113n20
air pollution, 59n60, 232. *See also* smokehouses
Alaska Native Claims Settlement Act (ANSCA), 33–34
Alaska Native Fund, 33–34
alienation: economic, 138–41; federal trust responsibility and, 106–11; historic aspects, 95; incorporation and, 95, 106–19, 147–48; model of tribal political community, *109*; modified model of, *110*
allotments. *See* General Allotment Act of 1887
Ambler Realty Co., Euclid v., 55
American Indian Movement, 118
Amin, Samir, 101
Anderson, United States v., 182, 191–92
anti-Indian movement, 129–32
Arapaho Indian Tribe, 51, 133n14
Arizona Public Service Co. v. EPA, 59n60
Arizona State Tax Commission, McClanahan v., 41, 191
Arizona v. California, 127n3
assets, restricted access to, 138–41
assimilation: acculturation and, 76, 103, 105, 147–48; cultural, 79–80, 136–37; incorporation and, 120, 132–34;

assimilation (*cont.*)
   policies, 24–25, 30–31, 33, 112, 122,
      124–25, 290; process of, 79–80, 114,
      119–20
Atkinson, John, 193
Atkinson Trading Co. v. Shirley, 135
Atlantic Richfield Company, 114n21
authority: constitutional, 18–19; critical
   theory and, 102–3, 103n8; implications for planning, 141–42; inherency
   of, 13, 14–15, 133–34, 234; origins
   of, 35–36; political, 40–48, 113n19,
   155. *See also* jurisdiction; regulatory authority; self-determination;
   sovereignty

banking industry, 66
Barry, Janice, 166
Barth, Frederick, 73
Bartlett, Solem v., 49n44
beliefs. *See* cultural value systems; reli-
   gious and spiritual traditions
Bennett, Robert, 30
BIA. *See* US Bureau of Indian Affairs
   (BIA)
bi-culturation, 76
Boldt decision. *See United States v.*
   Washington (*Boldt* decision)
boundary maintenance, 79, 79n6
Bourland, South Dakota v., 49n44
Boyer, Christine M., 96, 119–20
Brendale, Philip, 49n44, 51–57
Brendale v. Confederated Tribes and
   Bands of Yakima Indian Nation,
   51–57; defining *essential character*,
   54–56, 69–71, 134, 135, 160, 160n9,
   289; isolation as preferred outcome,
   149; limits of tribal authority and,

   49n44; planning interpretations of,
   90, 141–42, 214–15, 215n11
Bryan v. Itasca County, 28
Bugenig v. Hoopa Valley, 50
building codes and standards, 240,
   243–44, 257–58. *See also* zoning
Burlington Northern, Inc., 179n15
Bush, George H. W., 32
Bush, George W., 33
"Buy Indian," 140–41

California, Arizona v., 127n3
Campbell, Donald T., 73n2
captive nationhood, 112–13, 113n19
carbon monoxide, smokehouses and,
   247–51, 253–57
Cascade Natural Gas, 179n15
casinos. *See* gaming enterprises
Castells, Manuel, 96
Centennial Accord, 172, 176, 196, 201–2,
   213, 214, 235
Champagne, Duane, 28
Chelan Agreement, 200–201
Cherokee Nation v. Georgia, 20–22,
   38–39
Christianity, 77–79, 79n5
Church Council of Greater Seattle, 79n5
Citizens Equal Rights Alliance (CERA),
   130–32
civil jurisdiction: defined, 27n31; inherent power and, 43, 44, 48; non-Indians and, 45–46, 49–57, 133–34, *177*,
   190–94; overlapping, 126; Public Law
   280 and, 27–28, 31, 46n39, 52n52;
   regulatory jurisdiction vs., 27n31
civil rights, 30–31, 44, 192
Civil Rights Act of 1968, 44
Clean Air Act, 59n60

Clean Water Act, 60, 230, 268

Clinton, Bill, 32, 264

"closed areas," 51–57, 70, 113n19, 149, 215

Coast Salish Indian communities: allotments and, 210–12, 217; conveyance of honor and thanks, 89; cultural values in, 75–76, 84; early settlers and, 77–79; ethnic assimilation and fusion in, 79–80; Salish Sea area defined, 210n3; taxation rights, 193. *See also specific tribe*

codes. *See* building codes and standards; zoning

coercive relations, 151n2

collective theory, 104–7

Collier, John, 25

Columbus River Gorge National Scenic Area Management Plan, *206*

Colville Confederated Tribes v. Walton, 181–82, 183

Colville Tribe, 46, 61, 181–82, 183, 193–94

communication patterns, 86–90

community cohesiveness, 85

community development. *See* development and underdevelopment

community development financial institutions (CDFIs), 65–66

Comprehensive Cooperative Resource Management (CCRM), 197–99, 200, 205

Comprehensive Environmental Response, Compensation, and Liability Act (CERCLA) (Superfund), 60, 262, 263, 271–86

Confederated Salish and Kootenai Tribes, Moe v., 193

Confederated Tribes and Bands of Yakima Indian Nation, Brendale v.

See Brendale v. Confederated Tribes and Bands of Yakima Indian Nation

Confederated Tribes of the Colville Indian Reservation, Washington v., 46, 193–94

conflict resolution. *See* negotiation and mediation

confrontation tactics, 148–50

contracting, preferential treatment, 140–41

cooperation. *See* intergovernmental relations; negotiation and mediation

Cornell, Stephen, 115, 162

Corntassel, Jeff, 116

corporations. *See* incorporation

Council of Energy Resource Tribes (CERT), 114n21

country government, survey of planning departments, 214–17, 214n9

criminal jurisdiction, 39, 41, 44, 47–48, 133

Critical Areas Ordinance, 226, 226n15

critical theory, 102–3, 103n8, 121–22

Crow Tribe, 178

cultural development, theories of, 95–98

cultural imperatives, 155–57

cultural revitalization movements, 117

cultural value systems, 72–91; acculturation and bi-culturation, 76; behavioral characteristics, 80–86; "culture" defined, 80; defining community goals and, 153; early settlers and, 77–79; emotional expression and, 89–90; ethnic assimilation and fusion, 79–80, 136–37; ethnic groups vs., 73–75; generalizations and, 72; implications for planning, 90–91, 257–61; inherent tension in, 72–73; institutional mechanisms disrupting,

cultural value systems (*cont.*)
237n1; landholding and, 76–77,
217–18; role in economic development, 136–37, 239–40; social fragmentation of, 136–37; suppression of,
77–79, 79n5, 242; tribal identity and,
239–40; values differences, 75–77. *See
also* religious and spiritual traditions;
smokehouses

dancing, ceremonial, 117, 117n26, 241,
242
Davidoff, Paul, 96
Dawes Act. *See* General Allotment Act
of 1887
decision-making, community, 85
Deloria, Vine, 136–37
dependency theory, 99–106, 114, 122
development and underdevelopment,
95–122; acculturation and modernization theories, 76, 103, 105,
147–48; alienation and incorporation, 106–19, 147–48; captive nationhood, 112–13, 113n19; collectivism
vs. individualism, 104–5; critical
theory and, 102–3, 103n8, 121–22;
defined, 98–99; dependency theory
and, 99–106, 114, 122; financing, 26,
62, 64, 65–66, 138–41, 239; forms
of, 141; internal colonies, 112–13;
neoclassical economic view of,
99n5; origins of, 239–40; reservation control of, 105n11; reservation
economy vs. political economy,
104–6; role of institutional power
relations in, 119–20; social fragmentation and, 136–37; stages of internal
colonization, 112–13; unequal
exchange and, 100, 101; urban

marginality and, 101–2. *See also*
gaming enterprises
discrimination, 140–41, 264. *See also*
economic justice
dispute resolution. *See* negotiation and
mediation
domestic dependent status, 22, 39–40, 41
Dyckman, John W., 96

economic alienation, 138–41
economic assistance, 99
economic conditions: effects of outside
economic markets on, 98–99; Indian
Reorganization Act and, 25–26; lifestyle and, 81; overview of, 16
economic development. *See* development
and underdevelopment
economic justice, 262–86; concept of,
264; cost and funding for, 262–63,
269; critical theory and, 102–3;
Executive Order 12898 (Clinton
1994a), 264; federal trust responsibility and, 265–66, 274–76, 282, 284;
implications for planning, 281–86;
PM Northwest remediation project,
269–86; reservations and, 263–65;
self-governance and, 268, 284–85;
tribal vs. non-tribal communities,
264–65; tribes as political communities, 265–69
economic theory, 95–98. *See also* political economy
Eleventh Amendment, 68
employment preferences, 140–41
Environmental Justice Strategy, 264
environmental protection and management: agreements, 61, 200, 231–33,
270–71, 280–81, 284; controlling,
57–62, 266–71; cooperative

mechanisms for, 60–62, 202–5; federal trust responsibility and, 59, 185; implications for planning, 281–86; jurisdictional approaches to, 59–62, 165–67, 266–68; self-determination and, 185; shift in approach to, 197; in Washington State, *177*, 184–87. *See also* fishing and gaming rights; pollution control; smokehouses; water resources and rights

EPA. *See* US Environmental Protection Agency (EPA)

"equal footing doctrine," 178, 178n11

essential character, of reservations, 54–56, 69–71, 134, 135, 160n9, 289

ethnic development, 118

ethnic groups, 73–75, 79–80, 79n6, 118

Etzioni, Amitai, 150, 151n2

Euclid v. Ambler Realty Co., 55

Evans v. Shoshone-Bannock Land Use Policy Commission, 49–50

exploitation, 104, 105, 112, 113–16, 147

federal policy, 13–34; acculturation approach of, 76, 103, 105; allotment and assimilation era (1887–1934), *17*, 23–25, 48–49, 54, 55, 104, 112, 124–25, 132, 147; definition of Indian, 13n1; early period agreements (1787–1828), *17*, 18–19; fiduciary role, 125; independence period (1492–1787), *17*, 18; land claim settlements, 33–34; organizing principles of, 154–57; plenary powers as cornerstone of, 36–37, 39, 174–75; Presidential Commission studying, 131; proliferation of programs, 37; protection vs. elimination of tribes, 16–17; relocation period (1828–1887), *17*, 19–23;

reorganization period (1934–1953), *17*, 25–26; report on state of Indian affairs (1968), 31; report regarding failure of (1928), 25, 114n22; requirements for federal recognition, 13–16; reversal of, 25–26, 32, 115; self-determination era (1968–), *17*, 29–34, 37–38, 113–14, 125, 154–57, 173–74, 237–40; self-governance period (1990–), *17*; summary of, *17*; termination policy, *17*, 27–28, 32, 104, 114–15, 114n22, 122, 124–25, 290. *See also* treaties and treaty-making

federal trust responsibility: alienation and, 106–11; courts' extension of, 38n7; cultural protection and, 137; defined, 37–38, 42; economic justice and, 265–66, 274–76, 282, 284; environmental protection and, 59, 185; failure of, 38, 104; legal representation and, 42; as organizing principle, 155–57; origins of, 36–38; tribal financial resources and, 138–41. *See also* termination policies

fee lands, defined, 24

fee patents, 44, 194

fee simple title, 24, 106, 125, 132, 135, 168, 212n6, 217, 218

Feuerback, Ludwig, 107n13

Fidalgo Island, 229

Fifth Amendment, 40

financing, 138–41; development standards and, 239; estimated annual need in Indian country, 62n64; gaming revenues, 67; for incorporation, 26; for pipeline rights, 114n21; settlement claims, 33–34, 33n50; sources of in 1980s, 269; Superfund (CERCLA), 60, 262, 263, 271–86. *See also* taxation

First Nations Development Institute (FNDI), 62n64

fishing and gaming rights, 186–90; agreements, 197–98, 199, 232–33; cooperative fisheries management, 197, 202–3; historical dependency and, 178; Northwest coastal tribes and, 106n12, 119, 127; Puyallup case, 174, 174n5, 175, 187; salmon fishing, 131, 187–90, 197–98, 204; Swinomish case, 180; *Winters* case, 127, 180, 181, 183. *See also United States v. Washington* (*Boldt* decision)

fission, ethnic fusion and, 79, 79n6

Forester, John, 96

forests/forestry, 198–200, 231. *See also* timberlands

Foucault, Michael, 119–20

Frank, Andre Gunder, 99n5, 100n6

Friedmann, John, 96, 120, 157

fusion, ethnic, 79–80, 79n6

gaming enterprises, 66–68, 115–16, 115n24, 118, 138n18, *177*, 194–95

gaming rights. *See* fishing and gaming rights

Gardner, Booth, 201

General Allotment Act of 1887: ending of, 26; as form of resource expropriation, 112, 147; origins and intent of, *17*, 23–25, 48–49, 104, 132; Puget Sound tribes and, 168–69; Salish Sea region tribes and, 210–12; Swinomish tribe and, 217; zoning and, 54, 55

Georgia, Cherokee Nation v., 20–21, 22, 38–39

Georgia, Worcester v., 20–23, 133

Ghost Dance, 117, 117n26

Gobin and Madison v. Snohomish County v. The Tulalip Tribes of Washington, 212n6

Goeppele, Craighton, 50, 55, 133, 160, 225, 268

Goldberg, Carol, 28

Gorton, Slade, 130–31

governance. *See* self-governance; sovereignty; tribal governance

groundwater. *See* water resources and rights

Growth Management Act, 209, 229–30

Guemes Island, 242

Habermas, Jurgen, 90n10, 102–3

Hagen v. Utah, 43n29

Hall, Thomas D., 117n26

hazardous waste disposal, 184–86, 262–63. *See also* economic justice

health. *See* public health and safety

Hegel, Georg W., 107n13

Hicks, Nevada v., 44n32

historic preservation, 137

Hobbes, Thomas, 107n13

home ownership, concept of, 87

Hood Canal Coordinating Council, *207*

Hoopa Valley, Bugenig v., 50

House Resolution 108 (1953), 27, 31

HUD. *See* US Department of Housing and Urban Development (HUD)

Human Development Index, 98

human development theory, 98

immunity, sovereign, 44, 140

incorporation: alienation and, 95, 106–19, 147–48; assimilation and, 120, 132–34; dependency theory vs., 114; financing of, 26; forces of, 123–*24*;

historic aspects, 4, 95; powers of, 26, 26n28, 44, 45, 140–41; process of, 49, 75, 95, 111–16; Puget Sound tribes and, 167–71, 205, 212; responses to, 117–19, *118*; settlement claims and, 33–34; theory of, 111–15, 147–48; of water associations, *221*, 230

Indian Child Welfare Act of 1978, 47–48

Indian Christianity, 78–79

Indian Civil Rights Act (1968), 30–31, 44, 192

Indian Commerce Clause, 36

Indian country, defined, 19n10

Indian Finance Act of 1974, 65

Indian Freedom of Religion Act of 1978, 78–79, 137, 237n1

Indian Gaming Regulatory Act (1988), 67, 116, 138n18, 195

Indian Land Tenure and Economic Development Project, *207*

Indian Litigation Coordinating Committee, 173

Indian Policy Review Commission, 38

Indian Removal Act (1830), 19–20

Indian Reorganization Act (IRA) (1934), 25–26, 43, 44, 78, 140, 168, 238n1

Indian Self-Determination and Education Assistance Act (1975), 4, 32, 140–41, 148, 154

Indian Shaker Church, 78

Indian title, doctrine of, 21–22, 21n16, 106

Indian tribes: definition of, 13n1, 35, 265; federal recognition of, 13–16

individualism, 105–6

informality, social involvement and, 84

infrastructure planning, 228, 229–31

institutional power, 119–20

integrated site assessment (ISA), 277

inter-family relations, 84–85

intergovernmental relations, 47–48, 209–10, 214–17, 222–25, 233–36. *See also* negotiation and mediation

internal colonies, 112–13

Interstate Congress for Equal Rights and Responsibilities (ICERR), 129–32, 130n8

intrusion, 79, 79n6

investment, financial, 26, 62, 64, 65–66, 138–41, 239

Itasca County, Bryan v., 28

Jicarilla Apache Tribe, Merrion v., 63, 193–94

Johnson, Lyndon B., 30

Johnson v. McIntosh, 20–22, 38

Jojola, Theodore S., 148, 153, 166

Jorgensen, Joseph G., 112, 121–22, 147

Josephy Report (1969), 31

jurisdiction, 145–52; congressional power over, 36–37; criminal, 39, 41, 44, 47–48, 133; environmental, 59–62, 165–67, 266–68; multijurisdictional planning and, 60–62, 124–27, 165–67, 169, 289–91; Ninth Circuit Court of Appeals on, 184, 212n6, 267; non-Indians and, 44–45, 47–48, 49–50; preemption test for, 191; Public Law 280 and, 27–28, 31, 46n39, 52n52; short-term economic gain vs. conceding, 116; taxation and, 46–47; uncertainty of, 34. *See also* civil jurisdiction

jurisdictional concurrency, 91

Kalt, Joseph P., 162

Kennedy, John F., 29–30

Kikiallus Indian Tribe, 240

Knight v. Shoshone and Arapahoe Tribes,
    51, 133n14
Kootenai Tribe, 193
Kukutali Preserve, 231

Laguna Pueblo Indians, 114n21
Lake Roosevelt Forum, *206*
land claims, 20–23, 33–34, 165–67,
    177–79
land ownership and use, 48–57, 129–36;
    differences in cultural views toward,
    76–77, 217–18; as first step in self-
    determination, 218; normative-based
    conflict and, 90–91; permanent
    homelands, 156; zoning, 44, 51–57,
    133n14, 218, 227n16. *See also* fee
    lands, defined
language, patterns of communication
    and, 86–90
leases, 113–14, 113n20, 114n21
Lee, Williams v., 41
LeVine, Robert A., 73n2
life expectancy, 16
litigation: cultural values and, 72–73;
    as form of conflict resolution, 128;
    incorporation and, 45, 140; as result
    of lack of cooperation, 210; shifts
    in focus of, 212; Washington State
    Indian policy and, 172, *177,* 212–13
local government, survey of planning
    departments, 214–17, 214n9
Long Live the Kings Project, 204
Lower Skagit Indian Tribe, 240
Lytle, Clifford M., 136–37

Mancari, Morton v., 140–41
Marshal trilogy, 20–23
Marx, Karl, 95–97, 107–8

Mashantucket Pequot Indian Tribe,
    116n25
*Match-E-Be-Nash-She-Wish Band of Pot-
    tawatomi Indians v. Patchak,* 45n33
McCarren Amendment, 182
*McClanahan v. Arizona State Tax Com-
    mission,* 41, 191
McFarland, Andrew W., 199, 199n68
McIntosh, Johnson v., 20–22, 38
mediation. *See* negotiation and
    mediation
melting pot theory, 76, 103
Menominee Tribe, reconstitution of, 115
Meriam Report (1928), 25, 114n22
Merrion v. Jicarilla Apache Tribe, 63,
    193–94
*Mescalero Apache Tribe, New Mexico
    v.,* 47
metropolis-satellite theory, 100n6
Millennium Accord, 201–2
Mitchell, United States v., 36–37, 126n2
modernization theory, 103, 147–48
*Moe v. Confederated Salish and Kootenai
    Tribes,* 193
Montana v. United States, 44–45, 49n44,
    50–55, 69, 133–36, 160, 178
Morton v. Mancari, 140–41
Muckleshoot Indian Tribe, 184, *206*

*Nance v. US Environmental Protection
    Agency,* 267
National Association of Gaming Tribes,
    118
National Congress of American Indians,
    118, 132, 154–55
National Indian Policy Center, 67
National Pollution Discharge Elimina-
    tion System (NPDES), 61, 232, 270
Native American Bank, 66

Native American Financial Officers Association (NAFOA), 140

Native American Graves Protection and Repatriation Act of 1990, 137

natural resources: alienation and subjugation of, 107–11; CCRM principles and, 197; cultural relationship with, 266; exploitation of, 113–16. *See also* environmental protection and management; fishing and gaming rights; timberlands; water resources and rights

Navaho, United States v., 265

Navajo Nation, 114n21, 135, 265

"navigable waters," 177–79

negotiation and mediation: as alternative to litigation, 213; circumstances precluding, 213n8; effective outcomes of, 233–36; implications for planning, 205–8; institutions for, 202–5; overall approaches, 145–52, 158–62, 165–67, 172–76, 197, 205–10, 213, 222–26, 290–91; since 1980, *206–7*, 213; structures for, 195–202; tribal approaches, 219, 225–26, 233–36, *235*

neoliberalism, 97, 97n3

Nevada v. Hicks, 44n32

New Mexico v. Mescalero Apache Tribe, 47

Ninth Circuit Court of Appeals: *Brendale* decision, 52–53; *Colville* decision, 181–82; fishing and gaming rights, 178, 187, 189; land jurisdiction issues, 184, 212n6, 267; regulatory authority of reservations, 49–50; *Snow* decision, 191–92; treaty rights vs. federal tribal recognition, 14n3; *Walton* decision, 183

Nixon, Richard, 4, 31

normative relations, 151, 151n2

Northwest Air Pollution Authority, 232, 247

Northwest coastal tribes: early settlers and, 77–79; ethnic assimilation and fusion in, 79–80; fishing and gaming rights, 106n12, 119, 127; values in, 75–76. *See also specific tribe*

Northwest Ordinance of 1787, 18–19

Northwest Renewable Resources Center (NRRC), 167, 167n1, 202–5, 214n9, 224n13

Northwest Water Resources Committee, 204

Obama, Barack, 33

oil industry, 114n21, 262–63, 269–86

Oliphant v. Suquamish Indian Tribes, 39, 44

OPEC, 114n21

"open areas," 51–57, 70

oppression, 25, 104, 120

Owens, Nancy, 105n11

Pacific Salmon Treaty, 197–98

Page, Vicki, 103, 147, 218

parks and recreation planning, 231

particularized inquiry test, 191–92

Patchak, Match-E-Be-Nash-She-Wish Band of Pottawatomi Indians v., 45n33

paternalism, 25, 30n37, 31

permanent homelands, 156

Pevar, Stephen L., 38n7

phenomenological approach, 147–48, 158, 290–91

planning: awards for, 223n12; challenges of, 1, 3, 34; defined, 2; effects of political-economic discourse on, 96–98; as instrument of public policy, 103, 119–20; plural planning construct, 210–11, 227–33, 235–36; survey of tribal and county planning departments, 214–17, 214n9. *See also* tribal planning; tribal planning model

Planning Enabling Act, 218

plenary power, 36–37, 39, 174–75

pluralism, regional, 148–49, 161, 166

pluralist theory, 117–18, 199, 199n68

plurality of interests, 48, 69, 70–71, 91, 134, 225, 236

plural planning construct, 210–11, 227–33, 235–36

PM Northwest (PMNW) remediation project, 269–86, *283*; background, 271–74; cleanup agreement, 280–81; cooperative efforts, 276–79; federal trust responsibility and, 274–76; implications for planning, 281–86; site assessment findings, *278–79*

political authority, tribal, 40–48, 113n19, 155

political economy, 95–122; collectivism vs. individualism, 105–6; concept of praxis in, 96–97; implications for planning, 96–98, 120–22; Indian dependency and, 99–106, 114, 122; institutional power relations in, 119–20; process of incorporation, 111–16; reservation economy vs., 104–6; theoretical origins of, 95–103

political imperatives, 155–57

pollution control, 59n60, 60, 184–86, 230, 232, 267, 268

population: non-Indian on reservation land, 126n1, 132–33, 212; tribal, 15–16, 167–71, 212

Porter, Libby, 166

post-development theory, 97–98, 101

post-structuralism, 95–96

poverty, 62

power: critical theory and, 102–3, 103n8; institutional, 119–20. *See also* authority

praxis, concept of, 96–97

preemption tests, 191

private sector, investment and, 62, 64, 138–41

property rights, 33–34, 48–57, 59–60, 72–73, 129–34, 165. *See also* fishing and gaming rights; land claims; land ownership and use; natural resources; water resources and rights

Protect Americans' Rights and Resources (PARR), 130–32

public health and safety: agreements, 228–29; alcoholism, 80, 81, 90n9; life expectancy, 16; planning for, 229–31; smallpox epidemics, 242; smokehouses and, 242, 247–51. *See also* economic justice; pollution control

Public Law 280, 27–28, 31, 46n39, 52n52

public safety planning, 228–29

Public Water System (PWS), 60

Puget Sound tribes, 165–208; incorporation and, 167–71, 205, 212; organization of, 168; political differences among, 167–68; population of, 167–71, 212; territorial alienation, 168–69; treaties and treaty-making, 167–68, 197. *See also specific tribe*

Puget Sound Water Quality Authority (PSWQA), 201

Puyallup Lands Settlement Agreement, *206*

Puyallup Tribe v. Washington State Department of Game, 174, 174n5, 175, 187

Quesnay, Francois, 95n1
Quinault Tribe, Snow v., 191–92

racial discrimination, 140–41, 264. *See also* economic justice
Reagan, Ronald W., 32
rebellion, incorporation and, 118
regionalism, 209–10, 219, 235–36
regional pluralism, 209–36; confrontational tactics and, 148–50; cooperative land use planning, 222–25; extending model to regional governance, 227–33; forming working relationships, 214–17; implications for planning, 233–36; origins of regional conflict, 210–13; Swinomish case study, 217–18, 217–22; testing, 225–27. *See also* intergovernmental relations; negotiation and mediation
regulatory authority: civil jurisdiction vs., 27n31; development theory and, 97, 105n11; dual, 115n24, 134, 222, 234, 291; environment and, 57–62, 128, 172, 181–82, 184–86, 187, 212, 267, 268; gaming enterprises, 66–68, 115n24, 116, 138n18, *177*, 195; implications for planning, 68–71, 135, 152, 234; inherency of, 39–40, 44, 44n32; limitations on, 35; origins of, 16, 18–19, 35–36; over non-Indians, 48–57, 135, *177*, 190–92, 194; private property and, 135; taxation and, 46–47, 62–66, 141, 194; of tribal assets, 138–39; in Washington State, *177*, 190–95
religious and spiritual traditions: dancing, 117, 117n26, 241, 242; and death of family member, 87n8; institutional mechanisms disrupting, 237n1; legislation regarding freedom of, 78–79, 137, 237n1; Seowyn ceremonial practice, 238–39, 240–43; suppression of, 77–79, 79n5, 242; tribal identity and, 239–40. *See also* smokehouses
relocation programs, 27, 112
representation, 173, 173n4
reservations: additions to, 26; defined, 15n6; dissolution of, 27–28; *essential character* of, 54–56, 69–71, 134, 135, 160n9, 289; as internal colonies, 104–5; non-Indian population on, 126n1, 132–33, 212; number and size of, 15–16, 24; post-1871 establishment of, 20
reservation status, 43n29
"reserved rights" doctrine, 180
Resource Conservation and Recovery Act (RCRA), 61, 273–74

respectfulness, tribal values and, 84, 88
Rhode Island Indian Claims Settlement Act, 33
roads and highways, 228
Roberts, Hayden, 150
Roberts, Natalie Andrea, 73n2, 74–76, 79–80, 87
Rucklehaus, William A., 184–85

Safe Drinking Water Act (1986), 60, 267
Salish Sea, defined area of, 210n3
Salish Tribe, 75–76, 193, 212
salmon fishing, 131, 187–90, 197–98, 204
Salmon-Steelhead Preservation Action for Washington Now (S/SPAWN), 131

Samish Indian Tribe, 240
Sandercock, Leonie, 96
Seaton, Fred A., 29
Seattle City Light, *207*
Seattle Water Department, *206*
self-determination: effects on self-governance, 15; encroachments on, 2–3, 4, 108; environmental management and, 185; federal policy era of, *17,* 29–34; Josephy report (1968) on, 31; as predecessor to economic development, 137; principles and imperatives of, 154–57; rebellion and, 118; scope of planning and, 152–53; Swinomish Indian Tribe and, 218–21
self-governance, 42–48; assessing threats to, 151–52; effects of self-determination policy on, 15; encroachments on, 2–3, 4; environmental justice and, 268, 284–85; federal abandonment of support for, 27–28; federal support for, 25–26; oppositional forces to, 123–24, 128–32; period of (1990–), *17;* as predecessor to economic development, 137, 148; sources of power, 15, 40
self-sufficiency strategy, 150–52
Seminole Nation v. United States, 42–43
Sen, Amartya, 98
Senghass, Dieter, 146n1
Seowyn ceremonial practice, 238–39, 240–43
Shaker Church, 78
Shakopee Indian Tribe, 116n25
Shell Corporation, 262–63, 269–86
shellfish, 189–90
Shirley, Atkinson Trading Co. v., 135
Shoshone and Arapahoe Tribes, Knight v., 51, 133n14

Shoshone-Bannock Land Use Policy Commission, Evans v., 49–50
Skagit County, 218, 219, 222–25
Skagit County Coordinated Water Supply Plan, 229–30, 230nn18–19
Skagit County Critical Areas Ordinance, 226, 226n15
Skagit River Agreement, *207,* 232–33
Skagit River tribes, 232–33, 240–43. *See also specific tribe*
Skagit Valley region, 219, 289–90
Skokomish Tribe-Mason County Government-to-Government Agreement, *207*
slave trade, 107, 107n13
smallpox epidemics, 242
Smith, Adam, 107n13
smokehouses, 237–61; banning of, 242; building codes and standards, 240, 243–44, 257–58; carbon monoxide measurements, 247–51, 253–57; ceremonial importance, 237–43; completion of, 247; design objectives, 243; features of, 245–46; first, 242–43; floor plans, *245;* funding for, 243, 253; health risks, 244–45, 247–48, 258–59; implications for planning, 257–61; particulate measurements, 250–51, 253–54, 255–56; photos of, *238, 241, 246, 254, 258;* planning model and stages, 259–61, *260;* post-construction fire pit test, 253–54; rebuilding, 243–45; smoke dispersion system, 244–45, *246,* 251–53, *252, 254,* 256–57; smoke plume, 238–39, 256–57; wood combustion and smoke control testing, 248–50
Snipp, Matthew C., 112–13, 113n19
Snohomish County, 212n6

Snohomish County Aquatic Resource Protection Program, *206*
Snow v. Quinault Tribe, 191–92
social exchange, communication patterns and, 89
social involvement, informality and, 84
social movements, economic justice and, 102, 102n7
social relations, forms of, 152n1
social status, 84
Solem v. Bartlett, 49n44
South Dakota v. Bourland, 49n44
South Dakota v. Yankton Sioux Tribe, 43n29
sovereignty, 35–71; alienation and, 106–11; end of treaty-making and, 20; environmental, 57–62; as evolving political concept, 34, 288; federal trust responsibility and, 36–38; immunity and, 44, 140; implications for planning, 34, 68–71, 152–57; inherent, 133–34; limits to, 43n28; oppositional forces to, 123–24; origins of, 22–23, 38–42; political authority and, 42–48; recognition of, 202; scope of planning and, 152–53; as source of governmental power, 15; status of, 35–36; tribal sovereignty-building process, 117, 118–19
spirit dance, 241, 242
spiritual traditions. *See* religious and spiritual traditions
state government, transfer of federal power to, 28–29, 31, 46n39, 52n52
State of Washington, Department of Ecology v. United States Environmental Protection Agency, 128n5, 231–32
Stevens Treaties, 168–69, 168n2, 197

Stratton, Wickliffe, 193n59
Suagee, Dean B., 264–65, 266–68
Superfund (CERCLA), 60, 262, 263, 271–86
Supreme Court. *See* US Supreme Court
Suquamish Indian Tribes, Oliphant v., 39, 44
surplus lands, 49
survey, of tribal and county planners, 214–17, 214n9
Sustainable Forestry Roundtable, 200
Sutton, Imre, 210, 212
Swinomish Culture and Environmental Protection Agency, 269–70
Swinomish Indian Reservation, defined, 240
Swinomish Indian Senate, 243
Swinomish Indian Tribal Community v. Washington State Department of Ecology, 180
Swinomish Indian Tribe, 210–36, *216*; approach to negotiation and mediation, 219, 225–26, 233–36, *235*; attitudes toward land ownership, 217–18; authority over land ownership and use, 218–21; environmental authority of, 269–71; intergovernmental relationships, 214–17, 219; land use planning strategies, 222–27; litigation regarding tidal properties, 178–79; map of surrounding jurisdictions, *211*; non-tribal interests in, 218; origins and descendancy of, 240–43; origins of regional conflict in, 210–13, 217–19; pollution discharge permit agreement, 61; self-determination and, 218–21; water rights agreements, 229–31
Swinomish Indian Village, 240

Swinomish Joint Comprehensive Plan, *207*, 222–27
Swinomish Mental Health Project, 90n9
Swinomish-Skagit Joint Comprehensive Plan, *207*
Swinomish Smokehouse Organization, 243, 247, 253, 259, 260

taxation: authority of, 134–35; domestic dependent status and, 39–40, 41; economic development and, 62–66; state jurisdiction and, 46–47; tribally chartered businesses and, 45; in Washington State, *177*, 192–94
termination policies, *17*, 27–28, 32, 104, 114–15, 122, 124–25, 290
territorial imperatives, 155–57
Texaco Corporation, 262–63, 269–86
tidelands, 177–79
Timber, Fish and Wildlife Agreement (TFW), 197–98, 199
timberlands, 104n10, 126n2, 197–98, 199, 232
titles, fee simple, 24, 106, 125, 132, 135, 168, 212n6, 217, 218
Trade and Intercourse Acts, 19, 37
Transmountain Pipeline Co., 179n15
transportation planning, 228
treaties and treaty-making: cultural values and, 72–73, 79–80; diminishment of tribal powers and, 124–25; end of, 20; exploitation of, 104; federal recognition and, 13–14; fishing and gaming, 197–98; incorporation during post-period of, 117; intergovernmental relations, 47–48; political economy during pre-, 111–12; Puget Sound tribes and, 167–68, 197; reversals of, 131n10; as source of power,

15, 36; Stevens Treaties, 168–69, 168n2, 197
Treaty of Medicine Creek, 168
Treaty of Point Elliott, 79–80, 168, 217, 240, 262
Treaty of Point No Point, 168
tribal employments rights ordinances (TERO), 141
Tribal Environmental Agreement (TEA), 231, 270
tribal governance, mistrust toward, 134–35. *See also* self-governance
tribal land and territory: decreases in, 24, 29; increases in, 26; protection of, 37; reconstitution of, 33–34; sales of, 19, 21, 24, 27, 29, 37, 104; Stevens Treaties and, 168–69, 168n2, 197; surplus lands, 49. *See also* land claims; land ownership and use; natural resources; reservations
tribal planning, 123–42, 287–91; awards for, 223n12; challenges of, 2–3, 48, 68–71, 90–91, 122, 160; first national tribal-county plan, 225; multi-jurisdictional aspects, 60–62, 124–27, 165–67, 169, 289–91; negotiated approach to, 205–8; objectives of, 1–2, 135; phenomenological approach to, 147–48, 158, 290–91; preconditions for, 35; private and institutional obstacles, 123–24; public policy obstacles, 123–28; scope of, 152–53; stages of, *208*; survey of tribal and county planning departments, 214–17, 214n9
tribal planning model, 150–62; adaptive approaches, 150–52, 158; constructing, 157–58; environmental planning model, *285–86*; as framework for understanding relationships, 161–62;

implications of, 161–62, 290–91; organizing principles, 154–57; overview of theoretical traditions regarding, 147–48; phases of, 158–61; political setting for, 145–47; scope of, 152–53; smokehouse planning model and stages, 259–61, *260*; use of confrontational tactics, 148–50

Tribal Self-Governance Act of 1994, 154

Tribes and Counties: Intergovernmental Cooperation Project, 204

trust allotments, defined, 23n21, 26

Trust for Public Land, 231

trust responsibility. *See* federal trust responsibility

Tulalip Indian Reservation, 181, 184, 212n6

Tulalip Tribes of Washington, Gobin and Madison v. Snohomish County v., 212n6

Tulalip Tribes of Washington v. Walker, 181

Twiwok, 240

Udall, Stewart, 30

underdevelopment. *See* development and underdevelopment

Underground Injection Control, 267

unemployment, 27

unequal exchange, 100, 101

Uniform Building Code, 240

United Property Owners of Washington (UPOW), 130–32, 190, 190n49

United States, Montana v., 44–45, 49n44, 50–55, 69, 133–36, 160, 178

United States, Seminole Nation v., 42–43

United States, Winters v., 127, 180, 181, 183

United States Environmental Protection Agency, State of Washington,

Department of Ecology v., 128n5, 231–32

United States v. Anderson, 182, 191–92

United States v. Mitchell, 36–37, 126n2

United States v. Navajo, 265

United States v. Washington (Boldt decision): agreements, 199; cooperative fisheries management and, 197; effects of on state Indian policy, 196–97, 202–3; environmental rights dispute and, 188–90, 196; origins, 129–32; Puyallup case and, 174; summary, 127; *Winters* and, 183

United States v. Wheeler, 39–40, 42–43

United States v. White Mt. Apache, 265

urban marginality, 101–2

US Bill of Rights, 40

US Bureau of Indian Affairs (BIA): agricultural leasing policies, 113–14, 113n20; encouragement of tribal dependency, 105; funding for environmental management, 269; PM Northwest remediation project, 273; role in managing tribal financing, 139; during self-determination era (1968–), 30; suppression of spiritual practices, 242; timberland mismanagement, 126n2

US Constitution, 18, 36, 40, 43, 68, 131–32

US Department of Housing and Urban Development (HUD), 30n38

US Department of Justice, 37

US Department of the Interior, 30, 37, 59

US Environmental Protection Agency (EPA): environmental agreements, 231–33, 270; Indian policy of, 57–62, 184–86; PM Northwest remediation project and, 263, 266–86, *283*; Swinomish smokehouse and, 250–51, 253

US Environmental Protection Agency, Arizona Public Service Co. v., 59n60

US Environmental Protection Agency, Nance v., 267

US House Resolution 108 (1953), 27

US Supreme Court: "equal footing doctrine," 178, 178n11; Indian tribes defined, 35, 265; interpretation of plenary power, 36–37, 39, 174; *Marshall trilogy,* 20–23; preemption test regarding jurisdiction, 191; "reserved rights" doctrine, 180; "tribal interest" test, 46; on trust doctrine, 36–37, 59. *See also specific case*

Utah, Hagen v., 43n29

utilitarian relations, 150–51, 151n2

values. *See* cultural value systems

Veblen, Thorstein, 96

Walker, Tulalip Tribes of Washington v., 181

Wallerstein, Immanuel, 105

Walton, Colville Confederated Tribes v., 181–82, 183

wardship, 37

"War on Poverty," 30n38

Washington State, 165–208; approaches to state-tribal conflicts, 173–76, 197, 213; cooperation between local governments, 209–10; current disputes, 176–95, 210–13; environmental programs, 61, *177,* 184–87; evolution of Indian policy in, 172, *177,* 210–13; institutions for mediation, 202–5; Native American population in, 15–16, 126n1, 132–33, 167–71, 212;

shift in approach to state-tribal conflicts, 197, 213; tribal-state mediation structures, 195–202; tribes as public agencies, 229n17

Washington State, United States v. See United States v. Washington (Boldt decision)

Washington State Commercial Passenger Fishing Vessel Association, Washington v., 188–89

Washington State Department of Ecology (WDOE), 128n5, 180, 231–32, 270, 272, 273

Washington State Department of Ecology, Swinomish Indian Tribal Community v., 180

Washington State Department of Fisheries, 204

Washington State Department of Game, Puyallup Tribe v., 174, 174n5, 187

Washington State Department of Health, 229

Washington State Department of Labor and Industries, 247

Washington State Department of Natural Resources, 202, 232

Washington State Department of Transportation, 228

Washington State Model Toxics Control Act (MTCA), 275

Washington State Parks and Recreation Commission, 231

Washington Supreme Court, 180

Washington v. Confederated Tribes of the Colville Indian Reservation, 46, 193–94

Washington v. Washington State Commercial Passenger Fishing Vessel Association, 188–89

wastewater treatment planning, 229–31

water resources and rights, *177*–84; adjudication proceedings, 182–84; agreements, 200-201, 229–33; Clean Water Act, 60, 230, 268; codes regarding, 180–82; co-management of, 109n16, 201; "navigable waters," 177–79; PM Northwest remediation project, 269–86, *283*; Safe Drinking Water Act (1986), 60, 267; *Winters* doctrine, 126–27, 180, 181, 183. *See also* fishing and gaming rights
West Point Secondary Upgrade Treatment Project, *206*
Wheeler, United States v., 39–40, *42–43*
Wheeler-Howard Act. *See* Indian Reorganization Act (IRA) (1934)
White Mt. Apache, United States v., 265
Wilber, Charles K., 99n4
Wildlife Network, 131
Wilkinson, Stanley, 52–53

Williams v. Lee, 41
Winters v. United States, 127, 180, 181, 183
Wisconsin, cooperation law in, 209n1
Witmer, Richard C., 116
Wood, Mary Christina, 265–66
Worcester v. Georgia, 20–21, 22–23, 133
world-systems theory, 100n6

Yakima Indian Tribe. *See Brendale v. Confederated Tribes and Bands of Yakima Indian Nation*
Yankton Sioux Tribe, South Dakota v., 43n29

zoning, 44, 51–57, 133n14, 218, 227n16. *See also Brendale v. Confederated Tribes and Bands of Yakima Indian Nation*